M000272463

R DATA ANALYSIS WITHOUT PROGRAMMING

This book prepares readers to analyze data and interpret statistical results using R more quickly than other texts. R is a challenging program to learn because code must be created to get started. To alleviate that challenge, Professor Gerbing developed *lessR*. The extensions provided by *lessR* remove the need to program. By introducing R through *lessR*, readers learn how to organize data for analysis, read the data into R, and produce output without performing numerous functions and programming exercises first. With *lessR*, readers can select the necessary procedure and change the relevant variables without programming. The text reviews basic statistical procedures with the *lessR* enhancements added to the standard R environment, complete with input, output, and an extensive interpretation of the results. Through the use of *lessR*, R becomes immediately accessible to the novice user and easier to use for the experienced user.

Highlights of the book include:

- *Quick starts* that introduce readers to the concepts and commands reviewed in the chapters.
- *Margin notes* that highlight, define, illustrate, and cross-reference the key concepts. When readers encounter a term previously discussed, the margin notes identify the page number to the initial introduction.
- *Scenarios* that highlight the use of a specific analysis followed by the corresponding *R/lessR* input and an interpretation of the resulting output.
- *Numerous examples of output* from psychology, business, education, and other social sciences, that demonstrate how to interpret results.
- *Two data sets*, provided on the book's website and analyzed multiple times in the book, provide continuity throughout.
- *End of chapter worked problems* help readers test their understanding of the concepts.
- *A website at www.lessRstats.com* that features the *lessR* program, the book's data sets referenced in standard text and SPSS formats so readers can practice using *R/lessR* by working through the text examples and worked problems, PDF slides for each chapter, solutions to the book's worked problems, links to *R/lessR* videos to help readers better understand the program, and more.

An ideal supplement for graduate or advanced undergraduate courses in statistics, research methods, or any course in which R is used, taught in departments of psychology, business, education, and other social and health sciences, this book will also be appreciated by researchers interested in using R for their data analysis. Prerequisites include basic statistical knowledge. Knowledge of R is not assumed.

David W. Gerbing is a Professor in the School of Business Administration at Portland State University. He has published extensively in psychology, sociology, education, statistics, and business.

R DATA ANALYSIS WITHOUT PROGRAMMING

David W. Gerbing

Routledge
Taylor & Francis Group

NEW YORK AND LONDON

First published 2014
by Routledge
711 Third Avenue, New York, NY 10017

and by Routledge
27 Church Road, Hove, East Sussex BN3 2FA

Routledge is an imprint of the Taylor & Francis Group, an informa business

© 2014 Taylor & Francis

The right of David W. Gerbing to be identified as author of this work has been asserted by him in accordance with sections 77 and 78 of the Copyright, Designs and Patents Act 1988.

All rights reserved. No part of this book may be reprinted or reproduced or utilised in any form or by any electronic, mechanical, or other means, now known or hereafter invented, including photocopying and recording, or in any information storage or retrieval system, without permission in writing from the publishers.

Trademark notice: Product or corporate names may be trademarks or registered trademarks, and are used only for identification and explanation without intent to infringe.

Library of Congress Cataloging in Publication Data
Gerbing, David W.
R data analysis without programming / David Gerbing.
   pages cm
1. R (Computer program language) 2. Mathematical statistics–Data processing. I. Title.
QA276.45.R3G46 2013
519.50285'5133–dc23   2013024185

ISBN: 978-0-415-64173-9 (hbk)
ISBN: 978-0-415-65720-4 (pbk)
ISBN: 978-1-315-85675-9 (ebk)

Typeset in Stone Serif and Stone Sans
By Cenveo Publisher Services

Printed and bound in the United States of America by Sheridan Books, Inc. (a Sheridan Group Company).

To the wonderful woman who is my wife

Rachel Maculan Sodré

Eu te amo

BRIEF CONTENTS

Preface		xiii
About the Author		xvii
CHAPTER 1	R for Data Analysis	1
CHAPTER 2	Read/Write Data	31
CHAPTER 3	Edit Data	53
CHAPTER 4	Categorical Variables	77
CHAPTER 5	Continuous Variables	99
CHAPTER 6	Means, Compare Two Samples	123
CHAPTER 7	Compare Multiple Samples	149
CHAPTER 8	Correlation	181
CHAPTER 9	Regression I	203
CHAPTER 10	Regression II	223
CHAPTER 11	Factor/Item Analysis	251
Appendix: Standard R Code		279
Notes		283
References		285
Index		287

CONTENTS

Preface   xiii
About the Author   xvii

■ **CHAPTER 1**   R for Data Analysis   1

1.1   Introduction   1
1.2   Access R   3
1.3   Use R   6
1.4   R Graphs   16
1.5   Reproducible Code   19
1.6   Data   20
      Worked Problems   28

■ **CHAPTER 2**   Read/Write Data   31

2.1   Quick Start   31
2.2   Read Data   32
2.3   More Data Formats   40
2.4   Variable Labels   45
2.5   Write Data   48
      Worked Problems   50

■ **CHAPTER 3**   Edit Data   53

3.1   Quick Start   53
3.2   Edit Data   54
3.3   Transform Data   55
3.4   Recode Data   62
3.5   Sort Data   66
3.6   Subset Data   68

3.7   Merge Data   72

Worked Problems   75

◾ **CHAPTER 4**   Categorical Variables   **77**

4.1   Quick Start   77

4.2   One Categorical Variable   79

4.3   Two Categorical Variables   87

4.4   Onward to the Third Dimension   93

Worked Problems   98

◾ **CHAPTER 5**   Continuous Variables   **99**

5.1   Quick Start   99

5.2   Histogram   100

5.3   Summary Statistics   105

5.4   Scatter Plot and Box Plot   110

5.5   Density Plot   114

5.6   Time Plot   118

Worked Problems   121

◾ **CHAPTER 6**   Means, Compare Two Samples   **123**

6.1   Quick Start   123

6.2   Evaluate a Single Group Mean   124

6.3   Compare Two Different Groups   130

6.4   Compare Dependent Samples   142

Worked Problems   147

◾ **CHAPTER 7**   Compare Multiple Samples   **149**

7.1   Quick Start   149

7.2   One-way ANOVA   150

7.3   Randomized Block ANOVA   158

7.4   Two-way ANOVA   166

7.5   More Advanced Designs   173

Worked Problems   180

◾ **CHAPTER 8**   Correlation   **181**

8.1   Quick Start   181

8.2   Relation of Two Numeric Variables   181

8.3   The Correlation Matrix   194

8.4   Non-parametric Correlation Coefficients   200

Worked Problems   202

■ **CHAPTER 9** Regression I   **203**

9.1   Quick Start   203
9.2   The Regression Model   204
9.3   Residuals and Model Fit   209
9.4   Prediction Intervals   212
9.5   Outliers and Diagnostics   216
      Worked Problems   221

■ **CHAPTER 10** Regression II   **223**

10.1   Quick Start   223
10.2   The Multiple Regression Model   224
10.3   Indicator Variables   234
10.4   Logistic Regression   239
       Worked Problems   248

■ **CHAPTER 11** Factor/Item Analysis   **251**

11.1   Quick Start   251
11.2   Overview of Factor Analysis   252
11.3   Exploratory Factor Analysis   254
11.4   The Scale Score   260
11.5   Confirmatory Factor Analysis   263
11.6   Beyond the Basics   275
       Worked Problems   276

Appendix: Standard R Code   279
Notes   283
References   285
Index   287

PREFACE

Purpose

This book is addressed to the student, researcher, and/or data analyst who wishes to analyze data using R to answer questions of interest. The structuring of the data for analysis, doing the analysis with the computer, and then interpreting the results are the skills to which this book is directed. Explicit instructions to use the computer for the analysis are provided, but using the computer is the easy part of data analysis, especially with the computer instructions provided in this book. By far, more content of this book is oriented toward the meaning of the analyses and interpretation of the results.

The computational tools discussed in this book are based on the open source and free R system that is becoming the world's standard for data analysis. Unlike commercial packages, R costs no money and can be installed at will on any Windows, Macintosh or Linux system. By itself, however, R presents a rather steep learning curve as it requires the ability to write computer code to do data analysis. To make data analysis with R more accessible, this book features a set of extensions to R called *lessR*. These extensions ease the transition of the new user into using R for data analysis and for many users contain the only computational tools they will need.

The ultimate goal of this book is to make R accessible to users of SPSS and similar commercial packages, and, indeed, help facilitate R to become the preferred choice of any data analysis system. For data analysts with a proclivity for program computer code, R has already emerged as the preferred choice. The *lessR* extensions to R remove the need to program and so are designed to provide access to R for all data analysts. To the extent that R becomes as straightforward to use and as comprehensive in its range of analyses as its commercial alternatives, then it becomes a viable choice as the preferred data analysis system both in the field and for instruction.

This is the first book that follows the format of the many SPSS based data analysis texts, with emphasis on both the instructions to produce the analysis, plus detailed interpretation of the resulting output. This book, however, applies the *R/lessR* system for conducting the analysis, made possible with the *lessR* extensions. Traditional R books on data analysis provide some interpretation, but much more space is required to explain the programming needed to obtain the output.

Intended Audience

This book is indented to serve as a supplementary text for graduate or advanced undergraduate courses in statistics, research methods, or any course in which R is used, taught in departments of psychology, business, education, and other social and health sciences. The book will also be helpful to researchers interested in using R for their data analysis. Prerequisites include basic statistical knowledge. Knowledge of R is not assumed.

Overview of Content

The first chapter shows how to download R and then *lessR* from the worldwide network of R servers, provides an example of data analysis, shows how data are structured for analysis, and discusses general issues for the use of R and *lessR*. Chapter 2 shows how to read the data from a computer file into R. Then the data often must be modified before analysis begins, the topic of Chapter 3. This editing can include changing individual data values, assigning missing data codes, transforming, recoding, and sorting the data values for a variable, and also sub-setting and merging data tables.

Chapters 4 and 5 show how to obtain the most basic of all data analyses, the counting of how often each data value or groups of similar data values occurred. Chapter 4 explains bar charts and related techniques for counting the values of a categorical variable, one with non-numeric data values. Also included are the analysis of two or more variables in the form of bar charts for two variables, mosaic plots for more than two variables and the associated cross-tabulation tables. Chapter 5 does the same for numeric variables, which include the histogram and related analyses, the scatter plot for one variable, the box plot, the density plot and the time plot, plus the associated summary statistics.

Chapter 6 explains the analysis of the mean of a single sample or of a mean difference across two different samples. Theses analyses are based on the *t*-test of the mean, the independent-samples *t*-test and the dependent-samples *t*-test. The non-parametric alternatives are also provided. Chapter 7 extends the material in Chapter 6 to comparison of many groups with the analysis of variance. The primary designs considered are the one-way independent groups, randomized blocks and two-way independent groups. Also illustrated are the randomized block factorial design and the split-plot factorial. Effect sizes are an integral part of each discussion.

Chapters 8, 9, and 10 focus on correlation and regression analysis. Chapter 8 introduces the scatter plot and the correlation coefficient to describe the relation between two variables. Both the usual parametric version and some non-parametric correlation coefficients are presented, as well as the correlation matrix. The subject of Chapter 9 is regression analysis of a linear model of a response variable with a single predictor variable. The discussion includes estimation of the model, a consideration of the evaluation of fit, outliers and influential observations, and prediction intervals. Chapter 10 extends this discussion to multiple regression, the analysis of models with multiple predictor variables, and also to logistic regression, the modeling of a response variable that has only two values.

The topic of Chapter 11 is factor analysis, both its exploratory and confirmatory versions. The primary examples are of item analysis, the analysis of items that form a scale such as from an attitude survey, and the corresponding scale reliabilities. For exploratory factor analysis the concepts of factor extraction and factor rotation are presented. Within this context a linkage between exploratory and confirmatory factor analysis for item analysis is provided, as well as a discussion of the covariance structure that underlies the confirmatory analysis. Analysis of scale development from published data on Machiavellianism appears throughout the chapter with the final development of the subscales with confirmatory factor analysis.

Distinctive Features

Every chapter after the first chapter begins with a brief Quick Start section. The function calls that provide the analyses described in the remainder of the chapter are listed and briefly described. The goal is that the user can immediately invoke the specified analyses and then, as needed, refer to the remainder of the chapter to obtain the details. Each Quick Start section also serves as a convenient summary of the data analysis functions described in that chapter.

This book makes extensive use of margin notes to highlight the concepts discussed within the main text. Each definition is placed in a margin note. The margin notes also provide a concordance, a cross-reference to where in the book a specific concept is first explained and illustrated. When the reader encounters a term previously discussed, the relevant section and page number appear in the margin notes.

The motivation for a specific analysis is presented in what is called a Scenario, highlighted by light gray rules. Following each Scenario is the R/*lessR* input for a specific analysis, also highlighted by light gray rules. The resulting output is then interpreted. A Listing is a literal copy of computer output, of which there are many throughout this book.

The analysis of many data sets illustrates the concepts discussed in the book. Two data sets, however, are analyzed multiple times to provide continuity throughout. One data set contains some of the typical information found in an employee database, such as each employee's Gender, Salary and so forth. The other data set regards the measurement of the attitudinal components of Machiavellianism, the tendency to manipulate others for one's own perceived personal gain. This data set is from a published study by the author in the *Journal of Personality and Social Psychology*. This study was one of the first applications of confirmatory factor analysis in the psychological literature, and here the analysis is detailed and illustrated to explain both exploratory and confirmatory factor analysis as an integrated strategy for scale development.

lessR Website

The website to support this book and the *lessR* package is www.lessRstats.com. The site includes a variety of reference materials to support your learning of data analysis, such as the data sets referenced in this book in both standard text and SPSS formats. This way you can practice using R and *lessR*, as you read this book and work through the examples and the included worked problems. Also included are videos on the use of R and *lessR*, a slide set for each chapter, and solutions, some of which are available only for instructors. The website also provides the opportunity to give your own suggestions and feedback with a place to request upgrades, a place to report bugs, and an interactive forum for asking and getting answers to questions.

Personal Acknowledgments

I would like to acknowledge the helpful people at Routledge/Taylor & Francis who have made this work possible. My editor Debra Riegert expressed an interest in this project from the start and has encouraged and guided the development of this book from its initial conceptualization. Miren Alberro managed the production process with good cheer and the helpful and needed assistance to turn a manuscript into a book.

I would also like to thank Jason T. Newsom, a colleague and Professor at the Institute on Aging, the School of Community Health, at Portland State University. Already a successful author at Routledge/Taylor & Francis, Jason introduced me to Debra, the introduction from which this book developed. Jason also provided two different forums for presenting my work on *lessR* at Portland State University: his informal seminars on quantitative topics for faculty and graduate students, and his annual June workshops on quantitative topics.

My students at Portland State University also deserve recognition for their role in the development of *lessR* and this book. In 2008 some of my students who used Macintosh computers asked me what software they could use for class assignments. I had primarily been using Excel, but at that time Microsoft deleted much of the statistical functionality from the Macintosh version of Excel. My answer was R, but the first classroom experiences with R were not satisfying. Students were frustrated because of all the programming work needed to get anything useful done, and spent more time learning how to use the computer than actually thinking about the meaning of the results – hence *lessR* and four years of undergraduate and graduate students who have used and contributed much feedback to the project from the beginning of its development through the current version.

Finally, I would like to thank the three reviewers who provided comprehensive insightful reviews: J. Patrick Gray, University of Wisconsin – Milwaukee, Agnieszka Kwapisz, Montana State University, and Bertolt Meyer, University of Zurich, Switzerland. The quality of their reviews illustrates how whatever one person does is facilitated by the thoughtful critiques of others who are also knowledgeable in the subject. Their reviews shaped the format of this book.

ABOUT THE AUTHOR

David W. Gerbing received his B.A. in psychology from what is now Western Washington University in 1974, where he did his first statistical programming on an IBM 360 mainframe. He obtained his Ph.D. in quantitative psychology from Michigan State University in 1979 as a student of John E. Hunter. He has been an Associate Professor of Psychology and Statistics at Baylor University, and is now Professor of Quantitative Methods in the School of Business Administration at Portland State University. He has published many articles on statistical techniques and their application in a variety of journals that span several academic disciplines including psychology, sociology, education, business, and statistics.

CHAPTER 1

R **FOR DATA ANALYSIS**

1.1 Introduction

1.1.1 Data Analysis

We ask many questions to which we seek answers. Some of these questions involve the way things work in our world, including our social processes and relationships, and our psychological selves. This book describes analyses based on observations that facilitate answering these types of questions. On average, do men make more than women managers at a particular company? Which of two pain medications is more effective? What College GPA do we forecast for an applicant who has a SAT score of 1130 and a High School GPA of 3.8? Do people generally have trust in others?

To answer questions such as these we seek *empirical* answers. We seek answers based on our observations of the world around us: What we see, hear, touch, taste, and smell, in particular, the measurements of what we observe. Our concern in this book is with observations in the form of *data*, the varying measurements of different people, organizations, places, things, and events.

Different measurements generally vary. For example, two different people have different heights, place differing amounts of trust in others, have different blood pressures, and earn different salaries. Height and blood pressure are two of the many variables that can be measured for anyone. For college students, College GPA and incoming High School GPA, and SAT score are measured variables.

Data analysis is the application of statistical concepts and methods to transform data, sometimes vast amounts of data, into usable information. This information is then used to form a conclusion regarding the people or organizations or places or whatever is the topic of interest. In the modern world data analysis is done exclusively on the computer. This book is about doing data analysis with one such computer software system, R, enhanced with lessR.

empirical:
Information based on observations acquired from our five senses.

data:
Measurements of different people or whatever the unit of analysis.

data analysis:
Application of statistical methods to transform data into usable information.

1.1.2 R **with** lessR

Our journey into data analysis with R begins with some good news, some bad news, and fortunately, some more good news. The first good news, as announced in an article in the *New York Times* (Jan 7, 2009), is that the world of data analysis is rapidly changing. At the heart of this change is the computer application R, extensively used, for example, in the *New York Times* graphics department. From software for data analysis on the computer becoming widely available in the 1970s until the early 21st century, data analysis was typically accomplished with expensive, proprietary statistical applications. Originally they ran only on IBM mainframe computers, but eventually migrated to PCs as the technology developed.

The cost and exclusivity of competent statistical applications for data analysis is becoming less relevant as the capability and popularity of the R system continues to grow. In terms of pure statistical power to analyze data, R compares favorably to the most expensive commercial applications available, providing all that virtually anyone could desire. The cost is exactly $0.00 USD to use R for the rest of your life on the computer or computers of your choice, for whatever purpose you wish to use the software. Feel free to choose any computer you wish, because R runs identically on Windows, Macintosh, and Linux/Unix. Use wherever and on whatever you wish because R is free for you and for the world.

The problem is that although R's capabilities and price are great, so is the effort required to learn what is generally considered a rather complex system with a steep learning curve. To get much done in R you need to write code. Sometimes you write a little code and sometimes a lot of code. The standard R environment has all the power you need, but is mostly for those who like, or at least tolerate, reading manuals, programming, and then debugging the resulting code. Get your code working right and you have harnessed the power of the program. Or, you might be staring at some cryptic error message you have no idea how to resolve.

Fortunately, R is not only open to the world, its creators designed the system so that anyone can contribute by adding extra functionality. Taking advantage of this opportunity, your author developed an extension to R called lessR. Compared to standard R, lessR requires much less R code to accomplish basic data analysis. The addition of lessR to the R environment does not diminish the standard R environment. On the contrary, the lessR enhancements are just added to what already exists.

R is a true programming language, so the flexibility of R allows almost anything that can be done with data. The reality, however, at least for the vast majority of the standard data analysis topics discussed in this book, is that certain specific steps must always be accomplished. There is no need for everyone to have to figure out and then repeat the same programming to accomplish those steps.

appendix with equivalent R functions, Section 11.6, p. 279

Instead, let lessR do the extra programming. For example, to do a comprehensive regression analysis with standard R begins with a dozen or so separate R statements, and then multiple lines of programming R code to organize the results. With lessR, as explained in Chapters 9 and 10, one instruction calls the Regression function to accomplish more than is accomplished with the dozen R statements and the extra programming. The lessR regression procedure taps directly into R's capabilities, and then organizes the output and delivers several graphs. The appendix illustrates the core R functions upon which lessR depends.

Two primary objectives underlie the lessR project to minimize the needed programming to use R for data analysis.

- A data analysis procedure should typically produce desirable output without any extra instructions or information other than the name of the procedure and the relevant variable name or names.
- If changes to the default output are desired, such as choosing a new background color for a graph, then simply scan a list of the available options to understand how to provide all the information needed to proceed without writing code.

Let's get started.

1.2 Access R

1.2.1 Download R

The best way to learn R is to start using R, which is available on many Internet servers around the world. These servers and the information on them comprise CRAN, the Comprehensive R Archive Network. Obtain the latest version of R at:

CRAN: Worldwide network of servers and information for the R system.

```
http://cran.r-project.org
```

To download files from the CRAN servers, first choose a server from the available CRAN servers worldwide. The website provides the following prompt.

```
--- Please select a CRAN mirror for use in this session ---
```

Presumably choose a server close to your physical location.

Then choose an operating system. The next web page displays the following list of three links, one for each operating system.

- Download R for Linux
- Download R for MacOS X
- Download R for Windows

Windows: Click the `Download R for Windows` link near the top of the page. On the top of the resulting new page, click `base`. Another new page appears. Click the first link on the page, which begins with `Download R`, followed by the current version number.

Macintosh: Click the `Download R for Mac OS X` link near the top of the page. On the resulting new page, click the first file to download, under the heading of `Files:`, which lists the version number followed by `(latest version)`.

Linux: Click the `Download R for Linux` link and follow the posted instructions. Or, for a Debian version of Linux, or Debian based versions such as Ubuntu and Mint, instead download R from the usual software repository available with the Debian package system.

After downloading R, follow the instructions from the installer program. For each prompt from the installer, the default, the choice that is already presented, works well for most people. According to the installer's prompts, decide if you wish the installer to place the R icon on your desktop.

During the installation process the following question may appear.

```
Would you like to use a personal library instead?
```

If asked, usually respond with a `y`, for yes, so that you have administrative access to the files created for and needed by R.

R does not prompt for updates to itself so occasionally re-visit the R servers and check the current version of R, usually downloading a new version if applicable. In particular, the use of the `lessR` procedures requires at least Version 2.15.0 of R, which was released March of 2012.

1.2.2 Start R

Windows and Macintosh users begin an R session as for any other application, of which there are various methods. For example, if you chose to have the R icon placed on your desktop during the installation process, then just double-click that icon to start R. To run R on Linux/Unix, at the system command line prompt simply enter the letter R.

console: The window for entering R commands and for text output.

As an R session begins on Windows or Macintosh, a window opens called the `console`, analogous to the command line prompt window in Linux/Unix. This window displays about 20 lines or so of information, beginning with the version number. The first and last part of this information appears in Listing 1.1, running on a Macintosh computer.

```
R version 3.0.1 (2013-05-16) -- "Good Sport"
Copyright (C) 2013 The R Foundation for Statistical Computing
...
Type 'demo()' for some demos, 'help()' for on-line help, or
'help.start()' for an HTML browser interface to help.
Type 'q()' to quit R.

[R.app GUI 1.61 (6492) x86_64-apple-darwin10.8.0]

>
```

Listing 1.1 Information provided by R at the start of a new session.

command prompt: The > sign, which signals that R awaits an instruction.

The last line of this introductory information that R displays contains only a >, the R *command prompt*, from which you begin to instruct R on what it is that you wish to accomplish.

function: A procedure that implements a specific task such as a data analysis.

Enter each R instruction in response to this command prompt. Then press the `Enter/Return` key and R immediately processes that instruction. Each instruction is a call to a *function*, a procedure to accomplish a specific task such as to calculate a mean of the data values for a variable or to display its data values. An R session is interactive. The session consists of sequential function calls, each entered in response to another command prompt, followed by any subsequent output from R.

continuation prompt: The + sign, which indicates the entered instruction is incomplete.

If the entered function call is not complete when `Enter/Return` is pressed, such as missing a closing parenthesis, then R responds with the *continuation prompt*, +. Enter the missing information and continue as usual.

A previously entered function call can be re-run and/or edited without re-entering it. After an R function call has been entered, push the ↑ key, which accesses the *command history* of your R session. After pushing ↑ the statement reappears as if re-entered from the keyboard. Then, if

command history: Recently entered R instructions.

desired, use the ← and → keys, or the mouse on the Macintosh, to move to a specific part of the R statement. If desired, edit the statement before pressing `Enter` or `Return`. Each time the ↑ key is pressed, the next previous R command reappears.

R opens on Windows and Macintosh systems within the familiar standard menu based interface, though this menu interface is of secondary importance when using the command prompt based R. These menu based commands, however, can for a limited set of instructions be used in place of the command line. For example, the standard menu sequence File ▷ Save is available to save the information in the corresponding window. Navigate these menus as you would any other application. These menus are, however, different for Windows and Macintosh.

The different menus are not such a concern because the R command line instructions for performing specific tasks are identical across all systems.

1.2.3 Extend R

R organizes its many procedures, its functions, into groups of related functions called *packages*. The initial installed version of R includes six different packages, including the stat package, the graphics package and the base package for various utilities. All of these packages are installed with R on your computer system and are automatically loaded into memory when an R session begins.

package: A set of related R functions.

Many more functions, which considerably extend the functionality of R, are available from *contributed packages*, packages written by users in the R community. Anyone can write and upload a properly formatted contributed package to the CRAN servers. The resulting functions work within the R environment just like any standard R function. The functions in a contributed package simply add to the large number of already available functions.

contributed package: An R package provided by the user community.

One contributed package is the lessR package written by your author and featured in this book. To access the functions within a contributed package, first download the package from the CRAN servers. To download the lessR package, start up R and invoke the install.packages function at the R command prompt, >.

 R Input *Install lessR and related packages*

```
> install.packages("lessR")
```

install.packages function: Download a package from the R servers.

The lessR functions rely upon standard R functions as well as functions that are part of other contributed packages. These packages include John Fox's car package (Fox & Weisberg, 2011), which is especially useful for analyzing regression models, and also leaps (Lumley & Miller, 2009), and MBESS (Kelley & Lai, 2012). Downloading lessR also automatically downloads these other packages.

Over time most packages are revised and re-posted on the CRAN servers. Use the update.packages function to update one or more packages on your computer.

update.packages function: Update the versions of the installed R packages.

 R Input *Update all installed packages*

```
> update.packages()
```

R does not prompt for an update when a package is revised on the CRAN servers, so on occasion update to obtain the most recent versions.

Thousands of contributed packages are available. You can find an alphabetical list of all available contributed packages on the CRAN servers at:

```
http://cran.r-project.org/web/packages
```

Many R packages are grouped into what are called task views to more easily locate packages that provide functions directed towards certain general areas of analysis, such as for the social sciences, multivariate statistics, econometrics, and psychometrics. Links to these task views are at:

```
http://cran.r-project.org/web/views
```

Visit the lessR website to explore lessR beyond the confines of this book.

lessR Website *Site to support this book and the lessR package*
lessRstats.com

The site includes data sets to practice using R and lessR, a place to request features, a place to report bugs, an interactive forum for asking and getting answers to questions, and a list of errata for this text.

1.3 Use R

Our primary tasks are to learn to use R to analyze data and then interpret the results. After installing R and lessR what should be entered in response to the >, the command prompt?

1.3.1 Access lessR

install R, p. 5

After installation, begin each new R session with the library function to access the over 40 lessR functions for data analysis, plus the included data sets.

R Input *First entry for a new R session*
```
> library(lessR)
```

library function:
Activate the functions of the specified package.

The library call is shown in Listing 1.2.

```
> library(lessR)

To get help, enter, after the >,  Help()

>
```

Listing 1.2 Access lessR with the R library function.

Or, create a text file .Rprofile that contains the call to the library function to automatically invoke lessR each time R is run. This file automatically runs the specified functions when an R session begins. For Windows, place the file in the top level of the

`Documents` folder. For Macintosh and Linux, place the file in the top level of the user's home folder.[1]

To learn more about what to do next, access the `lessR` help system.

1.3.2 Get Help

The `lessR` function `Help` offers guides to implementing procedures for data analysis and data editing. The most general call to `Help` is to call the function with no arguments, as suggested when loading the `lessR` system as shown in Listing 1.2.

Help function: Obtain an overview of `lessR` data analysis functions by category.

✒ **lessR Input** *Access the lessR Help system*

> `Help()`

The result is a list of topics for a variety of types of analyses provided by `lessR`, which appears in Figure 1.1. For example, one part of the output of `Help` covers basic graphs such as histograms, bar charts, and scatter plots. This help window remains open until explicitly closed.

Help Topics for `lessR`

Help(data) Create a data file from Excel or similar application.
Help(Read) and **Help(Write)** Read or write data to or from a file.
Help(library) Access libraries of functions called packages.
Help(edit) Edit data and create new variables from existing variables.
Help(system) System level settings, such as a color theme for graphics.

Help(Histogram) Histogram, box plot, dot plot, density curve.
Help(BarChart) Bar chart, pie chart.
Help(LineChart) Line chart, such as a run chart or time series chart.
Help(ScatterPlot) Scatter plot for one or two variables, a function plot.

Help(SummaryStats) Summary statistics for one or two variables.
Help(one.sample) Analysis of a single sample of data.
Help(ttest) Compare two groups by their mean difference.
Help(ANOVA) Compare mean differences for many groups.
Help(power) Power analysis for the t-test.
Help(Correlation) Correlation analysis.
Help(Regression) and **Help(Logit)** Regression analysis, logit analysis.
Help(factor.analysis) Confirmatory and exploratory factor analysis.

Help(prob) Probabilities for normal and t-distributions.
Help(random) and **Help(sample)** Create random numbers or samples.

Help(lessR) lessR manual and list of updates to current version.

Figure 1.1 Output from `Help()`.

To pursue any of the listed topics further, invoke the `Help` function with one of the listed topics as an argument, a specific value entered between the parentheses. The `Help` function takes only one argument, such as the word `Histogram`.

lessR Input *Access help for a histogram and related functions*

```
> Help(Histogram)
```

The result is shown in Figure 1.2.

Histogram, etc.

Histogram, hs Histogram.
Density, dn Density curve over histogram.
BoxPlot, bx Box plot.
DotPlot, dp Dot plot.

These functions graph a distribution of data values for a continuous variable
such as Time. Replace Y in these examples with the actual variable name.

A histogram, or hs, based on the current color theme, such as the default "blue".
```
> Histogram(Y)
```

Specify the gray scale color theme, a title, and a label for the x-axis.
```
> set(colors="gray")
> Histogram(Y, main="My Title", xlab="Y (mm)")
```

Specify bins, starting at 60 with a bin width of 10.
```
> Histogram(Y, bin.start=60, bin.width=10)
```

Density curve superimposed on the underlying histogram, abbreviated dn.
```
> Density(Y)
```

Box plot, abbreviated bx.
```
> BoxPlot(Y)
```

Dot plot, a scatterplot of one variable, abbreviated dp.
```
> DotPlot(Y)
```

Complete list of Help topics, enter: Help()

For more help on a function, enter ? in front of its name: ?Histogram

Figure 1.2 Output from `Help(Histogram)`.

The resulting help page provides a brief overview of `Histogram` and related functions that display the distribution of values for a numeric variable, the subject of Chapter 5. Access this same help page by entering the name of any of these other functions. This is one place in R where capitalization is ignored, the goal is to facilitate access to the correct help page, perhaps by just entering the name of an analysis without needing to first display the general help page shown in Figure 1.1.

From scanning these help pages, the instructions to accomplish any lessR data analysis, and some standard R analyses, are revealed. As can be seen from Figure 1.1, the functions for the different analyses are named accordingly. The `Histogram` function provides a histogram, the `BoxPlot` function a box plot, the `ScatterPlot` function a scatter plot, and the `SummaryStats` function basic summary statistics. Include as part of the function call the appropriate variable name or names and any other arguments in parentheses. Most functions can also be accessed with an abbreviation such as hs for Histogram, bc for BarChart, ss for SummaryStats, sp for ScatterPlot and reg for Regression.

More detailed help for any function is also available from the general R help system. Every package in the R system, such as the built-in stats package, or a contributed package such as lessR, is required to have a manual, available to any R user. The manual provides a detailed explanation of each function in the corresponding package. As indicated at the bottom of Figure 1.1, the complete lessR manual is available from the lessR function Help.

 lessR Input *Access the complete lessR manual*

> Help(lessR)

The standard R help system provides the section of the manual for a specified function. To access this help system, enter a question mark, ?, in front of the function name.

? function: R help to obtain the user manual for a specified function.

 lessR Input *Access standard R help for a specified function*

> ?Histogram

The resulting explanation includes a definition of all the parameter options for the function, a more detailed discussion of how to use the function, and most importantly, examples of using the function.

The R help function only works when the exact name of the function of interest is specified, including its capitalization. In contrast, the lessR help system presents an overview of different analyses with the function names. More specific help can then be obtained once the function name is known.

1.3.3 Data Analysis Example

Data analysis begins with, well, data. From within R locate a data file on your computer system or the web, and then read the data in the file for analysis into R. Read data into R with the lessR function Read.

Read function, Section 2.2.1, p. 32

To demonstrate a basic R analysis, begin with a data file included with lessR, the Employee data set. This data file is available on any computer system on which lessR has been downloaded. To read data into R is to read the data into a specific object that R calls a data frame, a rectangular data table. The name of this data frame could be any valid R name, but in general for lessR analyses use the name mydata. Assign the data read into R to the mydata data table with the *assignment operator*, <-, a "less than sign" followed by a "minus sign". The <- mimics an arrowhead to indicate the direction of the assignment, here for the data read from an external data file into the created data table within R that we called mydata.

Employee data table, Figure 1.7, p. 21

assignment operator: Use <- to assign the value of an expression to a variable or object.

To read the data, enter the following instruction after the command prompt, >. Make sure to follow the same pattern of capitalization.

```
> mydata <- Read("Employee", format="lessR", quiet=TRUE)
```

By default `Read` provides a variety of useful information to understand the data read into the data table. The `quiet=TRUE` option suppresses this output, which awaits discussion in the following chapter. To preview this information, omit this option from the preceding call to `Read`.

Employee data, Section 1.6.1, p. 20

The Employee data set is explained later in this chapter, but for now note that the data set consists of measurements for several variables for 37 different employees at one company. One of the variables is Salary, the annual Salary in USD recorded for each of these 37 employees. Now that the data values have been read into the current R session these 37 Salaries can be listed

values *function: List the values of a single variable.*

with the `lessR` function `values`, as shown in Listing 1.3. Enter `values(Salary)` in response to the command prompt, >, as shown in the first line of Listing 1.3. Or, enter the name of the data frame, `mydata`, in response to the command prompt to view the values for all of the

display data table all or part, Section 2.2.4, p. 36

variables in the data frame.

```
> values(Salary)
  [1]   43788.26   84494.58  101074.86   43772.58   47139.90   59441.93   89062.66
  [8]   62321.36   51356.69   46772.95   45545.25   71871.05   61084.02   56337.83
 [15]   85027.55   82681.19   81352.33  124419.23  112563.38   39704.79   73014.43
 [22]   39868.68   59624.87   56312.89   67714.85   39188.96   36124.97   51055.44
 [29]   59547.60   77785.51   62502.50   51961.29   62675.26   98138.43   41036.85
 [36]   46508.32   47562.36
```

Listing 1.3 The values of Salary for 37 employees as read from the Employee data file.

The R output in Listing 1.3 follows the call to the `values` function. Each line of the output begins with a number enclosed in brackets. The first line begins with a [1], which means that this line displays the first data value, the Salary for the first employee listed in the data set. The last line of the output begins with a [36], so this line begins with the 36th Salary. The last line only contains two values because there are a total of 37 values listed, one for each employee.

A basic analysis of the data values for a numeric variable such as Salary plots its histogram

Histogram function, Section 5.2, p. 100

and displays its basic summary statistics. The `lessR` function `Histogram` accomplished both of these tasks. As discussed in Chapter 5, a histogram groups similar values of a numeric variable into bins, and then plots a bar for each bin such that the taller the bar, the more values in the bin. The result is a graph of the shape of the distribution of values for that variable. The graph shows the values that occur most frequently, which occur less frequently, and everything in between these extremes.

To create the histogram and summary statistics for the 37 Salaries in Listing 1.3, follow the information from the help page in Figure 1.2. Just enter the variable name, Salary, as the argument to the call to the `Histogram` function. As is true of all `lessR` data analysis functions, the default name of the data table that contains the specified variable is `mydata`.

```
> Histogram(Salary)
```

The histogram appears in Figure 1.3 (in gray scale whereas the usual default involves color). We observe that the Salaries of these 37 employees range from below \$40,000 to above \$120,000, but most of the salaries are concentrated in the lower range, particularly between \$40,000 and \$60,000.

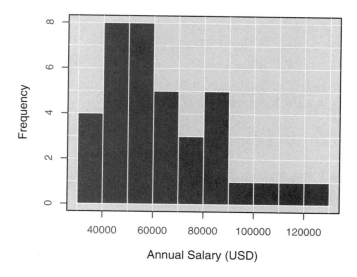

Figure 1.3 The gray color theme `lessR` histogram for Salary from the Employee data set.

The `Histogram` function also generates text output shown in Listing 1.4. The summary statistics appear first: the total sample size, number of missing values, and the sample statistics of the mean, standard deviation, minimum, median and maximum. Also provided is a list of any outliers and a frequency table based on all of the bins, along with the proportions, cumulative frequencies and cumulative proportions. Further discussion of this and other features of the `Histogram` function are deferred until Chapter 5.

summary statistics, Section 5.3.1, p. 105
outlier, Section 5.3.1, p. 106

```
--- Salary, Annual Salary (USD) ---

    n   miss         mean          sd         min         mdn         max
   37      0    63795.557   21799.533   36124.970   59547.600  124419.230
```

Listing 1.4 Summary statistics of Salary.

Our goal has been accomplished, our first R/lessR data analysis. As shown in the next chapter, to do data analysis of data stored in your own data file use `Read` to locate and then read a data file that you store on your computer system. The version of `Read` for this task is simpler in this more common situation, with only an empty set of parentheses. The empty parentheses inform R to allow you to browse, that is, navigate, your computer file system to locate the folder that contains your data file.

From the start of the R session to obtaining a histogram in color with various text output requires two or three statements, depending on whether the `library(lessR)` statement had previously been placed in the `.Rprofile` file. One R statement obtains the input needed for the analysis, which is to read the data into the R data table `mydata`. Then enter just one statement to generate the histogram and related analyses for the designated variable.

library function, Section 1.3.1, p. 6

.Rprofile, p. 6

```
> library(lessR)
> mydata <- Read()
> Histogram(Salary)
```

Listing 1.5 R/lessR instructions to generate a histogram of the variable Salary from a data file stored on the user's computer system.

If no argument is passed to the Histogram function, then a histogram is generated for *each* numerical variable in the data table, what R calls a data frame.

```
> Histogram()
```

The same result is obtained for both histograms and bar charts with the lessR function CountAll, again with no arguments.

CountAll
function: Bar chart or histogram and summary statistics for all variables.

```
> CountAll()
```

Each histogram or bar chart is written to its own pdf file and the corresponding statistical summaries are written to the R text window, the console. The lessR enhancements to R minimize the amount of work needed to accomplish data analysis and obtain meaningful, hopefully aesthetically pleasing results.

1.3.4 Quit R

Quit function:
End an R session.

To end an R session from the command line prompt, use the quit function, q.

> **R Input** *Quit R*
> ```
> > q()
> ```

Or, when running within the Windows menu system, choose the menu sequence File ▷ Exit as with virtually any other Windows application. The same applies for the Macintosh sequence R ▷ Quit R.

Unless the default settings have been changed, you are prompted after entering the quit command to save the working session, as shown in Listing 1.6.

```
> q()
Save workspace image? [y/n/c]: n
```

Listing 1.6 The quit R dialog.

Usually respond to this question with an n for no. If output needs to be saved, simply copy the output to another document, such as a word processing document. Or, unless the data set is exceptionally large and the computations particularly intensive, just re-run the analysis.

1.3.5 R **Functions**

All work is done in R with functions. Call a function with some information that is then processed by that function, such as data values for a function that processes data. The information passed to a function, referenced in between the parentheses of the function call, are the *arguments* of the function. In our histogram example, the one argument passed to the Histogram function is the variable name, Salary. Specifying the variable name as an argument makes the data values for that variable accessible to the function.

Some arguments of a function have *default* values, which are assumed but can be overridden. For example, lessR functions such as Histogram use the data argument to specify the name of the data frame, R's name for the data table that contains the variables of interest. The default value for the input data frame is mydata, so the following two function calls are equivalent.

> Histogram(Salary)   *or*   > Histogram(Salary, data=mydata)

For ease of use rely upon the default. Usually only invoke the data option when the input data frame is *not* mydata. If all the arguments in a function call are set to their default values, then no information needs to be passed to the function. The paired parentheses, however, are always part of the function call even if empty.

Functions may also have some arguments with no default value. These functions require the values of these arguments to be explicitly specified. To see the full list of arguments and default values for a function, along with other information, request the manual pages for the function. To obtain these pages, enter the function name preceded by a question mark, ?.

Types of Functions

There are at least three different types of functions within the R system. *Utility functions* provide information or set characteristics of the overall environment to facilitate data processing. An example of a utility function is the Help function.

The two other types of functions process data as illustrated in Figure 1.4, such as the lessR function Histogram. More specifically the type of data processing done by Histogram is data analysis. A *data analysis function* applies statistical methods to process the data to obtain the requested analysis, the output of the function. The Histogram function directs the resulting text output to the console and the graphics output to a graphics window.

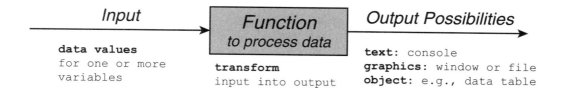

Figure 1.4 General procedure for functions that process data, either data analysis or data modification.

As we discuss in Chapters 2 and 3, another way to process data is to create or modify the data in preparation for subsequent data analysis. One example of a *data modification function* is

---

arguments of a function: Information used by the function.

default value: Assumed value for an argument of a function that can be explicitly changed.

data argument: The name of the data frame that contains the variables for analysis.

?function, the standard R help function, Section 1.3.2, p. 9

utility function: Inform or set characteristics of the data processing environment. *Help* function, Section 1.3.2, p. 7

data analysis function: Procedure to access and analyze data.

data modification function: Procedure to create or modify data.

Read, which reads data from an external data file and then directs the output to an R data table, usually named mydata as in the preceding example. Other examples of data modification are to sort the data, or to transform the data values of a variable such as by taking their logarithms. The modified data can then either be directed back to overwrite the original mydata, or to a new data table leaving the original mydata unmodified.

digits.d option: Explicitly set the number of decimal digits for the output.

The output from data analysis functions naturally involves numbers, which are displayed with a set level of decimal digits. By default lessR functions generally specify the number of displayed decimal digits as one more than the number of decimal digits for the input data values. Or two decimal digits are displayed if the input data values are all integers. If more or less decimal digits are desired, then specify with digits.d in the calls to the various lessR functions.

quiet=TRUE option: Suppress all text output to the console.

Suppress the text output to the console for the data modification functions and most other lessR functions with the quiet=TRUE option included as part of the function call. With the quiet option invoked these functions continue sending output to a special output object and/or a graphics window without sending any text to the console.

brief=TRUE option: Reduce text output to the console.

set function, Section 1.4.1, p. 16

The primary purpose of some functions is to display text output to the console. Suppressing their text output entirely is not meaningful. Instead the brief option set to TRUE reduces the amount of output to just the minimum amount needed to convey the most basic results. Both the quiet and brief options can also be set system wide with the lessR function set. Then their values remain in effect for all subsequent analyses unless explicitly changed.

Standard R Functions

Standard R functions tend to be very specific in terms of their output. Many of these functions do not provide any output to the console but instead send a returned object back into the R environment as the primary output. After running the function, access the output objects to extract the needed information.

$ notation: One application is to identify the relevant data frame.

R functions do not have a default data source, so the data table must always be explicitly referenced. For example, the standard R function to obtain a histogram is hist. To use the function the data frame that contains the variables of interest must first be identified. Unfortunately, there is no consistent method to identify this information. All lessR functions use the data option to identify the relevant data table. Some standard R functions use this option, but most do not. One way to indicate the input data table for functions that do not use the data option is to use the *$ notation* to prefix the name of the data table to the variable name.

```
> hist(mydata$Salary)
```

with function: Identify the relevant data frame.

Or, use the R with function to wrap around the function call.

```
> with(mydata, hist(Salary))
```

The resulting histogram has no default colors, no grid lines, and no text output.
To obtain numerical output, assign the output of the function to an object, such as h.

```
> h <- hist(mydata$Salary)
```

Analysis of the h object provides information such as the counts for each bin. The information can be displayed at the console by entering h at the command prompt, but this information is more intended as input for additional programming than it is for consumption as finished output. Then use R statements to extract and then apply the additional programming such as to arrange the numerical output for display at the console. Many lessR functions also return the same object as the corresponding R function that provides the computations, such as the Histogram function that can return the same object as hist.

The kind of programming that accesses this information is not covered in this book because the lessR functions do this work for you. Each lessR data analysis function runs one or more standard R functions, usually multiple functions, extracts the relevant information from each and then arranges and displays text output at the console and, if relevant, sends graphics to a graphics window. The standard R functions become a kind of tool kit that lessR functions rely upon to construct their output.

1.3.6 Lists of Values

When using statistical software such as R a frequent task is to specify a list of variables, or a list of constants of either numbers or character strings. For example, suppose you wish to have the histogram bars filled with two alternating colors, here two shades of gray, defined on a scale where "gray0" is black and "gray100" is white. The col.fill option specifies the color of the histogram bars.

col.fill option, Table 1.1, p. 17

```
> Histogram(Salary, col.fill=c("gray40","gray70"))
```

c function: Combine a list of values.

In R a list of individual values separated by commas is always enclosed in parentheses with the c function, which delineates a list of values from the rest of the information that surrounds the list.

Another example is the list of the first eight integers specified with the c function.

```
> c(1,2,3,4,5,6,7,8)
```

: notation: Specify a sequential set of integers.

If the items in the list are sequential the : notation can be used instead.

```
> 1:8
```

Or, the types of expressions for a list can be combined.

```
> c(1:4,5,6,7:8)
```

Enter any of the three preceding expressions at the command prompt to obtain the following output.

```
[1] 1 2 3 4 5 6 7 8
```

The [1] indicates that the first value in the output begins this line, the only line of output in this example.

list of variables,
Section 8.3, p. 195

The concept of a list applies not only to a list of numbers as illustrated here but also to lists of variables.

1.4 R Graphs

1.4.1 Color Themes

color theme: A
set of related colors
for graphic output.

Graphics from `lessR` functions are based on color themes, each with a pre-defined color palette. The default color theme is `blue`, so by default all graphs include color. This book is printed in gray scale (to save you money), so graphics here are printed with the gray scale color theme. The chosen gray color theme follows Hadley Wickham's design choices in his innovative graphics package `ggplot2` (Wickham, 2009).

In addition to `blue` and `gray`, other available color themes include `green`, `gold`, `rose`, `red`, `purple`, `dodgerblue`, `sienna`, `white`, `orange.black`, and `gray.black`. Most themes have lighter backgrounds, though any setting can be customized. The `orange.black` and `gray.black` themes have a black background by default.

set function: Select
a system option
such as color
theme and related
color choices.

Use the `lessR` utility function `set` to change the theme for all subsequent graphics. Enclose the name of the color theme in quotes.

 lessR Input *Set color theme for subsequent analyses such as gray scale*
```
> set(colors="gray")
```

.Rprofile, p. 6
trans.fill.bar,
trans.fill.pt
options:
Transparency levels
for the color of an
interior of a bar or
point.

If you prefer a specific theme over the default `blue`, add this `set` statement to your `.Rprofile` file to automatically invoke the preferred theme each time R is started.

The function `set` can also set the transparency of bars or points in a graph with the `trans.fill.bar` and `trans.fill.pt` options. The `lessR` default setting for the interior of plotted points is `trans.fill.pt=0.66`, a partial transparency. To plot points with a completely filled color, oblique, set the value of `trans.fill.pt` to 0. A value of 1 means complete transparency.

col.bg, col.grid
options: Set
background color,
grid color.

The default setting for filled rectangular regions such as the bars of a histogram is `trans.fill.bar=0`. That is, the default bars such as for a histogram are fully oblique. Set the background color and grid line colors with `col.bg` and `col.grid`, respectively.[2]

ghost option:
Create a ghost
effect for the
graphics.

The `ghost` option creates a black background, removes grid lines, and adds a transparency level to the bars, such as for a histogram. The following function call sets the color theme in subsequent graphs to `dodgerblue`, turns on the `ghost` option, and turns off the transparency of plotted points.

```
> set(colors="dodgerblue", ghost=TRUE, trans.fill.pt=0)
```

1.4.2 Individual Colors

Adjust color themes by setting options such as `col.fill.bar` with the `set` function. Customize beyond the color themes by tweaking individual components of a graph. To do so, apply a color name to the argument that corresponds to the relevant part of the graph, such as the bars of a histogram or the points of a scatter plot. To view the available options for any one graphics procedure, access help for that function by entering the function's name proceeded by a question mark.

R help function, Section 1.3.2, p. 9

Table 1.1 lists the color options available for most `lessR` graphics functions. Most of the graphics `lessR` functions use `col.fill` and `col.stroke` to define the interior of the relevant plotted object and its outline, respectively. For the histogram, these options refer to the color of the bars and the corresponding borders. For the plotted points in a scatter plot these options refer to the interior color of the points and their border color. Use the `set` function to set any of these colors to `"transparent"` to remove the color.

Table 1.1 Available color choices for `lessR` graphics functions such as `Histogram` and `ScatterPlot`.

Option	Meaning
col.fill	Color of bars or plotted points.
col.stroke	Color of the border of the bars.
col.bg	Color of the plot background.
col.grid	Color of the grid lines.
col.axis	Color of the font used to label the axis values.
col.ticks	Color of the ticks used to label the axis values.

One way to specify an individual color is to specify one of the 657 color names in R (though some names are just different spellings for the same color). To view the colors invoke the `lessR` function `showColors`.

 lessR Input *Display a sample of each R named color*

```
> showColors()
```

showColors function: Create an illustrated listing of all named R colors.

This function call generates a `pdf` file that contains all the color names and also a sample of each color and its corresponding `rgb` composition, that is, its defining red, green, and blue component.

For example, there is a color named `"aquamarine3"`, and a very pale color named `"snow"`. The following produces a histogram of Salary with the current color theme but modified colors for the histogram bars and background of the graph.

```
> Histogram(Salary, col.fill="aquamarine3", col.bg="snow")
```

In addition to all of the named colors, a color can also be customized in terms of its location within a color space. For example the `rgb` function specifies a color precisely according to its red, green, and blue component.

```
> Histogram(Salary, col.fill=rgb(102,205,170, maxColorValue=255))
```

The maxColorValue=255 option indicates to scale the colors from 0 to 255, the same scale used by Adobe Photoshop and also html, which forms the basis for web pages.

variable labels,
Section 2.4.1,
p. 46

1.4.3 Axes Labels

xlab, ylab
options: Custom
axis labels.

main option:
Optional graph
title.

If the data frame that contains the data for analysis contains the lessR feature of variable labels, then these labels automatically become the corresponding axes labels on the resulting graph. Otherwise the default labels are the variable names. Custom labels for the horizontal or x-axis, and the vertical or y-axis, are provided by the xlab and ylab options, respectively. The graph title is set with main.

color themes,
Section 1.4.1,
p. 16

To illustrate, re-do the histogram from Figure 1.3 with customized labels and also with a different color theme. One possibility is to choose a color theme that provides a black background by default, optimized for viewing when projected on a large screen.

 **lessR Input**

```
> set(colors="gray.black")
> Histogram(Salary, xlab="Salary (USD)", ylab="Count",
            main="Histogram of Salary")
```

The histogram displayed with this alternate color theme is in Figure 1.5. This color theme applies to all subsequent graphic output until explicitly changed, or until R is quit and then restarted.

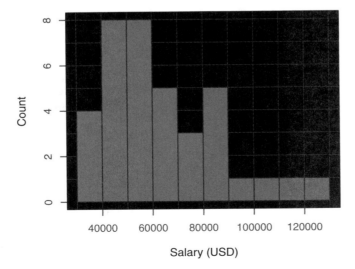

Figure 1.5 Histogram with the gray.black color theme, custom axes labels, and a title.

1.4.4 Save Graphs as `pdf` Files

After creating a graph such as a histogram, the graph can be saved to a file on your computer system. One option for Windows and Macintosh users is to right-click on the window that contains the graph, copy it and then paste it into the word processor that contains the report of the analysis. Another option is to write the graph directly to a `pdf` file as it is generated.

lessR Help function, Section 1.3.2, p. 7

The `lessR` graphics functions provide a means to save the graph directly to a `pdf` file, without interfering with any displayed help window from the `lessR` help system. Those routines such as the `Histogram` function that generate a single graph have an option `pdf.file` that provide for the name of the resulting file. Accompanying options are `pdf.width` and `pdf.height` to change the size of the graph from the default values of 5 inches by 5 inches.

pdf.file option: `pdf` file for which to direct a `lessR` function graphics output.

---

 lessR Input *Generate and save the histogram directly to a pdf file*

```
> Histogram(Salary, pdf.file="myHistogram.pdf", pdf.width=6)
```

Functions that generate multiple graphics, such as the `Regression` function, have a `pdf` option that is set to `TRUE` to generate the graphics. In this situation each of the file names is automatically provided.

pdf option: Set to `TRUE` to save `pdf` files for `lessR` functions that generate multiple graphics.

1.5 Reproducible Code

An analysis should be repeatable at some future time. To reproduce an analysis the code to generate the analysis must be able to be re-run, what is called *reproducible code*. The R statements to accomplish a specific analysis, such as in Listing 1.5, should generally be saved in a standard text file so that these instructions are reproducible. A *text file* consists of only standard characters, which consist of the upper and lowercase letters of the alphabet, digits, punctuation marks, and a few control codes. Text files are generally created with a *text editor*, a kind of simplified word processor that only works with the standard text characters.[3]

reproducible code: The instructions to generate an analysis can be repeated at some future time.

text file: A file that consists of only standard characters.

Several text editors integrate with the R environment so well that they become an extension of R itself. Your author exclusively uses a non-traditional, free text editor `vim`, which runs on Windows, Macintosh, Linux/Unix, iOS for the iPad and iPhone, and Android. An advantage of `vim` as a general text editor is that once having learned its insert and normal modes, and various keystroke combinations for navigating and editing text, writing and editing text is considerably faster than with a traditional word processor. `vim` also integrates with other environments. For example, this book was written with `vim` in conjunction with a powerful, cross-platform, open source and free typesetting system `LaTeX`.

text editor: An editor for editing a text file.

vim: General purpose text editor with excellent R compatibility.

Code integration, which transfers instructions from `vim` directly to R, is one means by which `vim` integrates with R. From within `vim` one keystroke combination starts an R session, or submits a single line, selected range of lines, or an entire file of R instructions directly into the running R session. All entering and editing of code takes place within a `vim` window, and all output flows into an adjacent R window.

code integration: Transfer code entered into an editor to an environment for executing the code, such as R.

Another form of integration of a text editor with R is *syntax highlighting*. Within the editor, R keywords are highlighted, as are numerical constants, quoted strings, and so forth, all usually in different colors. This highlighting makes the on-screen text considerably more readable and mistakes less likely. Figure 1.6 illustrates syntax highlighting, though only in gray scale.

syntax highlighting: Differently highlight different elements of the code to enhance readability.

```
1 library(lessR)
2 set(colors="dodgerblue", ghost=TRUE, trans.fill.pt=0)
3
4 Read()
5
6 Histogram(Salary, xlab="Salary (USD)", ylab="Count")
```

Figure 1.6 Excerpt of R instructions in the vim editor with gray scale syntax highlighting.

Alternatives also exist for a more traditional editing experience than vim yet that still provide a free editing product with code integration and syntax highlighting. The recommended traditional style text editor for Macintoshs is TextWrangler. Windows users have the Tinn-R editor and R development system that integrates with the R system, or the general purpose text editor and Notepad replacement Notepad++, with the NpptoR plug-in. Linux gnome users, as well as Windows and Macintosh users, have gedit with the RGedit plug-in. Many other possibilities exist as well, including the full editing and development environment provided by RStudio.

Rstudio, rstudio.com

At a minimum, use a simple, basic text editor to develop and store your R programs. An editor that links directly to R is the most elegant solution, but even without linking to R directly you can manually copy and paste your R instructions from an editor into R. Save your R instructions gradually so as to build a library of instructions to accomplish a variety of analyses. With this strategy you can reproduce the output of any one analysis when desired, or do a simple modification to obtain a related analysis.

1.6 Data

Data analysis begins, naturally enough, with data. This section presents two sets of data analyzed throughout this book, and a discussion of the different types of variables typically encountered in data sets. The rest of this book shows how to read a data set into R for analysis and then conduct a variety of analyses.

1.6.1 Data Example I: Employee Data

The human resources department of a company recorded the following information for each employee: Name, Years of employment, Gender, Department employed, annual Salary, Satisfaction with work environment, and Health Plan. Data such as these are naturally organized into a rectangular table for subsequent analysis. Consider a *data file* with measurements organized into a table for 37 employees, available on the web as an Excel worksheet.

data file: A file on a computer system that contains data, usually organized into a table of rows and columns.

```
http://lessRstats.com/data/employee.xlsx
```

Figure 1.7 displays the first nine lines of the Excel version of this data file.

A basic characteristic of a data table is the *unit of the analysis*, the object of study. In this example the unit of analysis is a person, an employee at a specific company. Other potential units of analysis include organizations, places, events, or things in general.

unit of analysis: The class of people, organizations, things or places from which measurements are obtained.

Each cell of this table represents a single *data value*, the value of a variable for a specific instance of the unit of the analysis, here a specific person. For example, the person listed in the first row of data, which is the second row of the worksheet, is Darnell Ritchie. The data value

data value: The value of a single measurement or classification.

	A	B	C	D	E	F	G
1	Name	Years	Gender	Dept	Salary	Satisfaction	HealthPlan
2	Ritchie, Darnell	7	M	ADMN	43788.26	med	1
3	Wu, James		M	SALE	84494.58	low	1
4	Hoang, Binh	15	M	SALE	101074.86	low	3
5	Jones, Alissa	5	F		43772.58		1
6	Downs, Deborah	7	F	FINC	47139.90	high	2
7	Afshari, Anbar	6	F	ADMN	59441.93	high	2
8	Knox, Michael	18	M	MKTG	89062.66	med	3
9	Campagna, Justin	8	M	SALE	62321.36	low	1

Figure 1.7 Variable names in the first row and the first eight rows of data from the employee data table as stored in an Excel worksheet.

for his annual Salary is $43,788.26. His data value for the variable Dept is admn, which indicates that he works in general administration. The data value for the Years employed at the company is not available for the second person, James Wu, and so the corresponding cell is empty.

Data analysis is organized around the concept of a variable. A *variable* is a characteristic of an object or event with different values for different people, organizations, etc. Each *variable name* is concise, usually less than 10 or so characters, and serves as the reference for the variable in any subsequent data analysis. The first row of the data table usually contains the variable names. The data values for each variable are within the same column. The data values of the first column in this particular data table, however, are not for a variable but are instead unique ID values that identify the employee for each row for which the data values are listed.

The data values in a single row of the data table in Figure 1.7 are the data for a single person. All the data values in a single row together are called a *case*, or by some authors, an *observation*. For example, the first case consists of the data values for Darnell Ritchie.

The form of the data table in Figure 1.7 is the *wide format*. One other data format is explored in Chapter 7, but the wide format is the format most commonly encountered in data analysis. All the data values for one case are in one row and all the data values for a variable are in one column.

variable: Attribute that varies from unit to unit (e.g., different people.)

variable name: Concise name that identifies a variable for analysis.

case (observation): Data values for a single unit such as a person, organization, thing or region.

data table, wide: Data values for each case are in a row and for each variable in a column.

1.6.2 The Worksheet Version

The data values are not usually entered into and then stored from the data analysis application, such as R. Data generally originate instead from some other application or source, perhaps a file saved in the form of a worksheet. Common worksheet applications include Microsoft Excel, which runs on Windows and Macintosh, and LibreOffice Calc, which is offered free of cost, is open source and runs on Windows, Macintosh, and Linux. Perhaps you manually entered the data into the worksheet, perhaps your IT department provided the data in that form, or perhaps you read the data values from some source directly into a worksheet to visualize the data and verify its integrity.

LibreOffice, libreoffice.org

The worksheet is a convenient container that matches the tabular structure of data. By its very nature a worksheet wonderfully organizes the data into the proper format of rows and columns. Do not underestimate the importance of the phrase "wonderfully organizes". It is not uncommon for the majority of work that underlies data analysis to be directed towards organizing and cleaning up the data for subsequent analysis. As opposed to most classroom data sets, real life data analysis is often messy, with the initial version of the data file far from ready for analysis. Except for very large data sets, viewing the data, manipulating the data, culling unreadable or nonsense data values, removing or correcting mis-formatted data values, and other such tasks are readily accomplished with Excel, Calc, or similar worksheet applications.

By default any type of data can be entered into any cell in a worksheet, but for a data table all the data values within each column should conform to the same specific format. For example, the data values for the Salary column in Figure 1.7 are all positive numbers with decimal digits and nothing else. It is not meaningful to include a value such as -3000.82 for a Salary, nor is it meaningful to include a salary of ABC, or >100,000.

data validation: Verify that all data values within the same column have the same format and conform to the same specifications.

Particularly when the data values are manually entered into a worksheet, activate the *data validation* option to verify a consistent format of the data values within each column. For example, in Excel go to the Data ribbon, choose the Validate pull-down menu, and then the Data Validation option. The resulting dialog box, illustrated in Figure 1.8, provides several options for selecting the specific type of data that can be accepted into the designated cells, such as a column of data values for a designated variable.

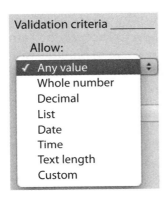

Figure 1.8 Validation option in Excel to specify the format of the data to be accepted in the designated cells.

Read function, Section 2.2.1, p. 32
Write function, Section 2.5.2, p. 50

A worksheet application and R are complementary tools for data analysis. Using the lessR functions Read and Write, for example, data stored in a worksheet can easily be exchanged with R and then returned to applications such as Excel or Calc just as quickly. For convenience, the data may have been initially entered into a worksheet, but the data analysis can take place in an application such as R. For example, it is generally much faster and less work, even when the data values are already in Excel, to export the data to R to compute a histogram than it is to obtain the histogram directly from the Windows version of Excel. With the Macintosh version of Excel, there is no histogram program available.

1.6.3 Types of Variables and Data Values

continuous variable: A variable with numerical values.

A distinction between two types of variables underlies all of data analysis. The values for *continuous variables* are ordered along a quantitative continuum, the abstraction of the infinitely dense real number line, in which an unlimited number of numeric values lie between any two values. Examples of continuous variables for a person are Age, Salary, or extent of Agreement with an opinion about some political issue; for a car, MPG, or Weight; and for a light bulb,

Mean Number of Hours until Failure, or Electrical Consumption per Hour (kilowatt hours). A continuous variable is sometimes also called a numerical variable or *quantitative variable*.

Another type of variable is the *categorical variable*, with values that define non-numeric categories. For example, the values of the categorical variable Gender are Male and Female. Other examples of categorical variables are Cola Preference, State of Residence, or Football Jersey Number. Yes, the number on the jersey consists of numeric digits, but in this context those digits are like any other characters and are not treated numerically. A categorical variable is sometimes also called a non-numerical variable or *qualitative variable*.

categorical variable: A variable with non-numeric categories as values.

The use of the word "variable" is somewhat ambiguous, though hopefully clear from context. There is a distinction between the values of a variable as they actually exist and the data values of the variable that result from the measurement of those values. This distinction follows from the important principle that the data values that result from measurement are *always* organized into discrete categories. This principle is most obvious for the data values of a categorical variable, which are classifications into discrete, unordered categories that correspond to the original, discrete values of the variable. The resulting data values are called *nominal data*. The association of the data values of a categorical variable with the underlying true value of the variable is so close as to almost render the distinction meaningless. A person lives in the state of California and the person marks California on a survey of where he or she lives.

nominal data: Data values grouped into unordered categories.

For continuous variables the distinction between the value of the true, underlying variable and the measurement of that value is more apparent. First, the value of the variable as it exists is always different from its measurement, the data value. Nothing, for example, weighs exactly 2 lbs, or 2.01 lbs or even 2.0000000001 lbs. The true weight of an object could be abstractly expressed to an infinitely large number of decimal digits. A measurement of weight, however, is expressed to a certain level of precision, such as the nearest pound, or the nearest ounce, or the nearest gram. The process of measurement places all similar weights into the same category, an approximation of the true weight, such as to the nearest pound.

The data values that are interpreted according to a numeric scale are one of two types. *Ratio data* follow a numeric scale with the usual properties that we assign to numbers. There is a fixed zero point and values on either side of zero scale proportionality. In particular, two different values can be compared by their ratios, such as to state that 20 is twice as much as 10. Also equal intervals of magnitude separate values that are an equal distance from each other. For example, the distance between 21 and 22 represents the same underlying magnitude of difference for 22 and 23.

ratio data: Numerical scale with fixed zero point and equal intervals.

A weaker numerical scale applies to *interval data*, which maintains the equal interval property of ratio data, but does not have a fixed, natural zero point. The classic example of two related interval scales are Fahrenheit and Celsius temperatures, which each have a different value of zero in terms of the actual magnitude of the temperature. Because the value of zero is arbitrary in either scale, ratio comparisons are not valid. For example, 20°F is not twice as warm as 10°F.

interval data: Numerical scale without a fixed zero point but equal intervals.

Another issue regarding measurement is that in some situations the measurement of the value of a continuous variable is so imprecise that instead of a numerical scale, only a small number of categories exist for which to place the measured values. Suppose admissions to the emergency room are quickly classified into one of only three categories according to the Severity of their Injury: Mild, Moderate, and Severe. The underlying variable regarding the Severity of Injury is continuous. This simple rating scale recognizes that some injuries are more severe than others, but the measurement of the severity is limited to only one of three categories.

Moreover, there is no assumption in this example that the distances of the magnitude of severity between adjacent categories are the same. The underlying progression of severity is assumed, but Moderate Severity of Injury as interpreted by the rater could be closer to Mild Severity than it is to Severe Severity of Injury. Another example is the outcome of a race with the winners ranked in order of finish: 1st, 2nd, and 3rd. The finish times of the each contestant represent a continuous variable, but simply ranking contestants by the order of their finish does not communicate if the race was extremely close or if the winner finished well ahead of his or her nearest competitor.

ordinal data: Ordered categories, rankings.

Data values grouped into ordered non-numeric categories, rankings, result in *ordinal data*. The potential confusion is that the underlying variable is continuous but the measurements only represent categories ordered along this continuum. There is no assumption that the distances between adjacent categories are the same.

1.6.4 The `csv` Formatted Data File

Excel data table, Figure 1.7, p. 21

There are many file formats in which to store the data table in a computer file. If saved from Excel with the usual File ▷ Save menu sequence, the data in Figure 1.7 would be stored in the native Excel format, `.xlsx`, or, if running an older version of Excel, `.xls`. There are also many other choices for the data format of tabular data, as can be seen from the `Format` pull down list of options available from Excel's or Calc's File ▷ Save As menu sequence.

text file: A file that is composed of only standard text characters.

One widely used standard for formatting a data table is to store the data as only standard text characters, such as letters, digits, and punctuation, a *text file*. One way to organize a text file is as a `csv` file, a comma separated values file. In a `csv` file, the contents are stored as ordinary text, commas separate adjacent data values, and the data for each new case (e.g., person) begins on a new line. One advantage of a text file is that the data in the file can be read by virtually any computer application that can read data, such as R, or any worksheet application or any word processor or text editor.

csv format: A format for a text data file with each adjacent pair of data values separated by a comma.

MS Excel:

1. Select all the columns of data, or at least the columns with numeric data values that need to have special formatting removed. Under the `Start` tab find the `Number` column. For versions of Excel prior to 2007, `Format ▷ Cells`. Click the `Number` tab and choose the `General` format to remove formatting.
2. From the `File` menu choose `Save As` and then choose the `Comma Separated Values (csv)` format.

LibreOffice Calc:

1. Select all the columns of data, or at least the columns with numeric data values that need to have special formatting removed. Choose `Format ▷ Cells`. In the `Format Cells` window click the `Numbers` tab in the upper left corner. Under the `Category` list of options in the top-left, choose `All`. In the adjacent option list labeled `Format`, choose `General` and then click the `OK` button.
2. `File ▷ Save As` and then click the arrow in the left margin towards the bottom labeled `File type`. From the available options, choose `Text CSV`. Then click the `Save` button and then the `OK` button.

The entire process should take no more than half a minute after you do this once or twice. The result of these actions is to have the same data stored in two different data files, one in the original native format such as Excel and the other in `csv` format, ready for R, and virtually any other application to read, including back into Excel or Calc or other worksheet application.

1.6.5 View the `csv` File Directly

Opening a `csv` file with Excel or Calc displays the data as a standard worksheet. For example, the commas that separate the adjacent data values are no longer viewable. As an option, to view the literal contents of the data file, view the file in a text editor such as NotePad (Windows), TextEdit (Macintosh) or gedit (gnome Linux). A word processor such as MS Word can also be used, but be aware that word processors sometimes change the displayed text, such as replacing straight quotes with curly quotes, or changing capitalization.

text editor, Section 1.5, p. 19

Viewing the text `csv` file directly is optional, and usually only done to provide diagnostic information when there is a problem with R reading the data. For illustrative purpose only, we look at the file here as it is literally stored. One way to do this for the Employee data is to point your web browser at the following web address.

```
http://lessRstats.com/data/employee.csv
```

Listing 1.7 shows some of the literal contents of the file that R actually "sees" when R reads the data in the `.csv` file named `employee.csv`. The first six rows of data from the `csv` file saved from Excel appear in Listing 1.7.

```
Name,Years,Gender,Dept,Salary,Satisfaction,HealthPlan
"Ritchie, Darnell",7,M,ADMN,43788.26,med,1
"Wu, James",,M,SALE,84494.58,low,1
"Hoang, Binh",15,M,SALE,101074.86,low,3
"Jones, Alissa",5,F,,43772.58,,1
"Downs, Deborah",7,F,FINC,47139.9,high,2
"Afshari, Anbar",6,F,ADMN,59441.93,high,2
```

Listing 1.7 Data as it exists in a computer file stored in the `csv` format.

Each person's Name in Listing 1.7 is enclosed in quotes. When saved as a `csv` file, Excel inserted the quotes because each name contains the same character that delimits or separates adjacent data values, the comma. The quotes indicate that all characters within a set of quotes are a single data value, even if one of the characters is a comma or a space.

Missing data values in this file are literally missing. For example, the data value for Years of employment, the first variable, which occurs immediately after the name, is missing for the second row of data, the data for James Wu. Following his name, instead of a comma, a number, and then a comma, there are just two commas with nothing in between. These adjacent commas result from the corresponding empty cell in the worksheet version of the file. Sometimes missing data values are represented by codes such as −99, which can also be accommodated.

missing data: A data value that is not available in the data table.

missing data codes, Section 2.2.5, p. 36

1.6.6 Data Example II: Machiavellianism

The data values described in this section are the responses to an attitude survey from Hunter, Gerbing, and Boster (1982). The topic is Machiavellianism. These data provide the basis for showing how to read and analyze survey data in `lessR`, and are referenced throughout this book.

These data values are also stored in a text file, but in a format different from that of a csv file.

Machiavellianism: Beliefs and values that endorse the cynical manipulation of others.

To introduce the concept of *Machiavellianism*, consider two different people with two radically different perspectives on life and human nature. One person believes in the inherent goodness of people, in living an ethical life, treating others with respect, trust, and honesty. The other person believes that a primary goal of life is to achieve as much power and material possessions as possible, by any means possible, that the "end justifies the means", to do whatever it takes. To "get ahead" may include lying and cheating. This second person tends to believe that either other people are like himself or herself, or they are naive and gullible, almost willing subjects for his or her manipulation.

This second perspective is aligned with the writings of Niccolo Machiavelli from the 1500s, who wrote extensively on the need for political leaders to do whatever is necessary to defend their political power and success, even if their goals are morally commendable. To be successful for good or for bad requires a cunning sophistication and tactics to achieve the desired goal. Machiavelli's most famous writing, *The Prince* (1902/1513), has become a manual of sorts for those seeking to implement his advice. The concept applies to both political power, in terms of government and organizations, as well as personal power, in terms of interpersonal relationships.

Christie and Geis (1970) introduced the concept of Machiavellianism to psychological researchers. Their Mach IV scale, a set of 20 items for assessing endorsement of Machiavellian beliefs, appears in Table 1.2.

Table 1.2 The Christie and Geiss (1970) Mach IV scale.

Mach IV Item
1.   Never tell anyone the real reason you did something unless it is useful to do so.
2.   The best way to handle people is to tell them what they want to hear.
3.   One should take action only when sure it is morally right.
4.   Most people are basically good and kind.
5.   It is safest to assume that all people have a vicious streak and it will come out when they are given a chance.
6.   Honesty is the best policy in all cases.
7.   There is no excuse for lying to someone else.
8.   Generally speaking, people won't work hard unless they're forced to do so.
9.   All in all, it is better to be humble and honest than to be important and dishonest.
10.   When you ask someone to do something for you, it is best to give the real reasons for wanting it rather than giving reasons which carry more weight.
11.   Most people who get ahead in the world lead clean, moral lives.
12.   Anyone who completely trusts anyone else is asking for trouble.
13.   The biggest difference between most criminals and other people is that the criminals are stupid enough to get caught.
14.   Most people are brave.
15.   It is wise to flatter important people.
16.   It is possible to be good in all respects.
17.   Barnum was wrong when he said that there's a sucker born every minute.
18.   It is hard to get ahead without cutting corners here and there.
19.   People suffering from incurable diseases should have the choice of being put painlessly to death.
20.   Most people forget more easily the death of a parent than the loss of their property.

One use of the term "scale" references the 20 items that define the Mach IV. Another use of the same word references the measurement scale by which *each* item is assessed, similar to the scale with which a person measures his or her weight. For the Mach IV the respondent assesses each item for the extent of agreement with the item along a continuum of Disagreement/Agreement.

As with thousands of other such scales devised by psychologists and social scientists, each item can be assessed on what is a *Likert scale*. A Likert scale consists of a small number of categories that vary from Disagree to Agree, usually 5, 6, or 7 categories. An odd number of categories allows for a neutral point in the middle, separating the Disagreement side from the Agreement side, whereas an even number forces the respondent to choose one side or the other, even if favored slightly. The Mach IV data were collected with the response to each of the 20 items provided on the following 6-point Likert scale.

Likert scale: Measurement of usually 4 to 7 scale points along the Disagree–Agree continuum.

```
Strongly    Disagree    Slightly    Slightly    Agree    Strongly
Disagree                Disagree    Agree                Agree
```

Hunter et al. (1982) administered the Mach IV items to college students as part of a longer attitude survey. The order of all items on the survey was randomized for presentation on the resulting questionnaire. Measurements were collected for 351 respondents. The responses to each of the items on the 6-point scale were numerically coded. A `Strongly Disagree` was coded as a 0, stepping through the integers for each successive category until reaching `Strongly Agree`, coded as a 5.

The first six rows of the resulting data file are shown in Listing 1.8.

```
0100004150541540000401324
0127001440330440111244310
0134121054405341400202401
0222105240444520001115440
0264123230222533101312320
0282022332323141312223321
```

Listing 1.8 First six rows of data for the 351 row Mach IV data file.

Included for each respondent is a four digit ID number, which occupies the first four columns of each row. The data values are sorted by the values of this ID field. The 5th column is Gender, encoded with 0 for Male and 1 for Female. Following are the 20 Mach IV responses, each response a single digit ranging from 0 to 5. Accordingly, there are 25 columns of data.

As opposed to a `csv` file, with a comma to delimit adjacent responses, there is no separation between any of the responses in the Mach IV data file. This data format is a *fixed width format*, abbreviated `fwd`. The data values for a single variable are allocated a specific number of columns, or width. Note the crucial similarity between `csv` and `fwd` files: both are *text files*. Both data formats as stored on the computer consist only of text characters, primarily letters and digits. The advantage of a text file is that the format is universal, accessible by virtually any application that can read data.

fixed width format: A text data file with data values for each variable in a specified number of columns.

The Mach IV fixed width data file is available on the web.

```
http://lessRstats.com/data/Mach4.fwd
```

The Mach IV data set is included as part of `lessR`, ready for analysis. The internal version does not include the four-digit ID number.

1.6.7 Who Owns the Data?

Who controls the rights to your data? Who has access to the data file on the computer? Another meaning of ownership regards the specific applications that can access your data. For example, a data table that exists only in a file saved in the default format of a worksheet, such as provided by Microsoft Excel or LibreOffice Calc, can only be read by an application that can decipher the encoding of the information in a worksheet file. This data is locked into a format that prevents it from being opened by any application not able to interpret the various usually hidden encodings of a worksheet file.

read fixed width data format, Section 2.3.4, p. 42

The perspective endorsed here is that you, not any specific application such as R, own your data. You always should be able to have any application that you choose read your data. Data stored in a text file, such as a csv or fwd file, are just pure text characters, accessible to virtually any application that can read text. You can always easily open your file in a worksheet application such as Excel or Calc, a data analysis application such as R or SPSS, a text editor, a word processor, a database application, and virtually anything else. When stored as a text file, the data are yours. You decide the applications that access your data.

Your operating system – Windows, Macintosh, or Linux – associates a specific file type with a specific application. For example, on Windows or Macintosh a file of type xls or xlsx will open in Excel by default, as will a csv file. You can, however, change this association. To open a data file in another application than the default follow these steps: view your computer's file system, locate the file of interest, right-click on the file icon, and then select Open With. You can also change an association permanently via Properties on Windows and Get Info on Macintosh, both also available by right-clicking a file icon.

Linux Mint free, open source operating system, linuxmint.com

The combination of LibreOffice with its worksheet application Calc, and R, in conjunction with user-friendly versions of the Linux operating system such as Ubuntu or Mint, is of particular interest. Most computer users have never seen, for example, Linux Mint, but the interface is so similar to Windows and Macintosh that most users could begin using a Linux Mint computer just by sitting down at one. All of this software is free and open source. All that is needed for data analysis and beyond: the operating system, the word processor and worksheet and other office applications, the R data analysis application, and much more. This free software also has the advantage of running well on older computers.

Worked Problems

1 Get and access R.
   - (a) Download the latest version of R for your computer.
   - (b) Start an R session and download lessR.

2 Get help.
   - (a) Generate the lessR general help menu.
   - (b) Using guidance from that menu, generate the help page for bar charts and pie charts.
   - (c) If a variable is named Gender, what is the instruction to generate its bar chart?
   - (d) Generate the pages from the manual that describe in detail the lessR function for bar charts.
   - (e) Briefly describe the option for changing the border of the plotted bars.

3 Colors.

    (a) Run the `lessR` function that shows all the named colors and a sample color patch.

    (b) List three of these colors. What are their corresponding `rgb` values?

    (c) Choose one of the colors and generate a histogram of Salary from the Employee data set with the bars colored with the chosen color.

    (d) Do the same, but now add transparency to the colored bars.

4 Data. Consider the data in Figure 1.9, randomly selected from a data file of the body measurements of thousands of motorcyclists.

	A	B	C
1	Gender	Weight	Height
2	F	150	66
3	F	138	66
4	M	240	74
5	M	178	71
6	F	130	64
7	M	200	74
8	F	140	70
9	M	220	77

Figure 1.9 Gender, Height, and Weight of eight motorcyclists.

    (a) Enter these values into a worksheet.

    (b) Describe how to create a `csv` file of these data, and then do so.

    (c) Open the `csv` file of data in an editor and display it in your homework document.

    (d) List each variable and classify each as continuous or categorical. If categorical, state if nominal or ordinal and specify the categories.

CHAPTER 2

READ/WRITE DATA

2.1 Quick Start

How to access `lessR` functions was addressed in Section 1.2.3. After R and `lessR` are installed, each time R is run, load the package into memory with `library(lessR)`.

A data file stored on your computer system consists of the measurements of one or more variables over many cases (observations), such as people. The organization of the data in the file considered here is in the form of a rectangular table called the *wide format*. The data for each observation (e.g., person) resides in a single row and the data for each variable in a single column. The first row consists of the variable names. Often, though not necessarily, the first column consists of a unique ID for each row of data, such as a person's name.

wide data format: The data for each row is all the data for a single person or unit of analysis.

A common and recommended file format to store data as text is a comma separated value or *csv* format, with adjacent data values separated by a comma. One way to save a file in a `csv` format is from a worksheet application such as Microsoft Excel or LibreOffice Calc. All numeric values in the data file should be free of all non-numeric characters such as $ signs, except for the character used as the decimal point. To analyze the data, first read the data in the data file into R. If this data file can be accessed by your computer's file system, just one call to the `lessR` function Read reads the data and then displays the relevant information.

csv format, Section 1.6.4, p. 24

```
> mydata <- Read()
```

This same R instruction also reads tab-delimited text data files, native SPSS data files with a file type of `.sav`, including any variable labels that may exist, and native R data files with a file type of `.rda`.

Read function, Section 2.2.1, p. 32

Additional refinements and considerations include the following.

✓ If the data file exists on the web, then enclose the full web address (URL) in quotes, including the `http://`, as the first value passed to Read.

```
> mydata <- Read("http://lessRstats.com/data/employee.csv")
```

✓ Identify a column of the data file that consists of unique row IDs with the `row.names` option, such as the following if the IDs are in the first column.

row.names option, Section 2.2.6, p. 37

```
> mydata <- Read(row.names=1)
```

✓ By default, missing data values are literally missing, that is, no data value is present for a specific cell in the data table. If a missing value is instead identified by one or more codes, such as -99 or XX, invoke the missing option.

missing option, Section 2.2.5, p. 36

```
> mydata <- Read(missing=c(-99,"XX"))
```

✓ If you are in a part of the world that uses a comma as the decimal separator instead of a period, then use the Read2 function to read a csv data file.

Read2 option, Section 2.3.2, p. 41

```
> mydata <- Read2()
```

✓ Read variable labels, such as from a separate text file, to add to a data table to provide more informative output than what is provided by the shorter variable names.

variable labels, Section 2.4.1, p. 46

```
> mydata <- Read(labels="myLabels.csv")
```

✓ Write the data file in native R format to save all information regarding the data such as any variable labels, which can then be quickly read back into R at a later time.

Write function, Section 2.5.2, p. 50

```
> Write("MyBestData", format="R")
```

2.2 Read Data

As a data analysis project progresses through various stages over time, the data table can simultaneously exist in several different forms. The data can be stored indefinitely on the computer in many different file formats, such as a universally readable text data file in csv format. The data can exist in a worksheet format specific to an application such as from MS Excel or LibreOffice Calc. The data table can also exist within an R session, what is called a *data frame*, and which can be saved as a computer file in native R format. As shown throughout this chapter, the data table can be easily transferred back and forth between these various forms.

csv format, Section 1.6.4, p. 24

data frame: A data table within an R session, ready for analysis.

2.2.1 Read Text, R or SPSS Data Files

To begin data analysis, usually first read the data from a data file into R. Except for two specific file types, the default format of the external data file is a text file with adjacent data values separated by either commas, csv, or tabs, tab-delimited. Data files created from within R are identified by the usual .rda file type for R data, and data files from the SPSS data analysis system by the usual .sav file type. Other file types and data formats are also accommodated when specific options are activated, as explained throughout this chapter.

 Scenario *Locate and read the data into R*
Browse your file system to locate a comma or tab-delimited text data file, or R or SPSS data file, then read the data in the file into R for subsequent analysis. Display relevant characteristics of the data to help guide this analysis.

Invoke the `lessR` function `Read` with the simplest possible function call, that is, with no arguments, to browse interactively for a file and then read the corresponding data. To *browse* for a file means that the usual window provided by your operating system automatically opens that allows you to locate the file within a specific directory (folder) on your computer or network. Then either double-click on the file name or click on the file name and then click on the `Open` button.

browse for a file: Navigate the file system to locate a file.

Once the file is identified, the `Read` function reads the data from the file. The data values that are read from an external file are usually directed into a designated internal R storage container for a data table, what R calls a data frame. Any valid R name for the data frame can be specified, though `mydata` is the usual choice. The R assignment expression, `<-`, indicates the object into which the data values are stored.

assignment statement, Section 1.3.3, p. 9

Read function: Read data from a file into an R data frame.

 lessR Input *Default read of csv or SPSS or R data from a local file*

> `mydata <- Read()`   *or*   > `mydata <- rd()`

Most `lessR` functions can also be referenced with an abbreviated name, such as `rd` for the function `Read`. Either form can be used, the full name to explicitly indicate the task performed by the function, or, an abbreviation to minimize keystrokes. Also, R pays attention to capitalization, so be careful to also do so. There are standard R functions based on the spelling `read` with a lower case r, but this refers to something other than the `lessR` function `Read` with the uppercase R.

Alternatively, locate the data file with the file's path name or full web address. List this name as the first argument within quotes in the call to the `Read` function. Here employee.csv is a `csv` data file stored in the data directory at the `lessR` website.

---

 lessR Input *Read data from a file on the web*

> `mydata <- Read("http://lessRstats.com/data/employee.csv")`

---

read data from `lessR`, Section 1.3.3, p. 10

For this particular file, another possibility is to read the employee.csv data directly from within `lessR` itself as it is included in the `lessR` installation.

Each `lessR` data analysis routine assumes, by default, that the data frame for which to apply the corresponding analysis is named `mydata`. So `mydata` does not need to be explicitly designated by a `lessR` data analysis function (by providing a value for the `data` option). All of the many, many standard R data analysis routines are also available to analyze the data in the `mydata` data frame. These procedures require the explicit statement of the name `mydata`, such as with the $ notation, because they make no assumption regarding the data frame name.

data option, Section 1.3.3, p. 13

$ notation, Section 1.3.5, p. 14

2.2.2 Types of Variables in R

The data analyst has a conceptual understanding of how the data values for a variable are structured. Are they numeric or non-numeric? What is their valid response range? The analysis of the data for the variables is done on the computer, so how the data are conceptually defined should align with the way in which they are stored within the computer, here within an R data frame.

Accordingly, when the data values are read into any data analysis application such as R, their structure and content as read by R should be examined and verified before their analysis begins. The analyst should confirm that the data were read correctly and are properly represented in the resulting data frame. Many things can go wrong. Perhaps errors occurred as the data values were entered into the data file. Perhaps the data values were not correctly read into R. Perhaps there is too much missing data to permit a meaningful analysis.

data storage type: How the data values of a variable are physically stored in the computer.

The *data storage type* is how the computer physically represents a data value in its memory. The storage type should match the conceptual definition of the variable. The common R data storage types for numeric variables are type `integer`, for numbers without decimal digits, and what R calls `numeric`, for numbers with decimal digits.[1]

Categorical variables usually have less than 10 or so unique values, and perhaps as few as two, such as for Gender. For a categorical variable different data storage types could be used both in the data file that stores the data or in the way that R represents the data within a data processing session, its data frame. For example, the data values can be integers with a different integer assigned to each level, that is value, of the categorical variable, such as 0 for Male and 1 for Female. Or, the values could be stored as non-numeric characters, what R calls type `character`, such as M for Male and F for Female. R, however, has a separate data storage type expressly dedicated to represent categorical variables. This storage type is a *factor*, which combines these two representations such that the data are internally stored as integers but displayed in terms of descriptive labels.

factor: R data storage type for categorical variables.

When R reads the data from an external file it scans the characters that form the data values for each variable. If it finds only digits for the data values of a variable, R defines the variable as `integer`. If only digits are found and at least one data value has a decimal point, the variable is defined as `numeric`. Based on the data in Figure 1.7 on p. 21, after R reads the data values, the variable Years is represented in the data frame as `integer` and Salary as `numeric`.

When R reads the data and finds *any* non-digit character except a decimal point in any data value for a variable, then R by default concludes that the variable cannot be numeric and so must be categorical. Accordingly, R defines the variable as a *factor*. From Figure 1.7 on p. 21, the data values for Gender, Dept and Satisfaction consist of non-numeric characters, and so each is interpreted as a `factor`.[2]

These coding interpretations imply that numeric data values in a data file should not include commas or dollar signs. Otherwise R would interpret the resulting variable as a factor, presuming an underlying categorical variable. Then its data values would not be amenable to any numerical statistical operation such as the computation of their mean. If the data values are in an Excel or other worksheet, remove the commas and dollar signs in the formatting before saving the data as a `csv` data file for analysis with R.

save a csv file, Section 1.6.4, p. 24

2.2.3 Output

Unless the option `quiet` is set to `TRUE`, the function `Read` displays a summary of the data frame before proceeding with the subsequent data analysis. The output from `Read` is from an internal call to the `lessR` function `details`. This function can be manually called at any time after a data table has been read into R with the specified data frame name. The default data frame is `mydata`.

details function: Provide many details about a data table.

The first part of the output, shown in Listing 2.1, displays the dimensions of the data table.

The next section of output is a summary of the row names, presented here in Listing 2.2. Every data frame, the R container for the data table, always has a unique identifier or ID for

```
Basics
-----------------------------------------------------------
Number of Variables in mydata:    7
Number of Rows of Data in mydata:  37
```

Listing 2.1 Initial output of `Read`.

each row in the data table, a *row name*. This ID can be assigned from a column of the data table. Or, the ID can be assigned by R, in which case the IDs are just the integers from 1 to the last row of data, as in Listing 2.2.

ID field, Section 2.2.6, p. 37

```
Row Names
-----------------------------------------
First two row names: 1     2
Last two row names:  36    37
```

Listing 2.2 The row names of the data frame are the consecutive integers from 1 to 37.

A description follows of each of the variables that have been read into R, including the data storage type. A brief dictionary of common data storage types is first presented, illustrated in Listing 2.3.

```
Variable Names and Types of the Values Read
------------------------------------------------------------------
factor: Non-numeric categories, which, as read here, are unordered
integer: The values are numeric and integers
numeric: The values are numeric with decimal digits
```

Listing 2.3 Some interpretations R makes of a variable.

`Read` then displays the variable names, as shown in the first column of Listing 2.4. Pay particular attention to the variable names, including the pattern of capitalization, because it is by its name that the variable is referenced in any subsequent data analysis. These names appear in the first column, under the heading `Variable`.

variable name: The reference for a variable in subsequent data analysis.

To help validate that the data table was read correctly, `Read` lists some of the first and last values of each variable. It is recommended to match some of these data values against the contents of the file from which the data were read. Before beginning the subsequent data analyses, make sure that you are analyzing the data you intend to analyze.

```
                          Missing  Unique
     Variable     Type  Values  Values  Values   First and last values
     ------------------------------------------------------------------
        Years  integer    36      1      16    7   NA  15 ... 1   2   10
       Gender   factor    37      0       2    M   M   M ... F   F   M
         Dept   factor    36      1       5    ADMN  SALE  ... SALE  FINC
       Salary  numeric    37      0      37    43788.26 ...  47562.36
 Satisfaction   factor    35      2       3    med  low  ... low   high
    HealthPlan  integer    37      0       3    1  1   3 ... 2   2   1
```

Listing 2.4 The summary of the variables read into the data frame `mydata` with the variable names listed in the first column.

NA: Data value
that is missing.

The data value of Years for the second row of data, the data for James Wu, is NA, R's missing data code for numeric data, which, for non-numeric data, is displayed as <NA>. The NA means "Not Available".

2.2.4 Display an R Object

To display the contents of any R object in its entirety, simply enter the name of the object in response to the command prompt.

 R Input *Display the contents of an object such as the data frame mydata*
```
> mydata
```

print function:
Display the
contents of an R
object at the
console.

Enter the name of the data frame, mydata, to display all the data. Entering just the name of the R object, such as a data frame, calls the print function. Explicitly evoke the print function to achieve more control of the listing.

```
> print(mydata)
```

head, tail
functions: List the
first or last lines of
the specified
object.

See ?print for more specifics.
List just the first or last lines of the data frame with the R head and tail functions.

 R Input *List the contents of the first and last six rows of the data frame*
```
> head(mydata)
> tail(mydata)
```

n option: Specify
the number of lines
to display with the
head and tail
functions.

The R head and tail functions are convenient for checking the form of the data without listing all rows of the data frame. The default number of lines listed can be changed from 6 with the n option.

2.2.5 Missing Values

missing data,
Section 1.6.5,
p. 25

Another issue is a consideration of missing data values. By default, Read interprets a data value as missing when it is actually missing, corresponding to a blank cell in a worksheet. Many if not most data sets have at least some missing data values. Via the details function, Read provides a comprehensive analysis of missing values, which includes how many values are missing for each row of data or case (observation), and how many are missing for each variable.

The variable summary provides number of missing data values for each variable, illustrated in Listing 2.4, under the column Missing Values. The complementary information, the number of non-missing values, is presented under the previous column, Values. The sum of these two numbers for any variable is the total number of rows of data, here 37. For example, the variable Satisfaction has two missing data values and 35 values that exist.

Read also reports the number of missing values for each *case*, also referred to as an *observation*. Identify each observation by its row name. Find this report for the Employee data set in Listing 2.5.

case or *observation*, Section 1.6.1, p. 21

```
Missing Data Analysis
---------------------------------------------------
n.miss  Observation
1       2
2       4
1       31


Total number of cells in data table:   259
Total number of cells with the value missing:   4
```

Listing 2.5 Number of missing data values for each row of data, that is, case.

From this analysis we see that the employee with the most missing data is the person listed in the fourth row of the data table. Here we see an advantage of more appropriately identifying the names of each person as an ID field. Then each person's name would be visible instead of his or her row number in this output.

row names, Figure 2.2.6, p. 37

R's code for missing data is NA, which indicates Not Available. Each NA code in the R data frame corresponds to a blank cell in a corresponding worksheet. R also makes it possible for missing data in the data file to be represented by codes instead of just leaving the cell blank.

example worksheet with missing data, Section 1.7, p. 21

 Scenario *Missing value codes in the data file*
The data file of interest stored on the computer system represents missing data with one or more designated codes, usually of data values that would not naturally occur, such as −99 for a numerical data value that only has positive values and XX for character data values. Read the data into R and interpret these codes to represent missing data.

Use the Read missing option to inform R as to what values define a missing value.

missing option: Designated data value to indicate missing data.

 lessR Input *Read data with both specified character and numeric missing data codes*
```
> mydata <- Read(missing=c("XX",-99))
```

c function, Section 1.3.6, p. 15

When presenting a list of multiple values with the values in the list separated by commas, always use the combine function c to group the values together. The result of this specification is that every XX and every −99 that exists in the data file read into R is replaced with an NA in the resulting R data frame, here mydata.

2.2.6 Row Names

By default R numbers each row of the data frame with a row number. An alternative is to have R label each specific row of data, a case, with a unique label from that row of data. Refer back to the Employee data table. The names in the first column are not values to be analyzed, but

Employee data table, Figure 1.7, p. 21

rather ID values that uniquely identify each row. Many different R analyses identify data by its row identifier, such as labeling points in a scatterplot, where an ID value from the data provides a more meaningful label than a row number.

The Read function provides some guidance regarding the implementation of row names, as shown in Listing 2.6. If Read detects in the data file a column of non-numeric data with unique values, then that column is noted as a potential ID column.

```
For the following 'variable', each row of data is unique. Perhaps
these values specify a unique ID for each row. To implement, re-read
with the following setting added to your Read statement: row.names=1
---------------------------------------------------------------
Name
```

Listing 2.6 A note from Read suggesting a possible ID column.

Read provides useful information when it recognizes a potential ID field.

 Scenario *Read the data and identify a column of data as the row names*
One column in the data table of interest consists of unique names, that is, each name uniquely identifies a specific row. Read the data into R and identify this column as row names to identify specific data values in the R output.

Use the row.names option in the Read statement to indicate the column number that contains the IDs. To interactively browse for this data file on the local file system or network, indicated by not specifying a file name, include here only the row.names option.

lessR Input *Read data and assign the first column as row IDs*
```
> mydata <- Read(row.names=1)
```

The following example applies when the row names in the data file are in the first column in the call to Read and the file name and location are specified.

```
> mydata <- Read("http://lessRstats.com/data/employee.csv", row.names=1)
```

The result of specifying the row names in the first column is that R now correctly no longer regards the first column of information as a variable, as shown in Listing 2.7. As opposed to the previous Read output, now only 6 variables are recognized in the analysis instead of the previously listed value of 7 from Listing 2.1.

```
Basics
---------------------------------------------------------------
Name of data frame that contains the data:  mydata
Number of Variables in mydata:     6
Number of Rows of Data in mydata:  37
```

Listing 2.7 Initial output of Read, here after the first column of the data file is specified as the row names.

If a column of the data table is not a variable but an ID field, then R should be properly informed of this structure. R will then accordingly use this information to enhance the quality of its output, as in Listing 2.8. The names of each employee are now listed instead of the row number.

```
Missing Data Analysis
----------------------------------------
n.miss  Observation
1       Wu, James
2       Jones, Alissa
1       Korhalkar, Jessica
```

Listing 2.8 Row-wise missing value analysis after the first column of the data file is specified as the row names.

One meaningful constraint regarding the row names is that they should be unique for each row of data. If not, the read is not successful. Nor should the read be allowed to be successful without unique IDs because confusion would result from linking two or more rows of data to the same ID.

2.2.7 Categorical Variables

A primary distinction among variables is the distinction between continuous and categorical variables. A categorical variable has relatively few unique data values, called *levels*. For example, the variable Gender typically has two values, Male and Female.

variable types, Section 1.6.3, p. 22

levels: Values of a categorical variable.

Another consideration is how the variable is stored on the computer. A potential confusion is that the values of categorical variables are not numeric, yet they can be stored as numbers, usually integers, on the computer. A common example is that the values of Gender may be coded numerically, such as a 0 and 1, as in the Mach IV data set. Or, for the Employee data set, each employee's choice of a health plan is coded as a 1, 2, or 3 instead of the actual names of the health plans.

computer storage, Section 2.2.2, p. 33

Mach IV data, Listing 1.8, p. 27

The computer program, R or anything else, cannot know without additional information if the numeric values are measurements of a continuous variable, or if they are numeric codes for non-numeric categories. Fortunately, there is a clue that suggests that a variable is categorical: only a small number of integer values. Read can check for this criterion, with a system parameter defined by lessR called n.cat, an abbreviation for "number of categories", which defines the maximum number of unique integer values for which to consider a variable as categorical.

Employee data set, Section 1.6.1, p. 20

n.cat option: The maximum number of unique values to consider a numeric variable as categorical.

By default, n.cat is turned off, set to 0, but can be specified to any value in one of two ways. A value of n.cat such as 4 can be passed to a relevant lessR data analysis function, such as for summary statistics, so that the value is applicable just for that specific analysis. An analysis of summary statistics, for example, of an integer variable in this situation with 4 or less unique values yields a frequency table rather than numeric summaries such as the mean. Or, a value can be set for all subsequent analyses with the lessR function set.

 lessR Input *Set maximum number of unique values to interpret as categorical*

```
> set(n.cat=4)
```

set function, Section 1.4.1, p. 16

For example, as shown in Listing 2.9, having set `n.cat` at the value of 4 defines, for all subsequent analyses, all numerical variables with 4 or less unique values to be interpreted as categorical.

```
Each of these variables is numeric, but has less than or equal
4 unique values. If these variables are categorical consider to
transform each variable into a factor with the Transform and
factor functions. To see examples enter:  > ?trans
Or, specify a value for n.cat, such as:  > set(n.cat=4)
--------------------------------------------------------------------
HealthPlan
```

Listing 2.9 The variable HealthPlan is likely categorical even though coded numerically.

factor function,
Section 1.6.3,
p. 22

A more formal solution to the issue of a categorical variable represented as type `integer` is to invoke the R function `factor` to define the variable as an R factor, R's variable type specifically designed for categorical variables.

2.2.8 No Text Output

Presumably the output of the `Read` function to the console is generally useful. However, if this information is not needed, such as when a data set is re-read at a later time for re-analysis, then the console output can be suppressed.

quiet option,
Section 1.3.5,
p. 14

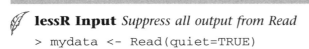

lessR Input *Suppress all output from Read*

> mydata <- Read(quiet=TRUE)

set function,
Section 1.4.1,
p. 16

This option applies to all the `lessR` functions that provide text feedback at the console, often where the primary task is to generate output elsewhere, usually to a graphics window or to a data structure such as `mydata`. The value of `quiet` can also be set at the system level with the `lessR` function `set`.

2.3 More Data Formats

The procedure of saving a data table stored as a worksheet file, such as from Microsoft Excel or LibreOffice Calc, into a `csv` formatted file with variable names in the first row provides a straightforward means of preparing data for entry into R. Sometimes, however, data are available in other formats that `Read` can also access.

2.3.1 Tab Delimited Data

delimiter:
Character that
separates adjacent
data values.

For a text file with the data values for each variable that do not occupy a pre-defined number of columns, a character called the *delimiter* separates adjacent data values. For a `csv` file the delimiter is a comma. Another common delimiter is a tab character. The `Read` function recognizes both of these file formats by default.

Any standard character, however, can also serve as a delimiter according to the R separator option, `sep`. The tab character, for example, can be explicitly specified as the delimiter. To browse for and then read from a data file of standard text with tab-delimited data values, invoke the following.

sep option: Specify the character that separates adjacent data values.

lessR Input *Read tab delimited data*
```
> mydata <- Read(sep="\t")
```

The tab character, itself invisible, is represented by the backward slash and the letter `t` in the function call. To read a file from the web, specify the first parameter option as the web address enclosed in quotes. Then include the `sep` option as the second option. More generally, set `sep=""` to indicate any white space for a delimiter, such as a space or other invisible character.

2.3.2 Decimal Comma Instead of a Decimal Point

Another `Read` option based directly on the options provided by standard R is to change the character that indicates the decimal digits in a number. Most English speaking countries, plus all of North America and China, use a period for the *decimal separator*, called the decimal point in this context. Another tradition, favored by Europe, Russia, and all of South America, uses a comma for the same purpose, and then, perhaps a semi-colon to delimit adjacent data values instead of a comma. Use the `dec` option to specify the character that indicates decimal digits, possibly in combination with the `sep` option.

decimal separator: The character in a numeric string that indicates where decimal digits begin.

Read2 function: Read data with a comma for a decimal point.

lessR Input *Read data with commas for the decimal separator*
```
> mydata <- Read(sep=";", dec=",")    or    > mydata <- Read2()
```

To simplify reading `csv` data files in this format, `lessR` includes the `Read2` function, which behaves just as `Read`, but with `sep=";"` and `dec=","` preset.

When reading data with `Read2` the display of the numbers in the R output still includes the decimal point as a period. To change the display on the output, invoke the `OutDec` option for the standard R `options` function.

OutDec option: Specify character for decimal point on R output.

lessR Input *Inform R to display a decimal separator as a comma*
```
> options(OutDec=",")
```

There are many other options that can also be set with the `options` function. Reference the help file with `?options` to view these options.

2.3.3 Skip Beginning Lines of Data File

skip option: Skip the specified number of lines at the beginning of a data file.

Sometimes a data file begins with comment lines that describe the purpose of the data and each of the variables contained in it. To read the actual data skip the first specified number of lines in the data file with the `skip` option.

---

 lessR Input *Skip the specified number of lines that begin a data file*

```
> mydata <- Read(skip=6)
```

In this example, the actual reading of the data begins on Line 7 of the data file. If the first line of information in the file beyond the comments contains the names of the variables, then that is what is read beginning on Line 7.

2.3.4 Fixed Width Data

csv data format, Section 1.6.4, p. 24

text file, p. 19

fixed width format: All data values for a variable occur in specified columns.

Mach IV data, Listing 1.8, p. 27

A `csv` file, where a comma or other specified character delimits adjacent data values, is a *text file*, a file of just plain alphabetical characters and the digits, and common punctuation characters such as a comma. A text file is a universal format, accessible to virtually all computer applications. Another kind of text file is a `fwd` file, the *fixed width format*, where the data values for each variable conform to a specified fixed number of columns in the data file.

The previously introduced example of a `fwd` formatted text file is the Mach IV data set. This file contains 25 digits for each row, the data for a single respondent. These data values for each row consist of a four-digit ID, a Gender column, and then 20 digits, the responses of each respondent to the 20 items on the Mach IV scale. Unlike a `csv` file, no delimiter separates the adjacent data values. There also are no variable names in the first row of the data table because the names do not fit into the allocated column or columns for the corresponding data.

 Scenario *Read fixed width formatted data into R*
The Mach IV data consists of responses to each of the 20 Mach IV items plus Gender, stored in a fixed width format, one column per response. Read this data table into R.

---

widths option: Specify the widths of the columns for the data values in each row of data.

rep function: Create a string of characters by repeating a specified set of characters.

The primary tool to specify the widths of the fields for `fwd` formatted data is the R `widths` option, which like most of the options for R read functions, such as `read.table`, also apply to the `lessR` function `Read`. We will also use other functions to reduce the work needed to accomplish this read of the Mach IV data.

First consider the standard R function, `rep`, for repetition. There are 20 columns for each row of the Mach IV responses, each response of width 1. To read the Mach IV data specify 20 1's to indicate the 20 column widths, a task best accomplished by `rep` with two arguments: the number to be repeated, 1, and the number of repetitions, 20, as shown in Listing 2.10. Wherever

R encounters `rep(1,20)`, it essentially processes 20 1's as if they were entered manually, one after the other.

```
> rep(1,20)
 [1] 1 1 1 1 1 1 1 1 1 1 1 1 1 1 1 1 1 1 1 1
```

Listing 2.10 Illustration of the R function `rep`.

A second function to assist reading the item responses on a multi-item scale such as the Mach IV is the `lessR` function `to`. This function simplifies naming a sequence of consecutive items. In this situation, we may name the first variable, or item, `m01`, the second item `m02`, and so forth until `m20`. The `to` function specifies this sequence without actually having to enter the name of each item, as shown in Listing 2.11. To use `to`, specify the prefix of each item within quotes and then the number of the last item. Optionally provide a third argument, the beginning value, otherwise assumed to be one.

`to` function: Name a sequential set of variables with consecutive numbers prefixed by a given character string.

```
> to("m",20)
 [1] "m01" "m02" "m03" "m04" "m05" "m06" "m07" "m08" "m09" "m10" "m11"
[12] "m12" "m13" "m14" "m15" "m16" "m17" "m18" "m19" "m20"
```

Listing 2.11 Illustration of the `lessR` function `to`, which names a sequence of consecutive items.

The next consideration for reading the data in a `fwd` formatted file is to name the variables as these names are not included in the data file. Use the R `col.names` option to specify the corresponding list of variable names, again specified in order of occurrence in the data file. As always, when presenting a list of multiple values with the values in the list separated by commas, use the combine function `c` to group or combine the values together.

`col.names` option: Specify the variable names.

The first argument listed in this example is the `widths` option. The four column ID takes up the first four columns, Gender the next column, and then one column each for the variables `m01` to `m20`. The variables are named with `col.names`.

`c` function, Section 1.3.6, p. 15

> *lessR Input* *Read fixed width formatted data with numbered variable names*
```
> mydata <- Read(widths=c(4,1,rep(1,20)),
      col.names=c("ID", "Gender", to("m",20)))
```

To specify the location of the file directly, such as a web address, this information appears as the first argument passed to `Read`. For example, insert the specified location before the `widths` option in the previous example.

```
> mydata <- Read("http://lessRstats.com/data/Mach4.fwd",
            widths=c(4,1,rep(1,20)),
            col.names=c("ID", "Gender", to("m",20)))
```

variable labels, Section 2.4, p. 45

2.3.5 Read Data Files Included in `lessR`

The primary purpose of `lessR` is to provide functions that simplify R data analysis. Also provided are some data sets for analysis so that data are always available on any computer on which `lessR` has been downloaded. These data files can be read into R with the `Read` option `format` set to `"lessR"`.

Employee data set,
Section 1.6.1,
p. 20

format="lessR"
option: Read a
data set included
in `lessR`.

Each `lessR` data file name begins with the prefix `data`, followed by the descriptive name that identifies the file. For example, consider the Employee data set `dataEmployee`. This data set can be read with the `format` option set to `"lessR"`.

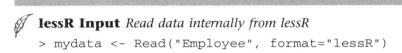

> **lessR Input** *Read data internally from lessR*
> ```
> > mydata <- Read("Employee", format="lessR")
> ```

The same format applies to any of the other internal `lessR` data sets, such as the Machiavellianism data set `Mach4`.

These built-in data files were created by first reading the corresponding text data files into R and then writing the resulting data frames as native R files with the `rda` file type. The `format="lessR"` option instructs the `Read` function to read the corresponding `rda` file stored within the `lessR` package into the current `mydata` data frame. The usual `Read` output that provides information regarding the data table is available, and because `mydata` is the data frame name, the data table is automatically accessed by the `lessR` data analysis routines for analysis.

2.3.6 Read SPSS Native Data

.sav filetype: A
native SPSS data
file.

The function `Read` can read data files written from the statistical package SPSS in their native format. If the data file's file type is the usual `.sav` for an SPSS file, then `Read` will automatically detect this attribute and automatically set the `format` option to SPSS. This option can also be set manually if the data file is a native SPSS file without the usual `.sav` file type.

All of the data sets analyzed in this book, including those included in `lessR`, are available in SPSS format at the `lessR` website.

```
http://lessRstats.com/data/SPSS
```

With these data files an SPSS user can run parallel analyses in SPSS and R on the same data to compare the ease of use and output from SPSS and R/lessR.

The data frame `mydata` created from reading the SPSS data file also contains any variable labels that are present in the native SPSS `.sav` file. The concept of variable labels is discussed in a following section.

2.3.7 Read Data Directly from an Excel File

*Worksheet
representation* of
data, Section 1.6.2,
p. 21

csv data file,
Section 1.6.4,
p. 24

A worksheet application such as Excel, as previously discussed, is an excellent way to enter and store data into a data table. To analyze this data, one strategy is to save the data as a `csv` text file. Another option is to read the data directly from the Excel file using, for example, the `read.xlsx` function from the `xlsx` package (Dragulescu, 2012). The reason why this option has not been promoted as the primary option is that there is an additional issue that must be addressed when reading data directly from Excel: some software in addition to R must be installed. The read.xlsx function relies upon java. So if java is properly installed, and the xlsx package is installed and then loaded with the library function, the following example reads data from the first worksheet from the specified Excel file stored on the lessR web server.

install.packages,
Section 1.2.3, p. 5
library function,
Section 1.3.1, p. 6

```
> read.xlsx("http://lessRstats.com/data/Employee.xlsx",
        sheetIndex=1)
```

With read.xlsx there is no need to first convert the data to the csv format before reading into R.

The problem is that the installation of java is not necessarily straightforward. One concern is that many consider java to be a security risk. Another issue is that there are 32-bit and 64-bit versions of java, just as there are 32-bit and 64-bit versions of R, and these architectures must be aligned. For example, if there is only a 32-bit version of java installed, and the 64-bit version of R is run, then the xlsx package will not work correctly. A related problem is that some applications other than R that depend on one version of java may cease to work correctly after installation of the second version. Yet another issue is that the company that provides the java software makes money when a particular search toolbar is installed along with the java software. There is considerable effort made to encourage the user to install this toolbar, and only careful reading of the prompts during the installation process will avoid the usually unwanted installation.

If these issues are addressed, then read.xlsx works well in reading data directly from an Excel file. The worksheet must be specified explicitly even if the Excel file contains only one worksheet. To do this, specify either the sheetIndex parameter, as in the previous example, or the sheetName parameter that specifies the name of the desired worksheet enclosed in quotes. To obtain the same feedback that the Read function provides regarding the newly created data frame, manually invoke a call to the lessR function details.

details function,
Section 2.2.3,
p. 34

2.4 Variable Labels

To analyze the data values of a variable requires a reference to the variable by its name. These names are as short as possible, usually around 10 characters or less. Long variable names are more difficult to type and the spelling of a variable name must be exact, including any capitalization, for the variable to be properly referenced. Shorter variable names simplify this reference to the corresponding variables. Also, the output tends to be more concise with shorter names. The names and values of many more variables can be listed in columns across a computer screen or printed with shorter variable names.

The disadvantage is that a short name may not adequately describe the meaning of the variable. Consider the sixth item on the Mach IV scale.

Mach IV scale,
Table 1.2, p. 26

Honesty is the best policy in all cases.

The corresponding variable name is m06, which is efficiently compact and communicates the location of the item on the Mach IV scale. The disadvantage is that by itself this name carries no indication as to the content of the item.

variable label: A
description of a
variable's meaning.

A *variable label* is a longer, more descriptive label that more fully describes the variable's meaning than its usually shorter name. For an item on a survey, an appropriate variable label is the content of the item. Reference the variables in the subsequent function calls with the shorter variable names, but the more descriptive variable labels appear on the output to help interpret the results.

Unlike standard R, lessR has a provision for variable labels, which are stored with the data in the data frame.

 Scenario *Read the variable labels into* R
Increase the interpretability of the graphics and text output of each data analysis procedure by displaying variable labels.

When using lessR functions, the existence of any variable labels in the data frame triggers their automatic use on the text or graphics output. For example, the label on the horizontal axis of the histogram for Variable m06 is ordinarily the variable name, m06. With a variable label present the axis label is the corresponding variable label, here the content of the item. When using standard R functions the variable labels can still be employed, though they must be manually invoked, such as in the specification of an axis label for a histogram. The details follow.

2.4.1 The Variable Labels File

The variable labels are read into R with the data. These labels for native SPSS and R files would have already been included in the respective data files. The SPSS user would have defined the variable labels within SPSS before writing the .sav data file. The R user would already have read the variable labels into the data frame and then written the data frame that included these labels to an external R data file. Reading either the resulting SPSS or the R native data file yields a data frame that includes both the data as well as any included variable labels.

How to read the variable labels when reading a text data file such as in csv or fwd format? Variable labels can be read from one of two text files. One possibility is a file dedicated specifically to variable labels, which is a csv file. Each row of the file consists of a variable name, a comma, and then the corresponding variable label. If there is a comma in the variable label, then the entire label must be enclosed in quotes, which a worksheet application such as Excel provides automatically when the file is saved to the csv format.

csv file,
Section 1.6.4,
p. 24

The example in Figure 2.1 shows how the Mach IV items are entered into Excel, one column for the variable names and one column for the corresponding variable labels. Save the worksheet in csv format so that the labels file is just another csv file. The organization of the information

	A	B	C	D	E	F	G
1	m01	Never tell anyone the real reason you did something unless it is useful to do so.					
2	m02	The best way to handle people is to tell them what they want to hear.					
3	m03	One should take action only when sure it is morally right.					
4	m04	Most people are basically good and kind.					

Figure 2.1 The Excel representation of the variable labels for Variables m01 to m04, the first four Mach IV items.

in this labels file is flexible. There is no need to list the variables in any particular order, nor do all variables in the corresponding data file need to have a variable label in the label file.

The variable labels are read with the lessR function Read at the same time the data values are read. To read the accompanying variable labels, specify the location of the file of variable labels with the labels option as part of the same Read instruction for reading the data. If the labels csv file is located in the same file directory (folder) as the data file, then just the file name in quotes need be specified. If the labels file is located somewhere else then the full path name needs to be provided.

labels option: Location of the variable labels.

In the following example the location of the data file is not specified, so the Read function will prompt the user to browse the file directory for the location of the file. The labels option in this example specifies just the file name of the corresponding variable labels file, so that file is presumed to be in the same directory as the data file.

 lessR Input *Read variable labels from the file called varlabels.csv*

```
> mydata <- Read(labels="varlabels.csv")
```

As usual with the Read function, if a full path name or web address (URL) is provided as the first argument of the function call, within quotes, then the file is read directly from the specified location.

2.4.2 Variable Labels in the Data File

A second option for providing variable labels is to include the labels in the main data file formatted as a csv or tab-delimited text file. Just place the labels in the second line of the data file, so that the first line contains the variable names and the data itself then begins on the third line of the file. Figure 2.2 provides an example.

	A	B	C	D	E	F
1	Mach_1	Mach_2	Mach_3	Mach_4	Mach_5	Mach_6
2	Never tell anyone	The best way to ha	One should take a	Most people are b	It is safest to assur	Honesty is the bes
3	0	4	1	5	0	5
4	0	1	4	4	0	3
5	2	1	0	5	4	4
6	0	5	2	4	0	4
7	2	3	2	3	0	2

Figure 2.2 A Mach IV data file with variable labels and the first four rows of data, opened in Excel.

The format of the information in Figure 2.2 is the format provided by the popular Qualtrics on-line survey software. This combined data/labels file can be constructed and/or modified in a worksheet application such as Excel. Or the file can be obtained directly from the Qualtrics on-line survey software with a download of the survey responses in csv format. To read the combined data/labels file, use Read with labels="row2".

Qualtrics on-line survey software, www.qualtrics.com

labels="row2" option: Read variable labels from the second row of a csv data file.

 lessR Input *Read data and variable labels from the same file*

```
> mydata <- Read(labels="row2")
```

Write function, Section 2.5.2, p. 50

Now that the variable labels have been read with the data values, they can be saved with the data to an external data file with the lessR function Write. Future Read statements to read the native R data file will automatically read the variable labels as well.

2.4.3 Using Variable Labels with Standard R Functions

If variable labels are present for an existing data frame, such as mydata, then standard R functions can also access the labels with the lessR function label. The argument of the function is the corresponding variable name.

label function: Use variable labels with R functions.

For example, the option to specify a title for a histogram, and virtually every other R graph, is main. The following function call is to the standard R histogram function, hist. The histogram is constructed for variable m06, the sixth item on the Mach IV scale. The label function accesses the corresponding variable label in the data frame, here for display on the graph title.

Unlike lessR functions, R functions cannot reference the variables directly by their name. Instead, each standard R function also needs the name of the data frame that contains the data. One way to provide this name is to precede the variable name with the name of the data frame that contains the variable and a $ sign, as follows.

$ notation, Section 1.3.5, p. 14

hist function: Standard R histogram.

```
> hist(mydata$m06, xlab=label(m06))
```

Histogram function, Section 5.2, p. 100

The result is that whatever variable label is in the data frame for variable m06 is displayed as the label for the horizontal or x-axis of the resulting histogram. In general, however, the lessR histogram function Histogram provides more pleasing aesthetics, more information regarding the underlying distribution, improved error diagnostics, and directly references the variable by name.

2.5 Write Data

The function Read reads data from an external file into a specified R data frame. The matching function Write writes a specified data frame within R, usually mydata, to an external file. One format for the file that is written is as a native R format file, readable only by R, but a relatively fast read, which also includes any variable labels present in the data frame. For compatibility with other systems the data can also be exported as a csv text file.

2.5.1 Write a Data Frame in Native R Format

The contents of a data frame necessarily include the data values read into R. The contents also include related information such as the storage type of each variable. The complete contents of a data frame can be written to an external file on your computer system as a virtual literal copy of the data frame as it is stored within an R session. The data table can then be re-read back into R for later analysis. The format of the resulting file is called a native R data file, which can only be read by the R system.

One advantage of saving the complete contents of a data frame is that, especially for large data files, re-reading a previously saved data frame in the form of a native R data file is much faster than reading a text file. The issue is that without prior information R spends a relatively large amount of time reading a text file column by column while attempting to interpret the type of data contained within each column.[3] Plus, the format of the saved R data frame is more compact than an equivalent text file, such as a `csv` file. Modern computers are fast, but particularly for large data sets, the time difference is noticeable. The larger the file, the greater the benefit from reading a native R data file instead of a text data file.

For example, consider a relatively large `csv` file of 69.8MB with over 4.2 million rows of data and 6 integer variables. This file was stored on your author's MacBook Pro with an Intel i5 processor and a solid state drive. The total elapsed time to read the over 4 million of rows of data was just under 31 seconds. The data were then written in native R format as an `.rda` file. The total time to read the same data in this format was reduced to just under 11 seconds. Further, the size of the written file reduced to 16.5MB.

After reading the data it is often worthwhile to perform one or more transformations of the existing data, the topic of the next chapter. For example, convert a variable with measurements in inches to measurements in centimeters, or analyze the logarithm of a variable. These subsequent modifications of the data values are saved when the updated data frame is saved. The alternative is to re-read the initial text file and then re-do the transformations.

data editing,
Chapter 3, p. 53

⭐ **Scenario** *Write the contents of a data frame in native R format*

Data and the variable labels were read into an R data frame and edited, with several transformations applied to the data. Write the complete contents of the edited data frame in R native format.

To write the complete contents of the `mydata` data frame to an external file, including all internal R specific formatting, use the lessR function `Write` with the option `format="R"`. To simplify the input, the abbreviation `wrt.r` automatically sets this option. Specify a file name, to which `Write` automatically appends the file type `.rda` for R data if the file type is not explicitly specified.

Write function: Write contents of a data frame to an external data file.

type="R" option: Write the data frame as an R native file.

---

 lessR Input *Write an R native data file called MyGoodData*

```
> Write("MyGoodData", format="R")    or    > wrt.r("MyGoodData")
```

Where does R write the data file? The answer is what R calls the *current working directory*, the directory to which output files are written. In Windows, the default location is your Documents folder. In Macintosh and Linux systems the default location is the top level of your home folder.

For example, the following call to `Write` was done on your author's Macintosh. Here the contents of the `mydata` data frame are written to the file called `MyGoodData.rda` in the `gerbing` folder, as indicated by the output of the `Write` function. Note that the file type, `.rda`, is not part of the information entered to the `Write` function, but is automatically appended to the file name.

current working directory: The location of where R writes files.

```
> wrt.r("MyGoodData")

The mydata contents was written at the current working directory.
     MyGoodData.rda   in:    /Users/gerbing
```

Listing 2.12 Input and output for the `Write` function for the `mydata` data frame.

Then, just move the new data file to the desired location on your computer's file system, such as by dragging the file's icon to the desired folder. Optionally, the current working directory can also be changed so that output files can be directly written to the desired location from R. In Windows go to the `File` menu and choose `Change dir...`, and on a Macintosh go to the `Misc` menu and choose `Change Working Directory...`. The R function to do this from the command line, applicable to all R users, is `setwd`, for set working directory. Enter `?setwd` for more information.

setwd function: Set the working directory where files are written.

2.5.2 Write a Data Frame in `csv` Format

The contents of a data frame can also be written to an external file in `csv` format as a text file. Here use the `Write` function with `format="csv"`, the default value. Obtain the same effect by simply omitting the option. One advantage of writing to the `csv` format is that data can be read into R, modified, written as a `csv` file, and then read into another application such as a worksheet.

lessR Input *Write a csv data file called MyGoodData*

```
> Write("MyGoodData")        or        > wrt("MyGoodData")
```

The `Read` and `Write` functions allow data to freely flow into and out of R.

The `Write` function by default also writes to the `csv` formatted file the row name for each row of data. Particularly for data tables read into R that already have row identifiers, such as the Employee data table, this default is generally appropriate. However, for data files without an explicit row ID contained in the data file, R assigns a row ID, which is just an integer from 1 to the number of rows. By default, then, this row number will be written to the output data file even though it was not included in the data file originally read into R. To suppress the writing of the row names, add the `row.names=FALSE` option to the `Write` statement.

row.names option: Suppress the writing of row names by setting to FALSE.

One other issue that relates to how well an output text file of data matches the input text file relates to missing data. As discussed, missing data by default in an input text file of data is represented as literally missing: for a `csv` text file there are two commas with nothing in between, and for a `fwd` text file there is simply an empty space in the corresponding column. Once read, internally R represents this missing data as `NA`. When writing data to an external text file, R retains these missing data codes, which are written to the output data file instead of literally being missing. To read this text file back into R, make sure to include the `missing=NA` option to the `Read` statement so that R will, once again, interpret these values as missing.

Worked Problems

1 Consider the data in Figure 2.3, randomly selected from a data file of the body measurements of thousands of motorcyclists.

   (a) Enter these values into a worksheet and create a `csv` file of these data. (See problem #4 for Chapter 1.)

   (b) Read the data into R.

   (c) Confirm that the data were read correctly.

	A	B	C
1	Gender	Weight	Height
2	F	150	66
3	F	138	66
4	M	240	74
5	M	178	71
6	F	130	64
7	M	200	74
8	F	140	70
9	M	220	77

Figure 2.3 Gender, Weight, and Height of eight motorcyclists.

    (d) List the data within R.

    (e) Write the data to an R native data file.

2 Variable labels.

    (a) In a worksheet application, construct a variable labels file for the data in Figure 2.3. For example, include the units of measurement along with the variable name.

    (b) Convert the labels file to a csv file.

    (c) Read the labels file into R.

    (d) List the labels within R.

3 Suppose the data from Figure 2.3 were stored in the fwd format, as shown in Listing 2.13.

```
F 150 66
F 138 66
M 240 74
M 178 71
F 130 64
M 200 74
F 140 70
M 220 77
```

Listing 2.13 Data for eight motorcyclists in fixed width format.

This data set is also available on the web at:

    http://lessRstats.com/data/HtWtEg.fwd

    (a) Read the data into R directly from the web. (Hint: To read the data, treat the blank space in front of each number as part of its field width.)

    (b) Create the data file on your computer system.

    (c) Confirm that the data were read correctly.

    (d) Write a csv version of the data file, without the imputed row names, 1 through 8.

4 The following web address (URL) specifies a file in fixed width format with 351 rows of data, the data for the Hunter, Gerbing, and Boster (1982) analysis.

    http://lessRstats.com/data/Mach4Plus.fwd

The codebook for the data follows.

```
ID, 4 columns
Gender, 0 for Male, 1 for Female, 1 column
Mach IV, 20 items, 1 column each
Dogmatism, 20 items, 1 column each
Self-esteem, 10 items, 1 column each
Internal locus of control, 8 items, 1 column each
External locus of control, Powerful others, 8 items, 1 column each
External locus of control, Chance, 8 items, 1 column each
```

(a) Read the data in an R data frame.

(b) List the variable names and the first 6 rows of the data frame.

CHAPTER 3

EDIT DATA

3.1 Quick Start

First install R and lessR as explained in Section 1.2. At the beginning of each R session access lessR with library(lessR). Then read your data into an R data frame with Read(), the subject of Chapter 2.

After you have read the data you may be ready to proceed directly to data analysis, the topic of the following chapters. If you are ready to begin analyzing data right now, feel free to proceed to one of the following chapters to learn to use lessR for a specific analysis, such as bar charts (Chapter 4), or histograms and related graphs (Chapter 5).

The values of a variable, however, can be edited and transformed in many ways. Sometimes certain transformations facilitate data analysis, or are even necessary for data analysis to proceed. These types of data editing and modifications are the topic of this chapter. Data modifications are usually followed by writing the revised data frame to an external file so that the revised data can be directly read, ready for analysis in a new R session.

✓ Edit individual data values with the R function fix, which presents a table of the specified data frame that resembles a worksheet.

fix function,
Section 3.2, p. 54

```
> fix(mydata)
```

✓ The values of a numerical variable may be transformed according to some arithmetic operation. For example, create a new variable called Weight.root by taking the square root of the existing values of Weight.

Transform function,
Section 3.3.1,
p. 56

```
> mydata <- Transform(Weight.root=sqrt(Weight))
```

✓ If the data values for a categorical variable are coded with integers, consider converting to the R data type for categorical data, a factor, using the factor function.

factor,
Section 3.3.2,
p. 59

```
> mydata <- Transform(Gender=factor(Gender,
            levels=c(0,1), labels=c("Male","Female")))
```

The levels argument refers to the integer values of the variable as read into R. The labels argument refers to their value labels.

✓ If the levels of a categorical variable are to be presented in an order other than alphabetical, then use the `factor` function to inform R of the correct order, either with ordered or unordered levels.

ordered option,
Section 3.3.2,
p. 60

```
> mydata <- Transform(Satisfaction=factor(Satisfaction,
                   levels=c("low", "med", "high"), ordered=TRUE))
```

✓ Up to around half of the items on a survey may be written so that to agree with the item is to disagree with the underlying measured attitude. When the scale responses are converted to numbers, reverse score these items.

Recode function,
Section 3.4.1,
p. 63

```
> mydata <- Recode(m03, old=0:5, new=5:0)
```

Sort function,
Section 3.5, p. 66

✓ To sort the rows of data in a data frame, use the `lessR` function `Sort`.

```
> mydata <- Sort(c(Gender, Salary), direction=c("+", "-"))
```

Here sort the data first by Gender, and then by Salary for men and women separately. Gender is sorted in ascending order and Salary in descending order. Ascending sorts are the default.

✓ To extract only a portion of a data frame, use the `lessR` function `Subset` to delete rows and/or columns.

Subset function,
Section 3.6, p. 68

```
> mydata <- Subset(Gender=="M" & Years<10, columns=c(Years, Salary))
```

Here retain in the data set only men who have worked in the company for less than 10 years, and only retain two variables, the number of years worked and salary.

✓ The opposite of `Subset` is to merge data frames with `Merge`, which combines two different data frames into one. First a horizontal merge, here on `row.names`, but any variable common to both data sets would work.

merge function,
horizontal,
Section 3.7.1,
p. 72

```
> mydata <- Merge(dataH1, dataH2, by="row.names")
```

A vertical merge applies where both data frames contain the same variables.

merge function,
vertical,
Section 3.7.2,
p. 73

```
> mydata <- Merge(dataV1, dataV2)
```

3.2 Edit Data

On occasion, after the data have been collected and read into R, individual data values need to be changed.

Scenario *Edit individual data values*
After the data were read into an R data frame, it was discovered that several of the values were incorrectly entered. Revise the data for subsequent analysis.

R provides a data editor that presents the specified data frame in tabular form that resembles a worksheet. Access this editor with the R function `fix`. Here apply the `fix` function to the Employee data set, read into the data frame `mydata`.

 R Input *View and edit individual data values*

```
> fix(mydata)
```

fix function: Edit individual data values.

Figure 3.1 presents the result, the R data editor as it appears on the Macintosh.

row.names	Years	Gender	Dept	Salary	Satisfaction	HealthPlan
Ritchie, Darnell	7	M	ADMN	43788.26	med	1
Wu, James	NA	M	SALE	84494.58	low	1
Hoang, Binh	15	M	SALE	101074.9	low	3
Jones, Alissa	5	F		43772.58		1
Downs, Deborah	7	F	FINC	47139.9	high	2
Afshari, Anbar	6	F	ADMN	59441.93	high	2

Figure 3.1 First six rows of Employee data in the Macintosh version of the R data editor.

The data table in Figure 3.1 looks like but does not have the flexibility and programmability of a worksheet. What is possible with the R data editor is to edit individual data values. To do so, click on the appropriate cell and enter the desired value. Also, individual columns and rows can be added or deleted, either by clicking on the icons in the top-left corner, or by right-clicking on the cell at the intersection of the appropriate row and column.

To exit the editor and save any changes, click on the close-window button at the top of the window, on the left side for Macintosh users and the right side for Windows users. Do *not* click on STOP to exit if the changes should be saved. Clicking on the STOP button quits the editor and cancels any changes.

Any changes made in the R data editor refer to the current version of the corresponding data frame, such as `mydata`. This storage container for the data is the subject of subsequent analysis, but it disappears when the R session ends. To save the data frame so that it exists independent of any one R session, write the edited contents of the data frame to your computer's file system, such as with the `lessR` abbreviation `wrt.r` for the `Write` function.

Write function, Section 2.5.1, p. 48

3.3 Transform Data

A standard procedure in data analysis is to transform the values of a variable into different values according to a specified formula. A transformation may transform values of an existing variable into a new variable, or overwrite an existing variable. These transformations are the topic of this section.

3.3.1 Transformations by Formula

For example, the values of Salary may be expressed in dollars, but for purposes of display such as in graphs that display the results of the analysis, the values are to be expressed in thousands of dollars. For example, a value of $64,000 becomes $64. Or a variable measured in hours can be expressed in terms of minutes. Or the logarithm of a variable can be analyzed instead of the original measurements.

To transform the values of a variable use the lessR function Transform, also expressed in terms of its abbreviation, trans.

Transform
function:
Transform the
values of an
existing variable.

> mydata <- Transform(*Variable*=expression with *Existing_Variable*)

If the variable name on the left side of the equals sign, =, has the same name as the variable on the right side, then the transformed variable replaces the existing variable. If the name of the transformed variable is different, a new variable is created. If the variable to be transformed is not in the mydata data frame, then specify the data frame with the data option.

data option,
Section 1.3.5,
p. 13

Arithmetic Operators

To construct the expression that defines the transformation, the usual arithmetic operators apply: +, −, *, and /, for addition, subtraction, multiplication, and division, respectively. R uses the caret symbol, ^, for exponentiation. Accordingly, for variable x, x*60 transforms the values of x by multiplying each by 60. And x^2 squares the values of variable x.

Employee data set,
Figure 1.7, p. 21

As an example, again consider the Employee data.

 Scenario *New variable from arithmetic*
An existing variable in the Employee data table is Years, the number of years employed at the company. Define a new variable, the number of months employed at the company.

Use the Transform function to create a new variable, the number of months worked.

 lessR Input *Arithmetic transformation*
> mydata <- Transform(Months=Years*12)

The output includes some data from the data table before and after the transformation to facilitate comparison. First, however, is a brief description of the data, in Listing 3.1.

```
Number of variables of mydata to transform: 1
Number of cases (rows) of mydata: 37
```

Listing 3.1 One variable to be transformed over 37 rows of data.

The data values listed before the transformation are just the first six rows of data of the Employee data set. Multiple transformations can be specified in a call to Transform, so a summary of the requested transformations is presented next, here only one in Listing 3.2.

Then, the first four rows of just the transformed data in the data frame, mydata, are displayed, as shown in Listing 3.3. Now there is a new variable in mydata, Months. For the

```
Transformation Summary
----------------------
     create new variable:  Months = Years * 12
```

Listing 3.2 The requested transformation.

second row of data the value of Years is missing, so this value is also necessarily missing for Months.

```
After, First five rows of transformed data for data frame: mydata
-----------------------------------------------------------------
                  Months
Ritchie, Darnell    84
Wu, James           NA
Hoang, Binh        180
Jones, Alissa       60
Downs, Deborah      84
```

Listing 3.3 The first four rows of the transformed data for the new variable Months.

Mathematical Functions

Transformations can also be defined from mathematical functions such as standardizing the values of a variable or calculating the logarithms of the values. Common functions for transformations are listed in Table 3.1.

Table 3.1 Some R mathematical functions applied here to the variable x.

Operation	Usage
round to n decimal digits	round(x,ndigits)
standard or z-score	scale(x)
natural logarithm	log(x)
square root	sqrt(x)
absolute value	abs(x)
cos	cosine(x)
sin	sin(x)
tan	tan(x)

As an example, consider the responses to the 20-item Mach IV scale. As we see in Chapter 11, there are some advantages to considering subsets of Mach IV, such as an Honesty subscale that consists of Items m06, m07, m09 and m10.

Standardization of the values of a distribution yields a transformed distribution with a specified mean and a standard deviation. Usually the mean and standard deviation of the standardized distribution are 0 and 1, respectively, yielding what are called *z-scores*. With a common mean and standard deviation, the transformed values of each of the four variables are more comparable. In the standardized distribution of z-scores, each data value is no longer expressed on an absolute scale from Strongly Disagree to Strongly Agree, but instead in terms of how many standard deviations it is from its own mean.

Honesty subscale, Section 11.10, p. 273

standardization: Transformation of a variable to have data values with a specified mean and standard deviation, usually 0 and 1.

Scenario *Standardize variables*

An analyst wishes to standardize the items before summing them, so that the responses to the different items are more comparable before the summation. This is required when the items are from different response scales, but sometimes done even when all the items are answered on the same scale.

scale function: Standardize the values of a variable.

Accomplish standardization in R with the R function scale. In the following, all four standardization statements for the four variables are included in a single Transform statement, with successive statements separated by a comma. The newly created standardized variables were chosen to all begin with the letter "z".

lessR Input *Transformation with functions*

```
> mydata <- Transform(z06=scale(m06), z07=scale(m07),
           z09=scale(m09), z10=scale(m10))
```

Listing 3.4 shows the first four rows of the transformed data.

```
After, First four rows of transformed data for data frame: mydata
-----------------------------------------------------------------
          z06         z07         z09          z10
1 -1.30348450 -0.8317862 -0.6707109 -0.007512965
2  0.05013402 -0.1528165  0.1948021 -0.007512965
3 -0.62667524  1.8840925  1.0603151 -0.007512965
4 -0.62667524 -0.8317862 -0.6707109  1.750520786
```

Listing 3.4 Newly created standardized variables.

For the values of a normally distributed variable, approximately 95% of the values are within two standard deviations of the mean. Because a z-score indicates how many standard deviations the original value is from its mean, most z-scores from normal distributions are between -2 and 2. Distributions of responses on a 0 to 5 scale for each item are not necessarily normal, but a general rule is that most z-scores look like the values in Listing 3.4. There are usually few such values larger than 2 or especially 3 and smaller than -2 or -3.

With the z-scores defined, the new scale scores on the Honesty subscale can now be calculated for each of the 351 respondents. A limitation of the Transform statement, however, is that multiple transformations can be specified in a single call to Transform, but a new transformed variable cannot be created out of other newly created transformed variables in the same Transform call. Accomplish the calculation of the subscale score from the newly created z-score variables in a separate statement.

```
> mydata <- Transform(Honesty=z06+z07+z09+z10)
```

All of these transformations only apply to the specified data frame, mydata. Once the R session ends, so does each data frame. To access the transformed data for future R sessions, one possibility is to write the data frame to your computer's file system as a native R file, with file type .rda, such as Mach4.rda.

Write function, Section 2.5.1, p. 48

```
> wrt.r("Mach4")
```

In a subsequent new analysis session, use Read() to browse for the new file and read it into R for additional analysis.

Save R code, Section 1.5, p. 19

data storage type, Section 1.6.3, p. 22

variable type, Section 1.6.3, p. 22

3.3.2 Define Categorical Variables as Factors

A potential confusion in data analysis exists between variable type and data storage type. The issue is that the values of a categorical variable, the non-numeric, discrete categories, can be represented in the computer as numeric digits, usually integers. It is often just as easy, and likely less confusing, to use mnemonic alphabetic characters to represent these non-numeric categories. Encoding Gender with an M and an F instead of a 0 and 1, for example, avoids confusion regarding the meaning of each code, and no one will try to compute the mean of a column of M's and F's.

Convert an Integer Variable to a Factor

A common data analysis scenario is to recognize some integer coded variables as categorical variables and then convert these variables to the explicit R storage type for categorical variables, factors.

factor, Section 2.2.2, p. 34

 Scenario *Recognize integer codes as non-numeric categories*
The values of Gender in a data file are coded as 0 for Male and 1 for Female. Create a new variable explicitly defined as a categorical variable and provide the labels of Male and Female in place of 0 and 1.

To transform a variable to the R representation of a categorical variable, a factor, the factor function relies upon two different parameters, levels and labels. The *levels* option specifies the values of the variable before the transformation. The *labels* option specifies the usually non-numeric names of the levels. To accomplish the creation of the new factor in the data frame of interest, usually mydata, embed the factor statement inside the Transform statement.

Consider the 0/1 coding of Gender in the Mach IV data set, with 0 for Male and 1 for Female. The goal is to create a factor variable with value labels Male and Female instead of the integers 0 and 1, the levels in this context. The labels are Male and Female.

We have no need to retain the 0/1 coding for subsequent analyses, so the following Transform statement uses the same variable, Gender, on both sides of the equals sign, =, which overwrites the data values. To improve readability and better keep track of the multiple parentheses, write this Transform statement on multiple lines.

factor function: Create or define the properties of a factor variable.

levels option: The original values of a categorical variable.

labels option: The labels of the variable after transformation.

lessR Input *Add value labels to a numerically coded categorical variable*
```
> mydata <- Transform(
    Gender=factor(Gender, levels=c(0,1), labels=c("Male","Female"))
  )
```

The result of this transformation appears in Listing 3.5. The first four values of Gender were originally the integer values 0, 0, 1, 1. Now they are the factor levels, Male, Male, Female, Female. All subsequent analyses will display the new factor levels, Male and Female, on the resulting output, instead of 0 and 1. Accordingly, the factor levels can be thought of as *value labels*, which label the corresponding categorical values as part of the output of any subsequent data analysis.

value labels: The values of a categorical variable.

```
After, First four rows of transformed data for data frame: mydata
-----------------------------------------------------------------

   Gender
1    Male
2    Male
3  Female
4  Female
```

Listing 3.5 Transformed Gender as a factor with new levels Male and Female.

On subsequent output for data analysis, R displays the output ordered by the levels in the `factor` statement. For example, the bars of a bar graph would now be displayed with Male listed before Female because the level for Male is listed before that of Female in the previous `factor` statement. Change this order with the `factor` function by changing the order of the listed levels in the `levels` specification.

To define Gender as a factor with Female listed first in the subsequent data analyses, switch the order for both the `levels` and the `labels` arguments in the `factor` statement. With the `factor` function, the labels must be listed in the same order as their levels. In this situation, the levels are the corresponding integer codes as read from the data file.

```
> mydata <- Transform(
    Gender=factor(Gender, levels=c(1,0), labels=c("Female","Male"))
  )
```

bar chart,
Section 4.2.1,
p. 79

On a bar graph, for example, the bar for Female now displays before the bar for Male. These value labels both enhance the interpretability of the output of subsequent analyses, and inform the R data analysis procedures that the variable to be analyzed is categorical and not numeric.

Convert Nominal Data to Ordinal Data

When R reads a data table into an R data frame, any variables with non-numeric data values are automatically converted to factors. This conversion is usually appropriate because unlike integer categorical variables, variables with non-numeric values cannot be numerical.[1] R goes as far as it can to infer characteristics of the data from the way that the data values are encoded.

nominal data,
Section 1.6.3,
p. 23

ordinal data,
Section 1.6.3,
p. 24

Employee data set,
Section 1.6.1,
p. 20

The issue of ordering the levels of a categorical variable goes beyond the ordering of the levels of the output for a data analysis. This more fundamental distinction refers to two types of data that consist of categories, nominal and ordinal. *Nominal data* are unordered, discrete categories. *Ordinal data* are ordered, discrete categories or rankings. For example, the data for Gender are nominal as Male is neither less than nor greater than Female.

Consider the data for the Satisfaction variable in the Employee data set with three categorical levels: `low`, `med`, and `high`. Although the levels are not coded on a numeric scale, the levels are ordered because they reflect different locations along a continuum of Satisfaction. The levels are ranked as: `low` < `med` < `high`. That is, the continuous variable of Satisfaction is coded with ordinal data. Unless this ordering is accounted for, R would misleadingly label subsequent output with the level `high` listed first because it alphabetically precedes `med` and `low`.

Data analysis routines can use this additional information inherent in ordinal data, the ordering of the data values. For example, when presented with an ordinal variable for analysis, the lessR function `BarChart`, abbreviated `bc`, presents the proper order of the categories, and then displays the bars in a graded shade of the same hue, from light to dark, to indicate the underlying ordering. Again, the structure of the data in the data frame should align with the structure of the data as it is conceptually defined.

BarChart function, Section 4.2.1, p. 79

 Scenario *Provide order to unordered categories*
R initially recognizes Satisfaction as categorical, but with unordered categories, that is, nominal data. The categories, however, should be ordered as `low`, `med`, and `high`. Redefine the Satisfaction variable within R as ordinal, with ordered, non-numeric categories.

Specify ordinal data with the `factor` function. Invoke the `levels` option to obtain the desired order of the levels displayed on subsequent output. This specification only changes the output order, leaving the status of the categorical variable as nominal. To define the variable as ordinal, also specify the `ordered=TRUE` option.

ordered option: Specify ordinal data.

---

 lessR Input *Specify the order of the value labels and define as ordinal*

```
> mydata <- Transform(Satisfaction=factor(Satisfaction,
            levels=c("low", "med", "high"), ordered=TRUE))
```

The output of the `Transform` function provides both the first four rows of the data before transformation, and then after transformation. However, there is no change in the values of Satisfaction in either listing. Instead, the change in the preceding transformation is a property of the data, not the data values themselves.

Likert Data Defined as Ordinal

The responses to the 20 Mach IV items are coded as integers on a 6-point scale from 0 to 5. Many researchers, your author included, analyze these data on a numeric scale. The resulting numerical data are subject to a wide variety of numerical analyses such as means, standard deviations, correlations, and factor analysis. These analyses are not meaningful when applied to categorical data.

Mach IV data, Listing 1.8, p. 27

There is no guarantee, however, that the respondents interpret the distances between equal scale points as equal. To interpret Likert data as numerical is to imply that the data values are *interval data* with the perception by the respondents of equally spaced categories on the underlying continuum of Disagree/Agree. If Likert data are interval, then the psychological perception of the distance between `Strongly Agree` and `Agree` is the same as between `Agree` and `Slightly Agree`. These psychological perceptions are presumed equal because the

interval data, Section 1.6.3, p. 23

corresponding integer encoding of 5 (Strongly Agree) and 4 (Agree) and then 4 (Agree) and 3 (Slightly Agree) specify equal distances, 1, between each of the two pairs of response categories.

Some researchers prefer to analyze Likert data as ordinal data, as ordered categories without the underlying specification of a numerical scale.

> ⭐ **Scenario** *Convert integer Likert data to ordinal categories*
> Respondents provided answers to Likert data attitude items, here on a 6-point scale from `Strongly Disagree` to `Strongly Agree`. The six possible responses to each item were coded as integers from 0 to 5, with 5 representing `Strongly Agree`. Convert these integer coded responses to each item to ordinal categories with each category appropriately labeled.

Mach IV data, Listing 1.8, p. 27

Consider the six response categories with which respondents answered each Mach IV item. To simplify these expressions save the Likert response category names into an object we choose to call LikertCats. The `<-`, the *assignment operator*, indicates to insert that whatever is on the right of the expression into whatever is on the left. The object LikertCats contains the six category names.

assignment operator, Section 1.3.3, p. 9

```
LikertCats <- c("Strongly Disagree", "Disagree", "Slightly Disagree",
                "Slightly Agree", "Agree", "Strongly Agree")
```

Instead of individually listing all six integers, use the colon notation to generate them. Now apply the factor transformation to each item of interest. Create factor versions for each of the four items on the Mach IV Honest subscale.

colon notation, Section 1.3.6, p. 15

```
> mydata <- Transform(
    m06.f = factor(m06, levels=0:5, labels=LikertCats),
    m07.f = factor(m07, levels=0:5, labels=LikertCats),
    m09.f = factor(m09, levels=0:5, labels=LikertCats),
    m10.f = factor(m10, levels=0:5, labels=LikertCats)
  )
```

After these transformations are run, subsequent data analysis routines will recognize the new variables such as `m06.f` as categorical variables with the specified value labels. By not replacing the original variables, such as `m06`, both the original integer variables and the newly created factor versions of the item responses remain available for analysis.

3.4 Recode Data

Transformations change all of the values of a variable according to a specified formula, such as standardization or taking the logarithm of each value. Transformations can be applied to continuous variables with many different values. Categorical variables, or continuous variables with a small number of possible data values, can have their values changed by specifying how each existing value is converted to a new value, what is called a *recode*.

recode: Map each value of a data variable into a new value.

3.4.1 Reverse Score Items

A common recode application relates to the computation of a scale score from a survey questionnaire. Consider the 20-item Mach IV scale. Some of the items are written so that an Agree response indicates a Machiavellian attitude, a pro-attitude item. The 15th item on the scale provides an example.

Mach IV scale, Table 1.2, p. 26

15. It is wise to flatter important people.

Other items are written so that Agreement with the item indicates the opposite of a Machiavellian attitude, a reversed-attitude item. An example here is the 3rd Mach IV item.

3. One should take action only when sure it is morally right.

To encourage the respondent to read and comprehend the meaning of each item, up to around half of the items on a scale are written such that agreement indicates the opposite of the attitude of interest. Otherwise, as applied to the Mach IV scale, a Machiavellian individual would respond `Agree` or `Strongly Agree` to each of the 20 items, perhaps then reading each item less critically.

To calculate a total score on the scale, all the item responses for a respondent must be scored so that summing over them consistently indicates endorsement for the attitude of interest. In the case of the Mach IV data, code a reverse-scored item such that a 0 indicates `Strongly Agree`, whereas for a pro-attitude item a 0 indicates a `Strongly Disagree`. Every `Strongly Agree` response is initially coded as a 5. In this situation the reverse scoring must adjust the coding of the relevant items before this analysis of the data values.

reverse score: Reverse the scoring of an item so that high values indicate Disagreement.

⭐ **Scenario** *Reverse score Likert data*
The responses to an attitude survey are coded as integers 0 through 5, which corresponds to the response categories of `Strongly Disagree` through `Strongly Agree`. However, about half of the items are written so that disagreement with the item indicates agreement with the attitude of interest. Reverse score these items so that, for example, a response of 0 that corresponds to `Strongly Disagree` is transformed to a 5 to indicate `Strongly Agree`.

To implement this reverse scoring, use the `lessR` function `Recode`, abbreviated `rec`. The first argument is a list of one or more variables, such as items, that are to be recoded. The `old` parameter specifies the list of existing values. The `new` parameter specifies the corresponding list of recoded values listed in the same order as the values in the `old` list. The optional argument is `new.var`, the name of a newly created variable to contain the recoded values. If omitted, then the recoded values are written over the original values of the variable of interest. If the variable to be recoded is not in the `mydata` data frame, then specify the data frame with the `data` option.

Recode function: Accomplish a recode of designated variables.

old argument: List of existing values.

new argument: List of new values.

new.var option: Name of the new variable.

data option: Data frame with the variable to be recoded, default is `mydata`.

In the case of the Mach IV data with responses to a 6-point Likert scale, the recoded values are written over the original values. The responses here are coded from 0 to 5. As always for a list of multiple values with the values in the list separated by commas, use the combine function `c` to combine the values together. This list could be written as `c(0,1,2,3,4,5)`, or, without the

*c function,
Section 1.3.6,
p. 15*

commas in the abbreviated form using the equivalent expression `0:5`. The reverse scoring flips this coding, so a 5 goes to a 0, a 4 goes to a 1, and so forth. This recoded list could be specified as `c(5,4,3,2,1,0)`, or, more simply, `5:0`. This recoding for the reversed-attitude item `m03` follows.

✒ **lessR Input** *Reverse score a Likert item*

```
> mydata <- Recode(m03, old=0:5, new=5:0)
```

---

*list of variables,
Section 8.3, p. 195*

The variable `m03` could be replaced with list of variables to be recoded.

The `Recode` function first lists the first several values of the variable or variables to be recoded, as in Listing 3.6.

```
First four rows of data to recode for data frame: mydata
----------------------------------------------------------
    m03
1    4
2    1
3    5
4    3
```

Listing 3.6 Some data from the variable to be recoded.

Next, `Recode` displays the implemented recode specification, as shown in Listing 3.7. Also provided are the total number of rows of data to be recoded, and also a note that the values of the original variable are replaced with the new values.

```
Recoding Specification
----------------------
    0 --> 5
    1 --> 4
    2 --> 3
    3 --> 2
    4 --> 1
    5 --> 0

Number of cases (rows) to recode: 351

Replace existing values of each specified variable,
   no value for option: new.var
```

Listing 3.7 The mapping of existing values to recoded values.

`Recode` then provides some information, the number of unique values, the number of values that are to be recoded, and each variable to be recoded, as shown in Listing 3.8.

As a final verification of the recode, in Listing 3.9, the first several data values of the recoded variable are displayed. These values can be compared to the values before the recode to verify that it worked as intended.

```
---   Recode: m03  ---------------------------------
Number of unique values of m03 in the data: 6
Number of values of m03 to recode: 6
```

Listing 3.8 Overview of recoding for Variable (Item) m03.

```
First four rows of recoded data for data frame: mydata
--------------------------------------------------------
   m03
1    1
2    4
3    0
4    2
```

Listing 3.9 First four recoded values of m03.

The Recode function also allows multiple variables to be specified in the recoding. Again, the items could be listed individually, or a range of consecutive items in the data frame could be specified with the colon notation for a variable list. The complete list of Mach IV items to be recoded follows.

```
> mydata <-
  Recode(c(m03,m04,m06,m07,m09,m10,m11,m14,m16,m17,m19),
        old=0:5, new=5:0)
```

Because Items m09, m10, and m11 occur consecutively in the data frame, this expression could be shortened a little by using the : notation to specify the sequence of these three items, replacing m09,m10,m11 with m09:m11.

3.4.2 Missing Data

By default missing data in the data file indicates data values that are literally not present. In addition, the missing argument of the Read function informs R of missing data codes such as −99, which although physically present in the data, indicate that the corresponding value is missing. It is also possible to assign these codes after the data values are read.

 Scenario *Assign missing data codes after the data values have been read*
After the data have been read, assign new codes to data that have been previously defined as missing, or, redefine specific existing values as missing.

missing option, Section 2.2.5, p. 36

To define missing data after the data values are read, use Recode with the value of "missing" for either the old or new specifications. The Recode function can assign missing data from a given data value or values, or it can assign missing data to a specific data value or values.

For example, returning to the Employee data set, suppose the value of 1 for HealthPlan indicates a missing data value. If this coding was not specified when the data values were read, then use Recode to assign the missing value.

 lessR Input *Recode an existing value to missing*
```
> mydata <- Recode(Years, old=1, new="missing")
```

Or suppose values originally coded as missing now should be assigned some other code. Here, assign missing values for the variables Years and Salary a value of 99.

 lessR Input *Recode missing data to another value*
```
> mydata <- Recode(c(Years, Salary), old="missing", new=99)
```

factor function,
Section 3.3.2,
p. 59

Note that these assignments cannot be done with variables that are factors. The reason for this is that applying Recode to a factor removes the factor attribute, so that after the transformation the variable is no longer a factor. Manipulating the values of a factor should be instead accomplished with the factor function.

3.5 Sort Data

One way to organize data is to sort the rows of the data frame by some criterion based on the data values.

3.5.1 Sort by Variables

Consider first sorting the data by the values of one or more variables. When multiple variables are specified, the second variable is sorted within each level of the first variable, and so forth. Each variable can be sorted in ascending or descending order, that is, from smallest to largest or largest to smallest.

 Scenario *Sort the data according to the values of one or more variables*
To facilitate a visual inspection of the data, sort the rows of data according to the values of Gender. List all the data rows for the women first, where the value of Gender is "F", and then again for the men, where Gender is "M". Within the data rows for each value of Gender, sort by Salary in descending order, listing first the women who make the most money, and then the men.

Sort function: Sort
the rows of a data
frame by specified
variables.

data option,
Section 1.3.5,
p. 13

To sort the rows of data in the data frame, usually mydata, use the lessR function Sort, abbreviated srt. Invoke the data option to specify a data frame with a different name. For example, to sort the data by Gender, enter the following.

✒ **lessR Input** *Sort the data frame by the specified variable*
```
> mydata <- Sort(Gender)      or      > mydata <- srt(Gender)
```

Consider a sort first by Gender and then, within each level of Gender, sort by Salary. To sort by multiple criteria such as these, list the multiple variables in the order of their sort. Unless otherwise specified the variables are sorted in the default ascending order from smallest to largest values. Because there is more than one specified variable, that is, a list of variables, use the combine function, c, to combine the multiple variables into a single list.

c function, Section 1.3.6, p. 15

```
> mydata <- Sort(c(Gender, Salary))
```

To sort at least one of the specified variables in descending order use the `direction` option for each variable to be sorted. To use this option, list the order of the sort for each variable. A "+" indicates an ascending sort, from smallest to largest values. A "-" indicates a descending sort, from largest to smallest values. For example, to sort by Gender in ascending order, and then Salary in descending order, enter the following.

direction option: Specify the direction of the sort for a variable.

✒ **lessR Input** *Sort the data frame by specified variables and directions*
```
> mydata <- Sort(c(Gender, Salary), direction=c("+", "-"))
```

Here the output of this sort instruction begins in Listing 3.10. The first output is a specification of the sort.

```
Sort Specification
------------------------------
  Gender -->  ascending
  Salary -->  descending
------------------------------
```

Listing 3.10 Sort specification for sorting Gender in ascending order followed by Salary in descending order.

Listing 3.11 displays the first rows of sorted data. All four rows are data from women, and the salaries are listed in descending order beginning with the highest women's salary of $112,563.38.

```
After the Sort, first four rows of data for data frame: mydata
-----------------------------------------------------------------
                 Years Gender Dept    Salary Satisfaction HealthPlan
James, Leslie       18      F ADMN 112563.38          low          3
Kralik, Laura       10      F SALE  82681.19          med          2
Skrotzki, Sara      18      F MKTG  81352.33          med          2
Billing, Susan       4      F ADMN  62675.26          med          2
```

Listing 3.11 Employee data sorted by Gender in ascending order and then Salary in descending order.

3.5.2 Sort by Other Criteria

In R the row names of a data frame are conceptually distinct from the variables. Unlike the variables, the row names are not subject to statistical analysis, such as computing a mean. Instead their purpose is to identify each unique row and to appear on the output to facilitate interpretation, such as to label individual points in a graph.

row.names
option: A criterion for sorting the data frame by row names.

The Sort function provides a way to sort by row names, the name of the employees in the Employee data set. To do this specify row.names as the criterion by which to sort.

```
> mydata <- Sort(row.names)
```

The value of each row name occurs only once. When row names are to be sorted there is no reason to first sort by values of the variables within each row, so if row.names is specified as the sort criterion then no variables are specified. The direction of the sort, however, can be specified. The default is ascending. If a descending sort by row names is desired, include the direction="-" option.

> **lessR Input** *Sort the data frame by row names in descending order*
> ```
> > mydata <- Sort(row.names, direction="-")
> ```

random option: A criterion for sorting the data frame randomly.

The Sort function also has an option to randomly shuffle the rows of data. To do so, specify random as the criterion for the sort.

```
> mydata <- Sort(random)
```

This option is useful if the data have been previously sorted by some criterion that is no longer relevant.

3.6 Subset Data

3.6.1 Select Rows and/or Columns

The analysis of interest may be directed towards only part of the original data table. Perhaps only some of the rows of data are to be analyzed, such as only the data for Females. Or, perhaps one or more of the variables are not needed for the analysis, and can be discarded. Or, maybe the goal is simply to identify and list some subset of the data frame.

Subset function: Create a subset of the original data frame.

data option, Section 1.3.5, p. 13

☆ **Scenario** *Retain only the rows of data for specific data values*
For some analyses, analyze the data for men and women separately. From the primary data table create new data tables for men and for women.

To create a subset of the original data frame, use the lessR function Subset. If the data frame of interest is not mydata, then specify with the data option. To locate rows of data but leave the original data frame, usually `mydata`, unmodified, leave off the `mydata <-` assignment at the beginning of the `Subset` statement. Or, assign the output from `Subset` to any desired data frame.

As is true of all functions defined in R, if the order of the arguments in the function call matches the order in the function definition, then the argument names can be deleted. To get the arguments of a function, either refer to the manual for that function, here `?Subset`, or call the function name with the R function `args`, as in Listing 3.12. The first two arguments to the `Subset` function are `rows` and then `columns`. So, if the rows to be retained or deleted are listed as the first argument, then the `rows=` specification can be omitted.

args function: List the arguments that can be specified in a function call.

rows argument: Specify the rows to retain or discard.

columns argument: Specify the columns to retain or discard.

```
> args(Subset)
function (rows, columns, data=mydata, brief=FALSE, holdout=FALSE, ...)
```

Listing 3.12 The arguments of the `Subset` function.

To specify the subset, use the double equals sign, `==`, which indicates a test for equality. For example, reduce the Employee data table to include only data for Females.

==: Test two expressions for logical equality.

 lessR Input *Select and then retain only the rows of data from women*
```
> mydata <- Subset(Gender=="F")
```

The function `Subset` lists the first five rows of data before the subset, then the last four rows of data after the subset. The function also reports the number of rows and columns in the data frame before and after the subset procedure. As can be seen in Listing 3.13, the first rows after the subset have a Gender value of `"F"`.

```
Number of variables in mydata: 6
Number of cases (rows) in mydata: 19

First four rows of data for data frame: mydata
----------------------------------------------------------------
                Years Gender Dept    Salary Satisfaction HealthPlan
Jones, Alissa     5      F  <NA> 43772.58     <NA>          1
Downs, Deborah    7      F  FINC 47139.90     high          2
Afshari, Anbar    6      F  ADMN 59441.93     high          2
Kimball, Claire   8      F  MKTG 51356.69     high          2
```

Listing 3.13 First four rows of data after the subset that specifies only women be included in the revised data frame.

The expression for the rows to be retained can specify multiple criteria, using the logical operators in Table 3.2.

To locate some data without modifying the original data frame, do not assign the output of the function to a data frame. For example, in the Employee data set the following expression locates only women with more than 10 years employment, and then displays the resulting data.

Table 3.2 Logical operators.

Operator	Meaning
==	equals
!=	not equals
>	greater than
<	less than
&	and
|	or

 lessR Input *List selected rows of data but do not change the data frame*

```
> Subset(Gender=="F" & Years>10)
```

row.name
function: Identify a
single row of the
data frame.

A row of data can also be located with the R `row.name` function, such as the data for employee Scott Fulton.

```
> Subset(row.names(mydata)=="Fulton, Scott")
```

Note that the name of the data frame, usually `mydata`, must also be specified in the call to `row.names`. The function `row.names` is an R function, and hence does not default to `mydata` for the input data frame as do the `lessR` functions. Listing 3.14 displays the row of data for Scott Fulton.

	Years	Gender	Dept	Salary	Satisfaction	HealthPlan
Fulton, Scott	13	M	SALE	77785.51	low	1

Listing 3.14 Locate a row of data based on the row ID, in this case the employee's name.

The `columns` option is the second parameter in the definition of the `Subset` function, as seen from entering `?Subset`. If `columns` is the second argument in the call to `Subset`, then the `columns=` specification can be omitted.

For example, the following retains all of the rows of data, but only the data for the columns that contain the data values for the variables Years and Salary.

 lessR Input *Select and retain only the specified variables*

```
> Subset(columns=c(Years, Salary))
```

*c function,
Section 1.3.6,
p. 15*

Columns can also be deleted from the data frame of interest. To indicate that data for all variables are retained except the variables Years and Salary, put a minus sign, −, in front of the c for the combine function. Or, if there is only a single variable and no combine function, put the minus sign directly in front of the variable name.

```
> mydata <- Subset(columns=-c(Years, Salary))
```

The rows and columns arguments can also work together.

```
> mydata <- Subset(Gender=="F" & Years>10, columns=c(Years, Salary))
```

Here rows of data are obtained only for women with more than 10 years work experience, and only for two variables, Years and Salary.

3.6.2 Randomly Select Rows

The previous uses of the Subset function generated subsets based on logical criteria, such as selecting only those rows of data for the subset in which Gender is equal to "F". Another possibility is to have Subset randomly select the rows of data to retain, such as to evaluate the stability of a statistical result by doing the same analysis on a different data set. If the original sample is sufficiently large, this dual analysis can be performed on both a random subset of the original data, and then again on those remaining rows of data not included in the original data table.

 Scenario *Random selection of rows of data*
Create a data set that consists of 60% of the original data and then a second data set of the remaining 40% of the rows of data.

To create these data sets, specify the rows argument either as an integer to indicate the number of rows to retain, or as a proportion to indicate the proportion of rows to obtain. For example, the following generates a randomly selected subset of 60% of the rows of data in the default mydata data frame. Leave the original data table mydata unmodified by directing the subset of the data to a data frame called mydata.sub.

rows argument: Specify the number or proportion of rows to retain.

 lessR Input *Randomly select a percentage of the rows of* mydata *data table*
```
> mydata.sub <- Subset(.6, holdout=TRUE)
```

To analyze the data in this subset in a subsequent analysis, specify data=mydata.sub, the name of the data frame chosen to assign the output of the Subset function.

The output of this random selection process in Listing 3.15 includes the usual Subset output previously described. Also included is a brief description of the selection process, which results from applying the previous statement to the Mach IV data.

Mach IV data,
Listing 1.8, p. 27

```
Rows of data randomly extracted
-------------------------------------------
Proportion of randomly retained rows:  0.6
Number of randomly retained rows:  211
```

Listing 3.15 Rows retained in the random selection.

hold-out sample:
A percentage of the original data table extracted and then retained for later analysis.

`Subset` also provides the code to construct a second data frame, known as a *hold-out sample.* The name of this constructed data frame is the name of the original data frame with the characters `.hold` appended to the name. The resulting name for the usual `mydata` data frame is `mydata.hold`. After randomly extracting 60% of the rows of the 351 rows of data in the Mach IV data set, the output in Listing 3.16 shows how to construct a data frame for the remaining 40% of the original data.

```
mydata.hold <- Subset(
   row.names(mydata)=="3"
 | row.names(mydata)=="5"
 | row.names(mydata)=="6"
 | row.names(mydata)=="8"
 ...
 | row.names(mydata)=="349"
 | row.names(mydata)=="351"
 )
```

Listing 3.16 Excerpt of the code to create from the `mydata` data frame a hold-out sample called `mydata.hold`.

To create the hold-out sample named `data=mydata.hold`, run this code on the original data frame, usually `mydata`. Or, if the original `mydata` has been overwritten, re-read the data to reconstruct the original data table before extracting the hold-out sample. To analyze this hold-out sample with the `lessR` data analysis routines specify `data=mydata.hold` in the subsequent calls to the corresponding functions.

3.7 Merge Data

A *merge* of two data sets combines both data sets into one. Within R the data table is called a data frame. The two basic ways to merge data frames are with a horizontal merge or vertical merge.

3.7.1 Horizontal Merge

horizontal merge: Join two data frames by variables.

A *horizontal merge* creates a new data frame by combining the variables from the two data frames to merge. In this situation the two data frames generally contain different variables, but the data values are for the same people. The two data frames also share a common variable, usually a row identifier, an ID field. A horizontal merge yields a new data frame with the variables of both of the input data frames.

 Scenario *Merge data horizontally*
One source of employee data provided the data values for the first four variables: Years, Gender, Dept and Salary. The second source provided the values for Satisfaction and HealthPlan. Merge these data sets into a single data frame for subsequent analysis.

In this situation, neither of the two data files to be read into R are the data file of primary interest. The data table for subsequent analysis is the merged data frame, typically called `mydata` for convenience to ease subsequent analysis by the `lessR` data analysis routines.

We wish to read data into R, but for the first time not directly into the `mydata` data frame. The two data frames created by reading the data are here called Emp1a and Emp1b. To keep the amount of data manageable for this example, only data from the first four rows of the Employee data set is included.

```
> Emp1a <- Read("http://lessRstats.com/data/Emp1a.csv", row.names=1)
> Emp1b <- Read("http://lessRstats.com/data/Emp1b.csv", row.names=1)
```

The resulting data frames appear in Listings 3.17 and 3.18.

```
> Emp1a
                 Years Gender Dept    Salary
Ritchie, Darnell    7       M ADMN  43788.26
Wu, James          NA       M SALE  84494.58
Hoang, Binh        15       M SALE 101074.86
Jones, Alissa       5       F <NA>  43772.58
```

Listing 3.17 Data frame with the first four variables of the Employee data set.

```
> Emp1b
                 Satisfaction HealthPlan
Ritchie, Darnell          med          1
Wu, James                 low          1
Hoang, Binh               low          3
Jones, Alissa            <NA>          1
```

Listing 3.18 Data frame with the last two variables of the Employee data set.

The goal is to merge horizontally the data frames Emp1a and Emp1b to create the primary data frame of interest. To accomplish this merge, use the `lessR` function `Merge`. The required `by` argument for a horizontal merge provides the ID field that dictates how the columns of data values are matched. Here the match is according to the `row.names`. A variable name for a variable that both input data frames have in common could also be specified.

Merge function: Merge two data frames.

by option: Specify the variable by which to join two data frames with a horizontal merge.

> **lessR Input** *Horizontal merge that combines columns of data*
> ```
> > mydata <- Merge(Emp1a, Emp1b, by="row.names")
> ```

The merged data is written to the data frame `mydata`. The contents of `mydata` appear in Listing 3.19.

3.7.2 Vertical Merge

A *vertical merge* combines the rows of data from the two data frames to create a new data frame in R.

vertical merge: Join two data frames by rows.

```
> mydata
          Row.names Years Gender Dept    Salary Satisfaction HealthPlan
1      Hoang, Binh    15      M SALE 101074.86          low          3
2     Jones, Alissa    5      F <NA>  43772.58         <NA>          1
3  Ritchie, Darnell    7      M ADMN  43788.26          med          1
4       Wu, James     NA      M SALE  84494.58          low          1
```

Listing 3.19 The horizontally merged data frame.

 Scenario *Merge data vertically*
The variables in the Employee data set are Years, Gender, Dept, Salary, Satisfaction, and HealthPlan. Two data frames contain data for these variables, but for two different groups of employees. Merge the two data frames into one.

First the two data frames must be created in R by reading the data for each. The merged data frame is the primary data frame of interest, to be analyzed by the subsequent data analysis routines. For convenience name the merged data frame the default name for the lessR data analysis routines, mydata.

The two data frames for the data to be merged are named Emp2a and Emp2b, respectively.

```
> Emp2a <- Read("http://lessRstats.com/data/Emp2a.csv", row.names=1)
> Emp2b <- Read("http://lessRstats.com/data/Emp2b.csv", row.names=1)
```

The resulting data frames appear in Listings 3.20 and 3.21. For purposes of illustration, each of these data frames is limited to only four employees each.

```
> Emp2a
                 Years Gender Dept    Salary Satisfaction HealthPlan
Ritchie, Darnell     7      M ADMN  43788.26          med          1
Wu, James           NA      M SALE  84494.58          low          1
Hoang, Binh         15      M SALE 101074.86          low          3
Jones, Alissa        5      F <NA>  43772.58         <NA>          1
```

Listing 3.20 A data frame for four employees of the Employee data table.

```
> Emp2b
                 Years Gender Dept    Salary Satisfaction HealthPlan
Knox, Michael       18      M MKTG 89062.66          med          3
Campagna, Justin     8      M SALE 62321.36          low          1
Kimball, Claire      8      F MKTG 51356.69         high          2
Cooper, Lindsay      4      F MKTG 46772.95         high          1
```

Listing 3.21 A data frame for another four employees of the Employee data set.

Vertically merge the data frames Emp2a and Emp2b to create the primary data frame of interest. Again use the lessR function Merge, but for the vertical merge do not specify a by variable. The merged data is written to the data frame mydata.

---

lessR Input *Vertical merge that combines rows of data*

```
> mydata <- Merge(Emp2a, Emp2b)
```

The contents of the merged data frame, `mydata`, appear in Listing 3.22.

```
> mydata
                 Years Gender Dept    Salary Satisfaction HealthPlan
Ritchie, Darnell    7      M  ADMN  43788.26         med          1
Wu, James          NA      M  SALE  84494.58         low          1
Hoang, Binh        15      M  SALE 101074.86         low          3
Jones, Alissa       5      F  <NA>  43772.58        <NA>          1
Knox, Michael      18      M  MKTG  89062.66         med          3
Campagna, Justin    8      M  SALE  62321.36         low          1
Kimball, Claire     8      F  MKTG  51356.69        high          2
Cooper, Lindsay     4      F  MKTG  46772.95        high          1
```

Listing 3.22 The vertically merged data frame.

Now the merged data, in the `mydata` data frame, is ready for analysis.

Worked Problems

1 The three values of HealthPlan coded in the data file – 1, 2, and 3 – correspond to three health plans, respectively named GoodHealth, GetWell, and BestCare.

(a) Is HealthPlan a continuous or categorical variable? Why?

(b) How is HealthPlan stored within the R data frame?

(c) Provide the R statement that transforms HealthPlan to a factor.

The `Cars93` data set contains much information on 93 1993 car models. One variable is Source with two values, 0 for a foreign car and 1 for a car manufactured in the USA.

?dataCars93 for more information.

```
> mydata <- Read("Cars93", format="lessR")
```

2 The variable Type is stored in the data file with non-numeric values.

(a) How is the data stored within the corresponding R data frame when the data file is read into R?

(b) Order the values of Type appropriately.

3 In the data file the variable Airbag is integer coded with values of 0, 1, and 2, which correspond to "none", "driver", and "driver+". The meaning of "driver" is driver only, and "driver+" means driver and passenger air bags, so there is an ordered progression across the three levels of Airbag.

(a) What is the formal name for this type of variable?

(b) Create the appropriate representation of these data in the R data frame.

4 Examine the values of horsepower, HP.

   (a) Sort the data by HP.

   (b) List the 10 most powerful cars in terms of horsepower.

5 The various modifications of the `Cars93` data set in the previous problems prepare the data for subsequent analysis, but the changes are only temporary to the R session in which the changes are made. Chapter 2 presents two strategies for making these changes available in a subsequent R session.

   (a) Discuss one strategy.

   (b) Discuss another strategy.

CHAPTER 4

CATEGORICAL VARIABLES

4.1 Quick Start

First install R and lessR as explained in Section 1.2. At the beginning of each R session access lessR with library(lessR). Then read your data into an R data frame with Read(), the subject of Chapter 2.

The data table, represented within R as the data frame, contains the data values for one or more variables, each variable characterized by either numerical values or non-numerical categories. This chapter describes some basic analyses that are routinely among the first analyses done after reading the data, the description of the variation of a categorical variable.

variable types, Section 1.6.3, p. 22

4.1.1 One-variable Summaries

Several lessR functions are available to describe the sample values of a variable, here illustrated for a variable named Y.

```
> SummaryStats(Y)
```

Summary statistics, p. 80

```
> BarChart(Y)
```

Bar chart, p. 79

```
> PieChart(Y)
```

Pie chart, p. 85

SummaryStats adjusts the type of summary statistics provided to describe the values of either numerical or categorical variables. If the values of Y are non-numerical categories formally identified by what R calls a *factor*, the result is a table that shows how often each value occurred, the corresponding proportions and total sample size. Or, for a categorical variable coded with numeric values, set the value of the n.cat option to indicate the maximum number of unique values of a variable for which to analyze the variable as categorical.

factor, Section 2.2.2, p. 34

n.cat option, Section 2.2.7, p. 39

SummaryStats also provides the results in a briefer form for BarChart and PieChart. Regardless of the variable's data type, BarChart and PieChart always analyze the data values as discrete categories. So it is only useful to apply these functions to a variable with a small number of unique values regardless whether the variable is numerical, a factor, or some other data type.

All the variables in the data frame can be analyzed with a single function call. As with all lessR functions that process data, the default data frame name is mydata. If the argument to the function is left blank, `SummaryStats` and `BarChart` analyze all the variables in the `mydata` data frame.

```
> SummaryStats()
> BarChart()
```

The resulting bar charts are written to their respective `pdf` files, the names of which are provided by the standard console output.

CountAll
function: A bar
chart or histogram,
with summary
statistics, for each
variable in a data
frame.

A related function is `CountAll`, abbreviated `ca`. This function does the complete summary analysis selectively invoking either `BarChart` for a categorical variable or `Histogram` for a continuous variable, and also provides the corresponding summary statistics from `SummaryStats`. `CountAll` provides a complete graphical and statistical summary of all the variables in the data frame.

---

 lessR Input *Histograms and bar charts for all variables (in mydata)*
```
> CountAll()          or          > ca()
```

`CountAll` only applies to data frames. The default data frame is `mydata`.

4.1.2 Two-variable Summaries

The `BarChart` function for two variables yields a corresponding bar chart. It also provides the corresponding joint frequencies, the cross-tabulation table, that is the numerical basis of the bar chart. In addition, the associated chi-square test of independence of the two variables follows the sample cross-tabulation.

bar chart for two
variables,
Section 4.3.1,
p. 87

```
> BarChart(X, by=Y)
```

For categorical variables X and Y, a call to `SummaryStats` yields additional summary statistics in the form of various ways of calculating the cell proportions.

*Two-variable
summary* of
categorical
variables,
Section 4.3, p. 87

```
> SummaryStats(X, by=Y)
```

No `lessR` function analyzes the relations among three categorical variables. To generate a cross-tabulation table of three variables, use the R function `table`. As with all standard R functions, the data frame name is not assumed and so must be explicitly specified, such as with the `with` function. Here the joint frequencies are computed for three variables, X, Y, and Z.

table function,
Section 4.4.1,
p. 94

```
> with(mydata, table(X, Y, Z))
```

The function `mosaic` from the `vcd` package provides a mosaic plot, a graphical representation of the relations of three categorical variables.

mosaic function,
Section 4.4.1,
p. 95

```
> mosaic(~ Dept + Satisfaction + Gender, shade=TRUE, data=mydata)
```

An alternative expression of the `mosaic` function directs the analysis to focus specifically on a response variable of interest.

4.2 One Categorical Variable

Consider first the description of the values of a categorical variable. To illustrate these analyses, we return to the Employee data set.

Employee data table, Figure 1.7, p. 21

```
> mydata <- Read("Employee", format="lessR")
```

The data set contains both numerical variables and categorical variables.

format="lessR" option, Section 2.3.5, p. 44

4.2.1 Describe the Sample with a Bar Chart and Statistics

The primary `lessR` function for the analysis of the sample values of a categorical variable is `BarChart`, abbreviated `bc`, which provides both a graph and a numerical analysis. The graph is a bar chart of the frequencies of the variable. The numerical analysis provides a table of these frequencies with the corresponding proportions and accompanying inferential analysis in the form of chi-square. The `BarChart` function enhances the standard R function `barplot` for graphics and also assesses the `table`, `addmargins`, and `chisq.test` R functions for the provided statistics.

BarChart function: Create a bar chart and summary statistics.

The function `BarChart` invokes the `lessR` function `SummaryStats` for the summary statistics of a categorical variable. If the graph is not of interest, then obtain the `BarChart` numerical output directly with `SummaryStats`. To analyze the variable as categorical with `SummaryStats`, the variable's data type either must be an R factor, the R data type for factors, or a numerical variable with a small number of unique values as determined by the setting of `n.cat`.

SummaryStats function: Compute summary statistics.

Ideally define each categorical variable in the data frame as an R factor, either by default after reading non-numeric data values or with the `factor` function. The `BarChart` function, however, does not enforce this criterion as it analyzes any variable as a categorical variable. So `BarChart` generally is only useful for the analysis of the values of a variable with relatively few unique values.

n.cat option, Section 2.2.7, p. 39

factor function, Section 3.3.2, p. 59

⭐ **Scenario** *Generate a bar chart for a categorical variable*

For a variable with a relatively low number of unique data values, generate a bar chart to show the frequency of occurrence of each category, and also a corresponding frequency table.

Consider the number of people who work in each of the five areas of employment as indicated by the value of the variable Dept. The data values that record the department in which an employee works form a categorical variable, composed of discrete, non-numeric categories such as ACCT for Accounting and SALE for Sales.

Employee data table, Figure 1.7, p. 21

lessR Input *Bar chart*

```
> BarChart(Dept)          or          > bc(Dept)
```

variable labels,
Section 2.4, p. 45

The resulting bar chart is shown in Figure 4.1. Because the variable labels were already read into R, the variable label for Dept by default appears as the title of the graph. As is true of almost all standard R graphics, including for lessR functions, a title can be manually created with the main option, such as main="My Title".

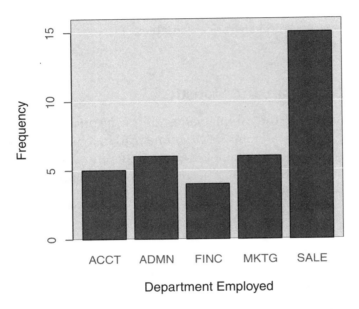

Figure 4.1 Default bar chart for a single categorical variable.

The statistics from BarChart in Listing 4.1 provide the frequencies for each of the categories, here the five categories of Dept. Also provided are the corresponding overall sample size and the proportions. By default R lists the order of the categories alphabetically. This ordering can be changed with the R factor function.

factor function,
Section 3.3.2,
p. 60.

```
--- Dept, Department Employed ---

               ACCT  ADMN  FINC  MKTG  SALE   Total
Frequencies:      5     6     4     6    15      36
Proportions:  0.139 0.167 0.111 0.167 0.417   1.000
```

Listing 4.1 Summary statistics from BarChart.

Far more people work in the Sales department, 15, than in any other of the four remaining departments. The corresponding sample proportion is 0.417, so 41.7% of all the employees in this sample worked in Sales.

4.2.2 Generalize Beyond the Sample with Inferential Analysis

The output of `BarChart` includes the inferential analysis of the sample frequencies in terms of the chi-squared hypothesis test. The underlying motivation of the inferential analysis is the generalization of the sample results to the population as a whole from which that sample was obtained. In this sample more people are in Sales than any other category. Would this same qualitative pattern of differences likely occur in a second sample of 37 *different* employees from the same population of employees from which the first sample was obtained?

chi-square goodness-of-fit test: Inferential test of a relationship between the values of a categorical variable.

Maybe in another sample Marketing would be the most frequently occurring group instead of Sales. Particularly for small samples the results are notoriously unstable from sample to sample, but hopefully the same qualitative pattern would be obtained in a new sample. The inferential analysis addresses the question whether the results are a true reflection of the underlying population values. Do the results persist over repeated samples, or are they a sampling fluke observed in this sample, but not the next?

Here the analysis is a test of the assumption that the cell frequencies are consistent with those expected under the *null hypothesis* of equal probabilities of group membership. Even if the null hypothesis of no association is true, the sample frequencies and associated probabilities will likely *not* be equal to the exact value expected under the assumption of equal probabilities. Given this assumption, are the obtained frequencies and their corresponding sample probabilities, the proportions, a "reasonable" outcome or not? If this assumption of no association is true, then the sample cell frequencies should be reasonably close to their expected values, which here is based on equal population proportions.

null hypothesis of equal group probabilities: Membership in each group is equally likely.

In this particular sample the sample probability of randomly selecting an employee in Sales is 0.417, much larger than the sample probability of 0.111 for Finance. This large discrepancy lends some credibility to the belief that the population probabilities are not equal, and suggests that Sales has the most employees. The large differences between the obtained sample probabilities indicate that this outcome has a low probability given the assumption of the null hypothesis.

 Scenario *Inferential analysis of the proportions of Departmental membership*
In this particular sample, the department with the most membership is Sales, with a proportion of 41.7% of all employees. Does this pattern likely exist in the population? Or is this sample result a sampling fluke with the reality that the probabilities of employment in all the departments are equal?

Are the probabilities equal in the population as a whole? Simply looking at the sample proportions and observing how discrepant they are from each other, however, cannot answer this question. This assessment requires the application of formal probability theory in the form of a *p-value*, the probability of the outcome at least as extreme *given* a true null hypothesis. In this example the null hypothesis is the assumption of equal probabilities for membership in the five groups. The result from `BarChart`, or `SummaryStats` upon which `BarChart` relies, follows.

p-value: Probability of the result at least as extreme given a true null hypothesis.

```
Chi-squared test of null hypothesis of equal probabilities
   Chisq = 10.94444,  df = 4,  p-value = 0.0272
```

chi-square test of equal probabilities: Evaluate if the probabilities of each category are equal.

If the sample proportions were all exactly equal to each other, then the chi-square value would be zero. Even if the true proportions are all equal, however, the sample proportions will generally not be equal. The issue is whether the chi-square statistic is so much larger than zero that the hypothesis of equal probabilities is no longer tenable. For this sample, the computed chi-square statistic is 10.944. What is the probability of obtaining a chi-statistic as large as 10.944 or larger in this situation, assuming that the true probabilities are all equal?

The probability of the outcome, or a more deviant outcome, given the assumption of the null hypothesis is the *p*-value, here reported as 0.028. The accepted value for what defines a low probability, the *alpha level* or α, is commonly set at 0.05. Define any probability value below $\alpha = 0.05$ as sufficiently unusual given the underlying assumption of the null hypothesis. The low probability of such an outcome, given the assumption, leads the analyst to conclude that the underlying assumption of the null hypothesis is likely not true.

alpha level: The definition of a low probability that specifies an unusual event.

$$\text{Equal probabilities test: } p\text{-value} = 0.027 < \alpha = 0.05, \text{ reject } H_0$$

If the assumption of equal group probabilities is true, then a sample with group probabilities this discrepant from equality to yield an obtained chi-square of 10.944 is only 0.028. We conclude that the null hypothesis of equal population probabilities of departmental membership is likely false. Some Departments have more employees than others. Informally we may conclude that Sales has the most employees because that pattern matches the sample result, but a precise evaluation of this later statement requires yet another analysis beyond our scope.

Note that the *p*-value does *not* inform us as to the probability that the null hypothesis of equal population probabilities of group membership is true. Rather it informs us that *if* the population probabilities are equal, then the sample result is a low probability event. From this formal probability result we take the additional step and conclude that the null hypothesis is unlikely. The true population probabilities are unlikely to be equal. This conclusion, however, is qualitative with the word "unlikely" not precisely defined with a numerical probability even though the *p*-value is a precise quantitative result.

4.2.3 Available Options for the One-variable Bar Chart

The chart shown in Figure 4.1 is the default chart produced by BarChart, but there are many more possibilities provided by the available parameter options. These different options are described next, organized into groups according to their functionality.

data option: The name of the input data frame.

Variable specifications. The variable plotted occupies the first position in the list of options. If the variable is in the data frame mydata, then the name of the corresponding data frame need not be specified. Otherwise, specify the relevant data frame with the data option.

color theme, Section 1.4.1, p. 16

color options, Table 1.1, p. 17

Colors. The default colors are from the current color theme, with a default of colors="blue" as specified by the set function. Colors of individual components of the graph can also be changed according to the col.fill, col.stroke, col.bg, and col.grid options.

To color each bar individually, specify a list of colors instead of a single color, usually one color for each bar. Consider a bar chart for Gender with values Female and Male. Specify plum and tan, respectively, for these values with no background color.

```
> BarChart(Gender, col.fill=c("plum","tan"), col.bg="transparent")
```

Whenever multiple values are specified for a single reference, the values must be enclosed by the combine function or c. Non-numeric character constants are included within quotes.

In addition to the color themes, there are three provided color palettes for the bar colors specified with the option `colors`. These palettes are `"rainbow"`, `"terrain"`, and `"heat"`. Randomly choose a color from the specified palette with `random.col=TRUE`.

General appearance. By default the bars of the bar graph are vertical. To display the bars as horizontal, set `horiz=TRUE`. The grid lines are by default behind the bars. To print the grid lines over the bars, set `over.grid=TRUE`. For a vertical bar graph, add more space between the top of the highest bar and the border by increasing the default value of `addtop=1`. To increase the default gap between the bars for a single variable, plot add a value to the default value of `gap=.2`. Frequencies are plotted by default. Set `prop=TRUE` to display proportions instead of counts.

To produce a bar graph requires the work of many R functions upon which `BarChart` relies, particularly the R function `barplot`. Most of the parameter options for any of these constituent functions ultimately used to produce a graph can also be passed directly to `BarChart`. Some of the relevant options from the R graphics function `par` are `col.main`, `col.axis`, and `col.lab` to specify the colors of the title, axes, and axis labels, respectively. To control the size of the axis labels, use `cex.axis` and `cex.names` for the size of the axis names, with the magnification factor of 1 as the default. Also, the graph's margins can be set with the `mar` option, as explained by entering `?par` at the command prompt.

Other options that can be passed to `BarChart` are from the base R function `barplot`. To fill the bars with shading lines instead of solid colors use `density` specified in lines per inch. Use `angle` to change the angle from the default of 45 degrees.

Figure 4.2 presents an example of the same analysis as from Figure 4.1, but with some `BarChart` options activated. The use of `main` specifies a custom title.

> **lessR Input** *Bar chart with several options*

```
> BarChart(Dept, horiz=TRUE, col.grid="transparent", density=18,
         main="Bar Chart of Employees in Each Department")
```

There are many available options to configure a specific graph. Find more examples at the end of the web page that results from `?BarChart`. These examples can be manually copied from the web page and then pasted into the R console, or run automatically with `example(BarChart)`. Presumably the default value for each of these options is reasonable in most situations, but regardless, re-specify as you wish, using the version of the bar graph in Figure 4.1 or Figure 4.2, or any version you can design from the available options.

4.2.4 A Bar Graph Directly from the Counts

In some situations the counts, frequencies, of each category are available, but not the original data.

Counts Manually Entered

First consider the situation in which the counts for each category are available, but manually entered into R.

---

c function, Section 1.3.6, p. 15

colors option: Three more available color palettes.

random.col option: Specify random colors.

horiz option: Orientation of graph.

addtop option: More vertical space.

gap option: Change the bar gap.

prop option: Specify proportions.

par function: R graphics settings.

barplot function: Standard R function that underlies `BarChart`.

main option: The title of a graph.

example function: Run each example in the posted manual for the specified function.

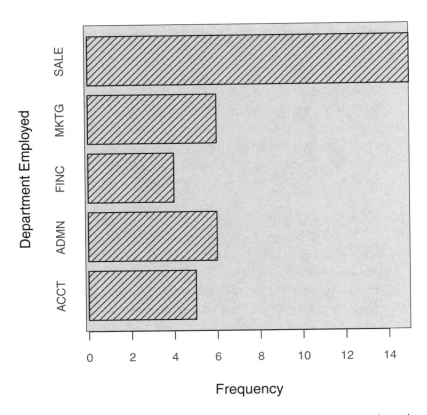

Figure 4.2 Bar chart for a single categorical variable with some activated options.

⭐ **Scenario** *Generate a bar chart directly from the counts*
The frequencies of occurrence of each of the values of the categorical variable Dept are available, but not the raw data from which the counts were obtained. Enter these counts into R and then generate the bar chart.

Construct a bar graph with `BarChart` from the frequencies of occurrence of each value, such as from the following frequencies.

	ACCT	ADMN	FINC	MKTG	SALE
Frequencies:	5	6	4	6	15

c function,
Section 1.3.6,
p. 15

names function:
Provide names for
the values of a
vector or columns
of a data frame.

To construct the bar chart, define two different vectors. The first vector contains the counts. As is always true in R, specify a list of multiple values wrapped within the combine function `c`. The second vector contains the names of each category, and uses the R `names` function to associate the category names with the category counts. Then call `BarChart` to graph the counts, which results in the same graph as shown in Figure 4.1.

lessR Input *Bar chart of one variable directly from counts*

```
> Counts <- c(5, 6, 4, 6, 15)
> names(Counts) <- c("ACCT", "ADMN", "FINC", "MKTG", "SALE")
> BarChart(Counts, xlab=label(Dept))
```

The `lessR` function `label` retrieves the variable label and here sets it equal to the label for the horizontal axis. If variable labels do not exist, or to specify another axis label, include the desired character string in quotes for the `xlab` argument.

variable labels, Section 2.4.1, p. 46

label function: Manually retrieve a variable label.

Counts Read Directly from a File

The counts can also be placed into a file and then directly read into R as a standard data file. Consider the data table in Listing 4.2 with two variables, Dept and Count. This information was read into R with the usual `Read` function.

```
> mydata
  Dept Count
1 ACCT     5
2 ADMN     6
3 FINC     4
4 MKTG     6
5 SALE    15
```

Listing 4.2 Counts for each category as read directly from a `csv` file.

To inform `BarChart` that the values read are counts, invoke the `count.levels` option, set equal to the name of the corresponding categorical variable that contains the counts.

count.levels option: The name of the variable for which the listed counts pertain.

 lessR Input *Generate a bar chart directly from counts read as data*

```
> BarChart(Count, count.levels=Dept)
```

The figure generated by this R input is identical to the bar graph generated from the data values in Figure 4.1.

4.2.5 Describe the Sample with a Pie Chart and Statistics

An alternative to the bar chart of one variable is the *pie chart* in which each slice of the pie represents a frequency of occurrence. In general the bar chart is considered easier to read than the pie chart, but the pie chart remains popular.

pie chart: Frequency plot of the values of a categorical variable according to the size of the slices of a pie.

PieChart

function: Generate a pie chart and summary statistics.

 Scenario *Generate a pie chart*

Generate a pie chart from the data, the recorded values of the categorical variable Dept, the department at which an employee works.

The `lessR` function for the pie chart is `PieChart`, with abbreviation `pc`.

 **lessR Input** *Pie chart*

> PieChart(Dept)   *or*   > pc(Dept)

The default `lessR` pie chart in gray scale is shown in Figure 4.3 for the categorical variable Dept.

Department Employed

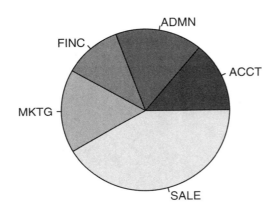

Figure 4.3 Gray scale pie chart for categorical variable Dept.

4.2.6 Available Options for the Pie Chart

Different options for the `PieChart` function are described next, organized into groups according to their functionality.

Variable specifications. The variable plotted occupies the first position in the list of options. If the variable is in the data frame `mydata`, then the name of the corresponding data frame need not be specified. Otherwise, specify the relevant data frame with `data`.

set function for color themes, Section 1.4.1, p. 16

Colors. The usual color themes do not apply to `PieChart`, except for the gray scale defined by `color="gray"`. There are also three more color palettes defined by R. To access these palettes set `colors` in the call to `PieChart` to either `"rainbow"`, `"heat"`, or `"terrain"`. Note that these palettes are not part of the system setting level from `set`, but instead are specific to only `BarChart` and `PieChart`.

Use `col.fill` to color each individual slice with its own color. Consider a bar chart for Gender with values Female and Male. In this example, specify `salmon3` and `seashell3`, respectively, for these values.

```
> PieChart(Gender, col.fill=c("salmon3","seashell3"))
```

To specify multiple values for a single reference, present the values with the combine function, `c`. Include non-numeric character constants within quotes.

c function, Section 1.3.6, p. 15

4.3 Two Categorical Variables

4.3.1 The Bar Chart and Joint Frequencies

The `BarChart` function for two categorical variables calculates and displays the associated joint frequencies and then constructs the bar chart from those frequencies.

 Scenario *Generate a bar chart for two variables*
To show the relation between two categorical variables, generate a bar chart for the department of employment and job satisfaction.

The primary variable plotted is always the first value passed to `BarChart`. If there is a second variable to plot, then either place it in the second position, or specify it with the `by` option, usually still in the second position although not necessarily.

by option: Specify a second variable.

The levels of each categorical variable are listed in alphabetical order by default. For Gender, that means that the values are listed as Female and then Male. The values of Satisfaction, however, are ordered and so Satisfaction should be defined as an ordinal variable with data values ordered from low to med to high. As this ordering is not alphabetical, employ the functions `Transform` and `factor` to specify the desired ordering and also to define Satisfaction as ordinal.

order levels of a factor, Section 3.3.2, p. 60

 lessR Input *Bar chart for two categorical variables with ordered levels*
```
> mydata <- Transform(Satisfaction=factor(Satisfaction,
          levels=c("low","med","high"), ordered=TRUE))
> BarChart(Gender, by=Satisfaction)
```

Figure 4.4 gives an example of a two-variable bar graph. Because variable labels are present, they appear instead of the shorter variable names.

Some of the text output of `BarChart` follows. First reported are the variable names in the analysis and, if present, the accompanying variable labels.

```
Gender, Male or Female
   by
Satisfaction, Degree of Satisfaction with Work Environment
```

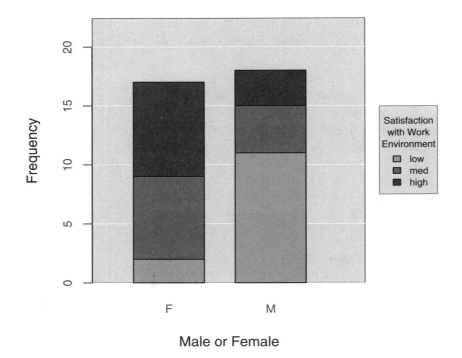

Figure 4.4 Default bar chart for two categorical variables, one variable with ordered values.

joint frequency: Frequency of occurrence of the combination of two values of a categorical variable.

cross-tabulation table: Table of joint frequencies.

The focus of analysis for the relation of two categorical variables is the *joint frequency*, the count of how many times two specific values in the same row of the data file, one for each of the variables, occur together. All of the joint frequencies for each pair of values are presented in the *cross-tabulation table*, the table of the joint frequencies of the values of two or more categorical variables, shown in Listing 4.3.

```
Joint and Marginal Frequencies
------------------------------
             Gender
Satisfaction  F  M Sum
         low  2 11  13
         med  7  4  11
        high  8  3  11
         Sum 17 18  35
```

Listing 4.3 Cross-tabulation table, the joint and marginal frequencies from BarChart.

For example, two women reported low Satisfaction, but 11 men reported the same low Satisfaction.

marginal frequency: Row or column sum of a cross-tabulation table.

grand total: The total number of observations in the table.

The cross-tabulation table from BarChart also contains the *marginal frequencies*. These marginal frequencies are the frequencies of each of the two variables considered in isolation from the other. In Listing 4.3 the marginal frequencies appear in the row or column labeled Sum.

The number in the bottom right corner of Listing 4.3, 35, is the sum of the row and column sums, the *grand total*. It is the total number of cases in the entire sample that have data values recorded for both specified variables. In this data set there are data for 37 employees, so two employees have at least one data value missing for either Gender or Satisfaction or both.

4.3.2 Generalize beyond the Sample with Inferential Analysis

As with the inferential analysis for one categorical variable, the inferential analysis for two categorical variables is also based on the chi-squared statistic. For two categorical variables the test evaluates their independence according to the null hypothesis that the variables are unrelated, or *independent*. Is the tendency to be classified in a particular category of the first variable related to a specific classification in the second category?

independent events: Occurrence of one event unrelated to the probability of the occurrence of another.

chi-square test of independence: Test to evaluate if two categorical variables are related.

⭐ **Scenario** *Evaluate the relationship between two categorical variables*
Gender has two categories, Male and Female. Do Males tend to be more or less satisfied with their job at this company than Females? Satisfaction here is assessed with responses of 1, 2, and 3, so both variables are categorical.

The test is of the relation between Gender and Satisfaction. If the variables are unrelated, that is, independent, then knowing a person's Gender conveys no information regarding his or her perceived level of Satisfaction. If the variables are related, then one of the Genders has a stronger tendency to be Satisfied than the other Gender.

Before performing the inferential analysis of the hypothesis test first look at the sample results. As seen from the bar graph and from the table, in this sample at least, men tended more to be dissatisfied and women tended toward more satisfaction. As always with inferential analysis, the question regards the extent the relationship observed in the sample generalizes to the population as a whole from which the sample was obtained.

The `BarChart` function for two variables also yields the chi-square test for independence. The chi-square test of independence is an example of an inferential test. This inferential analysis appears in Listing 4.4.

```
Chi-square Analysis
-------------------
Number of cases in analysis: 35
Number of variables: 2
Test of independence:    Chisq = 9.300699, df = 2, p-value = 0.0096
```

Listing 4.4 Inferential chi-square test of the null hypothesis of no relation between Gender and Satisfaction.

In this situation, the obtained chi-square statistic is 9.30. The assumption on which the test is based is the *null hypothesis*, denoted as H_0. If the cell proportions reflect no relationship between the two variables, then the chi-square statistic would be exactly zero. In real data, however, there is *sampling error*. Even when the null hypothesis of independence is true, the chi-square statistic is virtually always larger than zero. The question is how much larger than zero is reasonable *if* the null hypothesis of no relationship is true?

Assess how large the chi-square statistic is in terms of its probability of getting a chi-square value as larger or larger than what was obtained in this sample, assuming that there is no relation between Gender and Satisfaction. The *p-value* provides the answer. The *p*-value reflects

null hypothesis: Assumption of no relationship between the variables.

sampling error: Impact of the randomness inherent in any one sample.

p-value: If the null hypothesis is true, the probability of obtaining a result as deviant or more than the obtained result.

alpha level
function,
Section 4.2.2,
p. 82

the probability of what was obtained, which is then compared to usual cutoff value that defines a low probability, the *alpha level*, $\alpha = 0.05$.

If the *p*-value is larger than α, then the probability is sufficiently high that the obtained result is considered consistent with the null hypothesis. If the *p*-value is smaller than α, an unlikely event occurred assuming that no relation actually exists, so reject the hypothesis of no relation as implausible.

```
test of no relationship:
      p-value = 0.0096 < α = 0.05, so reject H₀
```

If the null hypothesis of no relation between Gender and Satisfaction is true, then the low *p*-value of 0.0096 indicates that an unlikely event occurred.

We conclude that the variables are related such that men are more dissatisfied with this work environment than women, not just in this sample, but in the population as a whole. The sample results generalize. Note, however, that although the *p*-value is precisely computed, it is a conditional probability in that it specifies the probability of the results *if* the null hypothesis is true. From the low *p*-value we conclude that the variables are likely related, but the probability of this relationship is not known. The *p*-value is quantitative, but the conclusion that the null is unlikely is qualitative. We do not know the probability that the null hypothesis of no relation is true.

4.3.3 Available Options for the Two-variable Bar Chart

General appearance. In addition to the option for displaying the bars horizontally, the bars at each level of the first variable may be displayed side by side instead of the default of stacked on top of each other. To display the bars side by side, set `beside=TRUE`.

Colors. Set the color of the bars individually with `col.fill`. Randomly choose a color from the specified palette with `random.col=TRUE`. With two variables, the usual color theme from the `set` function does not apply, but R defines three color palettes, which for `BarChart` only apply to two-variable bar charts. Access these palettes by setting `colors` as a `BarChart` option to `"rainbow"`, `"heat"`, or `"terrain"`. The most vivid color palettes are `rainbow` and `heat`.

Legend. A two-variable graph generates a legend, which indicates the color of the bars of the `by` variable when plotted at each level of the first variable. By default the legend appears to the right of the main graph. Change the location of the legend to somewhere on the graph itself with `legend.loc`, which can assume one of the following values: `"bottomright"`, `"bottom"`, `"bottomleft"`, `"left"`, `"topleft"`, `"top"`, `"topright"`, `"right"`, and `"center"`. To change to a horizontal orientation, set `legend.horiz=TRUE`. By default the labels in the legend are the values of the `by` variable. To specify custom values provide a list of values to `labels.legend`. A list must always be specified with the combine function `c`, such as `labels.legend=c("Label 1", "Label 2")`.

c function,
Section 1.3.6,
p. 15

Text output. The cell frequency can be divided by the total sample size or the corresponding row or column total. To obtain the corresponding three tables of proportions, set `brief=FALSE`.

Satisfaction is a categorical variable with ordered categories. Accordingly, `BarChart` plots the three levels of Satisfaction, from low to medium to high, as an ordered progression of a single hue.

4.3.4 A Bar Graph Directly from the Counts

As with the bar graph of a single variable, the bar graph of two variables can be constructed directly from the counts.

 Scenario *Construct a bar graph of two variables from the counts*
Given a table of joint frequencies for two variables, construct the bar graph.

Consider the table of counts, Table 4.1.

Table 4.1 Joint frequencies.

| | Gender | |
Satisfaction	F	M
low	2	11
med	7	4
high	8	3

Enter the table of joint frequencies directly into R with the `R matrix` function. With `byrow=TRUE`, the counts are entered row by row, with the specifications of 3 rows and 2 columns according to `nrow=3` and `ncol=2`. Use the `R colnames` and `rownames` functions to provide the names of the categories. The label on the horizontal axis is the name of the column variable. In this example, Gender is the column variable as specified with the `xlab` option. Call `BarChart` with the matrix of counts. The title of the legend is the name of the row variable, Satisfaction.

colnames function: Name the column values.

rownames function: Name the row values.

✒ **lessR Input** *Bar chart of two variables from counts*

```
> Counts <- matrix(c(2,11, 7,4, 8,3), nrow=3, ncol=2, byrow=TRUE)
> colnames(Counts) <- c("F", "M")
> rownames(Counts) <- c("low", "med", "high")
> BarChart(Counts, xlab="Gender", legend.title="Satisfaction")
```

The result of the preceding four lines of R code is the same graph that appears in Figure 4.4 with one difference. With the counts entered directly, `BarChart` is unaware that the corresponding counts represent ordinal data with the categories of Satisfaction ordered from low to med to high. The result is that the bar chart displays the levels of Satisfaction in a different hue for each level, as opposed to an ordered progression of hues when constructed from the data in which the levels of Satisfaction are ordered according to the `factor` function.

factor function, Section 1.6.3, p. 22

4.3.5 Cell Proportions

The purpose of `BarChart` for two variables is to provide their plot as well as the corresponding joint frequencies. The information provided by the joint frequencies, however, can be analyzed several different ways in terms of the way in which the sample proportions are calculated. The `SummaryStats` function provides these additional analyses.

by option: Specify a second variable.

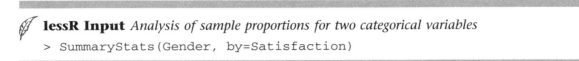

> 🖋 **lessR Input** *Analysis of sample proportions for two categorical variables*
>
> > `SummaryStats(Gender, by=Satisfaction)`

The first set of sample proportions, in Listing 4.5, are the sample probabilities that both the values of Gender and Satisfaction for a randomly sampled person will represent data in one of these 6 cells of joint frequencies.

```
Cell Proportions and Marginals
------------------------------
             Gender
Satisfaction    F     M    Sum
        low  0.057 0.314 0.371
        med  0.200 0.114 0.314
       high  0.229 0.086 0.314
        Sum  0.486 0.514 1.000
```

Listing 4.5 Overall cell proportions from `SummaryStats`.

Each cell proportion is the corresponding joint frequency divided by the entire sample size. For example, two women reported low Satisfaction, which is $2/35 = 0.057$ or 5.7%. Eleven men reported low Satisfaction, which is $11/35 = 0.314$ or 31.4% of all of the 35 employees represented in these data. We also see, for example, that 48.6% of all 35 employees are women and 51.4% are men.

Another way to compute the cell proportions is to express each cell value as the ratio of the corresponding joint frequency divided by the corresponding column marginal sum. If our interest is to compare Satisfaction levels for men and women, then this table in Listing 4.6 is relevant because we can see how the probabilities of different levels of Satisfaction change for women and men. These proportions represent sample *conditional probabilities*. Each probability for each level of Satisfaction depends upon, is conditioned upon, the respective event that the

conditional probability: Probability of one event assuming the occurrence of another event.

```
Proportions within Each Column
------------------------------
             Gender
Satisfaction    F     M
        low  0.118 0.611
        med  0.412 0.222
       high  0.471 0.167
        Sum  1.000 1.000
```

Listing 4.6 Column proportions from `SummaryStats`.

person is a woman or that the person is a man. For example, if the employee in this sample is a woman, then the probability that she reports low satisfaction is 0.118.

The table that presents the proportions within each row is based on the same logic as the previous table, but now focuses on the conditional probabilities with the Satisfaction level as the given, or conditioned, information. The result is in Listing 4.7. If a person has low Satisfaction, then the probability that the employee is a women is only 0.154, but rises to 0.846 for men.

```
Proportions within Each Row
---------------------------
              Gender
Satisfaction      F      M Sum
         low  0.154  0.846   1
         med  0.636  0.364   1
        high  0.727  0.273   1
```

Listing 4.7 Row proportions from SummaryStats.

4.4 Onward to the Third Dimension

The lessR functions BarChart and SummaryStats process one or two variables. To generate a cross-tabulation table of the joint frequencies of three variables requires moving directly to the R table function upon which BarChart relies.

table function: Generate a cross-tabulation table.

4.4.1 Example 1: Employee Data Set

To illustrate, consider the three categorical variables in the employee data set: Dept, Satisfaction, and Gender.

Employee data table, Figure 1.7, p. 21

 Scenario *Analyze the relation of three categorical variables*
What is the relationship of the variables Department of employment, Satisfaction, and Gender in the Employee data set?

First read the data into the R data frame mydata.

```
> mydata <- Read("Employee", format="lessR")
```

Because R does not directly reference variables in the data table by their names, use the R with function to indicate the name of the data frame so that the data frame name only has to be entered once.

 lessR Input *Create a three-way cross-tabulation table*
```
> with(mydata, table(Dept, Satisfaction, Gender))
```

with function: Identify the data frame for standard R functions.

The `with` function allows the variable names to be entered directly, which becomes convenient when multiple variables are referenced in a single function call. The result is Listing 4.8.

```
, , Gender = F                    , , Gender = M

        Satisfaction                      Satisfaction
Dept    low med high            Dept    low med high
   ACCT   0   1    1               ACCT   1   0    1
   ADMN   1   1    2               ADMN   0   2    0
   FINC   0   0    1               FINC   2   0    1
   MKTG   0   1    4               MKTG   0   1    0
   SALE   1   4    0               SALE   8   1    1
```

Listing 4.8 Cross-tabulation table for three categorical variables.

three-way cross-tabulation table: Joint frequencies of three categorical variables.

Listing 4.8 presents a *three-way cross-tabulation table* to display information from three dimensions with two-dimensional tables. Each table of joint frequencies displays variables Dept and Satisfaction at one level of Gender. The particular form of the resulting tables depends on the entered order of the variables in the call to the `table` function, here with Gender entered last.

At least in this sample we see from the first table of joint frequencies that women tend to have medium to high Satisfaction. Compare the two tables to observe that women are more prominent in the Marketing department than men. Men are concentrated in the Sales department with a deep level of dissatisfaction. Women also are well represented in the Sales department, albeit with a tendency to be more satisfied.

mosaic chart: Plot of joint frequencies based on rectangular regions.

We can also view this information graphically. A graphical analysis of three categorical variables is the mosaic chart, an extension of the stacked bar chart for two variables to the multidimensional equivalent of three or more dimensions. The *mosaic chart* breaks up a square into regions with the area of each region proportional to a frequency, either from a cell or a margin of a joint frequency table. The stacked bar chart for two variables essentially accomplishes this division of each bar in the bar chart. The mosaic chart extends this pattern to more variables.

mosaic function: Produce a mosaic chart.

install.packages function, Section 1.2.3, p. 5

library function, Section 1.3.1, p. 7

Although R contains a function for producing mosaic plots called `mosaicplot`, an improved version exists called `mosaic` in the `vcd` package. The abbreviation `vcd` is for Visualize Categorical Data. Of course this means that the package must first be installed with the `install.packages` function. Before accessing the function, invoke the `library` function.

The `mosaic` function generates the mosaic chart for Dept, Satisfaction, and Gender that corresponds to the three-way joint frequencies illustrated in Listing 4.8. To specify the variables, begin the variable list with a tilde, ~, found in the upper left hand corner of the standard keyboard and then the three variable names separated by plus signs. To highlight cells of the resulting graph that indicate a potential relationship, turn on the `shade` option. Specify the data frame with the `data` parameter, so set to `mydata`.

 lessR Input *Mosaic three-way association plot*

```
> library(vcd)
> mosaic(~ Dept + Satisfaction + Gender, shade=TRUE,
        data=mydata)
```

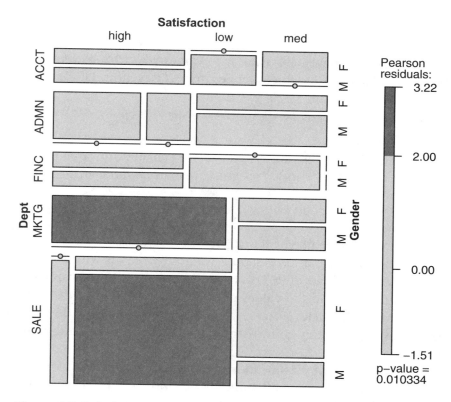

Figure 4.5 Default mosaic chart for three categorical variables.

The variable Dept is on the left side of the graph, Satisfaction on top, and Gender on the right side. The darker areas represent larger deviations from the expectation of the null hypothesis that there is no relation between the three variables plotted. The mosaic chart reveals that the largest deviations from the null are the low Satisfaction for men in the Sales department and the high Satisfaction of women in Marketing.

The graph also presents the p-value for the null hypothesis of no relationship.

```
test of no relationship:
     p-value = 0.0103 < α = 0.05, so reject H₀
```

If the null hypothesis is true, the low p-value indicates that an unusual event occurred. So conclude that the null hypothesis is likely *not* true, and that the variables are related as discussed.

R formula: An R expression that specifies a model.

response variable: The variable in a model that is explained by the remaining variables.

predictor variable: A variable used to predict or explain the response variable.

4.4.2 Example 2: Survivors of the *Titanic*

The next use of the `mosaic` function is our first use of an R *formula*, which provides a means for specifying a model, a functional relationship among variables. The expression of a model includes a variable of interest called the *response variable*, or outcome variable or dependent variable. This variable is explained in terms of one or more other variables called explanatory variables or *predictor variables*.

Scenario *Analyze survivors on the* Titanic *by Class of travel and Age*
Specify a model to explain one variable, Survived, with values Yes or No, in terms of two other categorical variables, the Class in which the person was traveling, 1st, 2nd, or 3rd, and his or her Age, a child or an adult.

The general form of a formula follows, here illustrated for two explanatory variables, where Y is the response variable of interest and X1 and X2 are the explanatory variables.

$$Y \sim X1 + X2$$

Models usually have anywhere from one to five or six explanatory variables.

The model from the previous example had no response variable, which is why the formula began with the tilde with no variable in front of it. This lack of a response variable implies that the purpose of the analysis is not to explain the values of one variable in terms of others, but just to visualize the resulting joint frequencies. Place a variable in front of the tilde to define a response variable, in which case the rectangles in the mosaic chart reflect the corresponding frequencies of this response variable.

In this example we look at the different classifications of the survivors of the *RMS Titanic*, the grand passenger ship that struck an iceberg and sunk in the North Atlantic on its maiden voyage on April 14, 1912. The data, in the form of cross-tabulation tables, is available as the data set called `Titanic` in the R `datasets` package, which is automatically loaded into memory when an R session starts. To view the variables and their levels as shown in Table 4.2, reference the corresponding help file for `Titanic`, that is, enter `?Titanic`.

Table 4.2 Categorical variables and their values for the *Titanic* data.

No.	Name	Levels
1	Class	1st, 2nd, 3rd, Crew
2	Sex	Male, Female
3	Age	Child, Adult
4	Survived	No, Yes

The goal is to account for, or explain, who survived on the basis of their Class of travel and their Sex, that is, Gender.

To implement the formula for this analysis, place the variable Survived to the left of the tilde. Class and Sex are the explanatory variables. In this situation the mosaic plot will shade each cell according to the percent who survived and those who did not. We use a dark gray value of `gray42` chosen to represent those who did survive and a lighter gray of `gray85` for those who did not. The values of the variable Survive, `No` and `Yes`, are ordered alphabetically so the first color listed is for those who did *not* survive.

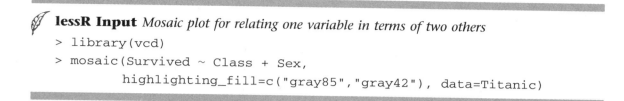

> **lessR Input** *Mosaic plot for relating one variable in terms of two others*
> ```
> > library(vcd)
> > mosaic(Survived ~ Class + Sex,
>          highlighting_fill=c("gray85","gray42"), data=Titanic)
> ```

The mosaic plot, the graphical version of the cross-tabulation table, is given in Figure 4.6.

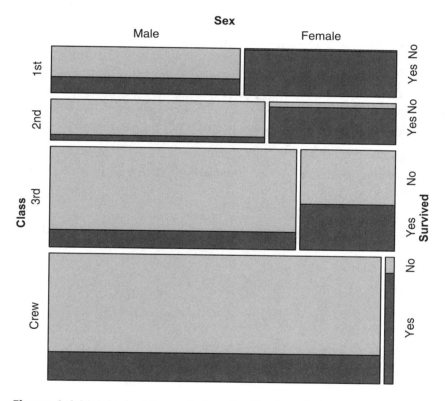

Figure 4.6 Mosaic chart for survival on the *Titanic* such that the darker gray indicates the proportion of the survivors.

One characteristic of the data revealed by the graph is the length of the top edge of the boxes for women in 1st, 2nd, and 3rd class. There were proportionally more women in 1st class than in 3rd class, a pattern necessarily reversed for the men. Almost all of the women in 1st class, and most in 2nd class survived, but not so for the women traveling in 3rd class. Regardless of the class of travel, more men died than survived. Still traveling 1st class was an advantage because the proportion of men who did not survive in 1st class was smaller. Only a small percentage of the crew were women, but unlike their much more numerous male counterparts, most survived.

The mosaic plot is an excellent visualization tool for viewing the relationship among multiple categorical variables, particularly compared to the alternative of staring at the numbers in, for example, a three-way cross-tabulation table.

3-way cross-tabulation table, Listing 4.8, p. 94

Worked Problems

The psychology department at a public university was interested in understanding more about their in-state and out-of-state students. The origin of their current students was classified as in-state, out-of-state-USA, and international. Also available was each student's gender and choice of major of either psychology as a social science or as a biological science.

The data are available at `http://lessRstats.com/data/psych.csv`

1 One categorical variable.

   (a) Show with statistics and a bar chart how many students fit each of the three classifications regarding origin.

   (b) Do the chi-square test of equal proportions. What is the conclusion?

2 Two categorical variables.

   (a) Is there a relation between gender and origin of student? Show with descriptive statistics and a bar chart.

   (b) Analyze with the chi-square test of independence. What is the conclusion?

3 Three categorical variables.
   Is there a relation between gender, origin of student, and choice of major? Show with descriptive statistics and a bar chart.

CHAPTER 5

CONTINUOUS VARIABLES

5.1 Quick Start

First install R and lessR as explained in Section 1.2. At the beginning of each R session access lessR with library(lessR). Then read your data into an R data frame with Read(), the subject of Chapter 2.

The data table, represented within R as the data frame, contains the data values for one or more variables, each variable characterized by either numerical values or non-numerical categories as discussed in Section 1.6.3. This chapter describes some basic analyses that are routinely among the first analyses done after reading the data. Here we focus on the analysis of continuous variables, those variables with numerical values.

Several lessR functions are available to describe the sample values of a variable, here illustrated for a variable named Y.

> SummaryStats(Y)

Summary statistics only, p. 105

> Histogram(Y)

Histogram, p. 100

> ScatterPlot(Y)

1-variable scatter plot, p. 110

> BoxPlot(Y)

Box plot, p. 112

> Density(Y)

Density (smoothed frequency) curve, p. 114

SummaryStats provides the summary statistics to describe the values of both numerical and categorical variables. For a continuous, that is, numerical variable, SummaryStats provides the mean, standard deviation, minimum, first quartile, median, third quartile, maximum, and inter-quartile range. Also listed are any outliers that would be identified by the corresponding box plot.

outlier, Section 5.3.1, p. 106

The function SummaryStats also implicitly provides the statistical summary for the histogram, scatter plot for one variable, box plot, and density functions. The function Histogram also provides the frequency table based on the histogram bins.

To obtain the summary statistics from SummaryStats for a variable at each level of a second variable, use the by option. The second variable is analyzed in terms of its categories, its

Statistics by category,
Section 5.3.5,
p. 109

unique values. So usually this second variable would be a true categorical variable with relatively few unique values.

```
> SummaryStats(Y, by=X)
```

If Y is numerical, SummaryStats provides the same summary statistics for a single numerical variable, but now reported for each level, that is, category of X.

To analyze all the variables in the data frame, substitute a data frame name for the variable name in the associated function call. As with all lessR functions that process data, the name of the data frame is assumed to be mydata. If no variable name is passed to the function call to SummaryStats, then all the variables in the mydata data frame are analyzed, whereas Histogram and BoxPlot analyze all the variables just for their corresponding data type.

```
> SummaryStats()
> Histogram()
> BoxPlot()
```

The resulting graphs are written to their respective pdf files, indicated as part of the standard output.

CountAll
function: A bar
chart or histogram,
with summary
statistics, for all
variables in a data
frame.

A related function is CountAll, abbreviated ca. This function does the complete summary analysis, selectively invoking either BarChart for each categorical variable or Histogram for each continuous variable, which also provides the summary statistics from SummaryStats. CountAll applies to the entire data set, providing a complete graphical and statistical summary of all the variables in the data frame.

 lessR Input *Histograms and bar charts for all variables*
```
> CountAll()              or            > ca()
```

CountAll only applies to data frames.

5.2 Histogram

The histogram is the standard graphical method for displaying the frequencies of a continuous variable such as Age, Salary, MPG, or Height. Measure a continuous variable, such as Years, Currency, Gallons, or Inches, on a numerical scale. The measurements are made to a specified level of precision, such as measuring to the nearest inch or the nearest 1/4-inch. The result, in contrast to a categorical value, is that there are typically many different unique values of a continuous variable. In this example for 37 employees, all 37 salaries are unique.

5.2.1 Default Histogram and Analysis

bin: An interval of
similar values of a
continuous
variable.

To construct the histogram, determine the range of the data values, from lowest to largest, and then partition the range into generally equal intervals called *bins*. Place each data value in its corresponding bin and then count the number of values, the frequency of the data values, in each of the bins. The list of the bins and the corresponding frequencies is the *frequency distribution*. From this distribution construct the histogram by placing the range of data values and bins on the horizontal axis, and then construct a bar over each bin to represent its corresponding frequency. Unlike a bar graph of a categorical variable, indicate the underlying continuity of the numerical scale with adjacent bins that share a common border.

> ⭐ **Scenario** *Construct a histogram*
> The variable of interest is Salary. To display the pattern of how often different salaries occur in this company, place similar values of Salary into the same bin. Then plot the resulting histogram.

The `lessR` function for a histogram is `Histogram`, abbreviated `hs`. To illustrate, consider the continuous variable Salary in our example data set Employee and its associated histogram in Figure 5.1 (and also Figure 1.3). Variable labels are present, so the variable label for the horizontal axis is automatically provided.

Histogram
function: Obtain a histogram, summary statistics, and a table of frequencies.

> 🖋 **lessR Input** *Default histogram*
> ```
> > Histogram(Salary)          or          > hs(Salary)
> ```

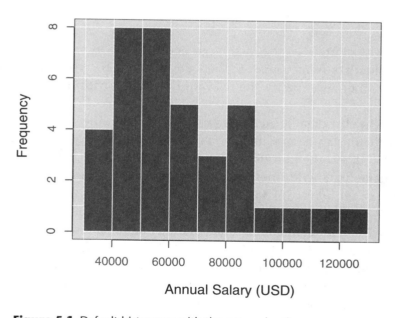

Figure 5.1 Default histogram with the gray color theme.

The histogram of Salary shows that for these 37 employees, the most frequently occurring salaries are from $40,000 to $60,000, with relatively few salaries over $100,000. The function `Histogram` also provides numerical output beginning with the same summary description of the specified variable that `SummaryStats` provides. This includes any values identified as outliers by a boxplot. `Histogram` also provides the *frequency distribution* upon which the graph is based, shown in Listing 5.1.

summary statistics,
Section 5.3, p. 105

frequency distribution: The values of a variable and corresponding frequencies.

```
Bin Width: 10000
Number of Bins: 10

-----------------------------------------------------------
        Bin          Midpoint  Count   Prop   Cumul.c Cumul.p
-----------------------------------------------------------
  30000 >  40000       35000      4    0.11       4    0.11
  40000 >  50000       45000      8    0.22      12    0.33
  50000 >  60000       55000      8    0.22      20    0.55
  60000 >  70000       65000      5    0.14      25    0.69
  70000 >  80000       75000      3    0.08      28    0.77
  80000 >  90000       85000      5    0.14      33    0.91
  90000 > 100000       95000      1    0.03      34    0.94
 100000 > 110000      105000      1    0.03      35    0.97
 110000 > 120000      115000      1    0.03      36    1.00
 120000 > 130000      125000      1    0.03      37    1.03
-----------------------------------------------------------
```

Listing 5.1 Frequency distribution from `Histogram` function.

The bins and their midpoints are identified, as well as the counts, the proportions, cumulative counts, and cumulative proportions. The > symbol for each bin indicates that all the values in the bin are larger than the first specified value, and include all values up to and including the second specified value.

5.2.2 Available options

Variable specifications. The variable plotted is the first argument in the function call to `Histogram`. If the variable is in the data frame `mydata`, then the name of the corresponding data frame need not be specified. Otherwise, specify the relevant data frame with `data`.

color themes, Section 1.4.1, p. 16

col.fill, etc., Table 1.1, p. 17

Colors. The current color theme, either the default theme or explicitly set from the `set` function, determines the colors. Any color theme can be modified by choosing an individual color of the bars, the bar borders, the background and the grid lines with `col.fill`, `col.stroke`, `col.bg` and `col.grid`, respectively. By default the grid lines are displayed underneath the histogram. To place the grid lines over the bars, set `over.grid=TRUE`.

breaks option: Set the bins based on the indicated algorithm.

Bins. Specify the bins exactly with the `bin.start` and `bin.width` options. R provides several possibilities, including the default specification `breaks="Sturges"`, which implements Sturges's formula for setting the bins. Other options include `breaks="Scott"` for Scott's algorithm and `breaks="FD"` for the Freedman–Diaconis option. The value of `breaks` can also be a single number that suggests, though does not explicitly set, the number of bins.

cumul="both" option: Obtain both a cumulative and a regular histogram.

Cumulative histogram. The cumulative histogram can also be displayed. To do so, set `cumul="on"`. To view both the regular and the cumulative histogram on the same graph, set `cumul="both"`. When both histograms are displayed, set the color of the cumulative histogram bars with the usual `col.fill` option, and the color of the bars of the regular histogram with the `col.reg` option. The default color for the regular histogram is `"snow2"`.

prop=TRUE option: Proportions on the vertical axis.

Proportions. Display proportions instead of frequencies by setting `prop=TRUE`.

5.2.3 Customize the Bins

The default histogram in Figure 5.1 is a little *undersmoothed*, that is, a little too jagged. The frequency for the bin for the range from beyond 70,000 up to and including 80,000 is lower than for both the previous bin and the successive bin, which likely reflects sampling error. That is, this is likely an arbitrary outcome of this particular sample and not a true property of the underlying process of assigning Salaries.

 Scenario *Adjust the bin widths to avoid undersmoothing*
The default bin width is too large for optimal display of the pattern of how often different salaries occur. To compensate for this undersmoothing, increase the bin size for the histogram of Salary from $10,000 to $15,000.

undersmoothed: A histogram with a bin width that is too small for the given sample size.

Set the widths of the bins with the `bin.width` option. Adjust the bin widths to be a little larger than the default bin widths, as shown in Figure 5.2.

bin.width option: Set the width of histogram bins.

```
> Histogram(Salary, bin.width=15000)
```

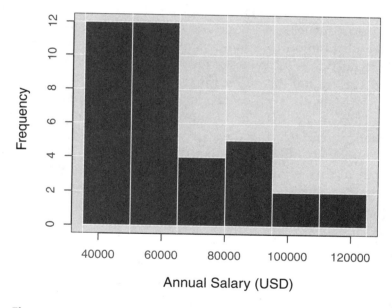

Figure 5.2 Histogram with specified bins and default starting value.

Set the starting point of the bins with the `bin.start` option. A problem with the histogram in Figure 5.2 is that the first bin, from beyond 20,000 up to and including 35,000 does not contain any values. To remedy this shortcoming, set the `bin.start` option to move the beginning of the first bin from $20,000 to $25,000.

bin.start option: Set the starting point of histogram bins.

 lessR Input *Histogram with specified bin width and starting value*
```
> Histogram(Salary, bin.start=25000, bin.width=15000)
```

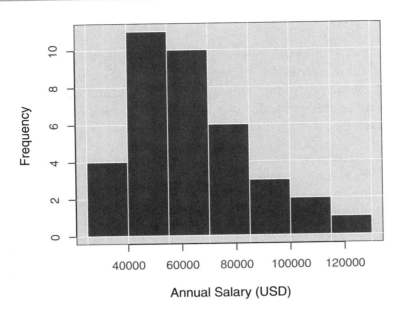

Figure 5.3 Histogram with specified bins and starting point for the bins.

This revised histogram in Figure 5.3 is an improvement over the previous versions in Figure 5.1 and 5.2 because the beginning bin now contains values, and the histogram represents a smooth progression from increasing frequencies to a peak, and then a progression of lowering frequencies. It is possible for a true distribution to assume many forms, but in practice most distributions are also increasing in frequency as the values of the variable increase, or decreasing in frequency, or, as shown here, increasing and then decreasing.

Tweaking the histogram bins is a standard procedure, especially for histograms based on relatively small sample sizes. There is no right or wrong or best histogram, but some represent data more effectively than others. Varying the `Histogram` options of `bin.start` and `bin.width` often shows a more desirable histogram than the given default. To construct a histogram, begin with the default histogram and then usually look at several alternatives. Choose the result that best displays the characteristics of the underlying distribution for the available data.

cumulative frequency: Sum of frequencies for all values up to and including the specified value.

cumulative histogram: Histogram of cumulative frequencies.

5.2.4 The Cumulative Histogram

Another `Histogram` option is to plot the *cumulative frequencies* or cumulative proportions instead of the frequencies. The resulting histogram is a *cumulative histogram*.

As indicated, there are two forms of the cumulative histogram offered by the `Histogram` function. The cumulative histogram may be offered by itself or in conjunction with the regular histogram. Figure 5.4 presents an example of both histograms on the same graph. The previous examples concluded with what is considered a better set of bins than provided by the default. Accordingly, retain these same bins for the cumulative histogram.

 lessR Input *Cumulative histogram (with bin width and start value)*

```
> Histogram(Salary, bin.start=25000, bin.width=15000,
            cumul="both")
```

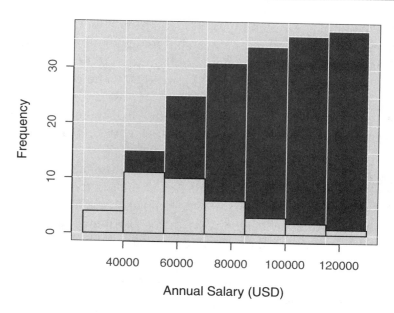

Figure 5.4 Cumulative and regular histogram with specified bins.

Frequencies are never negative, so as the values of the variable increase, a cumulative distribution always increases in value or stays the same.

The histograms in Figure 5.4 demonstrate that most of the salaries are in the lower range of the complete distribution of salaries. According to the text output, identical to that provided by the regular histogram analysis, the cumulative proportion of all the data values up through the bin $100,000 to $115,000 is 0.97. Only one value remains past this bin, that for the salary of $124,419.23.

5.3 Summary Statistics

Summary statistics describe characteristics of the distribution of sample data values. Summary statistics also describe characteristics of how two or more distributions relate to each other.

5.3.1 Overview of Summary Statistics

There are three different types of summary statistics: sample size information, parametric statistics, and order statistics. The sample size information is the number of actual data values present and the number of missing data values. The other types of statistics are described next. All three types of statistics are useful for summarizing a distribution, and all three should be examined for each variable of interest.

Parametric statistics only apply to variables with at least interval data values. Interval data have equal intervals of magnitude between any two values one unit apart. Numbers that represent a lower quality of measurement only specify a rank ordering of the data values. The most commonly applied parametric statistics are the mean and the standard deviation. Less frequently encountered are the skewness and kurtosis.

The *mean* is the usual arithmetic average, the sum of all the data values divided by the total number of non-missing data values. Its purpose is to provide an indicator of the middle of the distribution. The mean is probably the most widely reported characteristic of a distribution.

parametric statistics: Only apply to interval data values.

interval data, Section 1.6.3, p. 23

mean: Arithmetic average.

standard deviation: Indicator of variability.

The *standard deviation* is an indicator of the variability of a distribution about the mean. If the standard deviation is large, then the values tend to be spread out much about the mean. An example would be scores on a Final for a class that varied from 50% up to 100%, with scores equally distributed throughout this range. That is, many scores between 50% and 60%, between 60% and 70%, all the way up to many scores between 90% and 100%. If the standard deviation is small, then the values do not vary much about the mean. For the Final scores with a low standard deviation, most of the values might be between 85% and 95%, with only a few scores outside of this interval.

A key property of the standard deviation is that it relates closely to normally distributed data. For a population of normally distributed data, about 68.3% of all the data values are within one standard deviation of the mean. And about 95.5% of all data values are within 2 standard deviations of the mean. For example, height is normally distributed, and for US women, the mean is about 65.5 inches with a standard deviation of 2.5 inches. Two standard deviations equals (2)(2.5) or 5, so a little more than 95% of all US women have a height between 60.5 inches and 70.5 inches. This relationship between the standard deviation and the normal distribution lies at the core of much statistical analysis.

skewness: Indicator of symmetry.

Skewness is an indicator of the symmetry of a distribution of values. For a symmetric distribution, the right side of the distribution is a mirror image of the distribution's left side. Negative skewness values indicate that the distribution tends to have a tail on the left side and positive skewness values indicate a tail on the right side.

kurtosis: Indicator of the peakedness.

Similar to skewness, *kurtosis* is an indicator of the shape of a distribution, such as the measured data values for a variable. Specifically, kurtosis indicates a distribution's "peakedness" relative to the normal curve. A large value of kurtosis indicates that the values of the variable are more spread out so that the distribution has "fat" tails. A low value of kurtosis indicates that the values are concentrated around the mean, resulting in "skinny" tails.

order statistic: Specify position in an ordered set of data values.

Order statistics are applicable to a wider range of distributions of data values than are parametric statistics. An *order statistic* specifies some characteristic of the position of a specific value within that distribution, which may or may not be an actual data value. Compute an order statistic only after the values of a variable have been sorted from the smallest value to the largest. The most well-known order statistic is the *median*, the value literally midway between the smallest and largest values of the sorted distribution.

median: The value midway in an ordered distribution.

quartile: A value that separates the values of an ordered distribution into the first, second, third, or fourth quarter.

To derive the median, split the sorted distribution into two parts with the same number of values in each part. Generalizing, the *quartiles* split the ordered distribution into four equal parts. The median is the second quartile in this context. The first quartile cuts off the bottom 25% of the distribution and the third quartile cuts off the bottom 75% of the distribution.

IQR: Interquartile range, difference between first and third quartiles.

The most common order statistic for expressing variability is the interquartile range or IQR. The IQR is the difference between the third and second quartiles of a distribution. That is, the IQR specifies the range of the middle 50% of the data values, centered on the median.

outlier: A value far from most of the remaining data values.

An *outlier* is a value considerably different from most remaining values of the distribution. There are many ways to more precisely define an outlier. The definition applied here is based on the concept of a box plot, more fully described in the next section. Outliers always should be identified for any variable because their values could represent a coding error. Or, more fundamentally, an outlier could represent the outcome of a process different from the process that generated all or most of the other values of the distribution. If so, then mixing all the values into a single analysis may be accurate numerically, but may not represent any process that actually exists in the real world.

5.3.2 Summary Statistics for a Single Numerical Variable

All analyses of a variable should include its basic summary statistics.

 Scenario *Obtain summary statistics*

Obtain the summary statistics of the variable Salary in the Employee data set, both parametric and non-parametric, that numerically describe key characteristics of the distribution of Salary across the 37 employees.

The primary `lessR` function for numerical summaries of a variable is `SummaryStats`. Summary statistics can also be obtained from `Histogram` and `BarChart`, but a direct call to `SummaryStats` by default provides more statistics, without the graphics. To invoke `SummaryStats`, abbreviated `ss`, follow the usual pattern for `lessR` functions, illustrated here for the variable Salary.

SummaryStats function: Calculate summary statistics.

 **lessR Input** *Summary statistics*

```
> SummaryStats(Salary)          or          > ss(Salary)
```

In this example, the variable labels have been included in the analysis, and so the variable label for Salary is displayed as part of the output. The result appears in Listing 5.2.

variable labels, Section 2.4.1, p. 46

```
--- Salary, Annual Salary (USD) ---

   n  miss         mean            sd          skew          krts
  37     0     63795.557     21799.533         1.016         0.550


        min          Qrt1           mdn          Qrt3           max          IQR}
  36124.970     46772.950     59547.600     77785.510     124419.230     31012.560

Outlier: 124419.2
```

Listing 5.2 Parametric and order summary statistics for a continuous variable.

Or, invoke the brief version of `SummaryStats`, the version referenced by the functions `Histogram`, `BoxPlot` and the one variable version of `ScatterPlot`. Listing 5.3 shows the abbreviated form of the function call.

As can be seen from the output, the largest value in the distribution of data values is considered an outlier, apart from the remaining 36 values. None of the values are missing, so the value of Salary is present for each of the 37 employees. The mean is a little larger than the median, indicating that the distribution may have a tail in the upper side of the distribution, exhibiting skew, a lack of symmetry, consistent with the positive value of skew. The standard deviation is almost $22,000, so if the population from which the data were obtained is normal, roughly 95% of all the data values would be within two standard deviations, or a little less than $44,000 on either side of the mean of about $63,800.

```
> ss.brief(Salary)

--- Salary, Annual Salary (USD) ---

   n  miss        mean          sd         min        mdn         max
  37     0   63795.557   21799.533   36124.970   59547.600   124419.230

Outlier: 124419.2
```

Listing 5.3 Output of the brief version of summary statistics.

5.3.3 Available Options for Summary Statistics

Variable specification. The primary variable for analysis is always the first value passed to SummaryStats. If there is a second variable, a categorical variable, then either place it in the second position, or specify it with the by option, usually still in the second position though not necessarily. If the specified variable is in the data frame mydata, then the name of the corresponding data frame need not be specified. Otherwise, specify the relevant data frame with data.

digits.d function,
Section 1.3.5,
p. 14

n.cat option,
Section 2.2.7,
p. 39

Other options. A less complete version of the summary statistics can be obtained by setting the option brief=TRUE, or with the abbreviation ss.brief. The brief version limits the display to the sample size information, the mean, standard deviation, minimum, median, and maximum values. The number of displayed decimal digits can be changed from the default value by setting digits.d. The n.cat option specifies the maximum number of unique values of a numeric value that can be obtained and still be interpreted as a categorical variable.

5.3.4 Summary Statistics for All the Variables in a Data Frame

The most basic and usually first analysis of the variables in a data frame is to examine their distributions, both for continuous and categorical variables. The numeric summaries of a distribution are the summary statistics, which differ for continuous and categorical variables.

Scenario *Display the summary statistics for all variables*
For all numerical variables in a data frame, provide statistics such as the mean, median, standard deviation, and others. For all categorical variables, provide the values and the frequency and proportion of occurrence for each value.

If the first value in the call to SummaryStats is a data frame, all the variables in the data frame are analyzed. If there is no value passed to SummaryStats, then the data frame mydata is assumed.

lessR Input *Summary statistics for all variables in a data frame*
```
> SummaryStats()           or           > ss()
```

With this option, `SummaryStats` classifies each variable as either numerical or categorical. Then `SummaryStats` provides the appropriate summary statistics, either means, etc., or a table of the frequencies for each category. It is better, however, to declare all categorical variables in the analysis as R factors. If the variable is a factor, then `SummaryStats` always analyzes as a categorical variable.

factor function, Section 1.6.3, p. 22

There is also the `n.cat` option that can be passed to `SummaryStats` to denote variables with only a few unique values as categorical, even though the data type is numerical. The `n.cat` sets the definition of "a few". Numerical variables with only `n.cat` unique values, or less, are interpreted as categorical variables by `SummaryStats`. Here define *all* numerical variables with 7 or less values in a data frame as categorical solely for the purpose of calculating the appropriate summary statistics.

n.cat option, Section 2.2.7, p. 39

---

 lessR Input *Summary stats with n.cat option to define categorical variables*

```
> SummaryStats(n.cat=7)         or          > ss(n.cat=7)
```

If a variable with numerical values is interpreted as categorical according to the definition of `n.cat`, `SummaryStats` displays a message regarding its interpretation. Listing 5.4 shows this message for the variable HealthPlan, which has three numeric values, each corresponding to a different health plan.

```
>>> Variable is numeric, but only has 3 <= n.cat = 7 levels, so treat as
    categorical. To obtain the numeric summary, decrease  n.cat  to
    indicate a lower number of unique values such as with function: set.
    Perhaps make this variable a factor with R factor function.
```

Listing 5.4 A numerical variable with a small number of categories will be treated as a categorical variable.

The same `n.cat` parameter also applies to `BarChart` and `Histogram`. The value of `n.cat` can also be applied to all subsequent function calls if set with the function `set`.

set function, Section 2.2.7, p. 39

5.3.5 Summary Statistics of a Numerical Variable by Categories

Sometimes the summary statistics of a numerical variable are of interest for each of the values for each group defined by a categorical variable.

 Scenario *Compute summary statistics for each value of a second variable*
How does Salary vary by department? Display the summary statistics of Salary for each level of Dept.

For the statistics that summarize the sample, use the `by` option, usually for a categorical variable with relatively few unique values. The analysis of the summary statistics of Salary as they vary across the five different departments is shown in Listing 5.5. This version of the output is for the brief form of `SummaryStats`, specified by `ss.brief`, or by adding `brief=TRUE` in the call to `SummaryStats`.

 lessR Input *Summary statistics (brief) for each level of a second variable*

```
> ss.brief(Salary, by=Dept)
```

```
Salary, Annual Salary (USD)
  by
Dept, Department Employed
------------------------------
       n  miss        mean         sd         min      median         max
ACCT   5     0   51792.776   12774.606   36124.970   59547.600   62502.500
ADMN   6     0   71277.117   27585.151   43788.260   61058.595  112563.380
FINC   4     0   59010.675   17852.498   47139.900   51937.625   85027.550
MKTG   6     0   60257.128   19869.812   41036.850   51658.990   89062.660
SALE  15     0   68830.065   23476.839   39188.960   67714.850  124419.230
```

Listing 5.5 Brief version of summary statistics of Salary for each level of Dept.

Now compare each of the summary statistics across the different groups, one group for each value of the categorical variable. Of course this comparison applies only to this particular data set for the 37 employees. Do an inferential comparison of the means for the analysis of the more relevant population means. Invoke a *t*-test of the mean difference for two group means and, for multiple group means such as in Listing 5.5, a one-way analysis of variance, one-way ANOVA.

one-sample t-test,
Section 6.2, p. 124

one-way ANOVA,
Section 7.2, p. 150

5.4 Scatter Plot and Box Plot

The histogram is the traditional graphical presentation of the distribution of a continuous variable, but there are other possibilities.

5.4.1 One-variable Scatter Plot

Perhaps the simplest plot of a distribution of values for a continuous variable is its scatter plot, or dot plot. The *scatter plot* for a single variable is particularly appropriate for a relatively small number of data values. For each data value along a numerical scale, the scatter plot includes a mark, usually plotted as a dot. The scatter plot applies to the analysis of the employee data with measurements on 37 employees, but would be less effective for 370 employees. The distribution of a large number of individual data values is better expressed with the bins of a histogram.

one-variable
scatter plot: Each
value plotted such
as with a small
circle along the
value axis.

 Scenario *Obtain the one-variable scatter plot*
The salaries have been recorded for only 37 employees, a number small enough that the individual salaries could be successfully plotted as individual points. How are these 37 Salaries distributed?

Obtain the scatter plot of a variable as with any other `lessR` function, specify the function name, here `ScatterPlot`, and then the relevant variable name enclosed in parentheses. As with most `lessR` functions there is also an abbreviated form of the function name, here `sp`.

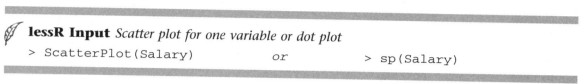

lessR Input *Scatter plot for one variable or dot plot*

> `ScatterPlot(Salary)`   *or*   > `sp(Salary)`

ScatterPlot
function: One- or
two-variable
scatter plot.

The output of `ScatterPlot` for the portrayal of the distribution of the 37 sample values of Salary is shown in Figure 5.5. To facilitate interpretation, each point by default is plotted with a transparent background so that the overlapped points display in a darker color to indicate the extent of the overlap.

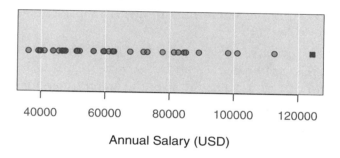

Figure 5.5 Gray scale `lessR` one-variable scatter plot, sometimes called a dot plot.

An *outlier* is a value in a distribution that is considerably different from most of the other values. For graphs with color, a *potential outlier*, following Tukey's (1977) definition explained on page 113, is displayed in dark red. *Actual outliers*, more extreme data values, are labeled in a more vivid red. For the gray scale plot in Figure 5.5, potential and actual outliers are displayed with a square and a diamond, respectively. The largest value in this distribution is considered a potential outlier according to this definition.

outlier,
Section 5.3.1,
p. 106

**potential
outlier**: A value
that could be an
outlier.

actual outlier: A
value that appears
to be an outlier.

5.4.2 Available Options for the `ScatterPlot` Function

Variable specifications. The variable plotted is the first position supplied to the `ScatterPlot` function. If the variable is in the data frame `mydata`, then the name of the corresponding data frame need not be specified. Otherwise, specify the relevant data frame with `data`.

Colors. The default colors are set by the current color theme from the `set` function. Any color theme can be modified by choosing an individual color of the bars, the bar borders, the background and the grid lines with `col.fill`, `col.stroke`, `col.bg`, and `col.grid`, respectively. The color of the points for outliers is set by `col.out15` with a default of `"firebrick4"` and by `col.out30` for more extreme outliers with a default of `"firebrick2"`. Set any of these colors to `"transparent"` to remove the color.

color themes,
Section 1.4.1,
p. 16

col.fill, etc.,
Table 1.1, p. 17

Plot symbols. For regular points, not outliers, the default plot symbol is a circle, with a default of partial transparency, as specified by the `set` function option `trans.fill.pt`. The plot symbol for outliers is a solid circle. The corresponding options, `pt.reg` and `pt.out`, are set equal to their default values of the numbers 21 and 19, respectively. Obtain the list of available plotting symbols and their corresponding reference numbers with `?points`. For example, an unfilled diamond is number 23.

Labels. As applies to most R graphs, the label for the x-axis is the `xlab` option. Set the graph title with the `main` option. If variable labels are present, then the axis label is set to the variable label unless overridden with the `main` option.

Other options. More options are available that are defined in the constituent R function `stripchart` upon which `ScatterPlot` relies for a one-variable plot. One default setting for `ScatterPlot` is `method="stack"`, which means that multiple points with the same value are stacked on top of each other instead of overprinting. Another possibility is to set `method="jitter"`, which randomly moves each point up or down so that points with the same value are not aligned over each other. Control the amount of jitter with a separate option, `jitter`, with a default setting of 0.1.

> **plot.method** option: Set to "jitter" to randomly move points.

As is true with all the graphic plots, more options from the graphics function `par` are also available. To control the size of the axis labels, use `cex.axis` and `cex.names` for the size of the axis names, with the magnification factor of 1 as the default. Also, the graph's margins can be set with the `mar` option, as explained in `?par`.

5.4.3 Box Plot

> *IQR, Section 5.3.1, p. 106*

The "box" in a box plot is based on the interquartile range or `IQR`, the positive difference between what are essentially the first and third quartiles. The `IQR` is the range of data that contains the middle 50% of all the data values. The width of the box is approximately the `IQR`, with a line through the median and perpendicular lines extending out from the edges. Tukey did not literally use the first and third quartiles, but rather an approximation called "hinges", apparently because they are easier to compute than quartiles, an important consideration with pre-computer technology. For our purposes, we consider the box plot based on the quartiles, which are almost if not equal to these hinges.

 Scenario *Generate a box plot*

The employee data set contains the salaries of 37 employees. What is the pattern of the distribution of these salaries? To visualize this distribution, generate the box plot of these salaries and identify any potential and actual outliers. Also display the basic summary statistics of Salary.

> **potential outlier**: An extreme value that may be an outlier.

> **actual outlier**: An extreme value that likely is an outlier.

The box plot is particularly useful to identify outliers. The inventor of the box plot, Tukey (1977), identified two types of outliers, based on the concept of an `IQR`. The *potential outlier* lies between 1.5 `IQR`s and 3.0 `IQR`s from the edges of the box. An *actual outlier*, according to this definition, lies more than 3.0 IQRs from either box's edge. Points past the *whisker* are likely outliers. There are many ways to define an outlier, but Tukey's definition appears to work well in practice.

whisker: A line from a box's edge that extends to the most extreme data value that is not a potential outlier.

Obtain the `lessR` box plot with `BoxPlot`, abbreviated `bx`.

✒ **lessR Input** *Box plot*
> BoxPlot(Salary)   *or*   > bx(Salary)

BoxPlot function: Generate a box plot.

The resulting box plot of Salary in Figure 5.6 shows one potential outlier beyond the right whisker. The plot also demonstrates some right-tailed skew with the right side of the box after the median bar, which is longer than the corresponding left side. Also the right whisker is longer than the left whisker. Variable labels are present to provide the label automatically for the horizontal or x-axis.

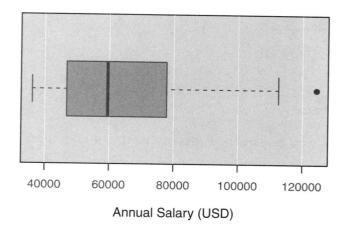

Figure 5.6 Default `lessR` box plot.

5.4.4 Available Options

Variable specifications. The variable plotted occupies the first position in the list of options, so list its name first. If the variable is in the data frame `mydata`, then specify the relevant data frame with `data`.

color themes,
Section 1.4.1,
p. 16

col.fill, etc.,
Table 1.1, p. 17

Colors. Either rely upon the default `blue` color theme, or set the colors with the current color theme from the `set` function. Modify any color theme by choosing an individual color of the bars, the bar borders, the background and the grid lines with `col.fill`, `col.stroke`, `col.bg`, and `col.grid`, respectively.

add.points=TRUE option: Super-impose a dot plot over the box plot.

Orientation. The default orientation is a horizontal plot. To plot vertically, specify `horiz=FALSE`. The concept of a box plot and a one-variable scatter plot, or dot plot, can be combined on the same graph. To do this, invoke the `add.points=TRUE` option for the box plot.

> **lessR Input** *Box plot with superimposed scatter plot*
> ```
> > BoxPlot(Salary, add.points=TRUE)
> ```

The combined box plot and dot plot in Figure 5.7 show in one graph the highlighted potential outlier, the overall shape of the distribution, and the specific values upon which the box plot is based.

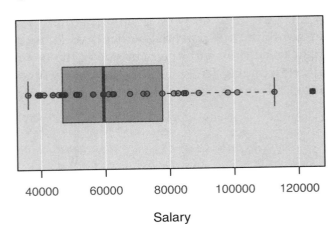

Figure 5.7 Box plot with superimposed scatter plot.

The text output in Listing 5.6 from `BoxPlot` reveals the value of the potential outlier.

```
--- Salary, Annual Salary (USD) ---

Present: 37
Missing: 0
Total  : 37
...
Outlier: 124419.2
```

Listing 5.6 Outlier identification.

Histograms also can be used to identify outliers, but the box plot explicitly identifies such data values as part of the plot.

5.5 Density Plot

density plot:
Smoothed out histogram, such as a normal curve.

A recent development that has become feasible with the advent of computer graphics, the density plot, extends the concept of the histogram to a more modern version. A *density plot* is a kind of idealized histogram in which the bin width of a histogram diminishes to zero, leaving a smooth curve instead of a jagged histogram. This smooth curve better represents the shape of the underlying distribution, which likely is not characterized by the sharp edges of rectangles, but rather a smooth continuity. The most well-known example of this smooth frequency-like density curve is the normal curve.

5.5.1 Default Density Plot and Analysis

A density curve can be estimated whenever a histogram is computed.

 Scenario *Obtain a density plot of a continuous variable*
From a sample of data values of Salary from the Employee data set, estimate the corresponding smooth curve, the density curve, that approximates the true shape of the underlying distribution of Salary without the jagged edges of histogram bins. Also simultaneously show the estimated density curve superimposed over a histogram of the data.

The lessR function for a density plot is Density, abbreviated dn. This function presents several enhancements over plotting the output of the corresponding R function density. The function Density by default imposes over a histogram both the normal densities as well as a general density curve.

To invoke the lessR function, just enter its name and the relevant variable name, enclosed in parentheses.

normal densities: The smooth normal curve.

Density function: Plot smoothed normal and general density distributions.

✒ **lessR Input** *Density plot*
```
> Density(Salary)          or          > dn(Salary)
```

This simple statement results in the histogram and two density curves in Figure 5.8. The data file includes the variable labels. That way, the more descriptive variable label appears on the graph instead of the more concise but less descriptive variable name.

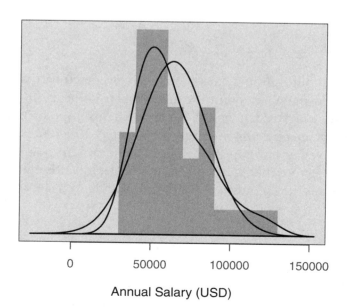

Figure 5.8 Default histogram with superimposed normal and general density curves.

The `Density` function also generates text output. One key aspect of data analysis is the actual sample size that underlies the analysis. There are 37 rows of data in the data table, but it is possible that there is much missing data for any one particular variable.

```
Sample Size:  37
Missing Values:  0
```

Here all 37 potential values of Salary are present.

 Scenario *Test the hypothesis that a distribution is normal*
A sample of data value is never perfectly normal. Is it reasonable, however, to conclude that the population from which the data values are sampled is normal? Use the Shapiro–Wilk statistic to test the null hypothesis that a distribution of data values is sampled from a normal distribution.

This text output includes the formal test of the null hypothesis that the distribution is sampled from a normal population.

```
Null hypothesis is a normal population
Shapiro-Wilk normality test:  W = 0.9117,  p-value = 0.0063
```

The test statistic based on the assumption of the null hypothesis that the population is normal is the Shapiro–Wilk statistic, $W = 0.9117$. How large is this value? The *p*-value provides the answer. *If* the null hypothesis is true, then the probability of obtaining a W statistic as large as or larger than $W = 0.9117$ is only *p*-value $= 0.006$, less than the usual alpha criterion of $\alpha = 0.05$, the definition of an improbable event. The value of W is too large to be consistent with the null hypothesis of normality, a result due in part to the slight right skew, the small tail on the right hand side of the distribution.

bandwidth:
Extent of diminishing influence of nearby values to calculate the position of a point on a density curve.

Also reported is the bandwidth used to construct the estimated density curve, which is $9229.

```
Density bandwidth for general curve: 9529.045
For a smoother curve, increase bandwidth with option: bw
```

bandwidth
option: Set the bandwidth used to estimate the density curve.

To estimate each point on the curve, the surrounding data values are considered with a set of diminishing weights. Data values close to the given point are given much influence in the location of the point on the density curve, whereas data values far from the given point have little if any influence on the location of the given position on the estimated curve. The *bandwidth option*, bw, specifies the influence that data values have on the location of the current point on the density curve depending on their distance from that point. Increasing the bandwidth option, bw, further smoothes the graph because more surrounding data values contribute to its location on the density curve.

5.5.2 Other Available Options

Variable specifications. The variable plotted occupies the first position in the list of options. If the variable is in the data frame `mydata`, then the name of the corresponding data frame need not be specified. Otherwise, specify the relevant data frame with `data`.

Colors. Either use the default `blue` color theme or choose the color theme with the `set` function. The individual color of the background and grid lines are set by `col.bg` and `col.grid`, respectively. Set the color of the histogram bars with `col.fill`. The borders of the curves default to `"black"`, but can be changed according to `col.nrm` and `col.gen`. The fill color for the normal curve, `col.fill.nrm`, and general density curve, `col.fill.gen`, are each set to be partially transparent so that their overlap can be directly viewed, as well as the histogram plotted behind them. Set any of these colors to `"transparent"` to remove the corresponding fill color from the graph.

set function,
Section 1.4.1,
p. 16

Bins. The default specification for setting the histogram bins is the same as `Histogram`, the `"Sturges"` algorithm. Obtain another set of bins with either one or both of `bin.start` and `bin.width`. The `breaks` option is not set at the user level as it is for `Histogram`.

bin.start, bin.width
options,
Section 5.2.2,
p. 102

To apply some of these options, revise the first density plot in Figure 5.8. First, the histogram is too jagged, so a new density plot is generated with a bin width for the histogram of $15,000. Also, the general density curve is a bit wobbly on its right side, a characteristic that probably reflects sampling error. Increasing the bandwidth to $12,000 further smooths this curve.

Generate the revised graph in Figure 5.9 according to the following function call.

✒ **lessR Input** *Density plot with specified histogram and bandwidth*

```
> Density(Salary, bin.start=25000, bin.width=15000,
          type="general", bw=12000)
```

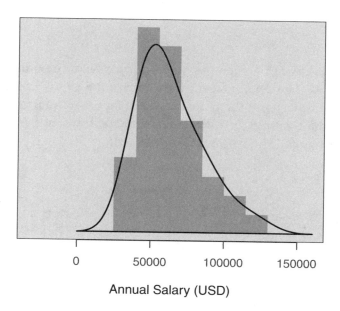

Annual Salary (USD)

Figure 5.9 Histogram with superimposed general density curve and customized histogram.

This graph succinctly summarizes the distribution of Salary for those 37 employees with a smooth curve. The plot reveals the minimum and maximum values and the relative size of nearby data values from our reference point upon which the hypothesis is based. The slight right skew is also apparent from this figure.

5.6 Time Plot

The previous analyses in this chapter applied to the distribution of values for a variable. The values were ordered from the smallest value to the largest with the frequencies of similar values noted. Here we continue to consider the distribution of the values of a variable, but now focus on the order of the values as they appear in the data table. When the entered order of the data values is of interest it is usually because the order reflects the time that each value was generated. The focus on time leads to a consideration of two different kinds of data.

cross-sectional data: Data for a variable collected at about the same time.

Cross-sectional data values are measurements of the same variable at about the same time over different people, or whatever is the unit of analysis. Administering an attitude survey one time to many different people generates cross-sectional data. The analysis of the frequencies of the data values ordered from smallest to largest is a primary analysis for these data. The graphs presented previously in this chapter all provide this type of analysis: a histogram, one-variable scatter plot, box plot, and density plot.

longitudinal data: Data for a variable collected at different times.

LineChart function: Plot points over time with a line segment that joins consecutive points.

Longitudinal data values are measurements of the same variable with variation obtained over different time periods. Data collected over time can, and usually should, be analyzed with graphs such as histograms. The frequency of different ranges of values usually is always of interest. Longitudinal data, however, also present the additional dimension of time for analysis.

To plot longitudinal data use the `lessR` function `LineChart`, abbreviated `lc`. The values of the variable appear on the vertical or y-axis, and some indicator of time defines the horizontal or x-axis. `LineChart` generates the indicator of time that scales the horizontal axis, so the only data passed to the function are the values of the variable to be plotted.

5.6.1 Run Chart

run chart: Values plotted and identified in the order that they occur.

One version of a time oriented plot is the *run chart*, in which the horizontal axis lists the ordinal position of each value, from 1 to the last value. The default label for the horizontal axis is `index`.

A primary purpose of the run chart is to understand the performance of an on-going process over time. For example, consider the student ratings of overall teaching performance for a professor who is about to be evaluated for tenure. The data set is on the web.

```
http://lessRstats.com/data/Ratings.csv
```

For the last 5 years the professor taught the same course once a term, four quarters a year. First the Dean examines the scatter plot of the mean ratings from these 20 classes. The variable name is Rating.

```
> ScatterPlot(Rating)
```

The result appears in Figure 5.10. The ratings are on a 10-point scale, where the most favorable rating possible is a 10.

The Dean concludes that the ratings are generally favorable, though some terms the students were relatively displeased. Are those less-well-received terms earlier in the professor's employment, or are they more recent, which would indicate a diminishing of performance in terms of student ratings. The run chart provides the visual answer to this question.

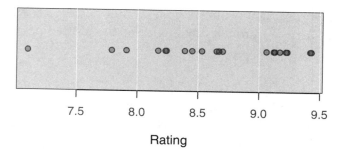

Figure 5.10 Distribution of the average student ratings over the 20 terms.

lessR Input *Run chart of the average teacher ratings for the last 20 terms*

```
> LineChart(Rating)
```

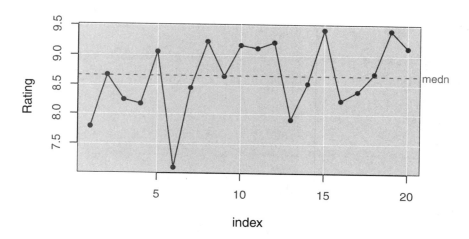

Figure 5.11 Run chart of the mean rating each term for a course.

Obtain the run chart with the `lessR` function `LineChart`, abbreviated `lc`. To facilitate comparison of values at different time periods, if the run chart does not exhibit pronounced trends up or down, then `LineChart` adds a horizontal dotted line at the median. For Figure 5.11, comparing the ratings against the plotted median line, the professor's ratings may exhibit a mild trend upwards, demonstrating some improvement over time. The worst ratings occurred toward the beginning of the professor's employment. For example, the worst mean rating, close to a 7.0, occurred for the sixth term. The best ratings occurred for Terms 15 and 19.

There are also several available options. As usual, to obtain the complete list of options enter `?LineChart`. As with all `lessR` graphic functions, the usual color choices apply. Use the `center.line` option to specify the reference line as the mean, `center.line="mean"`; the median, `center.line="median"`; turned off, `center.line="off"`; or through zero, `center.line="zero"`.

By default the `LineChart` function displays both the points for each individual data value and the line segment that connects each adjacent pair of points. To display only the line use the `type="l"` option. By default, the plotted point is a filled circle. Access alternative shapes that

color choices,
Section 1.1, p. 17

center.line
option: Specify the type of center line drawn, if any.

type option:
Specify to plot line segments (l), points (p), or the default both (b).

R provides with the `shape.points` option according to numeric codes. Enter `?points` to view all the possibilities. For example, `shape.points=23` provides diamonds as the plotted points.

shape.points
option: Specify the type of point to plot.

5.6.2 Time Series

Similar to a run chart, a time series chart also plots the values of a variable over time. The distinction is that for the time series chart the horizontal axis is labeled with times or dates that indicate when each data value was generated. To illustrate, the US Census Bureau provides historical estimates of the world population from 1950 and before, and results based on actual counts after that time (US Census Bureau, 2012).

Some of the data from the US Census Bureau website is extracted and reformatted, and available at the book's web site.

```
> mydata <- Read("http://lessRstats.com/data/WorldPopulation.csv")
```

time.start option, Starting time of the data values.

time.by option, Time increment with units of `"days"`, `"weeks"`, `"months"`, or `"years"` in the singular or plural.

The name of the variable of interest is Population. Inform `LineChart` of the variable to analyze and then specify the time periods from which `LineChart` will scale the horizontal axis. Specify the periods with the `time.start` and `time.by` options.

> **lessR Input** *Plot the time series of world population from 1900*
```
> LineChart(Population,
            time.start="1900/1/1", time.by="10 years",
            xlab="Year", ylab="World Population (millions)")
```

Figure 5.12 shows the explosive growth of the world population during the 20th century and into the 21st century.

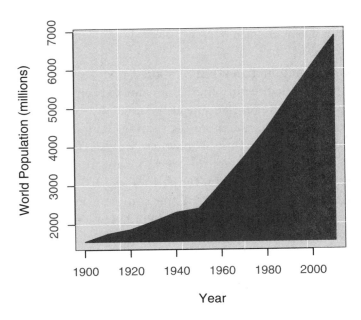

Figure 5.12 World population according to the US Census Bureau (2012).

If the data values are systematically changing over time, such as the dramatic increases in world population exhibited in Figure 5.12, then `LineChart` does not plot a center line by default but does fill in the area under the curve. To remove the filled-in area under the curve, set `col.area="transparent"` in the call to `LineChart`.

The data values for the time series chart need to be ordered from the earliest to the last data value. If they are ordered in the opposite direction, one possibility is to use the `lessR` function `Sort` to re-order the entire data frame. Another possibility is to set the `time.reverse` option to `TRUE` as part of the call to `LineChart`.

Sort function, Section 3.5, p. 66

time.reverse option: Applies to data values listed from last to earliest.

Worked Problems

1 Consider the Cars93 data set, available from within the `lessR` package.

```
> mydata <- Read("Cars93", format="lessR")
```

?dataCars93 for more information.

One of the variables in this data set is MPGcity.

(a) What is the sample mean and standard deviation of city MPG?
(b) Provide the histogram of city MPG.
(c) Provide the density curve of city MPG.
(d) Provide a box plot of city MPG. Are there are any outliers and potential outliers?
(e) Provide a scatter plot (dot plot) of city MPG.
(f) Describe the distribution of city MPG.

2 Consider the Mach4 data set, available from within the `lessR` package.

```
> mydata <- Read("Mach4", format="lessR")
```

?Mach4 for more information.

Now consider the ninth item, named `m09`, scored on a 6-point Likert scale from 0 for `Strongly Disagree` to 5 for `Strongly Agree`.

9. All in all, it is better to be humble and honest than to be important and dishonest.

(a) What is the sample mean and standard deviation of `m09`?
(b) Provide the histogram of `m09`.
(c) Provide the density curve of `m09`.
(d) Provide a box plot of `m09`. Are there any outliers and potential outliers?
(e) Provide a scatter plot (or dot plot) of `m09`.
(f) Describe the distribution of `m09`.

3 R provides several functions for simulating data. The function `rnorm` generates n simulated data values randomly sampled from a normal distribution with a specified population mean and population standard deviation.

```
> rnorm(n= , mean= , sd= )
```

When using the function, fill in the three blanks for the three respective values.

(a) Generate 20 randomly sampled values from a normal distribution with $\mu = 50$ and $\sigma = 10$.

(b) Generate another 20 values and store them into a data vector for later analysis with the R assignment statement. Call the data vector Y.

```
> Y <- rnorm( ... )
```

(c) List the simulated data values with > Y.

(d) Display their histogram. Describe the result.

(e) Compare the sample mean and sample standard deviation to their population counterparts. Are the sample values equal to the corresponding population values? Why or why not?

(f) Display their run chart. Describe the result.

CHAPTER 6

MEANS, COMPARE TWO SAMPLES

6.1 Quick Start

First install R and lessR as explained in Section 1.2. At the beginning of each R session access lessR with library(lessR). Then read your data into an R data frame with Read(), the subject of Chapter 2.

The focus of the first part of this chapter is to estimate the value of an unknown population mean based on a sample from that population. Next considered is the comparison of the unknown values of the population means that underlie two different samples. The latter test would be used, for example, to compare the average salary for men and women.

✓ Evaluate the mean of a single sample with a confidence interval and an hypothesis test to compare the sample mean to some pre-existing reference value. For example, is it reasonable that the average Salary for a given company is $75,000?

```
> ttest(Salary, mu0=75000)
```

one-sample t-test, Section 6.2, p. 124

✓ Use the independent-groups *t*-test to compare the means of the variable of interest across two different groups, such as the mean Salary for the values of Gender, men and women.

```
> ttest(Salary ~ Gender)
```

independent-groups t-test, Section 6.3, p. 130

✓ The non-parametric alternative to the independent-groups *t*-test is the Wilcoxon rank sum test.

```
> with(mydata, wilcox.test(Salary ~ Gender, conf.int=TRUE))
```

Wilcoxon rank sum test, Section 6.3.3, p. 135

✓ Instead of comparing the means of the two groups, do a dependent-groups *t*-test that directly compares a data value in one sample with a matched data value in the corresponding sample. Do this comparison by analyzing the differences between the corresponding matched scores invoked with the `paired` option.

```
> ttest(Before, After, paired=TRUE)
```

dependent-groups t-test, Section 6.4.1, p. 142

✓ The non-parametric alternative to the dependent-groups *t*-test is the Wilcoxon signed rank test, here run on the difference scores.

```
> with(mydata, wilcox.test(Diff, conf.int=TRUE))
```

Wilcoxon signed rank test, Section 6.4.2, p. 144

6.2 Evaluate a Single Group Mean

research design: The procedures for collecting and analyzing one or more samples of data.

To begin a research study, the researcher chooses a *research design* from which to obtain the measurements of people, or whatever is the unit of analysis. For the designs considered here the data values are either from one sample or are from different samples, which are then compared with each other.

The simplest research design is that of a single sample, the measurements of a single variable of interest. One characteristic often of interest is the mean. What is the average score on the class midterm? What percentage of people will vote for a particular candidate? What is the average score on an anxiety scale administered to clients about to undergo a particular type of therapy?

6.2.1 The Population Mean and a Sample Mean

inferential statistics: Analysis of sample data that provides conclusions regarding the true population values.

The focus of the analysis is not the sample statistics per se, but the corresponding population values of the variable of interest. For the analysis of the mean, the goal is to apply *inferential statistics*, to use information gleaned from the sample to evaluate the mean of the population from which the sample was drawn. So the population mean of the class midterm would be the mean if the same teaching conditions by which the class was taught were extended to many, many thousands of similar students. The usually hypothetical population values are denoted with Greek letters. Refer to the population mean of the variable of interest by the Greek letter μ.

The sample results are not of general interest because their values are unique to that specific sample. Usually take only a single sample for the group of interest. Hypothetically, more random samples of the same size from the same population could be taken. The key issue is that every random sample will yield different sample statistics. Every sample mean to some extent reflects the value of the true underlying mean, μ, and also the influence of random sampling error.

For example, flip a fair coin 10 times and you might get 6 heads. Flip the same coin another 10 times and you might get 4 heads. Which sample result is true? The answer is neither of them. What is true is the long run average of the population mean over an indefinitely large number of flips. The long run average for a fair coin is that 50% of the results are heads, a result that fluctuates from sample to sample, more noticeably for small samples.

Mach IV scale,
Listing 1.8, p. 27

Consider the responses to the Mach IV scale, in particular the responses to the 7th item, named `m07` in the data set.

There is no excuse for lying to someone else.

reverse score,
Section 3.4.1,
p. 63

Histogram
function,
Section 5.2, p. 100

variable labels,
Section 2.4, p. 45

The responses are numerically encoded from 0 to 5 with a 0 indicating `Strongly Disagree` and a 5 `Strongly Agree`. When considered as part of Mach IV, this item is reversed scored so that Disagreement is consistent with a high Machiavellianism score. For the analysis of this single item, however, leave the responses unmodified to simplify the discussion of the results.

The analysis of `m07` begins with a description of the sample results provided by the `Histogram` function. First read the data from the internal `lessR` data set `Mach4`, as well as the item content in the form of variable labels.

```
> mydata <- Read("Mach4", format="lessR")
```

First try the default histogram for `m07`.

```
> Histogram(m07)
```

Default histograms of Likert data are usually problematic because of the relatively small number of scale points that assess the underlying continuous variable, the extent of agreement with the item. In this example the default histogram of m07 has a bin width of only 0.5. Instead the bin width should be the increment between the successive scale values, here 1. Also, the histogram bars should be centered over the corresponding scale points. To accomplish these objectives, provide explicit values for the bin.start and bin.width options.

```
> Histogram(m07, bin.start=-.5, bin.width=1)
```

The histogram of the responses of the 351 respondents is shown in Figure 6.1.

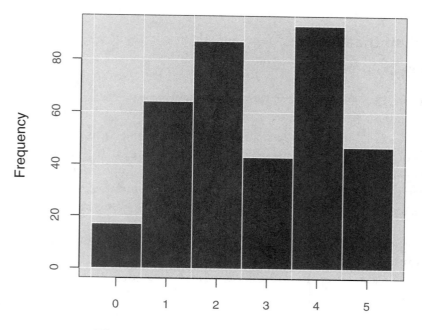

There is no excuse for lying to someone else.

Figure 6.1 Histogram for m07, the 7th Mach IV item, not reverse scored.

The histogram indicates that the responses vary across the possible range of values from 0 to 5. Values below 2.5 indicate Disagreement and values above 2.5 indicate Agreement. The summary statistics from Histogram in Figure 6.1 indicate that the sample mean of 2.8 is close to but larger than the midpoint of 2.5. In this particular sample the mean is 0.3 units above the dividing point of Disagree and Agree.

```
--- m07, There is no excuse for lying to someone else. ---

     n  miss   mean     sd    min    mdn    max
   351     0    2.8    1.5    0.0    3.0    5.0
```

Listing 6.1 Summary statistics for m07, the 7th Mach IV item.

The question of interest here is that of inferential statistics. Does this result of a sample mean larger than the midpoint of 2.5 generalize to the population? That is, is the true average response to m07 also in the Agreement region? If additional samples from the same population were obtained, would the mean generally be in the Agree region?

Considered from another perspective, *if* the true population mean is right at the midpoint of $\mu = 2.5$, then half the sample means would be below 2.5 and half would be above 2.5. The fact that the sample mean is larger than 2.5 does not imply that the true mean is larger than 2.5. Analysis of the underlying population value provides us with some probability information to evaluate the true value of the mean. There are two primary forms of inferential analysis, the confidence interval about the statistic of interest, and the hypothesis test of a specified value of the corresponding population value.

6.2.2 Inferential Analysis of the Mean

Apply this inferential analysis to the mean.

 Scenario *Inferential analysis of the mean*
The response to the Mach IV items follows a six-point Likert scale from 0 for Strongly Disagree to 5 for Strongly Agree. Evaluate the population value of the mean level of endorsement for the 7th item on the Mach IV scale. Base the hypothesis test on the scale value that separates the region of disagreement from agreement, 2.5.

Accomplish the lessR inferential analysis of a population mean with the function ttest, or its abbreviation tt. This function provides both classical forms of inference, the confidence interval about the sample mean and, if an hypothesized value is provided, the corresponding hypothesis test. Also provided is an indicator of *effect size*, the detected magnitude of the difference. An evaluation of the normality of the population from which the data values are sampled is provided for use when the sample size is small.

effect size: The magnitude of the difference between the sample and hypothesized results.

Use the mu0 option to specify the reference value for the hypothesis test. If mu0 is not specified, the confidence interval is calculated without the accompanying hypothesis test. The default confidence level is set with the conf.level option. The default value is 0.95.

mu0 option: Null hypothesis value.

The specifications of the null and alternative hypotheses depend on the deviations from the specified null value that are of interest. For the *two-tailed test* in which deviations in either direction from the null value are of interest, the rejection region of the test consists of values that are much larger than the null value and values that are much smaller. The two-tailed test is the default analysis, as specified by the default value "two.sided" for the alternative option.

two-tailed test: Rejection region consists of both + and − deviations from the null value.

For the one-tailed test, deviations from the reference value of the null hypothesis are of interest only in one direction from the null value. The issue is not if the researcher prefers a large positive or a large negative deviation, but rather what the researcher is willing to interpret. For example, a consumer protection agency interested in assessing a gas mileage claim by an automobile manufacturer does not care if the average fuel mileage betters the claim. Instead the agency is focused only on deviations significantly below the claimed mileage. If only deviations in one direction are of interest to interpret, then specify a *one-tailed* test, with the rejection on only one side of the null value. Specify the alternative hypothesis according to alternative="less" or alternative="more".

one-tailed test: Rejection region lies only on one side of the null value.

alternative option: Specify a one- or two-tailed test.

In this example the population mean value of interest is 2.5. For a two-tailed test the null hypothesis is $H_0 : \mu = 2.5$. The alternative hypothesis is that $H_1 : \mu \neq 2.5$. Specify the corresponding two-tailed test as follows.

✒ **lessR Input** *One-sample t-test*

```
> ttest(m07, mu0=2.5)          or          > tt(m07, mu0=2.5)
```

The first part of the output of `ttest` are the summary statistics of the variable of interest, the response variable. The `Histogram` output in Listing 6.1 includes these statistics. Included in this report is the sample mean of 2.8.

Next is an assessment of the normality of the population data from which the sample data values are obtained. If the sample size is greater than 20 or 30, or lower values if the population data values are not too skewed, then the *central limit theorem* ensures a normally distributed sample mean across many hypothetical repeated samples from the same population, each sample of the same size. This normality is needed to justify the use of the *t*-distribution as the basis of the statistical inference.

In this example the sample size is 351, well beyond the threshold of 30. Accordingly, `ttest` informs us that tests of normality are not needed, as shown in Listing 6.2.

central limit theorem: The sample mean is approximately normally distributed unless a small sample is taken from a non-normal population.

```
------ Normality Assumption ------

Sample mean is normal because n>30, so no test needed.
```

Listing 6.2 Consideration of the normality of the response to `m07`, the 7th Mach IV item.

The beginning of the inferential analysis follows in Listing 6.3, of which the first two lines are preliminary information for the analysis.

```
------ Inference ------

t-cutoff: tcut =   1.967
Standard Error of Mean: SE =   0.08
```

Listing 6.3 Preliminary information for statistical inference, both the hypothesis test and the confidence interval.

The first value is the *t*-cutoff for the specified confidence level, of which the default is 95%. This value can be changed from the default of `conf.level=0.95`. The *t-cutoff* specifies the range of sampling variability of the *t*-statistic over repeated samples, in terms of estimated standard errors. The value is around 2 except for very small samples, and always larger than 1.96, which is the baseline established by the normal distribution. Here the value of the cutoff for the two-tailed test is 1.967.

The *standard error* is the standard deviation of the sample mean over these repeated hypothetical samples and sets the baseline for the extent that the statistic fluctuates from sample to sample. The more fluctuation, the more error is likely to be in the estimation of the true mean, μ. The "magic" is that this information can be assessed from the information in only a single

conf.level option: The confidence level.

t-cutoff: Positive and negative values define the range of sampling variability.

standard error: Standard deviation of a statistic over usually hypothetical repeated samples.

sample, the sample of data subject to analysis by the `ttest` function. Here the standard error of the sample mean is 0.08, which is always less than the standard deviation of the data, here 2.8 as shown in Listing 6.1.

t-value of the mean: Number of estimated standard errors the sample mean is from the hypothesized mean.

The core of the inferential analysis follows, beginning with Listing 6.4. As specified by the obtained t-value, the corresponding sample mean of 2.8 is a considerable 3.497 estimated standard errors from 2.5.

```
Hypothesized Value H0: mu = 2.5
Hypothesis Test of Mean:   t-value = 3.497,   df = 350,   p-value = 0.001
```

Listing 6.4 Hypothesis test that the true mean response is 2.5 for `m07`, the 7th Mach IV item.

p-value: Probability of obtaining a sample statistic as deviant or more deviant from the null hypothesized value assuming a true null.

statistical decision: The rejection or not of the null hypothesis.

Given the degrees of freedom of $df = 350$, one less than the sample size of 351, the corresponding p-value is 0.001. The p-value is the probability of obtaining a sample mean that is 0.27 units away from the hypothesized mean of 2.5, here in either direction, *if* the null hypothesis is true. If the 2.5 is the true mean, the result of a sample mean of 2.8 is quite unlikely.

How low can the p-value be before the null hypothesis is considered unlikely and is therefore rejected. The definition of "unlikely" is the given value of α, usually 0.05, but sometimes 0.01 or 0.10. Here the *statistical decision* follows.

$$\text{Difference from 2.5: } p\text{-value} = 0.001 < \alpha = 0.05, \text{ so reject } H_0$$

significant difference: A likely difference has been detected between the true mean and the hypothesized mean.

Reject the null hypothesis as unlikely. A *significant difference* from 2.5 has been detected. Note that the probability of the truth of the null is not known. What is known is that if it is true, then an unlikely event occurred, so the null is probably not true. One limitation of the hypothesis test is that we do know the p-value, but we do *not* know the more useful probability of the truth of the null hypothesis. The p-value can be computed to as many decimal digits as desired, but our understanding of the likelihood of the null hypothesis is qualitative. We conclude that the null hypothesis is unlikely without any more specific probability information.

Listing 6.5 presents the confidence interval. Given our conclusion that the true mean is not 2.5, what is it? The randomness inherent in the sampling process prevents a precise answer. What is possible is to provide an interval that likely includes the true mean, μ.

```
Margin of Error for 95% Confidence Level:   0.15
95% Confidence Interval for Mean:   2.62 to 2.93
```

Listing 6.5 Confidence interval for `m07`, the 7th Mach IV item.

confidence interval: Range of values that likely contains the population value of interest.

The 95% confidence interval is from 2.62 to 2.93. The *confidence interval* is the range of values that likely contains the true mean, μ, at the specified level of confidence, 95%. Here the true average response is in the Agreement region.

The information from the confidence interval is consistent with that of the hypothesis test. The confidence interval indicates that the true mean response on the six-point scale from 0 to

5 for `m07` is likely between 2.62 and 2.93, of which all values in this range are larger than the null value of 2.5. Consistent with this information, the hypothesis test indicates that the mean value of 2.5 is unlikely, a value outside of the confidence interval.

Also of interest is the effect size. The *p*-value indicates if a difference between population and hypothesized values of the population has been detected, but provides no information regarding the extent of this difference. To report a significant *p*-value, that is, a *p*-value less than α, without reporting an effect size is to inform the reader that there is a difference, but with no indication as to its size.

effect size
Section 6.2.2, p. 126

The `ttest` function reports effect size in two different metrics. First, consider the units of measurement of the variable of interest. The difference of the sample mean from the hypothesized value of the mean estimates this difference, and can be extended to the lower and upper bounds of the accompanying confidence interval.

Another indicator of effect size is in standardized units, the sample distance of sample and hypothesized means divided by the standard deviation of the data. This standardized indicator is Cohen's *d* after Jacob Cohen (1969). Standardization is particularly useful when the original measurement unit is arbitrary, such as for Likert responses including the responses to the items on the Mach IV scale.

Mach IV data, Listing 1.8, p. 27

The function `ttest` reports both indicators of effect size, as shown in Listing 6.6. The raw distance of the sample from the hypothesized mean is 0.27 units on the six-point scale. The corresponding standardized value is 0.19, that is, the sample mean is 0.19 standard deviations above the hypothesized mean of 2.5.

```
------ Effect Size ------

Distance of sample mean from hypothesized:   0.27
Standardized Distance, Cohen's d:   0.19
```

Listing 6.6 Effect size for the distance of the sample mean of `m07`, the 7th Mach IV item, from the hypothesized value of 2.5.

To assist in the understanding of the distribution of the variable of interest, and the resulting effect size, `ttest` also provides a smoothed plot of the distribution, a density plot, shown in Figure 6.2. Included in the plot are vertical lines that represent the sample mean of the distribution and the corresponding hypothesized mean. The two indicators of effect size are also displayed. The bottom horizontal axis displays the original metric in which the variable is measured. The top horizontal axis displays the metric of Cohen's *d*, the standard deviation of the data.

density plot, Section 5.5, p. 114

For the responses to the Mach IV `m07`, the population mean is apparently in the Agree region, so that on average the respondents agree that lying to others is bad. However, the mean sample mean response is only 0.27 units above the midpoint of 2.5 on the six-point scale from 0 to 5. Even the upper end of the 95% confidence interval is below 3, with a value of 2.93. The histogram in Figure 6.1 and the density plot in Figure 6.2 indicate the responses vary over the complete range of data values. Further, the effect size is rather small. The true mean is in the Agree region, but the bimodal shape of the distribution implies that the mean is not an effective summary of all the data values.

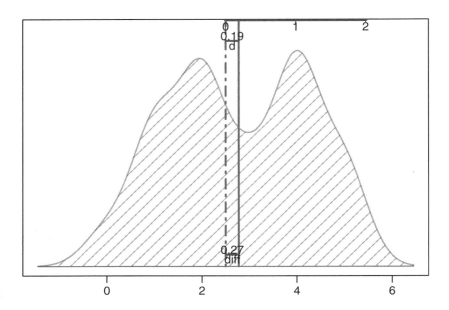

There is no excuse for lying to someone else.

Figure 6.2 Density plot of `m07`, the 7th item on the Mach IV scale, with sample mean and hypothesized mean and two effect sizes, not reverse scored.

6.2.3 Inference from Summary Statistics

The *t*-test can also be conducted directly from the three summary statistics that form the basis of the test. Just specify a value for n, m, and s, the sample size, the sample mean, and the sample standard deviation, respectively.

```
> ttest(n=351, m=2.77, s=1.47, mu0=2.5)
```

Invoking this statement results in exactly the same output as shown previously, except for the portions of the output that depend directly on the availability of the data. The density curves cannot be analyzed, nor is a test for normality of the data performed.

6.3 Compare Two Different Groups

A common data analysis procedure is to compare the means of two different samples of data from populations with potentially distinct characteristics. For example, is a newly developed therapy for depression equally effective for men and women? The number of men and the number of women in their respective samples do not need to be equal, although usually the goal is to have at least somewhat equal sample sizes.

6.3.1 Research Design for Two Independent Groups

Mach IV scale,
Listing 1.8, p. 27 Suppose a researcher investigates if men and women have different Machiavellian tendencies, such as assessed by the Christie and Geis (1970) Mach IV scale. The researcher is not advocating

that if there are different tendencies that all men are more Machiavellian than all women, or vice versa. Instead the issue is if the average male Machiavellian score is higher or lower than the corresponding average female score. Usually the means are compared, though other characteristics of the distributions may serve as the basis of the comparison. Here the researcher pursues a two-group design, with a sample of men and a sample of women, so as to compare, for example, the corresponding means.

The ultimate purpose of the study is the resulting inference to the population means from which the samples were obtained. The fact that in any one set of samples males had a higher average Machiavellian score than the average female score is not of general interest. What is of interest is if the pattern of one sample mean larger than the other generalizes to all men and women from the populations from which the samples were obtained. The purpose of such studies is to apply inferential statistics, to discover relationships and patterns that apply generally, beyond the random fluctuations of results found in specific samples.

inferential statistics,
Section 6.2.1, 124

A research design based on samples from two distinct populations is an *independent-samples* or independent-groups design. Another name for the separate samples design is a *between-subjects* design. The defining characteristic is that each data value in one of the samples is unrelated to any specific data value in the other sample. The examples explored here compare the means of two different samples. Later we generalize to a technique for comparing two or more means.

independent-samples design: Data values in each sample are unrelated to the data values in the other sample.

Compare two or more group means, Section 7.2, p. 150

6.3.2 Example 1: Compare Means of Two Existing Groups

To illustrate, consider the Deceit subscale on the Mach IV scale, which consists of Items 6, 7, 9, and 10. The analysis begins with reading the data and the corresponding variable labels, available from within the `lessR` package.

Mach IV Deceit scale, Listing 11.10, p. 273

variable labels, Section 2.4, p. 45

```
> mydata <- Read("Mach4", format="lessR")
```

In the context of the analysis of Machiavellianism, the four Deceit items are reverse scored. Each item is written such that agreement implies the endorsement of honesty, yet a Machiavellian would endorse a dishonest perspective. The following `Recode` and `Transform` statements reverse score the items and then calculate a Deceit score for each respondent, which is an average of the four constituent items.

Transform function, Section 3.3.1, p. 56

```
> mydata <- Recode(c(m06,m07,m09,m10), old=0:5, new=5:0)
> mydata <- Transform(Deceit = (m06 + m07 + m09 + m10)/4)
```

The values of the categorical variable Gender in this data table are encoded as integers, with 0 for Male and 1 for Female. To enhance the readability of the output, the following `Transform` statement invokes the `R factor` function to redefine Gender as a categorical variable with new values of `M` and `F`.

factor function, Section 3.3.2, p. 59

```
> mydata <- Transform(Gender =
        factor(Gender, levels=c(0,1), labels=c("M","F")))
```

Now consider a specific comparison of group means.

Scenario *Compare the means of two distinct groups*
Do men and women tend to differ regarding their endorsement of Deceit? Compare the responses of men and women on the Mach IV subscale Deceit.

ttest function: Applies to the analysis of the mean difference between two groups.

response variable: The continuous variable compared across the two groups.

grouping variable: The categorical variable with two unique values that defines group membership.

To compare men's and women's Deceit scores, invoke the independent groups *t*-test, with the lessR function ttest, or its abbreviation, tt. A form of the test is also available that provides an abbreviated output. To invoke this form, either specify brief=TRUE or the abbreviation tt.brief.

This comparison between the means of the two groups involves two different variables. Compare the *response variable* across the groups, here Deceit. The *grouping variable*, Gender, consists of two values, M and F.

The need for inferential analysis is that the sample means for each group will always differ, even *if* the null hypothesis of equal population means is true. The issue is if the sample means are so far apart that the null hypothesis of equality becomes untenable. To invoke ttest use the standard R formula, which is the response variable name, followed by a tilde, ~ , and here, the name of the grouping variable.

lessR Input *Independent groups t-test for the mean difference*

```
> ttest(Deceit ~ Gender)
```

The null hypothesis is that the two population means are equal, average Deceit is the same for Males and Females. Because the analysis focuses directly on the mean difference, express the null hypothesis as zero difference between the means.

$$H_0 : \mu_M - \mu_F = 0$$

alternative option, Section 6.2.2, p. 126

alternative option: Specify a one- or two-tailed test.

By default the test is two-tailed so as to evaluate differences in either direction. To change to a one-tailed test, change the default value of alternative="two.sided" to either "less" or "greater".

The default output of ttest includes the following topics: Description, Assumptions, Inference, and Effect Size. The first part of the output of ttest is the description of the sample results upon which the test is based, the sample size, mean and standard deviation for each group, and the number of missing data values, if any. This output is shown in Listing 6.7.

```
Compare Deceit across Gender levels M and F
------------------------------------------------------------

------ Description ------

Deceit for Gender M:   n.miss = 0,   n = 119,   mean = 1.588,   sd = 0.922
Deceit for Gender F:   n.miss = 0,   n = 232,   mean = 1.430,   sd = 0.970

Within-group Standard Deviation:    0.954
```

Listing 6.7 Descriptive statistics.

The within-group standard deviation is a kind of average of the two separate standard deviations for each group, here of the Deceit scores. The variance is the square of the standard deviation. The two variances are calculated as a weighted average, with the weights based on the two potentially different sample sizes so that the variance from the larger sample is given more weight. The square root of the resulting average is the within-group standard deviation, which is used in some of the following computations.

The *t*-test makes several assumptions, evaluated in Listing 6.8.

```
------ Assumptions ------

Null hypothesis, for each group, is a normal distribution of Deceit.
Group M: Sample mean is normal because n>30, so no test needed.
Group F: Sample mean is normal because n>30, so no test needed.

Null hypothesis is equal variances of Deceit, i.e., homogeneous.
Variance Ratio test:   F = 0.941/0.850 = 1.106,   df = 231;118,
                  p-value = 0.542
Levene's test, Brown-Forsythe:   t = 0.869,   df = 349,   p-value = 0.385
```

Listing 6.8 Evaluation of underling assumptions.

First, the sample mean of each sample must be normally distributed over the usually hypothetical multiple samples, a condition generally satisfied by the central limit theorem if the sample sizes are 30 or more. If this sample size is not specified for one or both of the samples, then normality tests are run.

Second, the classic *t*-test assumes that the population variances of the response variable, Deceit, are equal for the two groups, even though the test is if the population means are equal. Fulfillment of this assumption is not so crucial unless at least one of the samples sizes is small, perhaps 20 or less. There is no precise test of this assumption because the available hypothesis tests of this assumption do not perform well in small samples, which is the primary situation that the assumption need be formally evaluated.

Two hypothesis tests of the equality of variances for the two groups are provided. The first is the *variance ratio test*, literally the ratio of the two sample variances, the squared standard deviations. The variance ratio is an *F*-value. The second test is the *Brown–Forsythe version of Levene's test*. To perform this test, deviate each data value from its respective group median. Then perform a *t*-test on the two sets of deviated data values. If the difference is significant, consider the population variances unequal.

From Listing 6.8 the *p*-value of both equal variance hypothesis tests is larger than $\alpha = 0.05$. Accordingly, the null hypothesis of equal variances of Deceit for men and women cannot be rejected, and, while not proved, is shown to be consistent with the data. So proceed with the remainder of the analysis.

The first inference analysis, in Listing 6.9, is that of the classic *t*-test with the apparently correct assumption of equal population variances.

The degrees of freedom for this test, *df* = 349, is the sample size, 351, minus two, one for each group mean. The inferential analysis follows from the *standard error of the mean difference*, the standard deviation of the sample mean difference over the many hypothetical samples from the populations for the two different groups. In this example the standard error of the mean

assess normality assumptions, Section 6.15, p. 140

variance ratio, Brown–Forsythe tests: Evaluate equal population variances.

***p*-value**: Given equal population group means, the probability of a result as or more deviant in either direction than the sample result.

```
------ Inference ------

--- Assume equal population variances of Deceit for each Gender

t-cutoff: tcut =  1.967
Standard Error of Mean Difference: SE =  0.108

Hypothesis Test of 0 Mean Diff:  t = 1.471,  df = 349,  p-value = 0.142

Margin of Error for 95% Confidence Level:  0.212
95% Confidence Interval for Mean Difference:  -0.053 to 0.370
```

Listing 6.9 Inference for the classic *t*-test.

t-value of the mean difference: Estimated standard errors that separate the sample mean difference from the hypothesized mean difference.

conf.level option: Specify the confidence level.

difference is 0.108, considerably less than the standard deviation of the data for the response variable, 0.922 and 0.970, for the two samples, respectively.

The observed sample mean difference of 0.158, shown later in Listing 6.11, is $t = 1.471$ estimated standard errors from the null hypothesized mean difference of 0. If the null hypothesis of no population mean difference is true, then the probability of obtaining a sample mean difference that deviant or more from zero, in either direction, is given by the *p*-value of 0.142.

The 95% confidence interval of the mean difference is from -0.053 to 0.370, which crosses the boundary value of 0, so no difference is plausible. The default value for the confidence level is 95%, explicitly requested by setting `conf.level=0.95`. To change the confidence level, explicitly change the default value of `conf.level`.

Listing 6.10 presents the second inference analysis, which does *not* assume equal variances. Here, the variance of the response in each group is separately used to calculate the estimated standard error of the mean difference. In general it is better to make fewer assumptions. The problem, however, of using the variances separately is that the distribution of the resulting test statistic, the difference between sample means divided by the estimated standard error, only approximately follows the *t*-distribution. To compensate, there is a rather formidable expression that approximates the degrees of freedom, generally with non-integer values, here $df = 248.978$.

```
--- Do not assume equal population variances of Deceit for each Gender

t-cutoff: tcut =  1.970
Standard Error of Mean Difference: SE =  0.106

Hypothesis Test of 0 Mean Diff:  t = 1.496,  df = 248.978, p-value = 0.136

Margin of Error for 95% Confidence Level:  0.208
95% Confidence Interval for Mean Difference:  -0.050 to 0.367
```

Listing 6.10 Inference for the *t*-test that does not assume equal variances.

Which version of the *t*-test is preferred? Most researchers employ the classic *t*-test, which assumes equal variances. Precise guidelines are lacking, but the exception would be if at least one sample is small, and/or the group variances are quite different from each other. In that situation, not assuming equal variances may be the preferred alternative. In most situations the two versions of the test of the mean difference provide the same general result.

The concept of effect size was presented for a single sample analysis. Here the concept of *effect size* extends to two samples. Again, the *p*-value does not provide information regarding the extent of the difference between the population means. In most contexts, if a difference in means is detected, the natural follow-up question is how much?

The sample mean difference provides the sample estimate of effect size in terms of the original measurement units. The confidence interval provides the corresponding estimate in terms of the population. As with the single sample analysis, the mean difference can be standardized, providing the *standardized mean difference*, or *smd*, also called Cohen's *d* (Cohen, 1969). To standardize the mean difference divide it by the standard deviation of the data across the two separate groups, the within-group standard deviation, $s_w = 0.954$.

```
------ Effect Size ------

--- Assume equal population variances of Deceit for each Gender

Sample Mean Difference of Deceit:   0.158
Standardized Mean Difference of Deceit, Cohen's d:   0.166

95% Confidence Interval for smd:   -0.056 to 0.387
```

Listing 6.11 Effect size for the mean difference.

The value of *smd* for this sample is small. Less than 0.16 standard deviations separate the means for Men and Women's endorsement of Deceit in these samples. To estimate the value of *smd* in the population, the confidence interval for *smd* is obtained from a function (ci.smd) in Ken Kelley's MBESS package (Kelley & Lai, 2012), automatically downloaded with lessR. In the population, the corresponding 95% confidence interval ranges from −0.056 to 0.387. This indicates that the true value of *smd* may be as large as 0.387, but the interval also includes the value of 0, which indicates that no difference between the groups may exist.

The effect size can be best illustrated with the resulting graph of the overlapping distributions of endorsement of Deceit for Males and Females. This graph in Figure 6.3 directly demonstrates the extent of the overlap of the two distributions. This graph explicitly labels the mean difference and the standardized mean difference.

The small size of the standardized mean difference of 0.166 is apparent in the resulting graph. For this data set, there is a slight tendency for Males, on average, to endorse Deceit more than Females, but the result is not statistically significant, nor substantively large. No difference in endorsement of Deceit is detected for Males and Females. It may be that some difference in the average level of Deceit exists that this analysis failed to detect. Even so, if the difference does exist, it is likely to be small, of little or no practical importance.

6.3.3 The Non-parametric Alternative to Compare Two Groups

Parametric tests such as the *t*-test involve the estimation of parameters, such as from the assumption of a normal distribution. A *non-parametric test* of two samples does not compare parameter estimates, but rather compares the entire distributions from which the samples are obtained. A parametric test relies upon reasonably strong assumptions regarding the underlying distributions, such as the assumption of normality. A primary advantage of a non-parametric test is that it relaxes those assumptions.

---

effect size
Section 6.2.2, p. 126

effect size of the mean difference: The magnitude of the difference between the sample means for a null value of 0.

standardized mean difference: Standardized effect size for the mean difference.

within-group standard deviation, Section 6.7, p. 132

no significant difference: The conclusion is no difference detected, *not that* there is no difference.

non-parametric test: Inference without strong distributional assumptions.

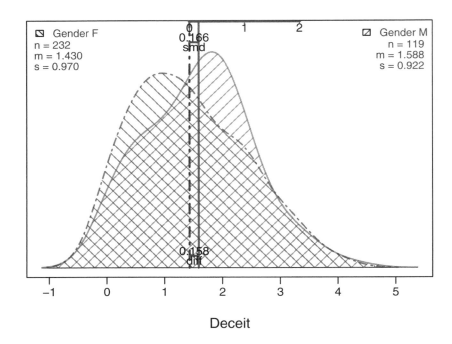

Figure 6.3 Density curves for Males and Females on Mach IV subscale Deceit.

Wilcoxon rank sum test: Non-parametric test from two independent samples that compares the corresponding population distributions.

The non-parametric test for two independent groups, the analogue of the independent groups *t*-test, is the two-sample *Wilcoxon rank sum test*. The test is equivalent to a related non-parametric test that compares two independent samples, the Mann–Whitney U-test. Either test gives exactly the same results.

The null hypothesis of the two-sample Wilcoxon rank sum test is that the two corresponding populations have the same continuous distribution. The alternative hypothesis is that one distribution is shifted to the right of the other distribution. The alternative hypothesis is that the values of one distribution are systematically larger or smaller than the value of the other distribution, though there still could be considerable overlap.

The two-sample Wilcoxon rank sum test requires the assumption of independent random samples, but the more stringent assumption of normality is dropped. Instead, the assumption is that the two distributions have the same shape, even if skewed. If the two distributions are of the same shape, but one is shifted to the right or left of the other, then the medians of the two distributions differ. This conclusion also applies to any cutpoint of the distributions other than the median, such as the third quartile. The test is not about the medians per se, but about the relative location of the distributions to each other. If the distributions are skewed, the mean is not the indicator of choice for non-parametric tests because its value is affected disproportionally by the skew.

As is typical of non-parametric group comparisons, the Wilcoxon rank sum test is based solely on the order of the data values from the two samples, the ranks. The transformation to ranks retains only the ordering of the data values, with no further consideration of their numerical values, and a diminished influence of extreme values of the distributions. The test is conducted by ordering all the values of both groups together. Each data value in this combined distribution has a rank, beginning with 1 for the smallest data value. The sum of all the ranks for the smaller of the two samples is the Wilcoxon rank-sum test statistic, *W*.

The R function for the Wilcoxon rank sum test is `wilcox.test`, illustrated here for the comparison of endorsement of Deceit for men and women. This is a standard R test, not modified through the lens of `lessR`. To inform R that the variables are in the `mydata` data frame, either place a `mydata$` in front of each variable name, or use the `with` function.

 R Input *Independent groups Wilcox rank sum test*

```
> with(mydata, wilcox.test(Deceit ~ Gender, conf.int=TRUE))
```

The same `conf.level` and `alternative` options from the `ttest` function apply to the `wilcox.test`. As with the `ttest`, the respective default values are 0.95 and `"two.sided"`. The confidence interval itself, however, must be explicitly requested.

The output of the two-sided test with the requested 95% confidence interval appears in Listing 6.12.

```
    Wilcoxon rank sum test with continuity correction

data:  Deceit by Gender
W = 15327, p-value = 0.08963
alternative hypothesis: true location shift is not equal to 0
95 percent confidence interval:
 -0.00001932667  0.49991749068
sample estimates:
difference in location
        0.2499937
```

Listing 6.12 R output from the two-sample Wilcoxon rank sum test.

To calculate the *p*-value, assuming the truth of the null hypothesis, requires knowledge of the distribution of the rank sum W over many usually hypothetical repeated samples. Probabilities from this distribution are expressed as the *p*-value. If the null hypothesis of no difference in the distributions of Males and Females for Deceit is true, then the obtained *p*-value of 0.090 indicates that the result is not sufficiently improbable to reject the null.

When requested with `conf.int=TRUE`, the output of `wilcox.test` also includes an estimate of the difference in location of the two distributions, as well as the corresponding confidence interval. The "location" does not refer to the median of the original data values, but rather to the following transformation. Calculate the difference between all possible pairs of the data values in the two groups. Then rank order this list of differences. The median of interest is the median of this list of sorted differences, about which the confidence interval is constructed.

The qualitative pattern of the results of the parametric independent groups *t*-test and the non-parametric Wilcoxon test are similar. For both tests, no difference in endorsement of Deceit is detected comparing Males and Females. The location difference from the Wilcoxon test of 0.25 is somewhat larger than the sample mean difference of 0.16, but in the same direction. The confidence intervals are from −0.05 to 0.37 for the mean difference and from −0.00002 to 0.50 for the location parameter in the Wilcoxon test. The mean difference and the location parameter are different statistics, so they are not expected to provide the same numerical result, especially for skewed distributions.

wilcox.test function: R function for the Wilcoxon rank sum test.

alternative option for a one-tailed test, Section 6.2.2, p. 126

conf.level option, Section 6.3.2, p. 134

6.3.4 Example 2: An Experiment

When studying for an exam there are two strategies by which to distribute study time. One strategy psychologists call distributed practice, in which the student distributes his or her study time over many relatively short study sessions. The alternative is mass practice with just one or two much longer study sessions. Students often informally refer to mass practice as "cramming" for an exam. According to the results of many research studies, distributed practice is the superior study technique for meaningful, long-term learning. Massed practice may succeed to some extent at fostering rote learning, which is quickly forgotten, but little else.

random assignment: Randomly assign participants to experimental groups.

To establish a baseline response before beginning a more extensive series of studies on distributed vs. massed practice, a researcher conducted the following experiment to compare the two learning strategies. Half of the participants were *randomly assigned* to the distributed practice condition, in which they studied in four 30-minute sessions. The other participants were randomly assigned to the mass practice condition in which their study time consisted of a single two hour session. Participants learned facts and information about a geographical region about which they likely knew little before the study began, a remote area in Indonesia.

The purpose of random assignment is to ensure that there are no systematic differences between two (or more) groups of participants on any variable. The two groups of participants should be equivalent on all variables so that all observed differences between the groups are due only to random sampling error. Then, after obtaining equivalence, the researcher administered the treatment condition. The researcher deliberately and systematically *manipulates* the local environment for the two groups of people. The experimenter controls the environment of the participants, so that some students experience distributed practice and the others experience massed practice. With random assignment followed by manipulation this study is a true *experiment*.

manipulation: Impose a treatment condition on the participants.

experiment: Random assignment to different groups followed by manipulation.

treatment variable: Variable manipulated to yield a different value for each group.

The variable manipulated across the defined groups, Number of Study Sessions, is the *treatment variable*, sometimes called the independent variable. In some contexts the treatment variable is instead called the grouping variable, particularly if the samples are drawn from pre-existing groups in place of random assignment. Gender, for example, cannot be randomly assigned. The *response variable* or dependent variable in an experimental study is measured and compared across the groups. In this study the response variable is the test Score to assess learning.

response variable: Measured variable compared across experimental groups.

The result of random assignment followed by manipulation is *experimental control*. Because the two (or more) groups differ only on one variable, the treatment variable, any difference in the response variable across the two groups can be explained by the different levels of the treatment variable. Is the difference in amount learned in the randomly assigned distributed and massed practice groups large enough to achieve statistical significance? If so, this difference can be attributed to the treatment variable, the type of study procedure.

experimental control: Two or more groups differ only on the value of the treatment variable.

confounding variable: Variable that causes changes in the response variable that is not the treatment variable.

Without some type of control the influence of other potentially influential variables, called *confounding variables*, cannot be assessed. Differences in the response variable across the two groups may be due to differences in the treatment variable, or to a confounding variable. For example, suppose the distributed practice group consisted only of men, or that the study sessions for this group occurred only in the early morning. Suppose the massed practice group consisted only of women, or the study sessions occurred only late at night. Then any difference in Learning across the two groups might be due to Type of Study, or perhaps instead due to gender or to time of day. A difference may have been observed, but in the absence of controls, the reason for this difference is not known.

The experiment is by far the most effective procedure to demonstrate a *causal relation*, that is, cause and effect. With random assignment and manipulation the researcher is reasonably well assured that there is only one variable that differentiates the experimental groups, the treatment variable. Then if the values of the response variable systematically tend to differ between the groups, such as by the group means, the treatment variable would appear to be the cause of the difference.

causal relation: A change in the value of one variable leads to a change in the value of another variable, with all other variables held constant.

 Scenario *Analyze the experimental results of Study Type on Learning*
Randomly assign participants to either a distributed or massed practice study type. When the study sessions are completed, administer a test to assess learning. Then examine any potential differences in the mean amount of material learned.

First read the data table, also available from within the `lessR` package called `Learn`.

```
> mydata <- Read("Learn", format="lessR")
```

An excerpt of the data, as it exists in the data frame `mydata`, is shown in Listing 6.13, with the variables StudyType and Score.

```
> mydata
    StudyType Score
1        Many    87
2         One    74
...
33        One    88
34       Many    93
```

Listing 6.13 First and last rows of data for the Learn data set.

The analysis is of learning, assessed by the response variable, test Score, for each value of the grouping variable, StudyType. Specify the analysis with the `ttest` function according to an R formula.

formula, Section 4.4.2, p. 96

```
> ttest(Score ~ StudyType)
```

The formula specifies that the value of the response variable, Score, depends on the value of the grouping variable, StudyType. Because this is a true experiment, the grouping variable is a treatment variable.

Listing 6.14 presents the first section of the output, the descriptive statistics for the two types of study sessions. For this set of samples the students in the distributed study sessions had higher average test scores than those students who only had one study session. The respective test scores are 87.58% and 81.27%. Now the question is whether this sample difference generalizes to the population so that the effect exists beyond the extent of sampling error.

To proceed with inference first requires verifying the assumptions upon which the analysis depends, normality of the sample mean difference over usually hypothetical repeated samples, and equality of population variances of the response variable in both groups. Listing 6.15

assumptions of the t-test, Section 6.8, p. 133

```
Compare Score across StudyType levels Many and One
---------------------------------------------------------

------ Description ------

Score for StudyType Many:  n.miss = 0,  n = 19,  mean = 87.58,  sd = 8.10
Score for StudyType One:   n.miss = 0,  n = 15,  mean = 81.27,  sd = 8.75
```

Listing 6.14 Descriptive statistics for the test score for each type of study sessions.

provides the evidence that both assumptions are tenable given the high p-values of the corresponding tests. Neither the null hypothesis of the normality of Scores for each group, nor the null hypothesis of equal variances, is rejected.

```
------ Assumptions ------

Null hypothesis, for each group, is a normal distribution of Score.
Group Many  Shapiro-Wilk normality test:  W = 0.960,  p-value = 0.567
Group One   Shapiro-Wilk normality test:  W = 0.898,  p-value = 0.090

Null hypothesis is equal variances of Score, i.e., homogeneous.
Variance Ratio test:  F = 76.50/65.59 = 1.17,  df = 14;18,  p-value = 0.747
Levene's test, Brown-Forsythe:  t = -0.347,  df = 32,  p-value = 0.731
```

Listing 6.15 Evaluation of normality and equal variance assumptions for amount learned depending on type of study.

The inferential analysis appears in Listing 6.16.

```
------ Inference ------

Hypothesis Test of 0 Mean Diff:  t = 2.179,  df = 32,  p-value = 0.037

Margin of Error for 95% Confidence Level:  5.90
95% Confidence Interval for Mean Difference:  0.41 to 12.21
```

Listing 6.16 Inference for amount learned depending on type of study.

The basic result of the analysis is to reject the null hypothesis of equal population means.

Type of Learning Effect: p-value $= 0.039 < \alpha = 0.05$, so reject H_0

If the value of the true mean difference is not 0, what is it? According to the confidence interval, we are 95% confident that the true mean difference is larger than 0, from 0.33 to 12.29.

The effect size in Listing 6.17 indicates that the mean test score for the distributed practice condition is 0.75 standard deviations larger than the mean for the massed practice condition. This represents a large effect according to Cohen (1969), indicating a prominent separation of the distributions.

```
------ Effect Size ------

Sample Mean Difference of Score:   6.31
Standardized Mean Difference of Score, Cohen's d:   0.75

95% Confidence Interval for smd:   0.05 to 1.45
```

Listing 6.17 Effect size for amount learned depending on type of study, assuming equal population variances of test scores.

This shift of the distribution of the distributed practice test scores 3/4 of a standard deviation to the right of the distribution of massed practice test scores is illustrated in Figure 6.4. This graph is part of the standard output of `ttest`.

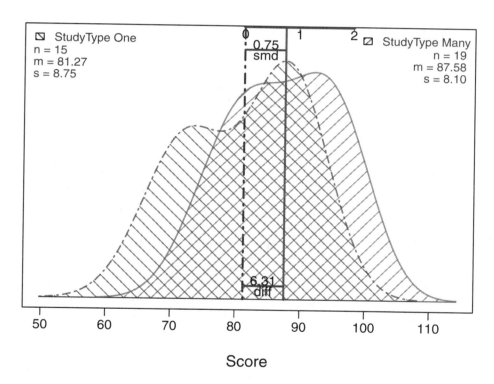

Figure 6.4 Density curves for distributed practice vs. massed practice on test Score.

We conclude that a true difference in learning exists between distributed and massed practice. According to the 95% confidence interval, the true average test score for distributed practice is from 0.33% to 12.29% larger than for the massed practice condition. The standardized mean difference for the sample data indicates that this is a separation of 0.75 standard deviations. Because the data were collected in the context of an experiment, with random assignment to treatment conditions and manipulation, the difference can be attributed directly to the type of studying. Distributed practice is shown to be more effective.

6.4 Compare Dependent Samples

The independent groups *t*-test discussed in the previous section compares the means of samples from two different groups. The groups are independent. The samples are drawn independently from each other, and there is no linkage between any specific data value in one sample with a specific data value in another sample. The analysis depends only on the means themselves, and also the two sample sizes and two sample standard deviations.

6.4.1 Dependent-samples *t*-test

block of matched data values: Match a data value to a data value in another sample.

dependent-samples: Two or more samples are organized in blocks of matched data values.

The alternative to independent groups is to collect the data in *blocks* of matched data values. The samples, then, are necessarily the same size. A *dependent-samples* design organizes data into these blocks. A block could be the data values of the same person before training and after training, or a block could consist of happiness measures from two different people, a husband and a wife, in a study of marital happiness.

A classic example of a dependent-samples design applies to treatments such as a therapy for depression or a program for weight loss. For weight loss, measure weight before the treatment program begins. Administer the program, and then re-assess the weight of each participant. The results are samples of two sets of measurements with each measurement from the first sample linked to the same person's measurement in the second sample.

dependent groups *t*-test: A *t*-test of the difference scores of the matched data values.

As with the independent groups design, there are still two sets of measurements with two sample means and two sample standard deviations. That is, the independent groups *t*-test could still be employed to analyze the mean difference for these two samples of data. The *t*-test for the dependent groups design, however, directly compares the matched scores, usually by subtracting one from the other. The analysis is not of the two means, but the mean of the differences of the two scores. For the pre- and post-measurements for a treatment program, the change in each person's score is analyzed directly, person-by-person.

power of a test: The ability to detect a real population difference.

The analysis of the direct differences can yield a more powerful test than the comparison of the overall means. A test with more *power* is more likely to detect a population difference that actually exists than a test with less power. The dependent-samples test is more powerful when the variable of interest, such as weight, exhibits much variability among the participants. Some people do initially weigh more than others. In an independent-groups analysis these variations in weight contribute to the variability within each sample of measured weights, which then masks the ability of the test to differentiate between the means. The dependent-groups analysis removes this variability of the participant's initial weights from the analysis. The focus shifts from the weights to a direct assessment of weight loss.

 Scenario *Evaluate the effectiveness of a weight loss program*
Ten people who desired to lose weight participated in a weight loss program with measurements of their weight before and after the program. Was the program effective, and, if so, how effective?

row.names option, Section 2.2.6, p. 37

The first task is to read the data. The name of each participant is in the first column, so these are identified as the row names for the `mydata` data frame.

```
> mydata <- Read("http://lessRstats.com/data/WeightLoss.csv",
                 row.names=1)
```

View all the data by entering the name of the data frame, `mydata`, illustrated in Figure 6.18.

```
> mydata
               Before After
Saechao, M.       220    206
Smith, D.         187    189
...
Jones, S.         298    291
Langston, M.      174    164
```

Listing 6.18 Weight before and after a weight loss program, in pounds, for the first few and last few blocks of data.

The analysis is of the difference between the Before and After weight for each participant. The null hypothesis is that, on average, there is no change from before and after the program. One way to accomplish the analysis is first to calculate these differences with the `Transform` function and do the usual one-sample *t*-test on the difference scores. The analysis can also be done directly by listing the two variables, in this case Before and After, and then specifying the option `paired` set to `TRUE`.

One-sample t-test, Section 6.2.2, p. 126

paired=TRUE option: Specify a dependent-groups t-test.

> ✒ **lessR Input** *Dependent-groups t-test*

```
> ttest(Before, After, paired=TRUE)
```

Specify the test as a two-tailed test even though the advocates of the weight loss program prefer to see a rejection of the null hypothesis in the direction of weight loss. Given this desire for a specific outcome, some authors recommend a one-tailed test, here with the value of `alternative` set to `"greater"`. However, setting a one-tailed test rules out any interpretation of results in the opposite direction. If the null hypothesis is not rejected, then the only conclusion is that the population mean difference is not greater than 0, even if the program had the opposite result than intended and actually leads to weight gain.

Yes, it would be somewhat strange for a weight loss program to result in weight gain, but sometimes our best intentions lead to results different from what we expect. Accordingly two-tailed tests are generally more appropriate unless there genuinely is no interest in a result that lies in the tail opposite the tail of a one-tailed rejection region. So the following test is run with the rejection region in both tails.

one-tailed test example, Section 6.23, p. 147

The descriptive statistics in Listing 6.19 indicate that the mean weight loss for these 10 participants is 8.20 pounds.

```
------ Description ------

Difference:  n.miss = 0,  n = 10,   mean = 8.20,  sd = 7.67
```

Listing 6.19 Descriptive statistics of the differences.

The normality assumption is assessed in Listing 6.20. The null hypothesis is that the population of difference scores from which these 10 scores were sampled is normal. This null hypothesis was not rejected as the resulting p-value of 0.573 is larger than $\alpha = 0.05$. As previously indicated, this test may not perform well in small samples, but at least the result is consistent with the assumption of normality.

```
------ Normality Assumption ------

Null hypothesis is a normal distribution of Difference.
Shapiro-Wilk normality test:  W = 0.939,  p-value = 0.541
```

Listing 6.20 Evaluation of the normality of the differences.

Listing 6.21 presents the inferential analysis, the hypothesis test and the confidence interval of the difference scores. The hypothesis test indicates that the population mean value of 0 is rejected.

$$\text{Weight Loss Effect: } p\text{-value} = 0.008 < \alpha = 0.05, \text{ so reject } H_0$$

The mean value of the differences is likely not zero, so what is it? There is no precise answer, but the 95% confidence interval indicates that the plausible range of values of the population mean indicates that the average weight loss for all participants is from 2.71 to 13.69 pounds.

```
------ Inference ------

t-cutoff: tcut =  2.262
Standard Error of Mean: SE =  2.43

Hypothesized Value H0: mu = 0
Hypothesis Test of Mean:  t-value = 3.380,  df = 9,  p-value = 0.008

Margin of Error for 95% Confidence Level:  5.49
95% Confidence Interval for Mean:  2.71 to 13.69
```

Listing 6.21 Inference of the mean population difference.

The plot of the data and the displacement of the sample mean of the differences of 8.20 are illustrated in Figure 6.5. Also illustrated is the displacement in terms of Cohen's d, which indicates that the sample mean of the differences is more than 1 standard deviation from zero.

The weight loss program appears to be effective. Most participants lose weight, and the average weight loss is somewhere between 2.7 and 13.7 pounds.

6.4.2 The Non-parametric Alternative for Dependent Samples

Just as the dependent-groups t-test directly analyzed the difference scores of matched data values with a one-sample test, so does the non-parametric alternative. This non-parametric alternative to the one-sample t-test is the *Wilcoxon signed rank test*. This test is first discussed in this section

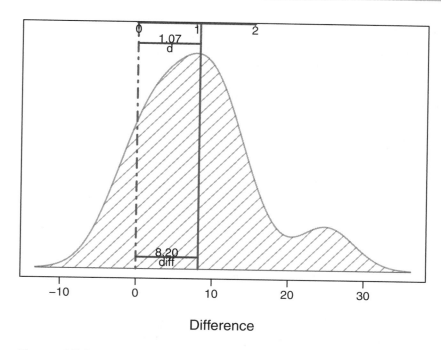

Figure 6.5 Density plot of the differences of weight loss, in pounds.

instead of the section on the one-sample *t*-test because the Wilcoxon test is most commonly applied to the analysis of difference scores.

To illustrate, return to the weight loss data in Listing 6.18, and the corresponding difference scores. The Wilcoxon test compares the size of the positive differences, in this case, weight loss, with the size of the negative differences, here, weight gain. Order the absolute values of the differences from smallest to largest. If weight loss predominates, then the size of the weight loss values should be larger than for the weight gain values. The test assesses the position of these weight losses in the overall distribution of ordered absolute value of differences scores. The basis of the test is the Wilcoxon signed rank statistic, the sum of the ranks of the positive differences.

Specify the Wilcoxon signed rank test for the analysis of a single variable with the same `wilcox.test` function that compares two independent samples. In this situation the difference of weight before and after the treatment program is the basis of the test. Again, since this is a standard R function, use the `with` function to inform R as to the location of the variable for analysis, here in the `mydata` data frame.

Wilcoxon rank sum test, Section 6.3.3, p. 135

The default value for the confidence level is 95%. The interval must be explicitly requested by setting `conf.int=TRUE`. To change the confidence level, explicitly change the default value of `conf.level=0.95`.

conf.level option, Section 6.3.2, p. 134

Also, by default the test is two-tailed to evaluate differences in either direction, regardless of what the desired direction. To change to a one-tailed test, change the default value of `alternative="two.sided"` to either `"less"` or `"greater"`.

alternative option for a one-tailed test, Section 6.2.2, p. 126

The null hypothesis is that there is no systematic difference within the matched data values for the two samples. The alternative hypothesis is that there is a systematic difference. For the default two-tailed test, the difference could be in either direction.

The test is run as the difference between matched data values implicitly calculated. Just specify the two variables that define the two matched samples, and include the `paired=TRUE` option, which informs R to analyze the difference between the corresponding data values.

paired *option: Set to TRUE to inform R to calculate and analyze a difference.*

✒ **R Input** *Wilcoxon signed rank test with implied Difference score*

```
> with(mydata, wilcox.test(Before, After, paired=TRUE,
        conf.int=TRUE))
```

The output is given in Listing 6.22.

```
    Wilcoxon signed rank test

data:  Difference
V = 53, p-value = 0.005859
alternative hypothesis: true location is not equal to 0
95 percent confidence interval:
  3 14
sample estimates:
(pseudo)median
          7.5
```

Listing 6.22 Output from the R function `wilcox.test` for analysis of a single variable.

From the output, reject the null hypothesis of no difference of Weight in the Before and After samples.

$$\texttt{Weight Loss Effect: } p\texttt{-value} < \alpha = 0.05$$

The sample estimate is of the (pseudo) median, a concept similar to, but not exactly equal to, the actual sample median. The 95% confidence interval ranges from 3 to 14 of these (pseudo) medians. These values are close to the lower and upper bounds of the confidence interval of the true mean of the difference scores, which are 2.71 pounds and 13.69 pounds.

These results follow from the two-tailed test, in which the mean of the differences in either the positive or the negative direction is interpreted. Some researchers prefer a one-tailed test when an outcome is predicted in a specified direction. For this example, a positive mean of the differences indicates a successful weight loss program. Carry out the one-tailed test to predict a positive difference by adding `alternative="greater"` to the function call to `wilcox.test`.

*one-tailed
alternative option,
Section 6.2.2,
p. 126*

✒ **R Input** *Wilcoxon signed rank test for a one-tailed test*

```
> with(mydata, wilcox.test(Before, After, paired=TRUE,
        conf.int=TRUE, alternative="greater"))
```

The result of this one-tailed analysis is given in Listing 6.23.

one-tailed test
results: The *p*-value
is half the size of
the two-tailed test,
and the confidence
interval is
one-sided.

The *p*-value of the one-tailed test is exactly half the size compared to that of the two-tailed test, and the confidence interval is one-sided. The smaller *p*-value makes the test more powerful in finding a difference from the null value that is real, because the one-tailed test might achieve a *p*-value less than 0.05 when the two-tailed version might not. That gain in efficiency is offset by not being able to conclude the opposite if the result is the opposite of what was intended.

```
    Wilcoxon signed rank test

data:  Difference
V = 53, p-value = 0.00293
alternative hypothesis: true location is greater than 0
95 percent confidence interval:
 3.5 Inf
sample estimates:
(pseudo)median
         7.5
```

Listing 6.23 Directional, one-tailed Wilcoxon signed rank test.

Moreover, the sample estimate, the (pseudo) median, could be an under or over estimate of the true value, a result more consistent with the concept of the standard confidence interval with both an upper and lower bound.

The conclusion from both the parametric t-test and the non-parametric `wilcox.test` dependent-samples analyses is that the weight loss program does appear to facilitate weight loss, likely somewhere between about 3 and 14 pounds.

Worked Problems

Answer the following questions in terms of the hypothesis test, confidence interval, and effect size.

1 Consider the Employee data set, available from within the `lessR` package.

?Employee for more information.

```
> mydata <- Read("Employee", format="lessR")
```

Two of the variables in this data set are Salary and Gender for employees at a specific company.

(a) Is it reasonable that the true mean Salary is $75,000?

(b) Are mean Salaries the same for men and women at this company? Answer with a parametric and a non-parametric procedure.

2 Consider the Cars93 data set, available from within the `lessR` package.

?Cars93 for more information.

```
> mydata <- Read("Cars93", format="lessR")
```

Some of the variables in this data set are MPGcity, MPGhiway, and Manual, a binary variable with a value of 1 for a manual transmission and a 0 for an automatic.

(a) Is it reasonable that the true mean city MPG is 22?

(b) Is city fuel mileage the same, on average, for cars with manual transmissions and cars with automatic transmissions? Answer with a parametric and a non-parametric procedure.

(c) Is there a difference in fuel mileage for city and highway driving? Answer with a parametric and a non-parametric procedure.

CHAPTER 7

COMPARE MULTIPLE SAMPLES

7.1 Quick Start

First install R and lessR as explained in Section 1.2. At the beginning of each R session access lessR with library(lessR). Then read your data into an R data frame with Read(), the subject of Chapter 2.

The topic of this chapter is to compare the means of a response variable across two or more groups for one or two different grouping variables. The response variable is also referred to as a dependent variable or an outcome variable. Particularly in the context of an experiment refer to the grouping variable as the treatment variable, factor, or independent variable. This chapter generalizes the *t*-tests for independent-groups and for dependent-groups from the last chapter. The *t*-test applies only to the analysis of two samples. The corresponding analysis for two or more groups, and multiple treatment variables as well, is the analysis of variance, or ANOVA.

experiment, Section 6.3.4, p. 138

A variety of designs for gathering data and their subsequent analysis with ANOVA are given in this chapter. In the following descriptions, Y represents the response variable, X is a treatment variable, and Blocks is the blocking variable.

✓ The one-way ANOVA generalizes the independent-groups *t*-test for two groups to as many groups as specified. Use the lessR function ANOVA for the between-groups, that is, independent-groups, one-way ANOVA of response variable Y evaluated across the levels of treatment variable X.

one-way ANOVA, Section 7.2, p. 150

```
> ANOVA(Y ~ X)
```

✓ ANOVA is a parametric procedure that compares means under the assumption of normality. Non-parametric analyses make less restrictive assumptions. Use the R function kruskal.test for the non-parametric alternative to one-way ANOVA, the Kruskal–Wallis rank sum test.

non-parametric one-way analysis, Section 7.2.7, p. 158

```
> with(mydata, kruskal.test(Y ~ X))
```

✓ Use the lessR function ANOVA to generalize the dependent-groups or within-groups *t*-test for two samples of matched responses to a randomized block ANOVA for as many samples as specified.

randomized Block ANOVA, Section 7.3, p. 158

```
> ANOVA(Y ~ X + Blocks)
```

non-parametric randomized blocks analysis, Section 7.3.6, p. 163

✓ The non-parametric alternative to the randomized blocks ANOVA is the Friedman rank sum test, accomplished with the R function `friedman.test`.

```
> with(mydata, friedman.test(Y ~ X|Blocks))
```

two-way ANOVA, Section 7.4, p. 166

✓ Use the `lessR` function `ANOVA` for the two-way factorial design, which specifies that each between-groups sample is a combination of the levels of the two treatment variables. The corresponding ANOVA provides an analysis of the effect of each treatment variable separately, plus their combined interaction.

```
> ANOVA(Y ~ X1 * X2)
```

randomized block factorial design, Section 7.5.1, p. 173

✓ The randomized block factorial design generalizes the randomized block design to two or more within-group treatment variables. Each effect is analyzed separately by the corresponding ANOVA, as well as the effect of the interaction of the two treatment variables on the response variable. Analyze data from this design directly from the standard R ANOVA function, `aov`, plus related functions.

split-plot factorial design, Section 7.5.2, p. 176

✓ The split-plot factorial design combines the concepts of the independent-groups or between-groups, design, with the dependent-groups or within-groups, randomized block design. One treatment variable is between-groups and the other is within-groups. Again, analyze with the standard R functions such as `aov`.

7.2 One-way ANOVA

Both the independent-groups and dependent-groups *t*-tests compare two samples of data. What if the research design specifies more than two groups to compare? Analysis of Variance, or *ANOVA*, generalizes the *t*-test to as many groups as specified. ANOVA also generalizes beyond a single variable to define the groups, the grouping variable, to analyze the simultaneous effects of multiple grouping variables on the response variable. Some of these more advanced designs are explored in further sections, as well as some non-parametric alternatives.

7.2.1 An Example with Data

For the one-way ANOVA there is one grouping variable that defines the groups. The data values in each group are not linked to the data values recorded for another group. This usually means that there are different people, organizations, laboratory rats, or whatever is the unit of analysis, in the different groups. Such a design is referred to as a between-groups or between-subjects design, or an independent-groups design.

 Scenario *Examine the effects of Dosage on task completion Time*
To what extent does arousal impact the ability to complete a task? To study this question, 24 laboratory rats were randomly and equally divided into three groups of eight, and then given one of three dosages of an arousal inducing drug: 0, 5, and 10 milligrams. Following the dosage, each rat completed a maze to obtain a food reward. The response (dependent) variable is the Time in seconds to complete the maze.

This study is an *experiment*, so the grouping variable in this analysis is a *treatment variable*, Dosage. The *control group* is not exposed to a treatment, here a drug dosage. The experimental groups receive a treatment, here a drug dose of 5 or 10 mg. The measured behavior, data values for the *response variable*, is task completion Time, analyzed across the groups. The one-way analysis of variance compares the means from each of the three samples. The lessR function ANOVA, abbreviated av, provides this analysis.

experiment and related terms, Section 6.3.4, p. 138

7.2.2 Data

First read the data stored as a csv file.

```
> mydata <- Read("http://lessRstats.com/data/anova_1way.csv")
```

Read function, Section 2.2.1, p. 32

Listing 7.1 presents the data table in two forms, encoded as a csv data file in the form read into R, and as the resulting data frame mydata as it exists within R.

```
                          > mydata
mg00,mg05,mg10              mg00 mg05 mg10
25.6,23.4,24.2           1 25.6 23.4 24.2
25.8,21.9,19.0           2 25.8 21.9 19.0
25.5,24.8,16.4           3 25.5 24.8 16.4
23.3,24.0,19.4           4 23.3 24.0 19.4
26.5,28.2,18.5           5 26.5 28.2 18.5
26.0,25.2,20.1           6 26.0 25.2 20.1
18.4,19.0,13.1           7 18.4 19.0 13.1
23.0,20.8,11.9           8 23.0 20.8 11.9
```

Listing 7.1 Data for the Time to complete a task at three different dosages, in the form of a csv data file and as the data frame mydata as read by Read.

The data values in Listing 7.1 demonstrate an issue often encountered in the analysis of experimental data. The data values are *not* in the form of a standard data table in which each row of data is from a single unit, here a laboratory rat, and each column contains all the data values for a single variable. Instead the data table lists the task completion Time values by group in three different columns. Each data value is *not* matched with the other data values in the same row. In this example the columns are all of the same length, but in general there can even be different numbers of participants in each treatment condition. R calls this data form *unstacked* data.

Another issue is that the standard R routine for analysis of variance, aov, upon which ANOVA relies, requires that the data be organized with one data value per row. This organization of a data table is called the *long* form, which contrasts to the more usual *wide* form in which all the data values for a particular unit, such as a person, organization or even laboratory rat, are included in a single row. If there is only one data value per unit, as in this situation, then the wide and long forms of a data table are the same.

The data must first be reshaped into a long form data table, here with the two variables, one for the Dosage and one for task completion Time. R calls this standard data table the *stacked* form because the data values are all stacked on top of each other. The most straightforward way to reshape a data table is to use Hadley Wickam's (2007) reshape2 package.

unstacked data: Groups of data values arranged according to a separate column for each group.

long form data table: One data value per row of data.

wide form data table, Section 1.6.1, p. 21

stacked data: Data in standard data table form.

reshape2 package: Hadley Wickam's package for reshaping a data table into another form.

The `reshape2` function `melt` transforms the data in Listing 7.1 into a stacked, long form data frame. This function "melts" the unstacked data down into its most basic shape, one data value per row of data. The result in this example is a long form data table with two variables, with all the data for each person, one data value, in a single row.

The `melt` function also provides for names of the resulting variables in the reshaped, now stacked data table. The original, unstacked version of the data in Listing 7.1 provides no information regarding the name of the response variable, nor is there a name for the grouping variable, also known in the context of an experiment as the treatment variable. Add the names specific to this analysis to the function call to `melt`. Specify the `value.name` option for the name of the response variable, and the `variable.name` option for the name of the grouping variable.

Because `melt` is from a separate package, first access the package with the `library` function. If not previously installed, then first install the package.

> **melt** function:
> From `reshape2`, unstack grouped data into a data table with one data value per row.
>
> **value.name** melt option: Name the response variable.
>
> **variable.name** melt option: Name the grouping or treatment variable.
> *library* function, Section 1.2, p. 6
>
> *install.packages* function, Section 1.2.3, p. 5
>
> *assignment operator,* Section 1.3.3, p. 9

```
> library(reshape2)
```

The function `melt` does not assume a name for the input data frame, such as `mydata`. To use the function enter the name of the data frame to be reshaped as the first argument in the function call. Assign the result of the reshaped data back to `mydata` with the R *assignment operator*, `<-`.

reshape2 Input *Reshape unstacked data to a standard data table*

```
> mydata <- melt(mydata, value.name="Time",
                 variable.name="Dosage")
```

The result is the data frame `mydata` organized as in Listing 7.2, which shows the first and last rows of the stacked form `mydata`, now a standard data table. Each column heading in the original, unstacked version in Listing 7.1 now becomes a value of the grouping variable in standard data table form.

```
> mydata
   Dosage Time
1    mg00 25.6
2    mg00 25.8
...
23   mg10 13.1
24   mg10 11.9
```

Listing 7.2 Stacked version of the dosage data, which simultaneously represents both the wide form and the long form of the data table.

7.2.3 Descriptive and Inferential Analysis

> **ANOVA** function:
> Includes analysis for one-way ANOVA.

The data frame, with variables task completion Time and Dosage, now is ready for analysis with the `lessR` function `ANOVA`. The syntax is the same as for `ttest`. List the response variable first, followed by the tilde, ~ , and then the treatment or grouping variable that defines the groups.

✒ **lessR Input** *One-way ANOVA*

```
> ANOVA(Time ~ Dosage)
```

The first part of the output describes the model, the variables in the model, the levels of the treatment variable, and the number of rows of data. The descriptive statistics appear next in tabular form, shown in Listing 7.3. The *grand mean* is the mean of all of the data.

grand mean: Mean of all of the data.

```
Descriptive Statistics
----------------------

        n    mean      sd     min      max
mg00    8   24.26    2.69   18.40    26.50
mg05    8   23.41    2.85   19.00    28.20
mg10    8   17.82    3.96   11.90    24.20

Grand Mean: 21.833
```

Listing 7.3 Descriptive statistics for each group of task completion Time data.

Figure 7.3 provides a scatter plot of the individual data values as well as the group means, plotted as diamonds. A horizontal line drawn through each plotted group mean enhances the comparison of the means. The mean of task completion Time for the group with the largest amount of dosage, 10 mg, is 17.82, quite a bit smaller than the remaining two means.

The ANOVA function automatically generates Listing 7.3 and Figure 7.1, which describe the task completion Times from for the three drug Dosage samples. This information can also be

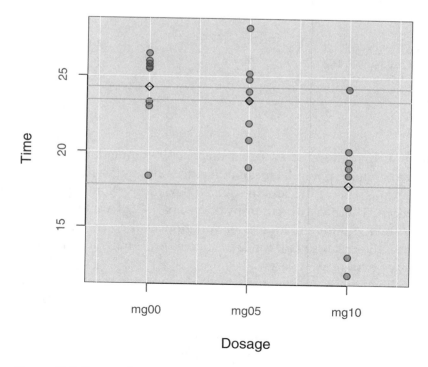

Figure 7.1 Scatter plot and means for each group of task completion Time data.

generated apart from the ANOVA function. For the graph, use the lessR function ScatterPlot, or sp, with the treatment variable listed first, followed by the response variable.

```
> ScatterPlot(Dosage, Time)
```

The lessR function SummaryStats, or ss, provides the summary statistics organized by group.

```
> SummaryStats(Time, by=Dosage)
```

Do these descriptive results generalize to the population as a whole? Inferential statistics address that question, beginning with the ANOVA table in Listing 7.4. The *null hypothesis* tested in this inferential analysis is the same population mean task completion Time for all three population groups.

null hypothesis
one-way ANOVA: All group population means are equal to each other.

$$H_0 : \mu_1 = \mu_2 = \mu_3$$

The alternative hypothesis is that at least two of the group means are not equal.

$$H_1: \text{At least two of the population group means are not equal}$$

This alternative hypothesis does not specify that all three means are equal to each other. Rather the hypothesis states that as a group they are not all equal, at least one group mean is not equal to the others. The results of the hypothesis test are presented in the ANOVA Summary Table, shown for this analysis in Listing 7.4.

```
ANOVA
-----
          Df  Sum Sq  Mean Sq  F-value  p-value
Dosage     2   195.7   97.85    9.462    0.0012
Residuals 21   217.2   10.34
```

Listing 7.4 ANOVA summary table.

The test statistic for the null hypothesis of all equal mean task completion Times is the *F*-value. The logic of the test is to evaluate potential mean differences by comparing two different variance estimates. A variance is the ratio of the sum of squared deviations about a mean to the corresponding degrees of freedom. The first two columns of an analysis of variance summary table specify these two values for the different sources of variation in the analysis. The third column is the variance estimate, the mean square for each source. An *F*-statistic is the ratio of two variance estimates, that is, of two mean squares.

residual in
one-way ANOVA: Deviation of a data value from its cell mean.

The analysis of variance follows from the comparison of the two variance estimates. For this one-way analysis, one estimate is for the variability of the mean completion times for the different dosages. The other variance estimate is for the residuals, the variation of each data value about its own cell mean. The importance of the cell mean is that it is the summary value of the data for that treatment level. The best prediction of a data value for a given treatment condition is its cell mean.

If the null hypothesis is true, then the distribution over hypothetical repeated samples of this statistic is known, so the p-value, the probability of an F-value as high or higher than the obtained $F = 9.462$, is calculated.

```
Dosage Effect:
        p-value = 0.0012 < α = 0.05, so reject H₀
```

Reject the null hypothesis. Conclude that at least two of the task Time group means differ from each other. Arousal, as induced by the administered drug, reduces task completion Time.

7.2.4 Effect Size

The p-value in relation to α indicates whether an effect is detected, yes or no. Effect size statistics assess the magnitude of the effect of the treatment variable on the response variable. Listing 7.5 presents the effect sizes of Dosage on task completion Time.

effect size, Section 6.2.2, p. 126

```
Association and Effect Size
---------------------------
R Squared: 0.47
R Sq Adjusted: 0.42
Omega Squared: 0.41

Cohen's f: 0.84
```

Listing 7.5 Indices for the magnitude of the effect.

The ANOVA function reports two classes of these effect size statistics. Indices of the first type are association indices, a type of correlation coefficient that assesses the extent of the relation between the treatment and response variables. The closer to 1.0, the stronger the association.

The association statistics of primary interest, which estimate the magnitude of the association in the population, are R squared adjusted, $R^2_{adj} = 0.42$, and omega squared, $\omega^2 = 0.41$. These two coefficients are more conservative than the unadjusted R^2 statistic, $R^2 = 0.47$, which only describes the association in the obtained sample. Some software packages report a statistic called eta-squared, η^2, which may appear in place of ω^2. However, η^2, like R^2, only describes the association in the sample. These sample values are larger than their population counterparts, but less useful because the population values are of greater interest.

The second type of effect size statistics directly assess the size of the group differences. An example is Cohen's f. This statistic is analogous to the standardized mean difference, Cohen's d, the number of standard deviations that separate the group means. To indicate the separation among multiple means, Cohen's f provides the average difference of each group mean from the overall mean of the data, standardized in terms of the standard deviation of the data in which each data value is deviated from its own cell mean. The obtained value of $f = 0.84$ indicates a substantial effect size. Cohen (1988) suggests that for most contexts a value of $f = 0.40$ or larger indicates what is generally considered a large effect, larger than 0.25 (a medium effect), and larger than 0.10 (a small effect).

Cohen's d, Section 6.3.2, p. 135

7.2.5 Post-hoc Multiple Comparisons

omnibus F-test: Assessment of a null hypothesis over all the treatment levels.

The null hypothesis of three population group means of task completion Time is rejected. This test from the ANOVA summary table in Listing 7.4 is called the *omnibus F-test* because it uses the F-value to assess simultaneously all the given levels of the treatment variable. *If* the omnibus F-test is significant, what specific population means are *not* equal to each other? The significant omnibus F-statistic indicates that not all population means are equal, but which specific means are not equal to each other?

To discover the population means different from the others, do *not* do a sequence of t-tests between all possible pairs of means assessed at $\alpha = 0.05$. The problem with this approach is that even if all population means are equal to each other, the sample means are not. By chance, some sample means will be larger than others, which skews the probabilities that the largest sample mean is significantly different from the smallest sample mean, an erroneous conclusion if all the population means are equal. Instead, the probabilities of the sequence of tests must be adjusted.

post-hoc test: A test following an omnibus F-test to isolate a pattern of differences between population means.

Post-hoc tests address this "taking advantage of chance" problem, which accounts for the additional possibilities of finding significant results simply because there are many tests to perform at the same time. The post-hoc tests ANOVA reports are Tukey's multiple comparisons, which simultaneously maintain $\alpha = 0.05$ for the entire family of tests.

The corresponding tabular output appears in Listing 7.6. Here two of three comparisons fall below $\alpha = 0.05$, those for mg10 vs. mg00 and mg10 vs. mg05. Time to complete the task is shown to differ for the group with the largest dosage and the two groups with the least dosage, but the two group means with the least dosage could not be separated from each other.

```
Tukey Multiple Comparisons of Means
Family-wise Confidence Level: 0.95
-----------------------------------
             diff     lwr    upr p adj
mg05-mg00   -0.85   -4.90   3.20  0.86
mg10-mg00   -6.44  -10.49  -2.38  0.00
mg10-mg05   -5.59   -9.64  -1.53  0.01
```

Listing 7.6 All pairwise Tukey multiple comparisons.

Figure 7.2 presents a graphic version of the same result with the corresponding confidence intervals held at the family-wise confidence level of 95%. The two intervals, which do *not* cross 0, are the two intervals with a p-value $< \alpha = 0.05$. Both the hypothesis test and the corresponding confidence intervals demonstrate a pairwise difference for these two intervals. Arousal does affect task completion Time, but only for a sufficient level of arousal, here induced by 10 mg of the drug.

7.2.6 Search for Outliers

Every analysis, descriptive or inferential, should investigate the possibility of outliers in the data. These values can represent errors in data entry or other aspects of data analysis and so should be corrected or deleted. They can also represent data from processes different than which generated the majority of the data, and so should be analyzed separately.

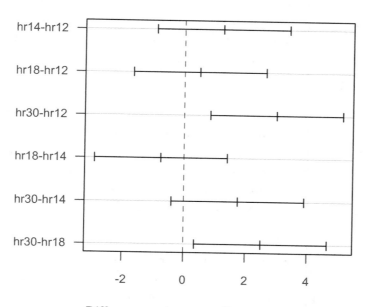

95% family-wise confidence level

Differences in mean levels of SleepDep

Figure 7.2 Tukey family-wise confidence intervals for each of three pairwise comparisons.

The `lessR` function `ANOVA` generates a table of the residuals and standardized residuals for each data value, the first three rows of which appear in Listing 7.7. By default the rows of data and residuals are sorted by the magnitude of the standardized residuals and only the first 20 are listed. A *residual* in a one-way ANOVA is the difference between a data value and its corresponding cell mean.

residual in one-way ANOVA: Difference of a data value and its cell mean.

```
Fitted Values, Residuals, Standardized Residuals
-------------------------------------------------
mydata <- melt(mydata, id.vars="Person",
               value.name="Reps", variable.name="Supplement")
     Dosage  Time  fitted  residual  z-resid
17    mg10  24.20  17.82      6.38     2.12
24    mg10  11.90  17.82     -5.92    -1.97
7     mg00  18.40  24.26     -5.86    -1.95
...
```

Listing 7.7 Residuals and related values.

For any normal distribution, around 95% of the data values are within two standard deviations of the mean. Assuming this normality for the residuals, each residual divided by the standard deviation of the residuals, the corresponding standardized score, should generally not be much larger than 2. Any standardized value larger than 3 is immediately suspect as a potential outlier. The largest standardized residual here is only 2.12. The data are judged to be free of outliers.

The default settings that control the display of the rows of data and other values can also be modified. The `res.rows` option can change the default of 20 rows displayed to any value up to the number of rows of data, specified by the value of `"all"`. To turn this option off, specify a value of 0. The `res.sort` option can change the sort criterion from the default value of `"zresid"`. Other values are `"fitted"` for the values perfectly consistent with the estimated model, and `"off"` to leave the rows of data in their original order.

res.rows option: The number of rows of data to be displayed for the residuals analysis.

res.sort option: The sort criterion for the residuals analysis.

7.2.7 Non-parametric Alternative

The standard non-parametric comparison of two or more samples is the Kruskal–Wallis rank sum test. As with the non-parametric analyses of differences in two independent and two dependent samples, the Kruskal–Wallis rank sum test is also based on the analysis of the ranks of the data instead of the original data values. All the data for all the samples are first ranked as one large sample, then the ranks are summed for the data values within each group. The more discrepant these sums, the more likely that the responses from one or more samples tend to be larger than the responses in other samples.

dosage study, Section 7.2.1, p. 151

To illustrate, return to the Dosage data. The non-parametric null hypothesis is that the distributions perfectly overlap. The alternative hypothesis is that at least one of the distributions of the data values is shifted to the right or left of at least one other distribution.

 R Input *Dependent samples Kruskal–Wallis rank sum test*

```
> with(mydata, kruskal.test(Time ~ Dosage))
```

The output appears in Listing 7.8.

```
    Kruskal-Wallis rank sum test

data:  Time by Dosage
Kruskal-Wallis chi-squared = 9.6204, df = 2, p-value = 0.008146
```

Listing 7.8 Non-parametric Kruskal–Wallis group comparisons.

To evaluate whether Dosage affects Task Time, compare the resulting *p*-value to $\alpha = 0.05$.

```
Dosage Effect: p-value = 0.0113 < α = 0.05, so reject H₀
```

ANOVA conclusion, Section lst:avtable, p. 154

The conclusion that Dosage decreases Task Time remains the same as the conclusion from the ANOVA.

independent samples Section 6.3.1, p. 130

7.3 Randomized Block ANOVA

dependent samples Section 6.4.1, p. 142

Previous sections compared the independent-samples *t*-test with the dependent-samples *t*-test. The distinction is between two samples of data without any linkage between individual data values versus data organized into two samples of blocks of matched data values. That distinction of two different types of samples generalizes to the analysis of variance, ANOVA, where now there are two *or more* samples, either independent, or dependent, organized into blocks. The dependent-samples design is a *randomized block design*, or a within-groups design. If the same experimental unit, such as the same person, provides a measurement for each sample, the design is also called a repeated measures design.

randomized block design: Two or more dependent samples with the data organized into blocks of matched data values.

7.3.1 An Example with Data

 Scenario *Evaluate the effectiveness of four different pre-workout supplements*
Seven people, with differing amounts of muscle strength, took one of four different pre-workout supplements and then did a bench press of 125 lbs as many times as possible. Each person did four workouts at four different times, with a different supplement before each workout. The experimenter randomized the presentation order of the supplements to each person to avoid any artifacts from presentation order. Do the supplements differ in promoting the number of repetitions of the bench press?

First read the data stored as a `csv` file.

```
> mydata <- Read("http://lessRstats.com/data/anova_rb.csv")
```

Listing 7.9 presents the data table in two forms, encoded both as a `csv` data file and a data frame as read by R.

Read function, Section 2.2.1, p. 32

```
Person,sup1,sup2,sup3,sup4            > mydata
p1,2,4,4,3                              Person sup1 sup2 sup3 sup4
p2,2,5,4,6                          1      p1    2    4    4    3
p3,8,6,7,9                          2      p2    2    5    4    6
p4,4,3,5,7                          3      p3    8    6    7    9
p5,2,1,2,3                          4      p4    4    3    5    7
p6,5,5,6,8                          5      p5    2    1    2    3
p7,2,3,2,4                          6      p6    5    5    6    8
                                    7      p7    2    3    2    4
```

Listing 7.9 Data in the form of a `csv` data file and as the R data frame `mydata` as read by `Read`.

The subsequent call to the `lessR` function `ANOVA` generated Figure 7.3. This figure is a graphical representation of the same data in Listing 7.9 from which the analysis begins. The data table and the corresponding graph both show that the fourth workout supplement resulted in the most repetitions, the fifth person has the least muscle strength, and the sixth person is the strongest performer.

As was true with the between-groups ANOVA in the previous section, the data values from each sample are organized to appear in a separate column, as shown in Listing 7.9. The distinction is that the data in Listing 7.9 form a true data table with variables in the columns and measurements for the same person in each row. The data are in the traditional *wide format*.

wide format data table, Section 1.6.2, p. 21

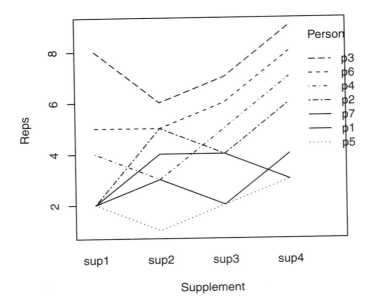

Figure 7.3 Plot of the four data values for each person.

long format data table,
Section 7.2.2,
p. 151

melt function,
Section 7.2.2,
p. 152

id.vars option:
Specify the name
of the variable that
identifies each row
of data.

library function,
Section 1.2, p. 6

For the analysis of variance, R requires the data in the *long format*, with one data value per row. In the current format the data for each person occupies four separate rows. To reshape this data table into the long form, again use the `melt` function from the `reshape2` package (Wickham, 2007). In addition to the `value.name` option for the name of the response variable that contains the data values, and the `variable.name` option, which names the treatment or grouping variable, there is a new option here called `id.vars` to name the blocking variable. The original form of the data in Listing 7.9 contains a row identifier, Person, also specified in the call to `melt`. Person is the blocking variable.

```
> library(reshape2)
```

🖋 **reshape2 Input** *Reshape data from wide to long format*
```
> mydata <- melt(mydata, id.vars=c("Person"),
            value.name="Reps", variable.name="Supplement")
```

The reshaped data in Listing 7.10 is now ready for analysis.

```
   Person Supplement Reps
1    p1        sup1     2
2    p2        sup1     2
...
27   p6        sup4     8
28   p7        sup4     4
```

Listing 7.10 Reshaped data for the randomized block design.

7.3.2 Basic Results

The purpose of the study is to evaluate the effectiveness of the workout supplements to maximize repetitions of the bench press. Type of Supplement is the treatment variable for the design. The omnibus null hypothesis is an identical population mean number of repetitions for all four supplements.

$$H_0 : \mu_1 = \mu_2 = \mu_3 = \mu_4$$

The alternative hypothesis is that at least two of the group means are not equal. The participants have different levels of muscle strength, so presumably there are also differences in abilities to do the bench press, but that relationship is secondary to the primary interest of the effectiveness of the workout supplements.

The lessR function ANOVA can analyze a one-treatment variable randomized block design with one blocking variable. Specify the response variable before the tilde, ~ , then the treatment variable, followed by a plus sign, +, and then the blocking variable.

ANOVA function: Includes analysis for the randomized blocks ANOVA.

> **lessR Input** *Randomized Blocks ANOVA*
>
> ```
> > ANOVA(Reps ~ Supplement + Person)
> ```

balanced design: Each combination of levels of the independent variables has the same number of responses.

The first part of the output lists the response variable, the treatment and blocking variables, the number of rows of data, and indicates if the design is balanced. A *balanced* design has the same number of responses in each combination of the levels of the grouping variables, of which there are two in this design. Each combination of Supplement and Person levels has exactly one response. If the design is not balanced, then a more sophisticated analysis is required.

The next part of the output, Listing 7.11, lists the means of the treatment variable for the samples, which are of primary interest. The output also includes the means for the blocking variable and the grand mean, not shown, which is 4.357 reps.

grand mean, Section 7.2.3, p. 153

```
Marginal Means
--------------
Supplement
sup1 sup2 sup3 sup4
3.57 3.86 4.29 5.71

Person
  p1   p2   p3   p4   p5   p6   p7
3.25 4.25 7.50 4.75 2.00 6.00 2.75
```

Listing 7.11 Sample statistics for the four different supplements.

The sample results indicate that the mean number of repetitions for the fourth workout supplement, 5.71, is considerably larger than the remaining three means. The question is whether this difference, and the other differences, are large enough to reject the null hypothesis, H_0. To evaluate the null hypothesis, Listing 7.12 presents the central output of an analysis of variance, the summary table that partitions the sum of squares across the various effects, and also provides the omnibus *F*-statistic and corresponding *p*-value for each testable effect.

```
Analysis of Variance
--------------------
              df    Sum Sq    Mean Sq    F-value    p-value
Supplement    3     19.00     6.33       6.71       0.0031
    Person    6     88.43     14.74      15.61      0.0000
 Residuals   18     17.00     0.94
```

Listing 7.12 ANOVA summary table for the randomized block design.

The primary *p*-value of interest is for Supplement. Reject the null hypothesis of equal group means for the repetitions response variable.

$$\texttt{Supplement Effect: } p\texttt{-value } = 0.0031 < \alpha = 0.05, \texttt{ so reject } H_0$$

We conclude that at least some of the supplements differ regarding their effectiveness. The *p*-value for the blocking variable, Person, is also less than $\alpha = 0.05$, so the participants do differ regarding performance on the bench press.

7.3.3 Effect Size

effect size,
Section 7.2.4,
p. 155

As always, a significance test that rejects the omnibus null hypothesis should be accompanied by an estimate of the corresponding effect size. The effect sizes in Listing 7.13 are for both the treatment effect and the blocking variable.

```
Effect Size
-----------
Partial Omega Squared for Supplement: 0.38
Partial Intraclass Correlation for Person: 0.79

Cohen's f for Supplement: 0.78
Cohen's f for Person: 1.91
```

Listing 7.13 Effect sizes for the randomized block design.

The effect sizes for differences in muscle strength for the different participants are larger than for type of Supplement. This means that people do differ in terms of strength and that blocking the participants in terms of strength is worthwhile. Both the correlation based measure for type of Supplement, the omega squared of 0.38, and also Cohen's *f* of 0.78, are, however, also large. The correlation based effect size for Person is not omega squared but the Intraclass Correlation coefficient. The reason for this other measure is that the Person variable is randomly sampled instead of set at fixed levels as are the four chosen supplements.

7.3.4 Post-hoc Multiple Comparisons

The omnibus *F*-value is significant and the value for Cohen's *f* of 0.78 indicates a relatively large effect. The supplements differ in regards to effectiveness, and the differences are relatively large.

So what specific mean differences can be isolated that contributed to these results? Listing 7.14 presents the Tukey multiple comparisons and their associated *p*-values for each Supplement.

Tukey multiple comparisons, Section 7.2.5, p. 156

Two comparisons are significant, with *p*-value $< \alpha = 0.05$. These comparisons are between the fourth workout supplement and the first and second supplements, with the mean repetitions larger for the fourth workout supplement. A third comparison, between the fourth and third supplements just misses significance, at *p*-value $= 0.06$.

```
Factor: Supplement
-----------
          diff   lwr   upr p adj
sup2-sup1 0.29 -1.18 1.75  0.95
sup3-sup1 0.71 -0.75 2.18  0.53
sup4-sup1 2.14  0.67 3.61  0.00
sup3-sup2 0.43 -1.04 1.90  0.84
sup4-sup2 1.86  0.39 3.33  0.01
sup4-sup3 1.43 -0.04 2.90  0.06
```

Listing 7.14 Tukey's multiple family-wise comparisons at the family-wide confidence level of 0.95 for the treatment variable in the randomized block design.

The primary finding of this analysis is that there are differences among the supplements to promote more weight lifted during a workout, but that these differences are due largely to the increased effectiveness of the fourth supplement. The effectiveness of the first three supplements has not been differentiated from each other.

7.3.5 Other Output

Although not shown here, the ANOVA function also displays the residuals and standardized residuals for the randomized block design, similar to the output shown in Listing 7.7. These values may indicate that a data value is a potential outlier. In this analysis, one residual, for the first person working out after taking the fourth workout supplement, was larger than 2.0 in magnitude, −2.06. Just one residual of this modest size indicates that there are no outliers in the data. Use the res.rows and res.sort options to control the display of the residuals.

residuals, Section 7.2.6, p. 158

The ANOVA function also provides a scatter plot with the fitted values, Listing 7.4. A *fitted value* corresponds to each data value in the analysis. It is the data value predicted for a specific condition, here the combination of type of Supplement and Person.

res.rows, row.sort options, Section 7.2.6, p. 158

As can be seen from Listing 7.4, the progression of repetitions steadily increases from the first to the fourth workout supplement. The omnibus *F*-test showed that not all the supplements are equal in terms of their mean effectiveness, and the Tukey multiple comparisons showed that only the fourth workout supplement was distinguished as different from the remaining supplements.

fitted value: Data value predicted from a combination of the values of the treatment and blocking variables.

7.3.6 Non-parametric Alternative

The non-parametric alternative to the randomized blocks ANOVA is the Friedman rank sum test. As with the other non-parametric tests, the Friedman test is based on the ranks of the data values instead of the data values themselves. This test for the randomized blocks design ranks the data values *within* each block of data across the different levels of the treatment variable.

Plot of Fitted Values

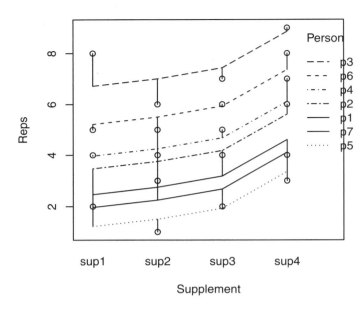

Figure 7.4 Scatter plot of the data with the values fitted by the model.

workout supplement data, Listing 7.9

For the workout supplement data, each of eight participants generates data values for each of four supplements. The Friedman test proceeds by ranking the data values for each person, here the number of repetitions of the bench press of 125 lbs after taking each workout supplement. Then rankings of each workout supplement are compared across all the people, with the mean rank of each workout supplement over the eight people calculated. The null hypothesis is that the distribution of repetitions for each workout supplement is the same. The alternative hypothesis is that at least one distribution differs from the others.

friedman.test function: Non-parametric analysis of a randomized blocks design.

The R implementation of this test is the function `friedman.test`. The syntax is slightly different from the ANOVA syntax. The vertical bar, |, replaces the plus sign, +. The treatment variable is listed first and the blocking variable follows the vertical bar.

> *R Input* *Non-parametric Friedman rank sum test*
```
> with(mydata, friedman.test(Reps ~ Supplement|Person))
```

The output follows in Listing 7.15.

```
    Friedman rank sum test

data:  Reps and Supplement and Person
Friedman chi-squared = 9.9545, df = 3, p-value = 0.01896
```

Listing 7.15 Output of the R Friedman rank sum test.

The results of the Friedman rank sum test parallel the results of the parametric randomized blocks ANOVA. The test statistic is chi-square. Under the null hypothesis the value of this statistic over repeated samples is known, so the corresponding probability of any result given the assumption of the null is also known.

Supplement Effect: p-value $= 0.0190 < \alpha = 0.05$, so reject H_0

The p-value is less than $\alpha = 0.05$, so reject the null hypothesis of no difference between the number of bench press repetitions for the four different supplements. The conclusion from this omnibus test is that at least one workout supplement has a different distribution of error values than the rest.

7.3.7 Advantage of the Randomized Block Design

Both the one-way ANOVA and the randomized block ANOVA have one treatment variable. The purpose of both analyses is to evaluate the differences among group means for this treatment variable. The distinction is that the randomized block design analyzes the data organized by blocks across the treatment levels, and so introduces a second grouping variable into the design.

The advantage of this analysis is evident from Listing 7.16. This analysis is of the same data for type of pre-workout Supplement as it relates to the ability to do the bench press, but here with the one-way ANOVA. That is, this analysis ignores the blocking structure.

```
Analysis of Variance
--------------------
              df    Sum Sq   Mean Sq   F-value   p-value
Supplement    3     19.00     6.33      1.44     0.2554
 Residuals   24    105.43     4.39
```

Listing 7.16 Evaluate effectiveness of type of Supplement with a one-way ANOVA, without consideration of the distinct blocks of data.

The result is a lack of statistical significance.

Supplement Effect:
p-value $= 0.2554 < \alpha = 0.05$, so do *not* reject H_0

No difference in effectiveness is detected among the supplements.

Why the distinction between the outcome of the one-way ANOVA and the randomized block ANOVA? In Listing 7.16 the sum of the squared residuals is 105.43. This is the level of error variation against which the variation of Supplement across the four different group means is evaluated. Compare this value with some sums of squares from the corresponding randomized blocks ANOVA in Listing 7.12.

$$SS_{\text{Residuals, 1-way}} = SS_{\text{Person, RndBlck}} + SS_{\text{Residuals, RndBlck}}$$

$$105.43 = 88.43 + 17.00$$

In the one-way ANOVA all the variation within each cell about the corresponding cell mean is defined as error variance, unaccounted for variation. The randomized blocks analysis, identifies and then partitions out some of the variance, assigning this source of the variation to the blocking variable, here Person. When there are noticeable individual differences among the participants, the remaining unaccounted for variation dramatically decreases.

This smaller residual variability leads to a more robust, powerful test, more likely to detect a difference that actually exists, such as in this analysis. A general theme in data analysis is that if there is a source by which to understand variation, then specify that source in the analysis. In this example include Persons as a blocking variable to obtain a more powerful test regarding the treatment variable of interest, type of Supplement.

7.4 Two-way ANOVA

independent-groups t-test,
Section 6.3.1,
p. 130
one-way ANOVA,
Section 7.2, p. 150

factorial design:
A design with two or more treatment variables.

The independent-groups *t*-test compares the group means for two different groups as indicated by two different values of the grouping variable, called a treatment variable in the context of an experiment. The one-way ANOVA generalizes this analysis to a design also with a single grouping or treatment variable, but possibly with more than two groups. The design introduced here generalizes the analysis to two different treatment variables. This more comprehensive design, a *factorial design*, provides for the simultaneous study of the effects of two different variables on the response variable. Other names for these variables are independent variables and factors. The values of each grouping variable are its categories or levels.

7.4.1 An Example with Data

 Scenario *Examine the effects of Dosage on task completion Time*
To what extent does the level of arousal impact the ability to complete a task? To study this question, laboratory rats were randomly and equally divided into groups, and then given one of three dosages of an arousal inducing drug: 0, 5, and 10 milligrams. Following the dosage, each rat completed either an easy or a hard maze to obtain a food reward. The response (dependent) variable is the Time in seconds to complete the maze.

cell: A specific combination of the values of the grouping variables in a study.

To evaluate the influence of drug Dosage and task Difficulty, 48 laboratory rats were randomly assigned to the 6 combinations of Dosage and Difficulty, resulting in 8 rats for each *cell*.

The first task is to read the data stored as a csv file.

```
> mydata <- Read("http://lessRstats.com/data/anova_2way.csv")
```

Read function,
Section 2.2.1,
p. 32

one-way ANOVA,
Section 7.2, p. 150

The first two and last two rows of this data table appear in Listing 7.17, for the variables Difficulty, Dosage, and Time.

Difficulty has levels of Easy and Hard. Dosage has values of 05mg, 10mg, and 15mg. The data values for the Easy task Difficulty are the same as for the one-way ANOVA previously illustrated. The data for this two-way ANOVA adds a Hard task Difficulty level, and so doubles the number of data values from 24 to 48.

```
> mydata
   Difficulty Dosage Time
1        Easy   mg00 25.6
2        Easy   mg00 25.8
...
47       Hard   mg10 39.3
48       Hard   mg10 43.0
```

Listing 7.17 Beginning and last rows of data for the two-way ANOVA.

By coincidence the levels of Difficulty, Easy, and Hard, are in the correct order for the R output according to their alphabetical ordering. The levels of Dosage are in their correct order because the labels include the numerical amount of the dosage. In many situations, however, this order will need to be explicitly specified. To re-order the values of a categorical grouping variable to the desired order that they should appear on the R output, refer to the R factor function.

order the categories of a variable, Section 3.3.2, p. 60

Each rat in the study has only one data value, the measured Time to complete the maze. The long form and wide form of this data table are the same. All the data for each participant appears in one row because there is only one data value per participant, so analysis is ready to proceed.

long form data table, Section 7.2.2, p. 151

7.4.2 Main Effects and Interaction Effects

There are several questions of interest in this study, each formally stated as a null hypothesis. The first such hypothesis is the statement of the equality of the mean completion time for each Dosage.

$$\text{main effect for Dosage } H_0 : \mu_{mg00} = \mu_{mg05} = \mu_{mg10}$$

Another null hypothesis is the equality of the mean response Time for each task Difficulty.

$$\text{main effect for task Difficulty } H_0 : \mu_{Easy} = \mu_{Hard}$$

The effect of each of the treatment variables or factors in the context of a factorial design is a *main effect*. A main effect occurs when the value of the response variable varies according to the levels of a treatment variable. For example, if there is a main effect of Dosage on task completion Time such that more arousal leads to improved completion Time, then average completion Time would decrease as Dosage increased.

main effect: Effect of a treatment variable on the response variable.

A factorial design provides analysis for a third potential effect, the *interaction*. For an intuitive illustration, consider two treatment variables or factors, peanut butter and jelly, with two levels each, present and absent. Four treatment combinations result: plain bread, a peanut butter sandwich, a jelly sandwich, and a jelly and a peanut butter sandwich. The response variable is the perceived taste of the resulting food. Plain bread is dull, perhaps with a taste rating of 1. Peanut butter makes plain bread taste better by a certain amount, say by 10 units. Jelly makes plain bread taste better by a certain amount, say by 8 units.

interaction effect: The effect of one factor is different at different levels of another factor.

The combined taste of peanut butter and jelly, however, produces much better taste than the combined effects of peanut butter and jelly by themselves, which would be $10 + 8 = 18$ units.

Peanut butter and jelly interact. Instead of 18 units, the taste of peanut butter and jelly is, say, 29 units. The interaction is the extra contribution of the two factors simultaneously beyond their individual, additive contributions. In the presence of an interaction, the main effect of either of the relevant factors is problematic because a general effect for each factor does not exist. In the peanut butter sandwich example, whatever effect peanut butter has on taste differs if jelly is present or not.

The null hypothesis for the interaction of Dosage and Difficulty is that it does not exist.

interaction effect H_0: Effect of each treatment variable is the same at each level of the other treatment variable

With no interaction, to the extent that Dosage raises or lowers completion Time, it would have the same effect regardless of the assigned Difficulty level. Dosage and Difficulty interact, however, if the effect of Difficulty differs depending on the Dosage. With an interaction, no one main effect for either Difficulty or Dosage describes all situations.

7.4.3 The Model and Descriptive Statistics

Randomized blocks design, Section 7.3, p. 158

The `lessR` function `ANOVA`, abbreviated `av`, provides the analysis. Both the two-way factorial design and the previously introduced randomized blocks design have two independent variables or factors. Both of the independent variables in the two-way factorial design, however, are treatment variables. This contrasts with the blocking factor in the randomized blocks design, which is generally not of substantive interest but rather is included to help minimize the error variability in the analysis of the one treatment variable.

The distinction in syntax in the function call to `ANOVA` for a factorial design is to replace the + in the model specification of a randomized block design with an asterisk, *. The asterisk instructs R to also include an interaction term in the analysis.

ANOVA function: Includes analysis for the two-way factorial ANOVA.

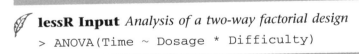

> **lessR Input** *Analysis of a two-way factorial design*
> ```
> > ANOVA(Time ~ Dosage * Difficulty)
> ```

balanced design, Section 7.3.2, p. 161

The first part of the output from `ANOVA`, not listed here, describes the variables and data in the analysis. Also assessed is whether the design is balanced. A balanced design has all treatment level combinations or cells with the same number of participants in each cell. If the design is not balanced, then a more sophisticated analysis is required, and so the present analysis terminates.

cell mean: The mean of the response variable for one cell in the design.

The analysis of variance compares the means of the cells in the design. The means for the individual cells in the design are called the *cell means*, shown in Listing 7.18.

```
Cell Means
----------
          Dosage
Difficulty  mg00   mg05   mg10
      Easy 24.26  23.41  17.82
      Hard 34.73  31.71  39.35
```

Listing 7.18 Cell means, one for each of the six treatment combinations in the experimental design.

The ANOVA function both provides cell means from Listing 7.18 and also their plot, Figure 7.5.

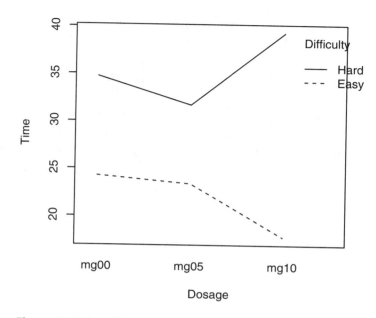

Figure 7.5 Plot of the six cell means of task completion Time for Dosage and Difficulty.

The means for each treatment level averaged across the treatment levels of the other treatment variable are the *marginal means*. ANOVA lists the marginal means separately, as in Listing 7.19. The mean of all the data is the grand mean, 28.548, which is also reported in the output though not included in Listing 7.19.

marginal mean: Mean of the response variable for a level of one treatment variable calculated.

```
Marginal Means
--------------
Dosage
 mg00  mg05  mg10
29.49 27.56 28.59

Difficulty
 Easy  Hard
21.83 35.26
```

Listing 7.19 The marginal means and grand mean of completion Time.

The marginal means in Listing 7.19 indicate, for these data, a substantial difference in task completion Time depending on the Difficulty level. The completion Times for the Hard Difficulty level is 35.26 sec, which drops to 21.83 sec for the Easy Difficulty level. In contrast, the Dosage means exhibit little difference, varying only from a high of 29.49 sec to a low of 27.56 sec. The patterning of the cell means in Listing 7.18 and Figure 7.5, however, clarifies this pattern. Rats who ran the Easy maze improved their completion Times as Dosage of the arousal drug increased. The pattern is much different for rats who encountered the Hard maze. The highest Dosage, and so the highest arousal, inhibited completion Time, yielding by far the largest cell mean of 39.35 secs.

This pattern indicates an interaction between assigned Difficulty and Dosage of training. The effect of one treatment variable on the response variable depends on the level of the other treatment variable. If corroborated by the inferential analysis of the corresponding population values, the effect of the Dosage of the arousal drug on task completion Time depends on the Difficulty of the task. An interaction here implies that there is no general effect of Dosage in isolation of task Difficulty. Without an interaction the two curves in Figure 7.5 would be parallel. Instead the lines that connect the 10 mg cell mean to the 5 mg cell mean for each level of Difficulty move in the opposite direction.

Also provided, in Listing 7.20, is the table of standard deviations of the response variable for all of the cells. The analysis of variance, like the classic t-test, assumes that the population variances of all the cells are equal. Even so, the sample variances, and their corresponding standard deviations, will not be equal. The analysis is reasonably robust against violations of this assumption, but the standard deviations should not be too widely divergent from each other, as is true of these standard deviations.

```
Cell Standard Deviations
-----------------------
          Dosage
Difficulty mg00 mg05 mg10
      Easy 2.69 2.85 3.96
      Hard 4.93 4.81 4.39
```

Listing 7.20 Sample standard deviations for each cell in the design.

7.4.4 Inferential Analysis

Following the descriptive statistics are the inferential tests, which ANOVA presents in the form of the traditional analysis of variance summary table in Listing 7.21. The purpose is to evaluate if the patterns observed in the descriptive statistics for the sample generalize to the population as a whole. There are three tests, each based on the p-value of the corresponding test statistic, the F-value. The first effect to examine is the interaction of the two factors, indicated by Dosage:Difficulty, which can subsume the main effects. The two main effects are for Dosage and Difficulty.

```
Analysis of Variance
--------------------
                   df    Sum Sq   Mean Sq   F-value   p-value
          Dosage    2     29.88     14.94      0.92    0.4076
      Difficulty    1   2164.11   2164.11    132.85    0.0000
Dosage:Difficulty   2    402.61    201.30     12.36    0.0001
       Residuals   42    684.17     16.29
```

Listing 7.21 ANOVA summary table.

The interaction of Difficulty and Dosage on completion Time is significant.

$$\text{Dosage Effect} \times \text{Difficulty:} \quad p\text{-value} = 0.0001 < \alpha = 0.05, \text{ so reject } H_0$$

The conclusion is that Difficulty and Dosage, jointly, affect task completion Time. Because the interaction exists, the main effects are of less importance. Neither Difficulty nor Dosage has a general effect on the task completion Time. Instead, the effect of one of the treatment variables depends on the level of the other treatment variable.

The interaction entirely obscures the Dosage main effect, which is not significant.

$$\texttt{Dosage Effect: } p\texttt{-value} = 0.4076 > \alpha = 0.05, \texttt{ so do } not \texttt{ reject } H_0$$

The interaction shows that contrary to the outcome of the test of the marginal Dosage means, Dosage does have an effect, but that the effect differs depending on the level of Difficulty. In the one-way ANOVA, which examined the effect of Dosage on completion Time, but only considered the Easy Task, the higher the Dosage the quicker the average completion Time. The two-way ANOVA adds the Difficult Task, in which case the largest Dosage of the arousal drug diminishes performance, resulting in the slowest completion Time. The high Dosage cell mean for the Difficult task is 39.35 secs, the largest of the six cell means.

The main effect for task Difficulty is shown to be significant.

$$\texttt{Difficulty Effect: } p\texttt{-value} = 0.0000 < \alpha = 0.05, \texttt{ so do reject } H_0$$

The Hard Difficulty task requires much more time to complete, on average, than the Low Difficulty task. Even so, this effect is modulated by the significant interaction effect. High Dosage of the arousal inducing drug has the opposite effect depending on the task Difficulty. The Easy task facilitates performance when highly aroused, and the Difficult task diminishes performance.

The significance of the interaction effect is the primary finding of this analysis, which implies that the interpretation of the main effect of each treatment variable is either obscured, as with Dosage, or at least modulated, as with Difficulty. Yes, the more Difficult task takes longer to complete, but a fuller understanding of this effect requires an understanding of the resulting interaction.

7.4.5 Effect Size

A follow-up to the detection of a significant effect is the estimation of the size of the effect, shown in Listing 7.22.

effect size,
Section 7.2.4,
p. 155

```
Effect Size
-----------

Partial Omega Squared for Dosage: -0.00
Partial Omega Squared for Difficulty: 0.73
Partial Omega Squared for Dosage_&_Difficulty: 0.32

Cohen's f for Difficulty: 1.66
Cohen's f for Dosage_&_Difficulty: 0.69
```

Listing 7.22 Magnitude of the two main effects and interaction effect.

Consistent with the lack of significance, the estimated association of Dosage with completion Time is zero to within two decimal digits. The population value of omega squared is constrained between 0 and 1, but the estimate of a small population value close to 0 may be negative, as is the case with the omega squared estimate for Dosage. The estimated associate of task Difficulty with completion Time is large, 0.73. The corresponding association for the interaction effect is moderate, 0.32.

There is no effect size statistic, Cohen's f, reported for Dosage because the corresponding omega squared value is less than 0. The value of f for Difficulty is substantial, 1.66, well beyond a generally large effect size of $f = 0.40$ suggested by Cohen (1988). The corresponding value for the interaction of $f = 0.69$ is also large, though much smaller than the Difficulty effect.

7.4.6 Post-hoc Multiple Comparisons

Multiple comparisons of main effects,
Listing 7.6, p. 156;
Listing 7.14, p. 163

The large separation between the cell means of the Easy and Difficulty conditions, and the strong interaction of Dosage and Difficulty, imply that most of the pairwise comparisons of the cell means are significant. The lack of significance of a main effect for Dosage, however, would imply that marginal means for Dosage are not distinguishable from each other. These results are verified by the Tukey post-hoc comparisons at the family-wise significance level of $\alpha = 0.05$.

The Tukey multiple comparisons are presented for the two main effects. All three pairwise comparisons for the three marginal means of Dosage are not significant, and the Hard–Easy marginal mean comparison is significant. The pairwise comparisons for the interaction effect, the latter of which are reported in Listing 7.23, are in terms of the cell means. Only three cell mean comparisons are not significant. There is no observed distinction between the two lowest Dosage levels at both the Easy and Hard Difficulty levels. Also there is no distinction between the lowest and medium Dosage levels at the Hard Difficulty level.

```
Cell Means
----------
                        diff    lwr    upr p adj
mg05:Easy-mg00:Easy    -0.85  -6.87   5.17  1.00
mg10:Easy-mg00:Easy    -6.44 -12.46  -0.41  0.03
mg00:Hard-mg00:Easy    10.46   4.44  16.49  0.00
mg05:Hard-mg00:Easy     7.45   1.43  13.47  0.01
mg10:Hard-mg00:Easy    15.09   9.06  21.11  0.00
mg10:Easy-mg05:Easy    -5.59 -11.61   0.44  0.08
mg00:Hard-mg05:Easy    11.31   5.29  17.34  0.00
mg05:Hard-mg05:Easy     8.30   2.28  14.32  0.00
mg10:Hard-mg05:Easy    15.94   9.91  21.96  0.00
mg00:Hard-mg10:Easy    16.90  10.88  22.92  0.00
mg05:Hard-mg10:Easy    13.89   7.86  19.91  0.00
mg10:Hard-mg10:Easy    21.52  15.50  27.55  0.00
mg05:Hard-mg00:Hard    -3.01  -9.04   3.01  0.67
mg10:Hard-mg00:Hard     4.62  -1.40  10.65  0.22
mg10:Hard-mg05:Hard     7.64   1.61  13.66  0.01
```

Listing 7.23 Multiple comparison of cell means.

Understanding these results emphasizes the importance of understanding and interpreting an interaction effect in a two-way ANOVA design. Collapsed across Difficulty levels, there is no Dosage effect, yet Dosage has a substantial relationship to task completion Time. This effect, however, is only evident from the corresponding interaction.

7.5 More Advanced Designs

The `lessR` ANOVA function can analyze the three designs previously illustrated in this chapter: one-way ANOVA, randomized blocks ANOVA, and two-way ANOVA. These designs and subsequent data analysis are among the most common in the analysis of experimental data, but many other designs are encountered, some of them considerably more complex, including unbalanced designs. Kirk (2013) comprehensively categorizes, explains and illustrates these more complex designs.

To analyze data from designs more complex than the three previously presented in this chapter requires direct use of the standard `R` functions upon which `lessR` relies. Such analysis is beyond the scope of this text. One excellent reference in the application of `R` to more advanced designs is Faraway (2004). For balanced designs the relevant `R` function is `aov`. For unbalanced and even more sophisticated designs, there is the function `lmer` in the `lme4` package.

lme4 package: Sophisticated functions for the analysis of data from unbalanced and complex designs.

When using `R` functions directly, two rules must be followed. First, unlike the `lessR` versions, the standard `R` functions make no default assumption regarding the data frame to be analyzed, which for `lessR` is `mydata`. For the `aov` function, specify the data frame with the same `data` argument as with the `lessR` functions, such as `data=mydata`.

Second, a complete analysis usually involves several to many `R` functions, and perhaps subsequent programming as well. The primary analysis of variance `R` function for balanced designs, `aov`, only specifies the initial analysis. Individual components of the analysis, such as the ANOVA summary table, must be explicitly referenced, here with the `R` function `summary`. By contrast the `lessR` functions weave these needed functions together and provide any needed ancillary programming. The `lessR` result is a more complete output from a single function call within the interactive `R` environment.

7.5.1 Randomized Block Factorial Design

The first more advanced design considered here is what Kirk (2013), p. 459, calls a randomized block factorial design, also referred to as a within-samples or within-subjects design. The randomized block design already presented yields a single data value for each block at each treatment level of the one treatment variable. The randomized block *factorial* design applies the same concept to more than a single treatment variable. In the factorial version, each block yields a single data value for each combination of levels of the treatment variables.

randomized block factorial design: Two or more within (dependent) groups design.

As with the randomized block design, the data values for the block can consist of repeated measures of the same experimental unit such as a person, rat, organization, thing, place, or event. Or, the block can consist of different units matched on some relevant characteristic. This example applies the latter approach with a re-consideration of the previously presented two-way between-subjects factorial design and corresponding analysis of variance.

The previous example of the two-way ANOVA examined the effect on task completion Time in response to one of three levels of Dosage of an arousal producing drug, and one of two levels of task Difficulty. The experimental subjects are laboratory rats. The task is running through a maze to obtain a food reward. The design is referred to as between-samples or between-groups or between-subjects design because each measurement of completion Time is provided by a different rat in one cell, one of $3 \times 2 = 6$ unique combinations of Dosage and Difficulty. The study has 8 replications per cell, that is, 8 different rats who are exposed to the same treatment conditions for each of the 6 cells in the design.

two-way ANOVA, Section 7.4, p. 166

The randomized blocks factorial version of this study partitions the 48 rats into 8 groups of 6 based on an initial assessment of each rat's ability to navigate a maze. That is, some rats in general do better than others. A trial maze served as a sort of a pre-test in which the rats were sorted on the basis of their ability to solve the maze. The first block of 6 rats ran the trial maze the fastest, and the last block the slowest. Within each block the rats were randomly assigned to each of the 6 treatment combinations. There are still 48 different rats in the study, but now each block of matched rats provides a score on each of the 6 treatment combinations. This design is referred to as within-subjects because similar rats in terms of maze running ability provide the data for each block of data values. Each rat in this block only experiences one of the 6 cells, but all the rats in a block are evaluated across all 6 combinations of the levels of the two treatment variables.

The first task is to read the data stored as a csv file in the long form with one data value per line in the data file.

```
> mydata <- Read("http://lessRstats.com/data/anova_rbf.csv")
```

Read function,
Section 2.2.1,
p. 32

The first and last rows of this data table appear in Listing 7.24. The data are the same data as from the two-way ANOVA, but here there is an additional variable, Block, with values that range from Blck1 to Blck8. Each block contains 6 data values, one for each combination of levels of the two treatment variables. The data values in Listing 7.24 illustrate the first 6 data values for the first block.

```
> mydata
   Difficulty Dosage Block Time
1        Easy   mg00 Blck1 25.6
2        Easy   mg05 Blck1 23.4
3        Easy   mg10 Blck1 24.2
4        Hard   mg00 Blck1 40.5
5        Hard   mg05 Blck1 40.3
6        Hard   mg10 Blck1 46.7
7        Easy   mg00 Blck2 25.8
...
47       Hard   mg05 Blck8 27.4
48       Hard   mg10 Blck8 43.0
```

Listing 7.24 Subset of data for randomized block factorial design.

The analysis proceeds from the R function aov.

R Input *Two treatment randomized block factorial design*
```
> fit <- aov(Time ~ (Dosage*Difficulty) +
              Error(Block/(Dosage*Difficulty)), data=mydata)
> summary(fit)
```

Note the similarity between the specification of the randomized block factorial design with aov and the two-way factorial design with ANOVA. The specifications are the same except for the addition of the Error term in the randomized block design. Both designs incorporate a complete factorial structure. In this example all 6 treatment combinations of 3 levels of Dosage and 2 Difficulty levels, with task completion Time as the response variable. Specify this aspect of the design with the following component.

```
Time ~ (Dosage*Difficulty)
```

The distinction between the designs is the blocking structure of the randomized block factorial design, indicated with the additional following `Error` term, which allows for the customization of the error terms in the analysis. Each error term in the analysis of variance summary table is labeled Residuals.

```
Error(Block/(Dosage*Difficulty))
```

This notation indicates that there are four error terms in the analysis. The first term is differences among the blocks, indicated by Block. The remaining three terms are for Dosage, Difficulty, and their interaction, all within blocks.

The standard `R` approach to linear models such as analysis of variance is to estimate the model and then store the results into an object named something such as `fit`. Then different functions are applied to `fit` to obtain different analyses of the model. The `summary` function provides the core analysis, the ANOVA summary table, shown in Listing 7.25.

```
Error: Block
          Df Sum Sq Mean Sq F value Pr(>F)
Residuals  7  316.6   45.23

Error: Block:Dosage
          Df Sum Sq Mean Sq F value Pr(>F)
Dosage     2  29.88  14.938   3.013 0.0816
Residuals 14  69.40   4.957

Error: Block:Difficulty
           Df Sum Sq Mean Sq F value   Pr(>F)
Difficulty  1 2164.1  2164.1   116.8 0.0000128
Residuals   7  129.7    18.5

Error: Block:Dosage:Difficulty
                  Df Sum Sq Mean Sq F value   Pr(>F)
Dosage:Difficulty  2  402.6  201.30   16.73 0.000195
Residuals         14  168.5   12.04
```

Listing 7.25 Randomized blocks factorial design summary table from R.

The primary feature of this randomized blocks factorial design compared to the two-way ANOVA is the same advantage for the one treatment variable randomized blocks design. The consideration of blocks of similar participants allows for the partitioning of the associated sum of squares, which are then removed from the sum of squares error term. The result is a more powerful test, more able to detect existing differences between population means, if there are differences among the blocks.

The primary result from the two-way ANOVA remains. The interaction of Dosage of the arousal drug and task Difficulty is significant.

```
Dosage x Difficulty Effect:
```
$$p\text{-value} = 0.0002 < \alpha = 0.05, \text{ reject } H_0$$

cell means plot example, Section 7.19, p. 169

The meaning of this interaction was previously explored in the cell means plot for these data. Similarly, task Difficulty is significant, and Dosage is not significant.

```
Difficulty Effect:
```
$$p\text{-value} = 0.0000 < \alpha = 0.05, \text{ reject } H_0$$

```
Dosage Effect:
```
$$p\text{-value} = 0.0816 > \alpha = 0.05, \text{ do } not \text{ reject } H_0$$

This R analysis was specified to evaluate each of the three effects, two main effects and the interaction, with its own error term, which is the interaction of Block with the corresponding effect. Some authors, such as Kirk (2013), p. 462, combine the residual terms for each of the three effects, to serve as a single error baseline from which to evaluate each of the three effects. The logic for this combined term is that each error term only reflects random error, so their combination is a single indicator of the extent of random error in the analysis.

To obtain an analysis with this combined error term, specify a new, simpler error term in the call to aov.

```
> fit <- aov(Time ~ (Dosage*Difficulty) + Error(Block), data=mydata)
```

The output from summary(fit) is given in Listing 7.26. The R output is slightly modified in that the p-values are reported only to four significant digits.

```
Error: Block
            Df Sum Sq Mean Sq F value Pr(>F)
Residuals   7  316.6   45.23

Error: Within
                  Df Sum Sq Mean Sq  F value  Pr(>F)
Dosage             2   29.9    14.9    1.422  0.2550
Difficulty         1 2164.1  2164.1  206.056  0.0000
Dosage:Difficulty  2  402.6   201.3   19.167  0.0000
Residuals         35  367.6    10.5
```

Listing 7.26 Analysis of the randomized block factorial design with a single within-subjects error term direct from the R function aov.

The Residuals degrees of freedom and sum of squares are just the sum of the corresponding three Residuals terms from Listing 7.25. The revised Error specification in the call to aov specifies only a Block error term. The remaining sources of error variation that are "left over" are now combined into a generic Within error term, which refers to the within-subjects variation.

split-plot factorial design: One between-groups treatment variable and one within-groups treatment variable.

7.5.2 Split-plot Factorial Design

A second more advanced design is the *split-plot factorial design*. The simplest such design is illustrated here, with two treatment variables. One treatment variable is between-groups, that is, with different sets of unmatched participants. The other treatment variable is within-groups, that is, the defining feature of a randomized blocks design. Each participant in the study forms a block of matched scores on the response variable across this within-groups treatment variable.

one-way between-groups design, Section 7.2, p. 150

The two-way split-plot factorial can be thought of as a combination of the one-way between-groups design and the randomized blocks design. The randomized blocks design has a data value for each block of responses for each level of the treatment variable. The split-plot factorial replicates this structure with a second treatment condition for the between-groups treatment variable.

randomized blocks design, Section 7.3, p. 158

To illustrate, return to the randomized-blocks design already presented. Each of 7 participants took one of four pre-workout supplements and then bench pressed 125 lbs for as many repetitions as possible. The design is randomized-blocks because each participant did this for each Supplement, a total of four times, which generated 28 data values. Supplement is a within-groups treatment variable because all four of its levels were administered to each participant. To generalize this design to the split-plot factorial, presume that all the participants in this previous study also had a controlled, highly nutritious breakfast exactly two hours before taking the pre-workout Supplement.

Now suppose that actually $7 \times 2 = 14$ participants were recruited for the study and then each participant was randomly assigned to one of two groups. Suppose the second group of 7 participants also followed the *same* randomized-blocks design. Each participant also took all four Supplements, one for each workout, in a randomized order, again resulting in a total of 28 data values. The distinction is that for this second group their breakfast was less nutritious. Type of Supplements is a within-groups treatment variable, but now the other treatment variable, Food quality, is a between-groups treatment variable. The participants in the Low Food quality group are different participants from those in the Hi Food quality group.

The first task is to read the data stored as a csv file in the long form with one data value per line in the data file, resulting in $7 \times 4 \times 2 = 56$ rows of data.

```
> mydata <- Read("http://lessRstats.com/data/anova_sp.csv")
```

Read function, Section 2.2.1, p. 32

Representative rows of this data table appear in Listing 7.27. There are 7 participants in the Hi Food quality level, and 7 in the Low Food quality level. For the split-plot design the identifier for each block of data, here for each Person, re-cycles the same values in the Low Food quality group, even though the reference is for different people. In Listing 7.27, for example, the identifier p1 appears in both the first row and the 29th row.

```
> mydata
    Person Food Supplement Reps
1       p1   Hi       sup1    2
2       p1   Hi       sup2    4
...
28      p7   Hi       sup4    4
29      p1   Low       sup1    2
...
55      p7   Low       sup3    2
56      p7   Low       sup4    4
```

Listing 7.27 Data for split-plot factorial design.

Descriptive statistics for the data table can be obtained with the lessR function SummaryStats, for which the brief form of the output from ss.brief suffices. The summary

SummaryStats function, Section 5.3, p. 105

statistics for Food quality appear in Listing 7.28. The mean repetitions of the bench press for the Hi Food quality participants is 4.36, which is 0.68 repetitions more, on average, than for the Low Food quality participants.

```
> ss.brief(Reps, by=Food)

        n   miss    mean     sd    min     mdn     max
Hi     28     0     4.36   2.15   1.00    4.00    9.00
Low    28     0     3.68   2.04   1.00    3.00    8.00
```

Listing 7.28 Marginal means and other summary statistics for the two levels of Food quality.

The marginal means for Supplement are found in Listing 7.29. The fourth Supplement led to the most repetitions of the bench press with an average of 5.36 bench presses.

```
> ss.brief(Reps, by=Supplement)

        n   miss    mean     sd    min     mdn     max
sup1   14     0     3.21   2.08   1.00    2.00    8.00
sup2   14     0     3.36   1.55   1.00    3.00    6.00
sup3   14     0     4.14   1.96   2.00    4.00    7.00
sup4   14     0     5.36   2.24   3.00    4.50    9.00
```

Listing 7.29 Marginal means and other summary statistics for the four pre-workout Supplements.

Do these differences observed in the sample also apply to the population? The inferential analysis for this split-plot factorial design proceeds from the R function aov. Food is the between-groups treatment variable and Supplement is the within-groups treatment variable. The interaction.plot function provides the graph of the cell means.

✒ **R Input** *Split-plot factorial design*
```
> fit <- aov(Reps ~ (Food*Supplement) +
                 Error(Person/Food), data=mydata)
> summary(fit)
> with(mydata, interaction.plot(Food, Supplement, Reps)))
```

The summary table obtained from the aov and summary functions is presented in Listing 7.30. In this split-plot design the Person variable defines the blocks.

From these results, the Food effect on Reps, the number of repetitions of the bench press, is significant.

$$\texttt{Food: } p\text{-value} = 0.0401 < \alpha = 0.05, \texttt{ so reject } H_0$$

The more nutritious breakfast does facilitate better performance, which in the sample is 0.68 more bench presses on average.

```
Error: Person
           Df Sum Sq Mean Sq F value Pr(>F)
Residuals   6  156.6    26.1

Error: Person:Food
           Df Sum Sq Mean Sq F value Pr(>F)
Food        1  6.446   6.446   6.811 0.0401
Residuals   6  5.679   0.946

Error: Within
               Df Sum Sq Mean Sq F value     Pr(>F)
Supplement      3  40.48  13.494  14.785 0.00000196
Food:Supplement 3   0.91   0.304   0.333    0.802
Residuals      36  32.86   0.913
```

Listing 7.30 Split-plot factorial design summary table direct from the R function aov.

The type of Supplement also is significant.

$$\texttt{Supplement: } p\texttt{-value } = 0.0000 < \alpha = 0.05, \texttt{ so reject } H_0$$

As in the analysis of the randomized blocks design, there are differences among the Supplements in terms of facilitating the bench press.

There is no detected interaction between Food and Supplement.

$$\texttt{Food x Supplement:}$$
$$p\texttt{-value } = 0.802 > \alpha = 0.05, \texttt{ so } not \texttt{ reject } H_0$$

This result means that whatever the effect of Supplement for the Hi nutrition breakfast, the same effect is present for the Low nutrition breakfast. To understand the meaning of this lack of interaction, consider the plot of the cell means in Figure 7.6.

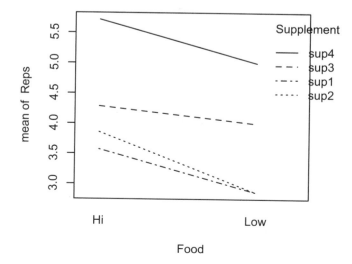

Figure 7.6 Cell means of bench press repetitions for two different Food types.

Analysis of Figure 7.6 reveals approximately parallel lines titled in a downward direction. Regardless of the type of Supplement, there is a shift downward in performance from the Hi to the Low nutrition Food groups. Eating a better breakfast facilitates performance in the gym, but the effects of the different Supplements remain the same regardless of the quality of breakfast.

Worked Problems

?dataEmployee
for more
information.

1 Consider the Employee data set, available from an internal `lessR` read.

```
> mydata <- Read("Employee", format="lessR")
```

Some of the variables in this data set are Salary, Gender, and Dept for employees at a specific company. Dept is a categorical variable with five levels: ACCT, ADMN, FINC, MKTG, and SALE.

(a) Are there differences among the average Salary across the five departments? Answer in terms of statistical significance, effect size, and confidence intervals among pairwise differences.

(b) Is this an experiment? Why or why not?

(c) The previous chapter analyzed the difference in average Salary for men and women with an independent-groups t-test. Do so with a one-way ANOVA. Compare the p-values from the t-value from the t-test and the F-value from the ANOVA.

2 Participants in a weight loss program had their weight monitored at the beginning of the program, and at the end of the first, second, and third months. The data are on the web.

```
> mydata <- Read("http://lessRstats.com/data/WeightLoss4.csv")
```

(a) Is the weight loss program effective? Answer with both a parametric and non-parametric procedure, and also effect size.

(b) Describe the pattern of weight loss over the three months of the study.

3 Two drugs were evaluated for the relief of anxiety. Each drug was administered in three different dosages. Participants in the study were randomly assigned to one of the six treatment combinations or cells. The data are on the web.

```
> mydata <- Read("http://lessRstats.com/data/Anxiety.csv")
```

(a) Is one drug more effective than the other? Answer with an analysis of statistical significance and also effect size.

(b) What is the pattern of effectiveness over time?

(c) Is this an experiment? Why or why not?

8.1 Quick Start

First install R and lessR as explained in Section 1.2. At the beginning of each R session access lessR with library(lessR). Then read your data into an R data frame with Read(), the subject of Chapter 2.

    The previous two chapters explored the relation between a continuous response variable and one or two categorical grouping variables that each defined two or more samples of data. For example, what is the relation between the response variable of annual Salary and the grouping variable Gender which defines two groups, Male and Female? This chapter generalizes these relationships to two continuous, that is, numeric, variables. The focus remains on the relationship between variables.

✓ Obtain the scatter plot and correlation of two variables with the lessR function ScatterPlot, such as for variables X and Y.

```
> ScatterPlot(X,Y)
```

Scatter plot function, Section 8.2.1, p. 182

Or, use Correlation of the two variables for no graph.

✓ Obtain the correlation matrix with the lessR function Correlation. With no specified variable list the correlation matrix is computed for all numeric variables in the mydata data frame. Set graphics=TRUE to obtain a scatter plot matrix and heat map of the correlations.

```
> mycor <- Correlation()
```

correlation matrix, Section 8.3, p. 194

✓ Non-parametric correlation coefficients are available with the method option, for either Spearman or Kendall correlations. These options can be specified for a scatter plot or an entire correlation matrix.

```
> ScatterPlot(X, Y, method="spearman")

> Correlation(method="kendall")
```

non-parametric correlations, Section 8.4, p. 200

relationship of numeric variables: As the values of one variable increase, the values of the other tend to either increase or decrease.

8.2 Relation of Two Numeric Variables

Do the values of two variables tend to change together or separately? Is there a relation between Salary and the number of Years employed at the company? First note that both of these variables

+ relation: The values of both variables tend to increase together.

− relation: As one variable increases, the values of the other variable tend to decrease.

are continuous. Two continuous variables are *related* if, as the values of one variable increase, the values of the other variable tend to either systematically increase, or systematically decrease. Relationships can be positive or negative. For a *positive relationship*, both variables tend to increase together, whereas for a *negative relationship* the values of the variables tend in opposite directions.

8.2.1 The Scatter Plot

To illustrate the positive relationship of Salary and Years consider again the Employee data set.

Scenario *Assess the relation between annual Salary and Years of experience*
At a specific company the data table is available for 37 employees, including the variables annual Salary and Years employed. What is the relationship, if any, between the number of Years employed and Salary?

Employee data table, Figure 1.7, p. 21

The employee data with the associated variable labels are available from within the lessR package.

```
> mydata <- Read("Employee", format="lessR")
```

scatter plot: Graph with one axis per variable, one plotted point for each set of data values.

one-variable scatter plot, Section 5.4.1, p. 110

Graphically express this relationship with a *scatter plot*, a plot of the values of one or more variables for each row of data, one axis for each variable. Previously we plotted the distribution of values for a single variable along a single axis with a one-variable scatter plot. The two-variable scatter plot illustrates the relation between two variables plotted with two axes. Plot each pair of data values as a single point with its two coordinates equal to the corresponding two data values.

ScatterPlot function: Draw a scatter plot for one or two variables.

Obtain the scatter plot of two variables with the lessR function ScatterPlot. The abbreviation is sp.

lessR Input *Default scatter plot of Years employed with annual Salary*
```
> ScatterPlot(Years, Salary)      or       > sp(Years, Salary)
```

The scatter plot in Figure 8.1 shows that working more Years tends to be associated with a higher Salary. Each plotted point represents one employee's data values for Years and Salary. There are 36 employees with data values for both variables, so the scatter plot consists of 36 points. By default the transparency level of each point is set at 0.66, on a scale from 0 to 1, from no transparency to complete transparency. The default partial transparency distinguishes overlapping points by darker colors.

Consider another version of the Figure 8.1 scatter plot.

lessR Input
```
> set(colors="gray.black", trans.fill.pt=0)
> ScatterPlot(Years, Salary, fit.line="loess")
```

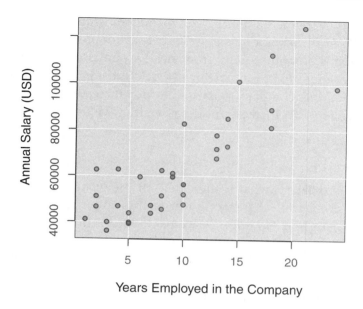

Figure 8.1 Default (gray scale) scatter plot of Years employed with annual Salary.

The version in Figure 8.2 illustrates the inverted gray scale color theme, optimized for projection onto a screen such as for a slide show. Use the `lessR` function `set` to choose the color theme with the `colors` options, and the option `trans.fill.pt` to set the transparency level, such as 0 for no transparency.

color themes, transparency, Section 1.4.1, p. 16

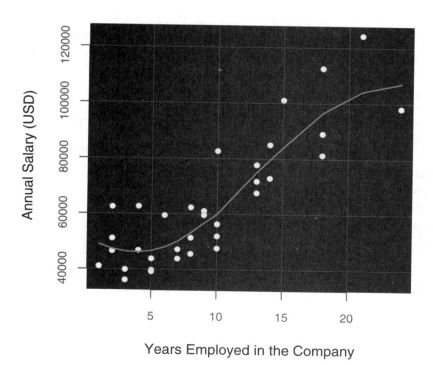

Figure 8.2 Scatter plot of Years employed and annual Salary and a loess curve with the gray.black color theme and no transparency for the plotted points.

A smooth curve fit through the points in Figure 8.2 summarizes the relationship between the two variables. The fitted curve is called a *loess curve* for locally weighted scatter plot smoothing. The position of each point on the curve is computed only from nearby points in the scatter plot. The result is a non-parametric procedure for summarizing the relationship between the two variables with a nonlinear curve. For this company, Salary does not increase much each year for the beginning levels of employment, but increases noticeably after five or so years.

fit.line option: Fit a curve through the scatter plot, either a least-squares line, `"ls"`, or `"loess"`.

8.2.2 The Correlation Coefficient

linear relationship: For a two-variable scatter plot, a straight line summarizes the relationship.

For two related variables, such as Years and Salary, what is the extent of the relationship? This assessment provided here is for a *linear relationship*. A perfect linear relationship means that all the points in the scatter plot lie on a straight line. No linear relationship means that there is no tendency for the value of one variable to systematically increase or decrease as the value of the other variable increases. As the value of one variable increases, the value of the other variable is just as likely to increase as decrease.

correlation coefficient: Index of the extent of the relationship between two variables, which varies from −1 to 0 to 1.

There are several implementations of a correlation coefficient. The correlation coefficient that gauges the magnitude of a linear relationship is the Pearson product-moment *correlation coefficient*, indicated in the sample with r. Pearson correlation coefficients of 1 and −1 indicate perfect positive and negative linear relationships, respectively. A correlation of 0 indicates no linear relationship between the variables.

Correlation function: Provides analysis of the correlation coefficient without the scatter plot.

Obtain the Pearson correlation coefficient, and its inferential analysis, from the `ScatterPlot` function. To obtain only text output, without the scatter plot, use the lessR function `Correlation`. The `Correlation` function also provides what is called the covariance, a version of the correlation coefficient in which the variables are expressed in their original measurement units. The abbreviation for `Correlation` is `cr`.

assignment operator, Section 1.3.3, p. 9

To illustrate, consider a scatter plot of two uncorrelated variables. Here we generate the data by simulating the process of randomly sampling from a normal distribution with the R function `rnorm`. Randomly generate 250 simulated data values for a variable X from a normal population with a mean of $\mu = 50$ and a standard deviation of $\sigma = 10$. Then randomly sample another 250 values from the same population for a variable Y. Use the R *assignment operator*, `<-`, to store the generated values in either X or Y.

> **R Input** *Generate randomly sampled data values from a normal distribution*
```
> X <- rnorm(n=250, mean=50, sd=10)
> Y <- rnorm(n=250, mean=50, sd=10)
```

To view the actual simulated data values, enter the name of the variable at the command prompt, >. The data values are randomly generated, so a different set of data values are generated for each repetition of these function calls.

user's workspace: Area to store data frames and other created objects.

ls function: List the contents of a workspace.

The creation of the variables X and Y illustrates another property of the R environment. The (simulated) data values for these variables do *not* exist in a data frame such as `mydata`. Instead they exist in a workspace called the *user's workspace*, or sometimes the *global environment*. This space can be used for creating variables and other objects apart from a data frame. The user's workspace is also where the default `mydata` data frame is stored. To view the contents of this workspace at any time during an R session use the list function `ls` without any arguments.

```
> ls()
```

Most `lessR` functions that process data can also access variables stored directly in the user workspace instead of within a data frame in that workspace. These functions by default automatically scan for the specified variables in both the specified or default data frame as well as the user's workspace. For example, `ScatterPlot` can access any variable in `mydata` as well as these variables X and Y in the user's workspace.

Consider the 95% data ellipse drawn around the points in the scatter plot. The purpose of this ellipse is to provide a visual summary of the extent of the relationship between the two variables. The narrower is the ellipse, the stronger is the relationship. For a perfect linear relationship the ellipse collapses to a line. For two uncorrelated variables measured on the same scale, the ellipse expands outward to a circle.

The function that draws this ellipse (`dataEllipse`) is from John Fox's `car` package (Fox & Weisberg, 2011), which is automatically downloaded when `lessR` is downloaded.[1] The `lessR` `ScatterPlot` function accesses the `car` ellipse function directly from its `ellipse` option, which is set to `TRUE` to draw the ellipse. Change the default color of the ellipse with the `col.ellipse` option. By default the ellipse is filled with a light, transparent color, which can be turned off with `fill.ellipse=FALSE`.

95% data ellipse: Contains about 95% of the points in a sample scatter plot of two normally distributed variables.

ellipse=TRUE option: Draw the 95% data ellipse around the values in a scatter plot.

col.ellipse, fill.ellipse options: Set the color of the ellipse and specify if to be filled.

---

 lessR Input *Scatter plot with ellipse*
```
> ScatterPlot(X, Y, ellipse=TRUE)
```

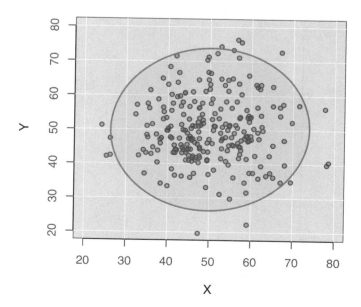

Figure 8.3 Scatter plot with ellipse for a correlation very near zero, $r = 0.016$.

The simulated data values for variables X and Y are randomly and separately sampled, so there is no correlation between X and Y in the population. Sampling error is always present, so the sample correlation differs from its corresponding population value of 0. For a sample of 250 paired data values there should be a sample correlation between the variables X and Y that is close to but not exactly equal to 0. The obtained correlation of $r = 0.016$ for this sample appears in the text output for ScatterPlot, partially reproduced in Listing 8.1.

```
Number of paired values with neither missing, n: 250
Number of cases (rows of data) deleted: 0

Sample Correlation of X and Y: r = 0.016
```

Listing 8.1 Descriptive statistics from ScatterPlot.

The 95% data ellipse in Figure 8.3 is almost a circle, which indicates the lack of relationship between the variables X and Y. For any one specific value of X, the corresponding value of Y is as likely to be larger than its mean near 50 as it is to be smaller than its mean. The circular form of this ellipse is the geometric expression of the corresponding correlation coefficient of almost zero, $r = 0.016$.

To view the data ellipse for a well-defined positive relationship, consider again the scatter plot of Years and Salary from Figures 8.1 and 8.2, but now in Figure 8.4 with a scatter plot added by setting ellipse=TRUE in the call to ScatterPlot.

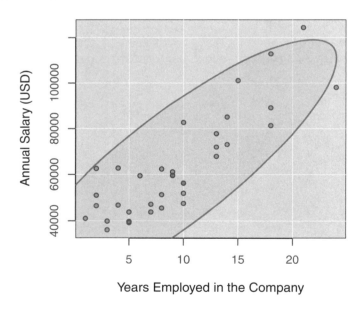

Figure 8.4 Scatter plot of Years employed and annual Salary with the default data ellipse.

One issue with including the ellipse in the scatter plot is that the default limits of both axes are set according to the range of the data values along each respective axis. Yet to include the entire ellipse often requires larger limits for the axes beyond the range of data. Explicitly set the limits of the axes with the standard R options xlim and ylim to specify both the minimum and maximum values of the axes.

xlim, ylim
options: Set the limits of the axes.

c function,
Section 1.3.6,
p. 15

> **lessR Input** *Scatter plot with explicit limits for each axis*
> ```
> > ScatterPlot(Years, Salary, ellipse=TRUE,
>                 xlim=c(-10,25), ylim=c(10000,125000))
> ```

As always with R, enclose a list of values separated by commas with the combine function c. The result appears in Figure 8.5.

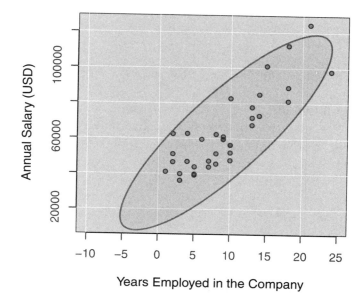

Figure 8.5 Scatter plot of Years employed and annual Salary with the data ellipse and explicit axes limits.

Compared to the almost circular ellipse in Figure 8.3, the ellipse in Figure 8.5 is much narrower. This narrow ellipse is the geometric representation of a large correlation, which for Years and Salary is $r = 0.852$, as reported in Listing 8.2.

```
Number of paired values with neither missing, n: 36
Number of cases (rows of data) deleted: 1

Pearson's product-moment correlation

Years, Annual Salary (USD)
Salary, Years Employed in the Company

Sample Correlation of Years and Salary: r = 0.852
```

Listing 8.2 Background information and sample estimate of the correlation coefficient from ScatterPlot and also Correlation.

Text output in Listing 8.2 is from either ScatterPlot or Correlation. The latter function does not provide the scatter plot.

8.2.3 Inferential Analysis

As is true of virtually any data analysis, the goal is not a description of a sample but information regarding the population from which the sample was obtained. The sample correlation is $r = 0.852$, but what is the population value of interest? As usual, address this question with a hypothesis test and/or confidence interval as in Listing 8.3 from either `ScatterPlot` or `Correlation`.

```
Alternative Hypothesis: True correlation is not equal to 0
  t-value: 9.501,  df: 34,  p-value: 0.000

95% Confidence Interval of Population Correlation
  Lower Bound: 0.727     Upper Bound: 0.923
```

Listing 8.3 Inferential analysis of the correlation coefficient from `ScatterPlot` and also `Correlation`.

The hypothesis test focuses on the null hypothesis of a population value of 0, of no linear relationship between the two variables. The analysis in Listing 8.3 is a two-tailed test in which substantially large differences in either the positive or negative direction from 0 lead to rejection of 0 as the population value.

$$\text{Years and Salary Relationship:}$$
$$p\text{-value} = 0.000 < \alpha = 0.05, \text{ reject } H_0$$

The rejection of the null hypothesis implies that Years and Salary are related. What is the extent of the relationship? The confidence interval for the population value of the correlation provides the answer as best can be ascertained from the available information. From Listing 8.3, we are 95% confident that the true correlation between Years and Salary is between 0.73 and 0.92, so the correlation is rather substantial.

alternative option, Section 6.2.2, p. 126

Specify one-tailed hypothesis tests in the R environment with the `alternative` option. The values for the `alternative` option that specify a one-tailed test are `"less"` and `"greater"`. The advantage of a *one-tailed test* is that a difference in the direction of the rejection region is easier to detect than the two-tailed alternative. The disadvantage of the one-tailed test is that if a difference in the opposite direction occurs, then the null hypothesis cannot be rejected, so the difference, even if substantial, is not detected. Usually the researcher would find a substantial deviation from the null in either direction to be of interest, regardless whether the deviation is predicted or desired, so usually a two-tailed test is preferred.

8.2.4 The Scatter Plot with a Classification Variable

Points in a scatter plot can also be plotted with different plotting symbols and/or colors according to different values of a third variable, usually represented by a few number of categories. Specify a third variable with the `by` option. For example, view the scatter plot of Years and Salary with different plot symbols for men and women.

by option: Specify a categorical variable for which to classify each point in the scatter plot.

 lessR Input *A scatter plot with Gender as a classification variable*

```
> ScatterPlot(Years, Salary, by=Gender)
```

The resulting scatter plot appears in Figure 8.6. By default, points for the first level, females, are plotted with a circle, whereas a diamond is used to plot paired data values for the second level, males. By default the color of the plotted points is that provided by the current color theme and transparency level.

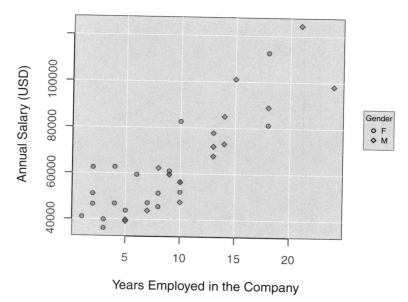

Figure 8.6 Scatter plot of Years and Salary with different plotting symbols for Gender.

The plot symbol used to plot the points at each level of the classification variable can be customized with the `shape.pts` option. Valid values are `"circle"`, `"square"`, `"diamond"`, `"triup"`, and `"tridown"`, which also apply to the point shapes when there is no `by` variable. The order of the specified symbols reflects the order in which the levels of the classification variable are defined. By default R defines the order of the levels alphabetically, though the order can be changed with the `factor` function.

shape.pts option: Plot symbol for each level of the by variable.

factor function for ordering levels, Section 3.3.2, p. 60

If the classification variable is a factor, verify the order of the levels with the standard R function `levels`. Because `levels` is an R function, the location of the referenced variable must be specified, which by default is the data frame `mydata`. For example, precede the name of the referenced variable with `mydata$` as in Listing 8.4.

levels function: Displays the levels of a factor variable.

```
> levels(mydata$Gender)
[1] "F" "M"
```

Listing 8.4 The `levels` function lists the levels of a factor.

According to Listing 8.4, the ordering of the levels for Gender is the default alphabetical order. To specify custom plot symbols with the `shape.pts` option, specify the order of the symbols with the symbol for females listed first. In this example use X for females and Y for males.

The size of these letters plotted as symbols tends to be a little large. Reduce their size using the standard R graphics option `cex`, which controls the size of the plotted symbols. The default value is 1.0, so to reduce the size to 80% of the default specify a value of `cex=.8`.

cex option: Specify the size of the graphics symbol in relation to 1.0.

⌇ **lessR Input** *Scatter plot with custom symbols for a classification variable*
```
> ScatterPlot(Years, Salary, by=Gender,
              shape.pts=c("X","Y"), cex=.8)
```

The resulting scatter plot appears in Figure 8.7.

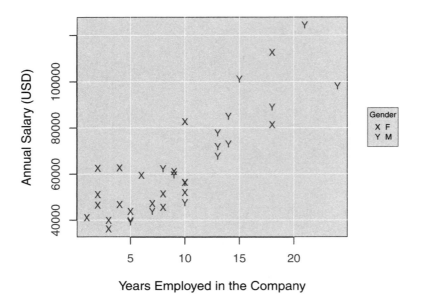

Figure 8.7 Scatter plot of Years and Salary with custom plotting symbols for Gender.

color choices,
Section 1.1, p. 17

An additional customization of a scatter plot with a classification variable is to provide custom colors for symbols plotted for each level of the variable. To do so use the option `col.stroke`, one color for each level of the `by` variable. If points are plotted, the default setting of the fill color is relied upon, which is the transparency level applied to `col.stroke`. Again, the order of the specified colors is the order of the values of the `by` variable.

Custom symbols and custom colors can be specified for the same plot. A loess or least-squares line of best fit can also be specified with the `fit.line` option. The line of best fit is plotted for each value of the `by` variable in the specified color. To emphasize the fit lines and deemphasize the points, plot the points at only 50% of the default point size.

⌇ **lessR Input** *Scatter plot with custom symbols and colors*
```
> ScatterPlot(Years, Salary, by=Gender, fit.line="loess",
              col.stroke=c("black", "gray60"),
              shape.pts=c("X","Y"), cex=.5)
```

Viewing Figures 8.6, 8.7, or 8.8 reveals that at this company three of the highest four salaries are for men and three of the lowest four salaries are for women. The scatter plot also reveals,

Figure 8.8 Scatter plot of Years and Salary with custom plotting symbols and color for Gender and loess lines of best fit.

however, that women tend to be concentrated at the lower end of the axis for the number of Years employed. The eight employees with the least Years of employment are all women.

8.2.5 Scatter Plot of Likert Data

Likert data are the responses to attitude items on the Disagree/Agree continuum, usually 4 to 7 different scale points, coded as integer values. A traditional scatter plot of two variables assessed on a Likert scale is not usually informative because of the small number of potential unique data values. A scatter plot of a 5-point Likert scale yields only 25 unique combinations of data values for the two variables. Without some transparency of the plotted points there is no way to tell if a plotted point, such as for a 3 on the first item and a 2 on the second item, represents one set of data values or many. Even with transparency most of the 25 positions for plotted points in this example may be filled over with many replications.

Likert data, Section 1.6.6, p. 27

The lessR solution to this problem automatically provides a form of a scatter plot called a *bubble plot* if there are less than 10 unique values for each variable. The larger the frequency, the larger the size of each plotted point, that is, bubble.

bubble plot: The size of each plotted point in a scatter plot reflects another value such as frequency.

To illustrate we return to the Machiavellianism data set where each item is assessed with values from 0 to 5. The two most highly correlated Mach IV items are m06 and m07.

Mach IV data, Listing 1.8, p. 27

⭐ **Scenario** *Investigate the relationship between Mach IV Items 6 and 7*

```
6. Honesty is the best policy in all cases.
7. There is no excuse for lying to someone else.
```

These items correlate $r = 0.53$. Explore their relationship graphically.

First read the Machiavellianism data directly from within lessR.

> mydata <- Read("Mach4", format="lessR")

Obtain the scatter plot with the ScatterPlot function. To further summarize the relationship, include a loess line.

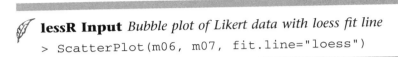

lessR Input *Bubble plot of Likert data with loess fit line*
> ScatterPlot(m06, m07, fit.line="loess")

Their scatter plot appears in Figure 8.9. Because there are only six unique values for each variable, which is less than the threshold of 10, the ScatterPlot function automatically provides a bubble plot form of the scatter plot.

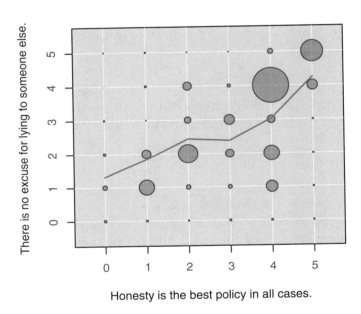

Figure 8.9 Scatter plot in the form of a bubble plot of Mach IV items m06 and m07 with the loess fit line.

The linear relationship of m06 and m07 is apparent from Figure 8.9 as the largest bubbles lie along the increasing diagonal axis. Consistent with this pattern, the loess fit line is approximately linear along this diagonal. The largest bubble is for the Agree response to each item, coded as a 4. Only one possible pair of data values did not occur at all for these 351 respondents, the pairing of Strongly Disagree coded as a 0 for m06 and Agree coded as a 4 for m07.

The ScatterPlot function kind option provides an override for the default style of the scatter plot. By default a regular scatter plot is produced when at least one of the two variables has 10 or more unique values. If both variables have less than 10 unique values, then a bubble plot is produced. For any analysis, to specify a regular plot, set kind="regular". The other values are "bubble" and "sunflower".

kind option: Specify the type of scatter plot, "regular", "bubble", or "sunflower".

The *sunflower plot* is an alternative to the bubble plot. A sunflower plot plots each point as an iconic sunflower such that the more petals the larger the value of another variable. Here the number of petals relates to the joint frequency of the paired data values for the corresponding point.

lessR Input *Sunflower plot of Likert data*

```
> ScatterPlot(m06, m07, kind="sunflower")
```

The sunflower plot of m06 and m07 appears in Figure 8.10. The point with the largest frequency, <4,4>, has so many petals that it almost appears as a filled circle.

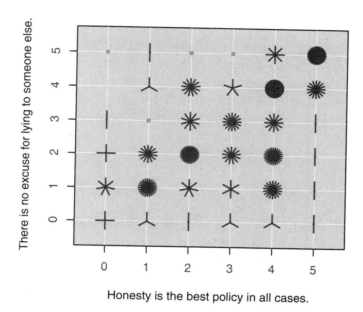

Figure 8.10 Scatter plot in the form of a sunflower plot of Mach IV items m06 and m07.

Figures 8.9 and 8.10 provide useful scatter plots of Likert data. Also of interest are the actual joint frequencies, the count of each possible pair of data values. The previously discussed lessR function BarChart applied to two categorical variables generates the cross-tabulation table of joint frequencies.

Cross-tabulation table, Section 4.3, p. 87

lessR Input *Cross-tabulation of Likert data*

```
> BarChart(m06, m07)
```

The text output of BarChart includes the cross-tabulations in Figure 8.5.

BarChart always tabulates the joint frequencies of the specified variables, regardless whether the type of variable is integer, real number with decimal digits, or a factor. This same cross-tabulation table can also be obtained from SummaryStats. An issue, however, is that

```
m06, Honesty is the best policy in all cases.
m07, There is no excuse for lying to someone else.
------------------------------------------------

      m06
m07     0    1    2    3    4    5  Sum
  0     4    3    2    3    3    2   17
  1     7   24    7    6   18    2   64
  2     4   14   30   13   24    2   87
  3     2    1   10   16   12    2   43
  4     0    3   13    5   56   16   93
  5     1    2    1    1    8   34   47
Sum    18   47   63   44  121   58  351
```

Listing 8.5 Cross-tabulation table for Mach IV items m06 and m07.

SummaryStats adjusts the provided analysis to the type of variable. The cross-tabulation table is by default only provided for categorical variables formally defined as factors, yet the Likert data in the Machiavellian data set are coded as integers.

n.cat option, Section 2.2.7, p. 39

To inform SummaryStats to treat the variables as categorical for purposes of this one analysis, include the n.cat=6 specification as part of the function call. To view only the cross-tabulation table, add the brief=TRUE option, or use the abbreviation ss.brief when calling the function.

```
> SummaryStats(m06, m07, n.cat=6)
```

The n.cat option provides for the treatment of an integer variable as categorical. Its value specifies the maximum number of unique values a variable can have and still be treated as categorical. Here the Likert data reflect a six-point Likert scale.

8.3 The Correlation Matrix

Up until this point in this chapter the focus has been on the linear relation of two variables with each other, in terms of their scatter plot and their Pearson correlation coefficient. Often there are many variables of interest such as the items on an attitude survey. In this situation the focus shifts from just two variables to the relations between all the pairs of variables of interest.

We begin with the correlation coefficients of all the pairwise combinations of the variables. The same lessR function Correlation that calculates a single correlation coefficient between two variables also calculates a *correlation matrix*, a table of all the possible correlation coefficients between all pairs of the specified variables. To calculate this matrix, in the function call to Correlation pass a single list of variables instead of two separate variables. Or, do not specify any variables.

assignment operator, Section 1.3.3, p. 9

Going one step further, if no arguments are specified in the call to the function Correlation, the correlation matrix for all numerical variables in the default data frame mydata is calculated. Usually write this matrix to the matrix mycor as specified by the R assignment operator, <-, though any valid name can be specified.

lessR Input *Correlation matrix from all numerical variables in mydata*

```
> mycor <- Correlation()
```

The `Correlation` function scans the input data frame for non-numerical variables, notes the existence of such variables, and then excludes them from further analysis.

By default, the variables to be analyzed are in the data frame `mydata`, which can be changed by the usual `lessR` option `data`. The matrix `mycor` is an R square matrix with the default name for the `lessR` factor and item analysis procedures. A *matrix* is a simpler version of a data frame in that all the columns in the matrix must be of the same data type. In `mycor` all the entries are real numbers, that is, numeric with decimal digits. By default the number of digits for each calculated correlation coefficient is two, a value that can be changed with the usual `lessR` option `digits.d`.

matrix: A storage container in which all the entries are of the same data type.

digits.d option, Section 1.3.5, p. 14

If not all numerical variables in the input data frame are to be included in the correlation analysis, specify a list of variables that exist within the input data frame. A *variable list* can be written several different ways. As always in R, if commas delineate any of the variables in the list, enclose the list with the c function. For example, list the four variables on the Mach IV Deceit subscale followed by the two items of the Flattery subscale.

c function, Section 1.3.6, p. 15

Mach IV subscales, Section 11.10, p. 273

```
c(m06, m07, m09, m10, m15, m02)
```

A list of contiguous variables in the data frame can be specified with the : notation instead of listing each variable name individually. Here specify the first 10 Mach IV variables.

```
m01:m10
```

Or, the c function and the : notation can be combined to specify a list.

```
c(m01:m05, m10, m13, m15:m18)
```

The rule is that if there is a comma in the list, then the c function must be used to enclose all the items in the list.

8.3.1 No Missing Data

Any of the preceding lists of variables can be passed to the `Correlation` function as a single argument. Here calculate the correlation matrix of the items of the Deceit and Flattery subscales. Access the data from the data frame `mydata` and write the computed correlations to the matrix `mycor`. This example contains no missing data, a topic to be discussed with a later example.

 lessR Input *Calculate a correlation matrix from a list of variables*

```
> mycor <- Correlation(c(m06, m07, m09, m10, m15, m02))
```

The first part of the output appears in Listing 8.6.

```
Correlation matrix calculated
   Name:  mycor
   Number of variables:   6
   Missing data deletion:   pairwise

>>> No missing data
```

Listing 8.6 First section of output for a correlation matrix with the `Correlation` function.

The correlation matrix follows in the output. An annotated version of the matrix appears in Figure 8.11. The matrix consists of three primary sections: the main diagonal and the lower and upper triangles.

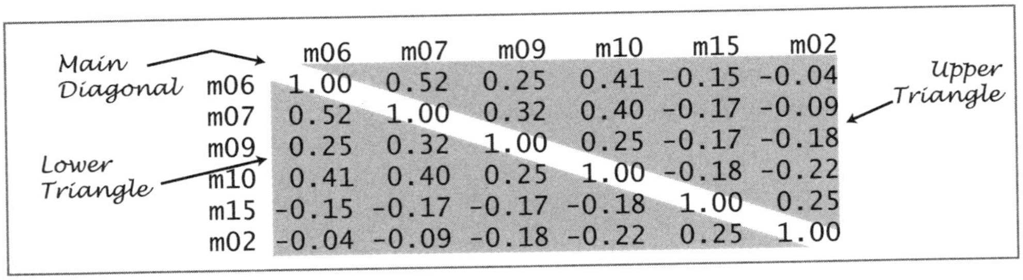

Figure 8.11 Annotated correlation matrix of six Mach IV items from the `Correlation` function.

The correlation coefficient is symmetrical. The correlation of Variable X with Variable Y is the same as the correlation of Y with X. As such, two correlations in the correlation matrix represent each pair of variables, once in the lower triangle and once in the upper triangle. For example, the correlation of `m06` and `m07` is 0.52, which appears twice in the top left of the matrix. Also, each item correlates with itself a perfect 1.0, the value that appears in the main diagonal.

8.3.2 Missing Data

fix function,
Section 3.2, p. 54

The Machiavellian data set has no missing data. To illustrate how the `Correlation` function addresses missing data, remove one value from the data set. With the R function `fix` applied to `mydata`, the data value for `m06` for the first row of data was removed. The result is shown in Listing 8.7, which displays the `NA` value for `m06` that indicates a missing data value in an R data frame.

```
> head(mydata)
  Gender m01 m02 m03 m04 m05 m06 m07 m08 m09 m10 m11 m12 m13 m14 ... m20
1      0   0   4   1   5   0  NA   4   1   5   4   0   0   0   0 ...   4
2      0   0   1   4   4   0   3   3   0   4   4   0   1   1   1 ...   0
```

Listing 8.7 First two rows of `mydata` from the `head` function.

Next the same call to the `Correlation` function is run that generated the correlation matrix in Figure 8.11. The additional output present for missing data appears in Listing 8.8. The default method for addressing missing data is *pairwise deletion* in which the data for each correlation is based on rows of data that both have non-missing data values.

pairwise deletion: Calculate each correlation coefficient from all non-missing data for the two variables.

```
     Missing data deletion:   pairwise

 --- Missing Data Analysis ---

                 350    351    Total
 Frequencies:     11     25      36
 Proportions:  0.306  0.694   1.000

       m06 m07 m09 m10 m15 m02
 m06  350 350 350 350 350 350
 m07  350 351 351 351 351 351
 m09  350 351 351 351 351 351
 m10  350 351 351 351 351 351
 m15  350 351 351 351 351 351
 m02  350 351 351 351 351 351
```

Listing 8.8 Sample size for each computed correlation coefficient.

The pattern of missing data can be different for different pairs of variables, so the sample size upon which each correlation is based can also differ. When the correlation matrix is calculated with pairwise deletion in the presence of missing data, the sample size for each correlation should be examined. In extreme cases some correlations could be based on much less data than other correlations, depending on the pattern of missing values. The data table contained only one missing value, for `m06`, in all 351 rows of data. This row of data is then dropped in the calculation of the correlation of `m06` with all other variables. The result is that the sample size for all the correlations of `m06` with other variables is reduced by 1 to 350.

Also present in Listing 8.8 are the summary statistics for the missing data counts. There are six variables in this correlation matrix, so there are $6 \times 6 = 36$ entries in the correlation matrix. Of these 36 entries, 25 are based on a sample size of 351. The 11 correlations that involve Item `m06` are based on a sample size of 350.

These summary statistics are particularly relevant for larger correlation matrices. For a correlation matrix with more than 15 variables the `Correlation` function does not by default display the sample size matrix nor the correlation matrix. In this situation the minimum sample size encountered in the calculation of any of the correlation coefficients in the matrix is evident in the summary statistics. To examine the individual sample sizes of each coefficient, the sample size matrix can still be displayed with the option `show.n=TRUE`.

Listwise deletion is another common method for addressing missing data. If a row of data has any missing data values, then that entire row of data is deleted from the analysis. Specify listwise deletion with the `miss` option set to `listwise`, of which the default value is `pairwise`.

show.n=TRUE option: Display the matrix of sample sizes for individual correlations.

listwise deletion: One missing data value in a row leads to the deletion of the entire row of data.

✎ **lessR Input** *Correlation matrix with listwise deletion*

```
> mycor <- Correlation(c(m06, m07, m09, m10, m15, m02),
        miss="listwise")
```

The relevant part of the `Correlation` output appears in Listing 8.9.

```
Missing data deletion:  listwise
Sample size after deleted rows: 350
```

Listing 8.9 Relevant output of `Correlation` for listwise deletion.

For listwise deletion all correlation coefficients are calculated with the same sample size. The value reported in Listing 8.9 is 350, the data that remain after deleting the first row of data from the analysis due to its one missing value.

Pairwise deletion is generally preferred over listwise deletion because of the loss of data from the listwise procedure. Many data values are deleted that were present in the original data table. The potential problem with pairwise deletion, however, is to ensure that there are not some correlations that are calculated from an extensively diminished sample size.

8.3.3 Graphics

graphics=TRUE: View correlation matrix graphics.

pdf=TRUE: Write correlation matrix graphics to pdf files.

scatter plot matrix: Table of two variable scatter plots.

Optional graphical portrayals of the correlation matrix are also available. One graphic is a scatter plot matrix and the other is a heat map. Set `graphics=TRUE` to view these graphics in the standard graphics windows, or set `pdf=TRUE` to write the graphics to their respective files.

A *scatter plot matrix* is a table of scatter plots, one for each correlation in the correlation matrix. The scatter plot matrix for the six Mach IV items is shown in Figure 8.12. Just as each correlation in the correlation matrix appears twice, each pair of variables is represented by two scatter plots in the scatter plot matrix. One plot is in the lower triangle and the other plot is in the upper triangle of the matrix.

The variables in the scatter plots have Likert data values so a small number of possibilities limits the configuration of plotted points. Fortunately, each scatter plot also contains a loess line of best fit, which can help gauge the extent of the relationship. For example, the scatter plots for the two highly most correlated items, `m06` and `m07`, contain a fit line of pronounced slope.

heat map: Graphical representation of a matrix with each number replaced by a colored square.

The other optional graph is a heat map of the correlation matrix, which appears in Figure 8.13. The *heat map* is a graphical portrayal of the matrix with each correlation coefficient replaced by a colored square. The larger the correlation, the darker is the color. The diagonal elements of the heat map are treated differently. To provide more color separation for off-diagonal elements, the diagonal elements of the matrix for computing the heat map are set to 0.

The largest correlation in the matrix, 0.52 between Items `m06` and `m07`, is represented with the two darkest colored squares, which are at the top left of the heat map. The lowest correlations in the matrix are between the items in the two different scales. These correlations are represented by white or very light gray colored squares in the second-to-last and last rows of the matrix as well as the second-to-last and last columns. The differentiation of the two different sub-domains of Mach IV items, Deceit and Flattery, is clearly visible in the Figure 8.13.

main option: Heat map title.

bottom, right options: Number of lines for each margin.

Specify a title for the heat map with the usual R graphics option `main`. Depending on the size of the variable names, the bottom and the right margins of the heat map might be too narrow to accommodate the full names. To widen the margins, use the `bottom` and `right` options, such as `bottom=5` to specify five lines for the bottom margin. The scatter plot matrix and heat map can be written to a `pdf` file instead of displayed in a graphics window. To do so,

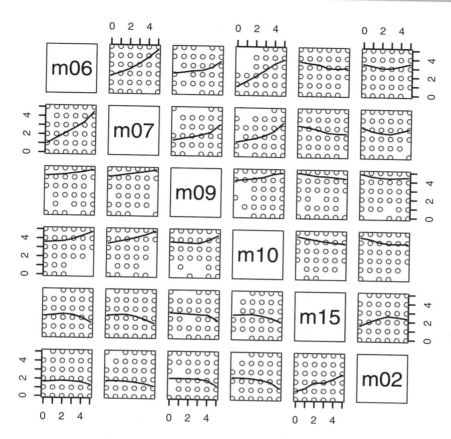

Figure 8.12 Scatter plot matrix of six Mach IV items.

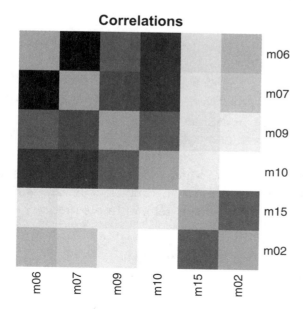

Figure 8.13 Heat map of the correlation matrix of six Mach IV items.

pdf options,
Section 1.4.4,
p. 19

invoke the usual lessR option pdf=TRUE, and if desired, the accompanying size specifications with pdf.width and pdf.height.

8.4 Non-parametric Correlation Coefficients

method=
"spearman"
option: Spearman
correlation.

method="kendall"
option: Kendall
correlation.

As seen in the chapters on group differences, common non-parametric analyses are of ranked ordinal data in place of the original data. The application to ranked data results in a statistic that is more resistant to outliers than the corresponding parametric statistic, and also does not assume underlying normality. The same principles apply to the two non-parametric correlation coefficients provided by R, the Spearman and Kendall coefficients. To invoke either of these coefficients, add method="spearman" or method="kendall" to the calls to the ScatterPlot and Correlation functions.

8.4.1 Spearman Correlation

**Spearman
correlation:**
Pearson correlation
of ranks.

The *Spearman correlation coefficient* is the application of the Pearson formula directly to the ranked data. A perfect Spearman correlation results when both sets of ranked data align perfectly, which occurs when each person has the same rank on each of the two variables. Because the data are expressed as ranks, any transformation that preserves ranks of the values of one of the variables leaves the Spearman correlation unchanged. As such, the Spearman correlation also applies to nonlinear relationships.

If the relationship of two normally distributed variables is linear, the Pearson and Spearman coefficients tend to approximate each other. But when there is nonlinearity that preserves order and/or outliers, the two correlation coefficients tend to diverge. Consider a variable and a transformed variable that is each of the original data values raised to the third power. The Pearson correlation between the two variables can be considerably less than 1, yet the corresponding Spearman correlation is exactly 1.0. As previously defined, two variables are related when as one variable increases, the other tends to either increase or decrease. This relationship is more generally assessed by the Spearman coefficient, which does not require linearity.

Calculate the Spearman coefficient in place of the default Pearson coefficient.

 lessR Input *Calculate the Spearman correlation coefficient*

```
> Correlation(Years, Salary, method="spearman")
```

The usual name for the Spearman coefficient is *rho*, which appears in the output in Listing 8.10. The output includes both the descriptive correlation coefficient in the sample, *rho* = 0.80, but also a hypothesis test that the population value is zero, or, more precisely, that the two variables are not related.

Reject the null hypothesis of no relation.

```
Test of Spearman population correlation of 0:
    p-value = 0.000 < α = 0.05, reject H₀
```

```
Spearman's rank correlation rho

Years, Annual Salary (USD)
Salary, Years Employed in the Company

Number of paired values with neither missing, n: 36
Number of cases (rows of data) deleted: 1

Sample Correlation of Years and Salary: rho = 0.800

Alternative Hypothesis: True rho is not equal to 0
  S-value: 1553.770,  p-value: 0.000
```

Listing 8.10 Analysis of the Spearman correlation coefficient for Years and Salary.

8.4.2 Kendall Correlation

The Kendall correlation coefficient is based on a direct analysis of what are called concordant pairs. Consider any two pairs of data values, X_i, Y_i and X_j, Y_j. If $X_i - X_j$ and $Y_i - Y_j$ have the same sign then the pair of data values is called *concordant*. Similarly, if $X_i - X_j$ and $Y_i - Y_j$ have the opposite sign, the pair of data values is called *discordant*. If the corresponding value of Y always increases as the value of X increases, all pairs of data values are concordant. Similarly, for an inverse relationship, if Y always decreases as X increases, all pairs of data values are discordant.

> **concordant** pair of data values: The two values for each variable change in the same direction.

> **discordant** pair of data values: The values for each variable change in opposite directions.

The numerator of the *Kendall correlation coefficient* is the number of concordant pairs minus the number of discordant pairs of data values. To normalize this result so that the resulting coefficient lies between -1 and 1, divide this value by the number of all possible pairs, $n(n-1)/2$, where n is the sample size. Achieve the maximum value $+1$ if all $n(n-1)/2$ pairs are concordant, and achieve the minimum value -1 if all pairs are discordant.

> **Kendall correlation**: Based on number of concordant and discordant pairs of data values.

To illustrate, return to the example for the correlation matrix of Pearson correlations in Figure 8.11. Now generate the corresponding matrix for the same variables but with Kendall correlation coefficients and store in `mycor`.

> **lessR Input** *Correlation matrix with Kendall correlations*
> ```
> > mycor <- Correlation(c(m06, m07, m09, m10, m15, m02),
>           method="kendall")
> ```

The matrix excerpted from the `Correlation` output appears in Listing 8.11.

```
      m06    m07    m09    m10    m15    m02
m06   1.00   0.47   0.24   0.34  -0.14  -0.06
m07   0.47   1.00   0.30   0.36  -0.15  -0.09
m09   0.24   0.30   1.00   0.27  -0.17  -0.18
m10   0.34   0.36   0.27   1.00  -0.17  -0.22
m15  -0.14  -0.15  -0.17  -0.17   1.00   0.22
m02  -0.06  -0.09  -0.18  -0.22   0.22   1.00
```

Listing 8.11 Correlation matrix of Kendall correlations.

In this example, the Kendall correlations in Listing 8.11 are approximately the same as the corresponding Pearson correlations in Figure 8.11. The largest discrepancy of these correlations is for the largest correlation, between Items m06 and m07. The Pearson correlation is 0.52 and the Kendall correlation is .05 lower, at 0.47.

Worked Problems

?Cars93 for more information.

1 Refer to the Cars93 data set, which is part of lessR.

```
> mydata <- Read("Cars93", format="lessR")
```

(a) Obtain the scatter plot and correlation for MPGcity and MPGhiway. Comment.
(b) Calculate the correlation matrix and scatter plot for the three prices for each car: MinPrice, MidPrice and MaxPrice. Comment.
(c) From the correlation matrix of all numeric variables, which five variables are most correlated with MPGcity?
(d) Why is the scatter plot matrix of all numeric variables not useful?

2 Compare the usual Pearson correlation with the corresponding non-parametric Spearman and Kendall correlations.

(a) Create a data vector X of 25 values of simulated data values from a random normal distribution with a mean of 0 and a standard deviation of 1. Create a second data vector, X3, which consists of the cubed values of X.
(b) Generate the scatter plot of X and X3. Comment. Is it linear?
(c) Calculate the Pearson correlation coefficient of X and X3, as well as the Spearman and Kendall correlation coefficients.
(d) Compare and account for the values of the three correlation coefficients.

CHAPTER 9

REGRESSION I

9.1 Quick Start

First install R and lessR as explained in Section 1.2. At the beginning of each R session access lessR with library(lessR). Then read your data into an R data frame with Read(), the subject of Chapter 2.

Chapters 6 and 7 compared the values of a response variable across different groups of data defined by one or more categorical grouping variables. Chapter 8 compared two continuous, that is, numerical, variables with each other. The current chapter on regression analysis generalizes the concepts presented in these earlier chapters.

Regression analysis always includes a response variable, but now the other variable, called a predictor variable in this context, can be numerical with many values. This chapter considers a single predictor variable. The consideration of multiple predictor variables is deferred to the following chapter. The focus remains on the relationship between variables, particularly the extent to which the values of the response variable can be understood in terms of the values of one or more predictor variables.

✓ For regression analysis, use the lessR function Regression, here for response variable Y and predictor variable X.

```
> Regression(Y ~ X)
```

one-predictor regression analysis, Section 9.2.2, p. 205

✓ In some situations, particularly when there is no intrinsic meaning to the units in which the variables are measured, standardize the variables in the regression equation before model estimation.

```
> Regression(Y ~ X, standardize=TRUE)
```

standardize, Section 9.2.2, p. 207

✓ Prediction generally involves new values of the predictor variable, values not contained in the original data from which the regression model is estimated. To obtain predictions for any specified values of the predictor variable and associated 95% prediction intervals, use the X1.new option. In this example predictions are obtained for values of the predictor variable of 10 or 25.

```
> Regression(Y ~ X, X1.new=c(10, 25))
```

prediction for new values of the predictor variable, Section 9.4.2, p. 214

In this chapter `Regression` is the only R function considered. It is all that is needed for a comprehensive regression analysis. The different sections of `Regression` output should generally be included in any analysis: estimation of the model, residuals and model fit, outliers, and prediction intervals for both existing and new data values. Because all of these analyses should be considered part of regression analysis, they are all conveniently provided by a single function call. To manage the resulting output, the default settings provide useful information regarding these different aspects of regression without copious output.

9.2 The Regression Model

prediction: Estimate an unknown value of the response variable.

explanation: Estimate the impact of a change of one variable on another.

response variable: Variable to be predicted.

predictor variable: Variable(s) from which the prediction is made.

The purpose of regression analysis is twofold. One goal is to *predict* the value of the variable of interest, the response variable, from the values of one or more predictor variables. A second goal is to *explain* the relation of each of the predictor variables to the response variable. Prediction and explanation are at the core of scientific research, and so regression analysis is a central concept in data analysis, subsuming all the previous chapters on studying relationships between variables.

The variable that is predicted, or explained, in terms of the predictor variables is the *response variable*. The variables from which the prediction is made are one or more *predictor variables*. These variables are referred to by different names in different contexts, some of which appear in Table 9.1.

Table 9.1 Alternate names for the response and predictor variables in a regression analysis.

Y variable	X variable
response	predictor
dependent	independent
outcome	explanatory
criterion	predictor

9.2.1 The Function

function: The value of one variable determines the value of another variable.

Regression analysis is based on the mathematical concept of a *function*, in which the value of one (or more) variables X determines the value of another variable Y. A function is typically expressed with an equation, of which the simplest expression is a linear equation, here with just one X variable.

The general equation for a linear function follows.

$$Y = b_0 + b_1 X$$

In this linear equation, b_0 and b_1 are specific constants such as 2 and -5. For these respective values the preceding general form of a linear equation can be written as a specific equation.

$$Y = 2 - 5X$$

With a specific equation the value of Y can be calculated from the value of X. For example, consider a value of the predictor variable of 10. To indicate a specific value of a variable, subscript the variable with an index such as i. For $X_i = 10$, the value of the corresponding Y_i can be computed.

$$Y_i = 2 - 5X_i = 2 - 5(10) = 2 - 50 = -48$$

Given the value of X, the function precisely determines the value of Y.

An equation in this form is a linear function because in general its graph is a linear surface, no curves, which for a single X variable is a straight line. When plotted in the coordinate plane in which the two axes correspond to the two variables, X and Y, the value of Y that crosses the Y-axis, where X=0, is b_0. For this reason b_0 is the *Y-intercept*. The slope of the plotted line is b_1, the *slope coefficient*.

Y-intercept: The constant value in a linear equation.

slope coefficient: The multiplier coefficient of a predictor variable in a linear equation.

9.2.2 The Estimated Model

For the linear function previously illustrated, a value of the variable Y is not a data value, but a value calculated from a function. The application of a linear equation to data analysis changes the meaning of Y. Regression analysis applies to a sample of paired data values, a value of predictor variable X and response variable Y for each case, each row of data. Each paired data value plots as a point in the corresponding graph, the scatter plot (for two variables) from Chapter 8. Accordingly, each set of paired data values is referred to as a *data point*. The regression analysis estimates the sample values of b_0 and b_1 for the corresponding linear function, which can be expressed as a *regression line* graphed through the scatter plot.

data point: A set of data values of the regression variables for a single case.

regression line: Graphical representation of the linear model estimated by a regression analysis.

An example follows. A variable of interest to many is the annual Salary earned working at a job. What are some factors that account for an employee's Salary?

 Scenario *Build a model to predict annual Salary from Years employment*
The more Years worked at a specific company, the larger tends to be the employee's annual Salary. How much does the annual Salary increase, on average, for each Year of employment? What information regarding Salary can potential employees be given for any specified number of Years employment?

t-test, Section 6.3, p. 130

Perform a regression analysis with the `lessR` function `Regression`, abbreviated `reg`. The syntax follows the same general form as the `ttest` and `ANOVA` functions, which follow the R rules for the formula that specifies a model. The response variable is on the left side of the equation, followed by a tilde, $\sim$, and then the predictor variables on the right side of the equation.

In this example, the response variable is Salary with one predictor variable, Years.

 lessR Input *Regression analysis with one predictor variable*

```
> Regression(Salary ~ Years)        or        reg(Salary ~ Years)
```

reg.brief: Specify a brief form of the regression output.

The call to the `Regression` function just described is the call to the full analysis. A briefer analysis is obtained from setting `brief=TRUE`, or use the abbreviation `reg.brief` when calling the function. The brief version gives just the basic analysis, whereas the full version provides a comprehensive analysis that is recommended as what should be part of the standard analysis. The material in this section is part of either version.

The output of the `Regression` analysis begins with a general summary of the variables in the model. This background information is then followed by the first section of output, which appears in Figure 9.1.

	Estimated Coefficients		Hypothesis Test of B=0		95% Confidence Intervals	
	Estimate	Std Err	t-value	p-value	Lower 95%	Upper 95%
(Intercept)	32710.898	3746.753	8.730	0.0000	25096.580	40325.216
Years	3249.552	342.030	9.501	0.0000	2554.463	3944.641

Figure 9.1 Annotated output of estimated regression coefficients, and their corresponding standard errors, hypothesis tests of values of zero in the population, and 95% confidence intervals.

The two values under the `Estimated` column are the estimated values of the regression coefficients, the values of $b_0 = \$32710.90$ and $b_1 = \$3249.55$ that specify the equation of the regression line. The notation $\hat{Y}$ indicates the value of the regression function for the specified value of X.

$$\text{model estimated from data: } \hat{Y}_{Salary} = 32710.90 + 3249.55 X_{Years}$$

fitted value: The value of the response variable calculated for a given value of X with the regression model, $\hat{Y}_i$.

The estimation of this model is the key to the regression analysis goals of prediction and understanding relationships. From this equation a value of Salary can be calculated for a given value of Years, such as for the tenth year of employment.

$$\text{fitted value for X=10: } \hat{Y}_{Salary} = 32710.90 + 3249.55(10) = 65206.42$$

The fitted value $\hat{Y} = 65206$ is the value consistent with the estimated regression model.

The relation of Years and Salary can be expressed with the corresponding slope coefficient of $b_1 = \$3249.55$. The meaning of the slope coefficient follows directly from the mathematics of a linear equation. The *slope coefficient* is the average change in the response variable Y for a one unit increase in the value of the predictor variable X. Without implying cause and effect, the slope coefficient informs us how changes in one variable, X, relate to changes in the response, Y. In this particular sample, for each additional Year employed at the company, Salary increases an average of $3249.55.

slope coefficient meaning: Average change in Y from a unit change in X.

model: An equation to explain the value of a response variable in terms of the values of predictor variables.

The equation of the line is the function that expresses the relation between the response variable Y and predictor variable X for the estimated values of b_0 and b_1. This equation is a *model*. The notation for the variable of the transformed data values that define the regression line calculated from the model is $\hat{Y}$. Distinguish between the measured data values of the variable Y and the variable that consists of the transformed data values according to the regression line, $\hat{Y}$.

The `Regression` function also provides the scatter plot of the response and predictor variables, Years and Salary, with the included regression line. The scatter plot in Figure 9.2

is from the brief version of the output from `reg.brief`. The enhanced scatter plot from the full version of `Regression` provides additional information.

Enhanced scatter plot, Section 9.7, p. 215

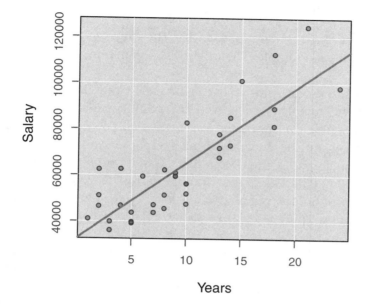

Figure 9.2 Scatter plot with best-fitting least-squares regression line from the brief output form of the `Regression` function, `reg.brief`.

Each value of Years employed, X_i, is associated with both its paired data value of Salary, Y_i, and its corresponding *fitted value* of Salary. This value of Y fit by the regression model, $\hat{Y}_i$ lies on the regression line. Figure 9.2 provides the graphical representation of the relationship between the variables X, Y, and $\hat{Y}$.

The model estimated in this section is estimated from the measurements, the data values, for each of the variables in the model. Particularly when the variables have no natural unit, such as the score on a psychological test or Likert scale attitude survey, the variables may be standardized first before the model is estimated. This transformation expresses each value of a variable in terms of how many standard deviations the value is from its mean so that the unit of the standardized variable becomes the variable's standard deviation instead of its original measurement scale. Standardization likely would not be applied to the Salary data in this section because the units of the variables in the model are meaningful and understood, $ in USD and Years employment. When desired, however, standardize the variables simply by setting the `standardize` option to TRUE.

standardization, Section 3.3.1, p. 57

standardize option: Set to TRUE to standardize the variables before estimating the model.

9.2.3 Inference of Regression Coefficients

As virtually always with data analysis, the goal is not to describe relationships in the sample, but rather in the population from which the sample data values were obtained. That is, the goal is to move beyond the description of the sample to inference of the corresponding values in the population as a whole. That means that each computed sample statistic of interest should be the basis for understanding the corresponding population value.

For regression analysis there is a population model that describes the relation of Years and Salary for the process by which Salaries are assigned at that company.

$$\texttt{population model:}\ \hat{Y}_{Salary} = \beta_0 + \beta_1 X_{Years}$$

Each sample of employees yields a set of data values for X and Y. The values of the estimated regression coefficients b_0 and b_1 differ for each sample. The unknown population values β_0 and β_1 are of primary interest.

inferential analysis,
Section 6.2.1, 124

standard error:
Standard deviation of the sample value of a statistic over usually hypothetical repeated samples.

As previously discussed, statistical inference from what can be called the classical model consists of two different techniques: the hypothesis test and the confidence interval. Both concepts follow from the standard error. The *standard error* of a regression coefficient sets the baseline for how much the corresponding statistic fluctuates from sample to sample.

Each statistic has a standard error. In Figure 9.1 the two statistics are b_0 and b_1, with respective standard errors of $3746.753 and $342.030. From these standard errors the corresponding *t*-test of the null hypothesis that the corresponding population value is zero can be constructed. As previously defined for the mean and mean difference, the *t*-value is the number of estimated standard errors the sample statistic is from the corresponding hypothesized value.

The two *t*-values for the two corresponding hypothesis tests are also found in Figure 9.1. Usually the meaning of the slope coefficient is more interesting than the meaning of the Y-intercept, the value of the response variable when the predictor variable is zero. In some situations that value may be interpretable, but in this example the b_0 represents a Salary with no Years of employment.

To focus on the slope coefficient, $b_1 = 3249.55$, the null hypothesis is that there is no average population change in Salary for a 1-year increase in Years employed.

$$\texttt{Null Hypothesis:}\ H_0\ \texttt{is}\ \beta_1 = 0$$

t-value,
Section 6.2.2,
p.128,
Section 6.3.2,
p.134
p-value,
Section 6.2.2,
p. 128

The corresponding *t*-value is the estimate of b_1 divided by its estimated standard error, $t_b = 9.501$. That means that the estimated sample coefficient of $3249.55 is 9 and one-half estimated standard errors from the null value of 0. This is an extremely improbable event given the assumption of a population value of 0, as shown by the accompanying *p*-value of 0.000 to three decimal digits.

$$\texttt{Effect of Years on Salary:}\ p\texttt{-value} = 0.000,\ \texttt{so reject}\ H_0$$

We conclude that a change in the Years employed does, on average, lead to change in Salary.

Given that the relationship exists, what is the extent of the relationship? In the sample each additional Year was worth an $3249.55 average increase in Salary. The estimated extent of the average change of Salary in the population is provided by the confidence interval for the slope coefficient found in Figure 9.1. Each 95% confidence interval is about two estimated standard errors on either side of the sample estimate, as specified by the *t*-cutoff value. This range of about two estimated standard errors contains about 95% of all sample estimates about the true value, though the estimate of the standard error fluctuates from sample to sample.[1]

t-cutoff,
Section 6.2.2,
p.127

Figure 9.1 reveals that there is 95% confidence that the true average change in Salary for each additional Year employed at this company is somewhere between $2554 and $3945. This range is the extent of our knowledge regarding the true impact on Salary depending on the number of Years employed. Again, the fact that a change in Years employed is associated with a change in Salary does not mean that change in Years directly causes the change in Salary. There could be common variables that correlate with both Years and Salary that would have the true causal impact.

9.3 Residuals and Model Fit

The points in the scatter plot, which represent the paired data values, tend not to lie on the regression line that summarizes the relationship between the specified variables. The vertical distance that separates each plotted point from the regression line is a key attribute of the analysis. This distance from the ith point on the regression line to the corresponding value of the response variable is the ith *residual*, denoted e_i.

residual: Given the value X_i, the difference between the data value Y_i and the fitted value, $\hat{Y}_i$.

$$\text{Residual of } i^{th} \text{ value of X, } X_i\colon \; e_i = Y_i - \hat{Y}_i$$

For example, consider the data in the Employee data set for the 16th row of data, the data for Laura Kralik, who has worked for the company for 10 years and earns $Y_{16} = \$82,681.19$. As previously computed, the fitted value of Salary for 10 years of employment is $\hat{Y}_{16} = \$65206.42$. From these values the 16th residual can be calculated, that is, for $i = 16$.

fitted value for X=10, Figure 9.2.2, p. 206

$$\text{Residual Ex: } e_{16} = Y_{16} - \hat{Y}_{16} = 82681.19 - 65206.42 = 17474.77$$

In this example her actual Salary is $\$17,474.77$ larger than the fitted value as illustrated in Figure 9.3.

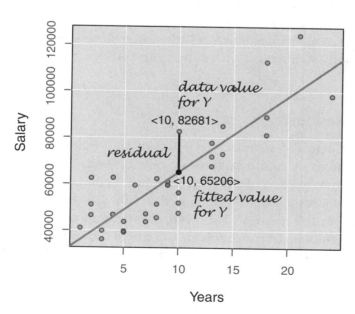

Figure 9.3 Example of a data value, fitted value, and associated residual.

least-squares estimation: Regression coefficients minimize the sum of squared residuals.

The residual is the basis for how the model is estimated, that is, how the regression coefficients are computed. According to the widely used *least-squares estimation* procedure, the estimated coefficients $b_0 = \$32,710.90$ and $b_1 = \$3249.55$ are the two numbers from all possible pairs of numbers that result in the minimization of the squared residuals for that specific data set entered into the regression analysis.

least-squares estimation: Choose b_0 and b_1 to minimize $\sum e_i^2$

Calculate the residual for each pair of data values in the data set analyzed by the regression program. Then square each residual and sum the squared values. The result is the smallest possible sum. In the Regression output this value appears in the Analysis of Variance section of the output, in Figure 9.4.

```
Analysis of Variance

              df          Sum Sq          Mean Sq      F-value   p-value
Years     1    12107157290.292   12107157290.292     90.265    0.0000
Residuals 34    4560399502.217     134129397.124
```

Figure 9.4 Annotated analysis of variance output for the regression model, with the sum of the squared residuals.

The sum of the squared residuals can be read directly from the output.

Sum of squared residuals: $\sum e_i^2 = 4560399502.217$

The resulting value is large, but the scale of the coefficient is due to the unit of analysis of only $1 with the salaries in the tens of thousands dollars. The hypothesis test in Figure 9.4 is redundant with the hypothesis test already discussed regarding the slope coefficient of Years.

Least-squares estimation ensures that the sum of squared residuals has been minimized, but a related issue is how good is this minimization. Is there much or little scatter about the regression line? Too much scatter and the line poorly summarizes the relationship between X and Y, even if it is the best line for the given data.

9.3.1 Standard Deviation of the Residuals

One method of assessing fit is to calculate the standard deviation of the residuals. A small standard deviation is an indicator of good fit, and a large value not so good. This standard deviation is $11,580 as reported in the next section of the Regression function, called Model Fit, shown in Listing 9.1. Assuming the residuals are normally distributed, then a range of two standard deviations on either side of their mean, which is zero, contains about 95% of the values of the distribution. The Regression function also reports the size of that range. Most of the values about the regression line vary across the considerable span of over $46,000.

9.3.2 R^2 Fit Statistic

The other primary fit statistic for a regression analysis is R^2, here reported as 0.726 from Listing 9.1. This statistic compares the scatter about the regression for two different models, the current model compared to the null model. The *null model* is the model without X or any

null model:
Regression model with no predictor variables.

other variable as a predictor variable. Prediction is still possible even without a predictor variable. The fitted value of Y for each value of X without X in the model is just the mean of all the

```
Standard deviation of residuals:   11581.42 for 34 degrees of freedom
If normal, the approximate 95% range of residuals about each fitted
   value is 2*t-cutoff*11581.42, with a 95% interval t-cutoff of 2.032
95% range of variation: 47072.57

R-squared:   0.726      Adjusted R-squared:   0.718

F-statistic for null hypothesis that population R-squared=0:   90.2648
Degrees of freedom:   1 and 34
p-value:    0.0000
```

Listing 9.1 Fit indices.

values of Y, $\bar{Y}$. The null regression line and two of the corresponding residuals are illustrated in Figure 9.5. As can be seen by comparing Figure 9.3 with Figure 9.5, the residuals are considerably reduced from the actual model compared to the null model.

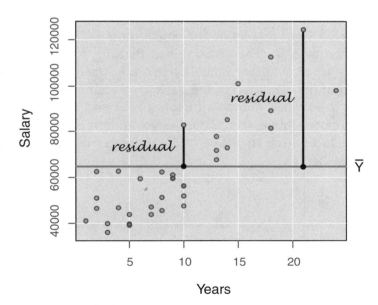

Years

Figure 9.5 Scatter plot with the null regression line and two illustrated residuals from that line.

The R^2 statistic assesses how much using X in the model reduces the amount of scatter about a $\hat{Y}$ generated for each value of X, the extent of the residuals, compared to the amount of scatter that results without X, the scatter about $\bar{Y}$. An additional interpretation follows from the meaning of the residuals of the data values of Y from the null model. This sum of squared residuals from $\bar{Y}$ is the basis for the variance and its square root, the standard deviation, of the response variable Y, which describes the total variability of Y. So R^2 is also referred to as the percent of variance accounted for in the response variable by the predictor variable.

Values of R^2 are generally considered rather high if above 0.5 or 0.6. Many published analyses have an R^2 in the 0.3 range or below. The corresponding hypothesis test is of the null hypothesis, H_0, that the population R^2 is zero. This value is usually significant, as is the case in this example.

Test of population $R^2 = 0$: p-value $< \alpha = 0.05$, so reject H_0

The sample $R^2 = 0.726$ is large. Further, the null hypothesis of a zero value is rejected. So conclude that the size and extent of the residuals for this sample is reduced by adding the predictor variable to the model.

Unfortunately, the size of R^2 does not straightforwardly reflect the improvement in predictive accuracy by including the predictor variable(s) in the model. R^2, and the standard deviation of residuals as well, are descriptive statistics. They describe properties of the sample but do not indicate performance of the model in new samples. That is, these fit statistics do not account for sampling error. A high R^2 is a goal, but is not sufficient to indicate a useful model for prediction.

The issue of sampling error is most salient for small samples. With R^2 there is the additional consideration that adding predictor variables to a model necessarily increases R^2 relative to the sample size. This bias increases to the extent that if the number of predictors equals the sample size then $R^2 = 1.0$. Particularly for a small sample size with a relatively large number of predictor variables, the estimation procedure minimizes the sum of squared residuals by taking advantage of random variation that will not replicate in another sample. To account for this upward bias, an adjustment is needed that explicitly accounts for the increase of R^2 as the number of predictor variables increases.

This companion statistic is the adjusted R^2, or R^2_{adj}, an improvement on the original R^2, and should always be reported in conjunction with R^2. The distinction is that R^2_{adj} adjusts for the size of the sample compared to the number of predictor variables. The adjustment is based on dividing each of the two sums of squares in the definition of the statistic by their corresponding degrees of freedom. The result is that R^2_{adj} provides a downward adjustment and more realistic assessment of the comparison of the proposed model to the null model. In very small samples the value of R^2_{adj} may be considerably reduced from the value of R^2. In larger samples R^2_{adj} will still be smaller, but usually not much smaller.

9.4 Prediction Intervals

One of the two primary purposes of regression analysis is to enter a value of the predictor variable X into the estimated model to calculate the prediction or forecast, $\hat{Y}$, of the value of the response variable Y. Up until this section the calculated value of $\hat{Y}$ is called a fitted value because it is calculated from the same data from which the model is estimated, the *training sample*. There is no prediction here in the calculation of $\hat{Y}$ because the value of the response variable Y is already known for training data. There is nothing to predict. Instead use the neutral term "fitted" value in this context in place of "predicted" value.

Accomplish true prediction by entering data values for the predictor variables from a new sample of data, the *test sample* or validation sample, into the model estimated from the training sample. By coincidence some of these new values of the predictor variable may duplicate values from the original data, but in general they will not. At the time the forecast is made the researcher knows the value of the predictor variable, but not the corresponding value of the response variable. The true value will not be known until some later time, when the accuracy of the prediction can be assessed.

As is true of any statistical result, such as a predicted value, the presence of error confounds the result. Unfortunately, two forms of error underlie a prediction. First, as discussed in the previous section, is the residual from the model, the distance in the training sample of the fitted value of the response variable Y from its actual value. These residuals, the plotted data

fitted value calculation, Section 9.2.2, p. 206

training sample: Sample of data from which the regression model is estimated.

test data: Sample of data from which the regression model generates predictions.

modeling error: The residual, the difference of the actual value and fitted value from the original data.

values scattered about the regression line, indicate a lack of fit of the model. The model does not account for all of the variation in the response variable, so another name for the residuals from the training sample is *modeling errors*.

The unfortunate reality of any statistical estimation process, such as for the estimation of b_0 and b_1 for the regression line, also necessarily involves *sampling error*. For each new sample of paired data values for the response and predictor variables, Y and X, a different set of estimates for the regression coefficients b_0 and b_1 would be obtained. The regression line randomly fluctuates from sample to sample, and then so does the point on the line for any single value of the predictor variable X.

Prediction necessarily involves new data, which means a new sample, the test sample. A problem here is that the regression model applied to the test sample to obtain the prediction was estimated from the original data, the training sample. So the regression model was optimized by choosing the regression coefficients that resulted in the smallest possible sum of the squared residuals, but only for the training sample, *not* the test sample.

The consequence is that the encountered level of prediction error for a true forecast of an unknown value of Y cumulates both modeling error and sampling error. The prominence of modeling error is summarized by the indicators of fit already discussed, the standard deviation of the residuals and R^2, preferably in its adjusted form. The extent of prediction error is larger than indicated by these fit indices because it will consist of the influences of both modeling error and sampling error. The smaller the sample, the more pronounced the effect of the sampling error on the size of the prediction interval.

prediction error: Difference between a prediction on new data and the actual value later obtained.

The concept of *prediction error* is made practical by providing a 95% interval, the *prediction interval*, for each predicted value. There is a 95% confidence that the actual value of Y later obtained will be contained within this prediction interval. The size of these intervals is not the same for all values of the predictor variable X. Instead, the closer the value of the predictor variable is to its mean, the smaller the interval. This is because as the regression line fluctuates across samples values the extremes of the line vary more than do values in its middle, similar to a teeter-totter where sitting on the end provides much more up and down motion than does sitting further inward.

95% prediction interval: Range of values that with 95% confidence contains the predicted value.

9.4.1 Prediction from Existing Data Values

The `Regression` function by default provides two different analyses for these prediction intervals. First the function displays the lower and upper bounds of the intervals as part of the standard text output. The intervals by default are sorted from the smallest lower bound of the prediction intervals to the largest lower bound. To leave the rows of data in their original order, specify the `pred.sort="off"` option. To avoid voluminous output only representative prediction intervals are provided, intervals for lowest values of the lower bound of the interval, middle values of the lower bound, and intervals for the largest values. If the sample is sufficiently small, less than 25, or if the `pred.rows` option is set to `"all"`, then all the prediction intervals for all the rows of data are displayed.

`pred.sort="off"` option: Do not sort rows of data by the prediction interval lower bounds.

`pred.rows` option: Number of displayed prediction intervals for first, middle, and last intervals, or set to "all".

Annotated output for the prediction intervals of Salary from Years appears in Figure 9.6. The fitted values and the 95% prediction intervals are highlighted. Also provided are the corresponding data values, the width of each prediction interval, and the 95% confidence intervals of the point on the regression line. To save space in this figure the decimal digits are not displayed, accomplished by setting `digits.d=0` in the function call to `Regression`.

digits.d option, Section 1.3.5, p. 14

	Years	Salary	fitted	ci:lwr	ci:upr	pi:lwr	pi:upr	pi:wdh
Hamide, Bita	1	41037	35960	28933	42988	11397	60524	49126
Singh, Niral	2	51055	39210	32747	45673	14803	63617	48815
Korhalkar, Jessica	2	62502	39210	32747	45673	14803	63617	48815
Anastasiou, Crystal	2	46508	39210	32747	45673	14803	63617	48815

... for the middle 4 rows of sorted data ...

	Years	Salary	fitted	ci:lwr	ci:upr	pi:lwr	pi:upr	pi:wdh
Kimball, Claire	8	51357	58707	54668	62747	34827	82588	47761
Saechao, Suzanne	8	45545	58707	54668	62747	34827	82588	47761
Tian, Fang	9	61084	61957	58025	65889	38094	85819	47725
Stanley, Grayson	9	59625	61957	58025	65889	38094	85819	47725

... for the last 4 rows of sorted data ...

	Years	Salary	fitted	ci:lwr	ci:upr	pi:lwr	pi:upr	pi:wdh
Skrotzki, Sara	18	81352	91203	84046	98359	66603	115803	49200
James, Leslie	18	112563	91203	84046	98359	66603	115803	49200
Correll, Trevon	21	124419	100951	91978	109925	75763	126140	50378
Capelle, Adam	24	98138	110700	99813	121587	84768	136633	51865

Figure 9.6 Annotated 95% prediction intervals for representative rows of data.

The confidence intervals in Figure 9.6 reflect the sampling error, the variation of the corresponding point on the regression line from sample to sample. Larger sampling errors contribute to larger prediction errors. Assuming normality, the 95% range of the residuals provide the extent of the modeling error, a value already reported as $47073 in Listing 9.1. Because the prediction intervals reflect both modeling and sampling error, they are larger than the corresponding 95% range of the residuals. From Figure 9.6, the smallest prediction interval is $47,725 wide, from $38,094 to $85,819 for 9 years of employment. The largest prediction interval is $51,865 wide, from $84,768 to $136,633 for 24 years of employment.

The second type of results the Regression function provides for prediction intervals is an enhanced scatter plot that illustrates the size of the prediction intervals. This scatter plot, in Figure 9.7 also contains the regression line, the confidence intervals that reflect variability of the regression line, and the wider prediction intervals. The two (slightly) curved lines that define the prediction intervals define many such intervals, the lower and upper bound of the interval for each value of the predictor variable, Years.

As is frequently encountered in the estimation of regression models, the prediction intervals are wide. Precise prediction is not easy. A larger sample will reduce the effect of the sampling error, but the effect of the modeling error can only be reduced by improving the model, such as adding new predictor variables, the topic of the following chapter.

9.4.2 Prediction from Specified Data Values

The prediction intervals provided by the Regression function are for each row of the data table, the existing values of the predictor variable. As noted, prediction occurs from new values of the predictor variable, which generally do not equal the existing values. There also needs to be a way to obtain these prediction intervals for specified new values.

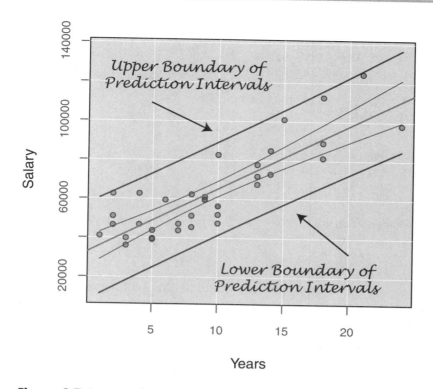

Figure 9.7 Annotated scatter plot with prediction intervals of Salary, and the regression line and the confidence intervals for the variability of the regression line.

 Scenario *Obtain predictions for new values of the predictor variable*
The data include employees who have worked at the company for each of 1 to 10 years. The interval from 10 to 20 years, however, contains gaps such as for 12 years and 16 years, for which the default analysis does not provide predictions. Generate a list of predictions for all integer values of Years from 10 to 20. Then a prospective employee can be provided an estimate of the Salary at the company after any specified number of Years employed.

The `Regression` function provides an option `X1.new` for listing specified values of the predictor variable from which to obtain a prediction of the response variable and associated interval. The `X1` refers to the first predictor variable, which is the only predictor variable in this example. Specify the range of values of the predictor variable as `10:20`. Or, invoke the `c` function to specify a more customized list of variables.

X1.new option: Obtain predictions for specified values of the predictor variable. *c* function, Section 1.3.6, p. 15

 lessR Input *Prediction intervals for specified values of the predictor variable*
```
> Regression(Salary ~ Years, X1.new=10:20)
```

The resulting predictions and associated 95% prediction intervals appear in Listing 9.2.

```
Years Salary fitted ci:lwr ci:upr pi:lwr pi:upr pi:wdh
  10         65206  61261  69152  41342  89071  47729
  11         68456  64377  72535  44569  92343  47774
  12         71706  67383  76028  47776  95635  47860
  13         74955  70298  79612  50962  98948  47985
  14         78205  73139  83270  54129 102280  48150
  15         81454  75923  86986  57277 105632  48355
  16         84704  78662  90746  60404 109003  48599
  17         87953  81367  94539  63513 112394  48881
  18         91203  84046  98359  66603 115803  49200
  19         94452  86705 102200  69674 119231  49557
  20         97702  89348 106056  72727 122677  49950
```

Listing 9.2 Specified predictions and prediction intervals for Salary for values of Years employed from 10 to 20.

The remainder of the `Regression` output is identical to what is obtained without the `X1.new` option. The only distinction is the section for the prediction intervals. This section now analyzes the new, specified values of the predictor variables. The value for the response variable in this section is blank because it is not yet known.

9.5 Outliers and Diagnostics

outlier,
Section 5.3.1,
p. 106

**bivariate
outlier**: An outlier
with respect to the
distribution of
paired data values.

Before accepting a model as a valid representation of the relationships among the specified variables, some conditions and assumptions should first be examined. To begin, consider the concept of an outlier, a value of a variable far from most of the data values, and its effect on the estimated model coefficients, b_0 and b_1. The outlier of interest here is a *bivariate outlier*, defined with respect to both variables. The bivariate outlier lies outside the patterning of the points in the two-dimensional scatter plot. As discussed in the previous chapter, this patterning is an ellipse for two normally distributed variables.

For the 37 employees in the Employee data set, estimate the following regression model to explain Salary in terms of Years employment.

$$\text{model estimated from data:} \quad \hat{Y}_{Salary} = 32710.90 + 3249.55 X_{Years}$$

fix function,
Section 3.2, p. 54

Now consider changing the value of Salary for just one person, Trevon Correll, the person who has worked the longest at the company, 21 years, and has the highest Salary, \$124,419.23. What is the impact on the estimated coefficients if that Salary is changed to \$40,000? With the `fix` function that one data value was changed and the regression analysis re-run. The result is the following model.

$$\text{model estimated from outlier data:} \quad \hat{Y}_{Salary} = 4537.62 + 2394.64 X_{Years}$$

The resulting scatter plot with both the original and new regression lines appears in Figure 9.8. The decrease in the estimated slope coefficient is \$854.91. The shift in one data value decreased the impact of each additional Year on Salary from an average of \$3250 down to \$2395.

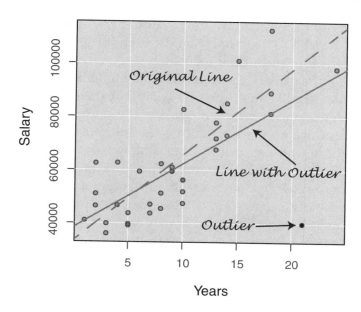

Figure 9.8 Regression line with the outlier compared to the original regression line.

As discussed, the least-squares estimation procedure for the regression coefficients minimized the sum of the squared residuals. The problem of outliers in this scenario is that it is the minimization of the *squared* distance of the actual and fitted values for the response variable. The result is that the large residual of the resulting outlier exerts a disproportionate influence on the estimated model. For this reason an estimated regression model may not well reflect an underlying process if an outlier generated by a different process is included in the analysis. For example, if an employee actually did work at the company for 21 years and still made little money, perhaps the employee is the only part-time employee in the analysis. The process of how to determine Salary for part-time and full-time employees is quite different and should be analyzed separately.

9.5.1 Influence Statistics

Some data values for the predictor and response variables have more impact on the estimation of the resulting model than do other data values. These data values may also be outliers. A way to assess these differential impacts would identify those data points with the most impact. A data point with disproportionate influence, an influential data point, always should be inspected, and its role in the analysis assessed. Sometimes an influential data point is just a data coding or entry error, yet one that would have changed the entire analysis had it remained. Sometimes a different process generates the influential data point than does the process that generates the remaining data values. In such a situation the data point should be analyzed separately. And sometimes an influential data point and may just represent an unusual event, analogous to flipping a fair coin 10 times and getting 8 heads.

Several different indices of influence are available for diagnostic checking (Belsley, Kuh, & Welsch, 1980). A large residual suggests the possibility of outliers and influential data points, but there are several difficulties with this use. One problem is to define the meaning of "large"? A way to address this problem is to standardize the residual so that, presuming normality, values larger than 2 or 3 likely indicate an outlier and perhaps an influential data point. Standardization of a

influence: Effect of a specific set of the values of the predictor variables and the response variable on the estimated model.

influential data point: A data point with considerably more influence than most other data points.

residual in this situation, however, is not quite so straightforward because its standard deviation depends on the value of the predictor variable. This proper standardization that makes this adjustment for the value of the predictor is the Studentized residual.

Another issue to consider is that the estimated regression coefficients minimize the sum of squares of these residuals. If a data point is influential, then by definition there is a greater adjustment than usual made to the regression estimates to achieve this minimization. To remedy this problem, a more useful set of diagnostics are the *case-deletion statistics*. To avoid the confounding of the residual adjusted to the data point, delete the data point and then re-compute the regression. Then calculate the residual of the deleted data point from this new model. Fortunately, formulas exist to make these adjustments without an actual physical re-computation. The result is an influence statistic based on a residual for a data point that does not contribute to the estimation of the model.

The version of the Studentized residual when adjusted for case-deletion is the externally Studentized residual, also called *R-Student*. This version of the residual has the additional advantage of following the *t*-distribution with degrees of freedom of $n - k - 1$, where n is the sample size and k is the number of predictor variables in the model. The *t*-distribution provides a standard for evaluating the size of R-Student. Except in very small samples, regardless of the original scale of measurement of the response variable Y, values of R-Student larger than 2 or smaller than -2 should be infrequent, and values larger than 2.5 or 3 or smaller than -2.5 or -3 should be rare.

Other case-deletion statistics directly assess the influence of a data point on the estimated regression model. One index, *Cook's Distance* or *D*, summarizes the overall influence of a data point on all the estimated regression coefficients. Data points with larger *D* values than the rest of the data are those that have unusual influence. Fox and Weisberg (1991, p. 34) suggests as a cut-off for detecting influential cases, values of *D* greater than $4/(n - k - 1)$, where n is the number of cases, rows of data, and k is the number of predictor variables.

Perhaps the most useful interpretation of Cook's Distance follows from a comparison of their relative sizes. When one or a few data points result in a large *D* value, both in terms of the overall magnitude, and also relative to the remaining values, then an influential case has been identified. These larger values of Cook's Distance or other influence statistics are more likely in smaller data sets.

Another direct index of the influence of a data point is its impact on the fitted value. *DFFITS* represents the number of standard errors that the fitted value for a data point has shifted when it is not present in the sample of data used to estimate the model. Large values of DFFITS indicate influential data points. A general cutoff to consider is 2, or, a recommended size-adjusted cutoff is $2\sqrt{(k + 1)/n}$. Perhaps a more useful approach, however, is to isolate those data points with large DFFITS values relative to most of the other data points and then try to understand why these data points are so influential.

The `Regression` function presents these three case-deletion influence indices, labeled `rstudent`, `dffits`, and `cooks`. Only those data points with relatively large values on these indices are of interest, so to conserve space these indices by default are listed only for the 20 data points with the largest value of Cook's Distance. Listed for each such row of data are the row name, the data values, the fitted value, the residual, and then the three indices.

The rows are by default sorted by Cook's Distance as shown in Listing 9.3. The case with the largest Cook's Distance is for Trevon Correll, who makes the highest Salary. The value of Cook's Distance, 0.409, is more than twice as high as the next highest value of 0.204. Also this case has the highest R-Student value of 2.330 as well as the largest dffits value of 0.961. The value

---

case-deletion statistic: A statistic for a data point calculated without the point in the analysis.

R-Student: A standardized residual calculated from the model estimated with the corresponding data point deleted from the data.

Cook's Distance, *D*, Summary of the distance between the regression coefficients calculated with a specific data point included and then deleted.

DFFITS: Scaled change in the fitted value for a specific data point when the point is deleted.

of the residual for Trevon Correll's Salary is \$23,467.73, which is the extent that the Salary is larger than the value fitted with the model. Further examination of this situation beyond the regression analysis may account for this considerably larger Salary than is accounted for by the model.

	Years	Salary	fitted	residual	rstudent	dffits	cooks
Correll, Trevon	21	124419.23	100951.50	23467.732	2.330	0.961	0.409
Capelle, Adam	24	98138.43	110700.15	-12561.725	-1.233	-0.643	0.204
James, Leslie	18	112563.38	91202.84	21360.540	2.022	0.645	0.191
Korhalkar, Jessica	2	62502.50	39210.00	23292.498	2.208	0.630	0.178
Hoang, Binh	15	101074.86	81454.18	19620.677	1.799	0.435	0.089
Billing, Susan	4	62675.26	45709.11	16966.153	1.535	0.364	0.064
Singh, Niral	2	51055.44	39210.00	11845.438	1.066	0.304	0.046
Skrotzki, Sara	18	81352.33	91202.84	-9850.510	-0.890	-0.284	0.041
Cassinelli, Anastis	10	47562.36	65206.42	-17644.061	-1.579	-0.268	0.035
Kralik, Laura	10	82681.19	65206.42	17474.769	1.563	0.266	0.034

Listing 9.3 Residuals and influence indices sorted by Cook's Distance.

The default settings that control the display of the rows of data and other values can be modified. The `res.rows` option can change the default of 20 rows displayed to any value up to the number of rows of data, specified by the value of `"all"`. To turn this option off, specify a value of 0. The `res.sort` option can change the sort criterion from the default value of `"cooks"`. Other values are `"rstudent"` for R-Student, `"dffits"` for the dffits index and `"off"` to leave the rows of data in their original order.

res.rows option: The number of rows of data to be displayed for the residuals analysis.

res.sort option: The sort criterion for the residuals analysis.

9.5.2 Assumptions

As with any statistical procedure, the validity of the analysis requires satisfying the underlying assumptions. The assumptions focus on the properties of the residuals, which ideally only reflect random error. Any systematic content of the residual variable violates one or more of the assumptions. If so, the model is too simple, so explicitly revise the model to account for this systematic information instead of relegating it to the error term. Often this correction includes adding one or more predictor variables, accounting for a nonlinear relationship, or using an estimation procedure other than least-squares.

The least-squares estimation procedure requires the following three assumptions.

✓ the average residual value should be zero for each value of the predictor variable
✓ the standard deviation of the residuals should be the same for each value of the predictor variable
✓ for data values collected over time, the residuals at one time value should not correlate with the corresponding residuals at other time values

A detailed analysis of the evaluation of the assumptions of regression analysis is well beyond the scope of this book. Fortunately, the first two assumptions can be at least informally evaluated by examining a scatter plot of the residuals with the fitted values. Figure 9.9 is the `Regression` scatter plot for these variables.

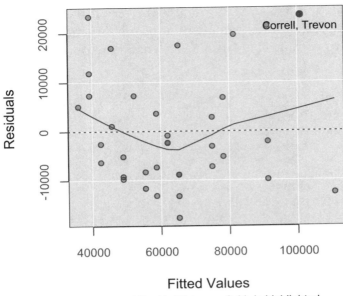

Figure 9.9 Scatter plot of fitted values with residuals with the data point with the largest Cook's Distance highlighted.

For each value of $\hat{Y}_i$, that is, for each vertical line drawn through the scatter plot, the residuals should be approximately evenly distributed in the positive and negative regions. To facilitate this comparison the graph contains a dotted horizontal line drawn through the origin. If the residuals for individual values of $\hat{Y}_i$ are not evenly balanced about the horizontal zero line, the relationship between response and predictor variables is likely not linear as specified.

The second assumption of least-squares regression is a constant population standard deviation of the estimation errors at all values of X, the equal variances assumption. The value of Y should be no more or less difficult to predict for different values of X. Any difference in the standard deviation of residuals for different values of X should be attributable only to sampling error. That is, the variability of the values of Y around each value of X should be the same. The violation of this equal variances assumption is *heteroscedasticity*. Often the pattern exhibited by heteroscedasticity is a gradually increasing or decreasing variability as X gets larger or smaller. When heteroscedasticity occurs, the corresponding standard errors of the regression coefficients and associated confidence intervals are also incorrect.

heteroscedasticity: Standard deviation of residuals differs depending on the value of the predictor variable.

The third assumption of least-squares estimation is uncorrelated residuals with any other variable, including each other. The correlation of successive residuals usually occurs over time and so typically applies to the analysis of time-oriented data. It is common that this assumption is violated in time-oriented data. For example, sales of swimwear peak in Spring and Summer and decrease in Fall and Winter. The residuals around a regression line over time would reflect this seasonality, systematically decreasing and increasing depending on the time of year. Analysis of time-oriented data typically requires more sophisticated procedures than simply fitting a regression line to the data.

A fourth assumption of regression is that the estimation errors are normally distributed for each value of X. This assumption is not needed for the estimation procedure, but is required for the hypothesis tests and confidence intervals previously described. To facilitate this evaluation `Regression` provides a density plot and histogram of the residuals, which appears in Figure 9.10. Both the general density curve and the curve that presumes normality are plotted over the histogram. The residuals appear to be at least approximately normal, satisfying the assumption.

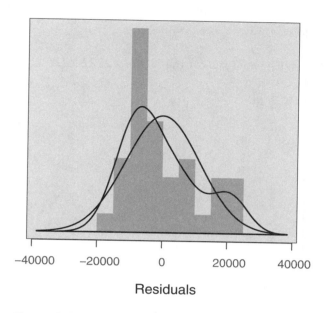

Figure 9.10 Distribution of the residuals.

Worked Problems

1 Consider the `BodyMeas` data set.

?dataBodyMeas for more information.

```
> mydata <- Read("BodyMeas", format="lessR")
```

(a) Predict Weight from Height. Specify the estimated model. Is the slope coefficient significant? Interpret.
(b) Identify the obvious outlier. What data value most contributes to the status of this case as an outlier?
(c) With the `Subset` function drop this case from the data table.
(d) Re-estimate the model. Is the model reasonably similar or qualitatively different from the model estimated with the outlier?

2 Separate data tables for men and women.

(a) With `Subset` create a data table with just women.
(b) Estimate a regression model of Weight from Height for just the women.
(c) With `Subset` create a data table with just men.
(d) Estimate a regression model of Weight from Height for just the men.
(e) Compare the models. (Note that the more formal way to provide this comparison is with the technique of indicator variables discussed in the next chapter.)

?dataCars93 for
more information.

3 The `Cars93` data set contains much information on 93 1993 car models.

```
> mydata <- Read("Cars93", format="lessR")
```

(a) Build a model to predict MPGhiway from the Weight of the car.
(b) Specify the estimated model and interpret the slope coefficient.
(c) Are there outliers?
(d) What is the prediction interval for MPGhiway for a car that weighs 2222 lbs?

CHAPTER 10

REGRESSION II

10.1 Quick Start

First install R and lessR as explained in Section 1.2. At the beginning of each R session access lessR with library(lessR). Then read your data into an R data frame with Read(), the subject of Chapter 2.

The previous chapter introduced the concept of regression analysis of models with a single predictor variable. This chapter introduces models with multiple predictor variables, multiple regression models. Most regression models in practice typically contain from two to five or six predictors. Usually we obtain more success with more than a single predictor, with diminishing returns after six or seven predictor variables.

✓ To do a multiple regression analysis again use the lessR function Regression. For more than one predictor variable separate each pair of predictor variables with a plus sign, +. The model here is for response variable Y and predictor variables V1 and V2.

```
> Regression(Y ~ V1 + V2)
```

multiple regression, Section 10.2, p. 224

If any of the predictor variables in the model are categorical and encoded as R factors, then R automatically treats the variable as an indicator variable so that the regression analysis proceeds.

indicator variables, Section 10.3, p. 234

✓ To obtain predictions and prediction intervals for any specified combination of values of the predictor variables and associated 95% prediction intervals, use the X1.new option to specify the values of the first predictor variable, X2.new for the second, and so forth up to X5.new.

```
> Regression(Y ~ V1 + V2, X1.new=c(10, 25), X2.new=c(2,4,6))
```

prediction for new values of the predictor variable, Section 10.3.1, p. 238

This example provides predictions for all combinations of values for the first predictor variable of 10 or 25 with the second predictor variable of 2, 4, and 6.

✓ For a binary response variable use logistic regression.

logistic regression, Section 10.4, p. 239

```
> Logit(Ybinary ~ V1 + V2)
```

Here Ybinary is a variable with only two values.

10.2 The Multiple Regression Model

The *multiple regression model* contains two or more predictor variables to account for the values of a single response variable. Express the fitted value of Y as a function, here linear, of a set of m predictor variables with corresponding regression coefficients b_0, b_1, ..., b_m.

$$\hat{Y} = b_0 + b_1 X_1 + b_2 X_2 + \ldots + b_m X_m$$

The form of the model remains the same as with the single-predictor models from the previous chapter, just more predictor variables.

residuals,
Section 9.3, p. 209

The estimation procedure is the same least-squares procedure defined for a single-predictor model. This procedure provides the regression coefficients that minimize the sum of the squared residuals. Define the residual for the ith data point as $Y_i - \hat{Y}_i$. The `lessR` function `Regression` provides the same output as from the single-predictor model, the model estimates, model fit, residuals, and prediction intervals. There are also some new considerations that result from multiple predictor variables that contribute to the output.

purposes of
regression
analysis: Forecast
unknown response
values and relate
the response
variable to the
predictors.

Why add more predictor variables to the model? As discussed in the previous chapter, the analysis of a regression model has two primary purposes:

✓ $\hat{Y}$: *Forecast* unknown values of Y, given of the value of each of the predictor variables
✓ b_j: *Relate* how the values of the response variable change as the values of the predictor variables change

These goals of regression analysis remain the same for multiple regression, which typically can better achieve these goals compared to the use of only a single-predictor model.

new predictor
variable
criterion: The
predictor provides
new, relevant
information.

To benefit from adding new predictors, ideally each new predictor variable adds new, relevant information to the model. That is, choose predictor variables that satisfy the following two conditions.

✓ *New Information*: A proposed predictor variable is relatively uncorrelated with the predictor variables already in the model.
✓ *Relevant Information*: A proposed predictor variable correlates with Y.

s_e, Section 9.3.1,
p. 210

R^2, Section 9.3.2,
p. 211

Each additional predictor variable generally leads to better fit with a decreased sum of the squared residuals. This decrease indicates improved fit with a lower standard deviation of the residuals, s_e, and a larger R^2. Unlike R^2, R^2_{adj} accounts for the number of predictor variables in the model relative to the overall sample size. As such, R^2_{adj} has the desirable property that adding predictor variables that do not contribute much to the overall reduction in the sum of squared residuals may even indicate worse fit with a lower value.

partial slope
coefficient b_j:
Average change in
Y for each unit
increase in X_j with
values of all other
predictors held
constant.

A distinguishing characteristic of multiple regression is that each additional predictor variable also changes the size and meaning of the slope coefficients for the remaining predictor variables. The regression coefficient b_j isolates the relation of predictor X_j to response Y with the effects of the remaining predictor variables held constant. The analysis controls the effects of the remaining predictor variables as if their values were identical for all rows of data in the analysis. Each slope coefficient partials out the effects of the other predictor variables in the model, so these slope coefficients are called *partial slope coefficients*.

Consider the slope coefficient in a simple (one-predictor) model. The slope coefficient indicates the impact of a one-unit increase in the value of the single predictor variable X on the average change in the response variable Y. The extent of this change, however, results from two different sources. First, the coefficient summarizes the effect of any direct causal impact that X has on Y. Second, the coefficient also summarizes the influence of all variables on Y related to X. Change the value of the predictor variable X and all the values of variables correlated with X also change. The changes in all of these related variables also influence Y. The subsequent average change in the value of the response variable, the *gross effect* of X on Y, reflects the cumulative impact of all of these changes.

gross effect: Effect of a change in the value of the predictor variable and all related variables on the average change of the response variable.

For a multiple regression model consider the partial slope coefficient for predictor variable X_j. The size of this partial slope coefficient reflects the impact of a change in predictor X_j on Y with the values of the other variables in the model held constant. As a result, the addition of a new predictor variable to a model generally changes the values of the remaining coefficients. As more potential extraneous influences are removed, the average change in Y that results from a change in X_j more resembles the direct causal impact of X_j on Y, referred to as a *net effect*. The extent of a net effect, however, is relative. If all variables correlated with X_j that impact Y are included in the model, then the net effect reflects the direct causal impact of X_j and Y. In reality some of these extraneous variables, perhaps most, are not included in the model and so are not controlled.

net effect: Effect of one variable on the response variable with the values of related variables held constant.

Which interpretation, net effect or gross effect, is preferred? The answer depends on the question asked. Is the focus on the effect of a direct change in X_j on Y for all other variables held constant? Or should this effect be assessed with the other predictors freely varying? If the goal is to understand the direct causal impact of a predictor variable on the response variable, then these other influences should be included in the model as additional predictor variables. If these other variables correlated with the predictor variable do not appear in the model, the corresponding slope coefficient, perhaps inadvertently, includes their impact on the response variable. If the goal, however, is to assess the overall change on the response variable, then the one-predictor model regression coefficient provides the desired estimate.

The control achieved with multiple regression is *statistical control*. For example, and illustrated later in more detail, consider the relation of primary interest between Gender and Salary. Statistical control allows for this relationship to be examined by holding variables constant such as the number of Years employed. When experimental control with random assignment is not possible, statistical control is the next best alternative to isolating direct causal influences. Unfortunately, not all potential confounding variables can be identified, measured and then entered into the regression model. Holding the values of the other variables constant is an attempt, usually not entirely successful, to achieve the equivalence attained with experimental control.

statistical control: Multiple regression controls the values of potentially confounding variables.

experimental control, Section 6.3.4, p. 138

10.2.1 Multiple Regression Example

An educational researcher investigates the conditions that contribute to reading success. As part of this (simulated) research project at the end of the school year, 100 students in the same grade were administered a test of their Reading ability with results on a percentage scale from 0 to 100. Verbal aptitude was measured with a separate test, again on a scale of 0 to 100. Also measured was the number of days Absent from school during the school year and family Income in $1000s. The data are in the file called Reading that is downloaded as part of lessR.

```
mydata <- Read("Reading", format="lessR")
```

Gross Effects

Separately regressing the measure of Reading ability on each of the remaining variables demonstrates a statistically significant relation between Reading ability and each predictor variable.

$$\hat{Y} = 38.407 + 0.523 X_{Verbal}, \quad \text{for } H_0 : \beta_{Verbal} = 0, \quad p\text{-value} = 0.000$$

$$\hat{Y} = 83.477 - 2.833 X_{Absent}, \quad \text{for } H_0 : \beta_{Absent} = 0, \quad p\text{-value} = 0.000$$

$$\hat{Y} = 62.282 + 0.170 X_{Income}, \quad \text{for } H_0 : \beta_{Income} = 0, \quad p\text{-value} = 0.000$$

The gross effect for each predictor variable is significant, with the corresponding p-value less than $\alpha = 0.05$. More specifically, each p-value is approximately equal to 0 to within three decimal digits.

A change in each of the predictor variables leads to a change in Reading ability as expressed by the gross effect for each predictor. In this sample of 100 students, an increase in one point on the Verbal aptitude test yields, on average, an increase of a little more than one-half point on the Reading test. Each additional day of being Absent yields an average decrease of more than 2.8 points on the Reading test. And each additional $1000 of family income results in an average increase of 0.17 points on the Reading test.

Net Effects

There is, however, no control on the estimation of each of these three slope coefficients of their respective gross effects. When one of these predictor variables varies, so do all the variables correlated with the predictor variable, including the values of the other two predictor variables in the study.

> **Scenario** *Statistically control for the effects of other predictor variables*
> Assess these relationships regarding Reading ability with the imposition of statistical control. Use multiple regression estimates that convey the net effect of each predictor on Reading ability, relative to the other predictor variables.

Only with a control that holds the values of these correlated variables constant can the underlying direct impact of a predictor variable on the response variable be estimated.

> **lessR Input** *Multiple regression*
> ```
> > Regression(Reading ~ Verbal + Absent + Income)
> ```

The resulting partial slope coefficients and the associated hypothesis tests and confidence intervals are found in Listing 10.1.

	Estimate	Std Err	t-value	p-value	Lower 95%	Upper 95%
(Intercept)	64.437	8.354	7.713	0.000	47.854	81.021
Verbal	0.204	0.096	2.120	0.037	0.013	0.395
Absent	-2.043	0.489	-4.176	0.000	-3.013	-1.072
Income	0.033	0.037	0.912	0.364	-0.039	0.106

Listing 10.1 Estimated model coefficients, hypothesis tests, and confidence intervals for the three predictor model of Reading ability.

The estimated multiple regression model follows.

$$\hat{Y}_{Reading} = 64.437 + 0.204X_{Verbal} - 2.043X_{Absent} + 0.033X_{Income}$$

The pattern of results of the estimated net effects with multiple regression differs from that obtained with the estimated gross effects from three separate one-predictor regressions. Consider Income, which has an estimated net effect coefficient considerably less than the corresponding estimated gross effect. The gross effect is significant, but the partial slope coefficient for Income is not significant, not statistically detectable from zero.

```
Net effect of Income on Reading:
    p-value = 0.364 > α = 0.05 so do not reject H₀ : β_Income = 0
```

For students who have the same Verbal aptitude and are Absent the same number of days of school, there is no detected effect of Income on Reading ability. The net effect of Income cannot be distinguished from zero.

The net effect for Verbal aptitude also drops considerably from the gross effect, less than half, from 0.523 to 0.204. The effect, however, does remain significant.

```
Net effect of Verbal aptitude on Reading:
    p-value = 0.037 < α = 0.05 so reject H₀ : β_Verbal = 0
```

When the effects of the variables Absent and Income are controlled, that is, held constant, a 1-point increase in the Verbal attitude test score results in an average increase of Reading ability of 0.2 points.

Controlling for Verbal aptitude and family Income only slightly mitigates the effect of days Absent on Reading ability. The estimate of the gross effect is −2.833. The net effect estimate is −2.043.

```
Net effect of days Absent on Reading:
    p-value = 0.000 < α = 0.05 so reject H₀ : β_Absent = 0
```

The effect of days Absent applies for all students with the same Verbal aptitude and family Income. Days Absent appears to be closer to having a direct causal impact on Reading ability than do the other two predictor variables. Days Absent probably directly contributes to less Reading ability because of missed classroom instruction and practice. The variable is also likely a proxy for a more abstract concept, general Motivation. The motivated student both is more likely not to miss class and is also more interested in learning, both attending class and paying more attention when in class. This additional hypothesis would be tested in a later study that also included measures of Motivation beyond just class attendance.

standardize option, Section 9.2.2, p. 207

The previous chapter introduced the `standardize` option, set to `TRUE`. The effect of this specification is to first standardize each variable before estimating the model. Though not applied here, this option applies to the multiple regression model and can be invoked for any analysis.

Model Fit and Validity

As discussed in the previous chapter, the estimated model coefficients cannot be properly interpreted without several other considerations satisfied. One consideration is the model fit in terms of the size of the residuals. The relevant output appears in Listing 10.2.

```
Standard deviation of residuals:  10.19 for 96 degrees of freedom
If normal, the approximate 95% range of residuals about each fitted
  value is 2*t-cutoff*10.19, with a 95% interval t-cutoff of 1.985
95% range of variation: 40.46


R-squared:  0.448     Adjusted R-squared:  0.430


Null hypothesis that population R-squared=0
  F-statistic: 25.934      df: 3 and 96      p-value:  0.000
```

Listing 10.2 Model fit in terms of fit indices based on the size of the residuals.

The population R^2 is apparently larger than zero because the corresponding p-value is equal to 0 within three decimal digits. Its sample value of $R^2 = 0.448$ is of moderate size and compares favorably with the value typically obtained in the social and behavioral sciences. The difficulty in precise prediction is also consistent with many other studies. Here the 95% range of variation based on the sample residuals spans over 40 points on a 100-point scale for Reading ability. The sizes of the actual prediction intervals are a little larger, up to a value of 42.85 from the `Regression` output.

In terms of influential data points and outliers there do not appear to be any in this data set. From the `Regression` output the largest R-student value in magnitude is 2.35 and the largest Cook's Distance is only 0.12. In terms of assumptions, the residuals are at least approximately normally distributed and, as shown in Figure 10.1, the plot of the residuals and fitted values does not indicate any noticeable patterns.

In terms of fit, influence, and assumptions the interpretation of the estimated coefficients appears valid.

10.2.2 Collinearity

collinearity: Property of two or more highly related variables.

Ideally, each predictor variable relates to the response variable and contributes new information compared to the remaining predictor variables in the regression model. A potential problem is that two or more highly related predictor variables provide redundant information. When a predictor variable linearly relates to one or more of the remaining predictor variables, the predictor variables are *collinear*. Little gain in predictive efficiency results from the addition to the model of a new predictor variable that substantially correlates with an existing predictor variable.

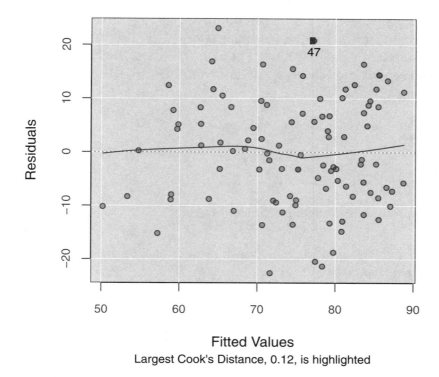

Figure 10.1 Diagnostic plot of Residuals vs. Fitted Values.

Conversely, dropping one of the redundant variables from the model does not substantially diminish predictive accuracy.

Another issue is that multiple regression analysis estimates the net effect of a unit change in each predictor variable on the response variable, with the value of all other predictor variables held constant. The more collinearity, the more difficult to separate the effects of the collinear predictor variables from each other. This difficulty in separation of effects increases the standard errors of the slope coefficients for the collinear predictor variables. When multiple predictor variables represent different names for essentially the same concept, the standard errors of the estimates are inflated because the effects cannot be easily disentangled from each other. The large standard errors for the individual coefficients preclude statistical significance.

null model, Section 9.3.2, p. 211

A large correlation between two predictor variables results in collinearity. A more general method for detecting collinearity considers the relationship between each predictor variable with all the remaining predictors. To evaluate this relationship, create a regression model in which the jth predictor, X_j, becomes the response variable, and all remaining predictors are the predictor variables. If X_j is collinear with one or more of the remaining predictors, then the resulting R_j^2 would be large, such as over the somewhat arbitrary but conventional threshold of 0.8.

From this value of R_j^2 for the jth predictor, define two equivalent indices of collinearity: Tolerance and the variance inflation factor or VIF.

collinearity indicators of a predictor variable: Tolerance and VIF, each based on the R^2 of regressing the predictor on all others.

$$\text{Tolerance}(b_j) = 1 - R_j^2 \qquad \text{and} \qquad \text{VIF}(b_j) = \frac{1}{\text{Tolerance}} = \frac{1}{1 - R_j^2}$$

Tolerance of the jth predictor variable is R_j^2 subtracted from 1. So R_j^2 larger than 0.8 stipulates the same threshold of collinearity for tolerance less than 0.2. *VIF* is just the reciprocal of Tolerance, so the same threshold is stipulated when VIF is larger than $1/0.2 = 5$.

The `Regression` function reports the values of Tolerance and VIF for each of the predictor variables, here shown in Listing 10.3.

```
        Tolerance     VIF
Verbal      0.600   1.667
Absent      0.463   2.158
Income      0.667   1.500
```

Listing 10.3 Collinearity indicators for each of the three predictor variables.

All the values of Tolerance are well above 0.2 and all the values of VIF, then, well below 5. Collinearity is not an issue for this analysis.

10.2.3 Model Selection

model selection:
Choose the minimal set of predictors that achieves satisfactory fit relative to all possible models.

R_{adj}^2, Section 9.3.2, p. 212

Collinearity occurs when one or more predictor variables do not add new information to the remaining predictor variables. A task related to collinearity analysis is to pare down an initial set of predictor variables to the minimal set of predictors that each provide new and relatively unique information, and also relate to the response variable. For example, if two predictor variables are collinear, one possibility is to remove the collinear predictor from the model that is the least related to the response variable. The task of selecting an appropriate set of predictor variables from a larger initial set of predictor variables submitted to a regression analysis is *model selection*.

all possible subsets: Model selection procedure that lists the fit of all possible models from the submitted model.

Several different procedures exist for model selection. Perhaps the most useful procedure is *all possible subsets*, an analysis of the fit of all possible models from a given set of predictor variables. The procedure computes a fit index such as R_{adj}^2 for every possible combination of predictor variables in the model. The procedure that provides this analysis is the function `leaps` written by Lumley and Miller (2009) from the package of the same name. The `leaps` package is automatically downloaded and installed with the `lessR` package. The `Regression` function automatically accesses the `leaps` function and then displays the modified output by default, as shown in Listing 10.4.

```
Verbal  Absent  Income    R2adj  X's
    1       1       0    0.431    2
    1       1       1    0.430    3
    0       1       0    0.411    1
    0       1       1    0.410    2
    1       0       1    0.334    2
    1       0       0    0.277    1
    0       0       1    0.177    1
```

Listing 10.4 All possible regression models evaluated in terms of R_{adj}^2.

Each row of the output in Listing 10.4 is for the analysis of a different model. A column with a 1 indicates that the considered model contains the corresponding variable and a 0 indicates the variable is deleted from the model. The `R2adj` column lists the model's R^2_{adj}, and the `X's` column lists the number of predictor variables in the corresponding model.

The goal of model selection is *parsimony*, to select the model that balances the two competing criteria of the best possible fit against the smallest number of predictor variables. If a complex model with many predictor variables achieves slightly better fit in the training data than a simpler model, the simpler model is preferred. Models should become more complex only when meaningful gains in fit are obtained and this improved fit extends to new situations with new data. It can be too easy to *overfit* a complex model to the training data, in which the improved fit only applies to the sample data from which the model is estimated, with little or no increased predictive power for new data, the test sample.

Each additional predictor variable in practice increments at least slightly the value of R^2 from the previous model without that predictor. R^2_{adj} typically, but not necessarily, increases for an additional predictor, but add a weak, new predictor variable to the model and R^2_{adj} may actually drop in value because it accounts for the loss of an additional degree of freedom from the model. Each additional predictor variable removes one more degrees of freedom.

This drop occurs in this example in which a two-predictor model of Verbal and Absent has an $R^2_{adj} = 0.431$. The fit index drops slightly to 0.430 for a model with all three predictors. This evidence indicates adding Income to the two-predictor model not only does not increase fit, there is a slight decrease. Dropping Income from the model is also consistent with the non-significant result for the estimate of its slope coefficient.

After Income is dropped from the model, should the model contain Verbal aptitude and Days Absent ($R^2_{adj} = 0.431$) or just days Absent ($R^2_{adj} = 0.411$)? In terms of the balance between fit and number of predictors, perhaps the model with just Absent as a predictor variable provides the best trade-off. The fit only drops from $R^2_{adj} = 0.431$ to 0.411, which is not much of a drop for deleting a single predictor variable.

A formal test of the contribution of one or more predictor variables to a model is an hypothesis test of a *nested model*, with deleted variables, compared to the full model with all of the predictor variables. The test of the nested model against the full model examines the contribution of the variables deleted to obtain the nested model. If the analysis detects no difference between the models, then the deleted variables did not significantly contribute to the model.

⭐ Scenario *Test the effectiveness of specified predictor variables*
Create a nested model with the specified predictor variables deleted from the full model. Then compare the two models.

The `lessR` function `Nest` accomplishes the test of the difference between the models. To use the function, list the response variable, the subset of the predictor variables for the nested model, and then the larger set of predictor variables in the full model. The `Nest` function directly compares the residual sum of squares of the two models. The process is similar to the concept underlying R^2 that compares the residual sum of squares of the full model to the null model. Here the result is more general in that the nested model is not as severe as the null model, but still not as complete as the full model.

The function `Nest` analyzes the full model first, and then analyzes the data for the nested model with the same data analyzed by the full model. The full model contains more variables

---

parsimony:
Model selection optimizes both fit and simplicity.

training sample, Section 9.4, p. 212

model overfit:
The model contains too many predictor variables, and so fits random error.

nested model:
Model with predictor variables that are a subset of the more complete model.

Nest function:
Compare a nested model with the corresponding full model.

null model, Section 9.3.2, p. 211

and some of these additional variables not in the nested model may have missing data. If the full data table was submitted to two separate analyses, any cases, rows of data, that *only* had missing values on the variables not present in the nested model would be deleted from the full model analysis, but not from the nested model analysis. The comparison between models is only valid when the same data are analyzed for both models.

Another strategy is to use the R function na.omit to purge all cases from the data frame with at least one missing data value.

na.omit function:
Remove all rows of
data with any
missing data
values.

```
mydata <- na.omit(mydata)
```

This strategy is too broad, however, because data values may be missing for variables in the data table not present in either of the models. The result is the deletion of too much data, leaving an analysis based on a smaller sample size than necessary.

Invoke the Nest function to compare a nested model to the full model.

✒ **lessR Input** *Test a nested regression model against the full model*
> Nest(Reading, c(Absent), c(Verbal,Absent,Income))

The result appears in Listing 10.5.

```
Model 1: Reading ~ Absent
Model 2: Reading ~ Verbal + Absent + Income
  Res.Df        RSS  df     SumSq      F  p-value
1     98    10529.0
2     96     9972.6   2    556.36  2.6778  0.07384
```

Listing 10.5 The comparison of a nested model to the more general full model.

From this analysis dropping both Verbal and Income yields a model that is not statistically significantly different from just a one-predictor model.

$$\text{Effect of both Absent and Income: } p\text{-value} = 0.074 > \alpha = 0.05,$$
$$\text{so do } not \text{ reject } H_0 : \beta_{Verbal} = \beta_{Income} = 0$$

The *p*-value, however, just misses the boundary of $\alpha = 0.05$. This situation is "backwards" from the typical test of a null hypothesis that leads to detection of a difference by rejecting the null hypothesis. In this situation *not* rejecting the null hypothesis leads to a conclusion to delete variables. So a lack of power, the lack of the sensitivity of the test to find a difference that truly exists, would lead to the conclusion there is a difference. Given the relatively small sample size of 100, a larger sample may, but not necessarily, lead to a significant difference.

cross-validation:
Re-estimate a
model on new data
to verify that the
original estimates
generalize to a new
sample.

Our conclusion is that solely in terms of the prediction of Reading ability, the days Absent in this sample of 100 data points is probably sufficient compared to a model with one or both of the remaining predictor variables. This conclusion, however, is tentative. In terms of understanding the relationships, and potentially the causes, of Reading ability or lack thereof, a model with both days Absent and Verbal ability is probably the best model for this situation.

Note, however, that whenever a model is re-specified and then re-analyzed with the same data from which it was originally estimated, the training data, the new model should be *cross-validated* on a new sample of data, the test data. The smaller the sample size of the training data, the more the need to apply the model to a new data sample, the test data. Models re-specified on small data sets are at risk of overfitting the model to the data, modeling random sampling error instead of components that apply to the population as a whole.

10.2.4 Three-dimensional Scatter Plot

A two-predictor model presents another option available from John Fox's `car` package (Fox & Weisberg, 2011), an option that can be referenced directly from the `Regression` function: An interactive three-dimensional scatter plot and associated regression plane. The vertical axis is for the response variable and the two horizontal axes are for the two predictor variables. The *regression plane* is the three-dimensional analogue of the two-dimensional line. The line is the linear graph in two dimensions and the plane is the linear graph in three dimensions.

regression plane: Three dimensional linear surface.

To access the `car` function for the scatter plot and regression plane from `Regression` set the `scatter.3D` option to `TRUE`.

scatter.3D: For a two-predictor model set to TRUE to specify a three-dimensional scatter plot and regression plane.

> 🖋 **lessR Input** *3D scatter plot about the regression plane*
>
> ```
> > Regression(Reading ~ Verbal + Absent, scatter.3D=TRUE)
> ```

The resulting graph appears in Figure 10.2. When viewed on the computer screen, rotate the entire graph as desired by dragging over an open area with the mouse. The graphics window can be re-sized by dragging one of its corners or edges.

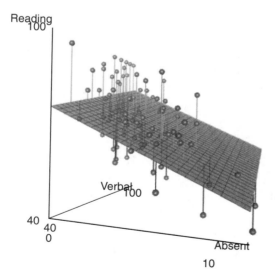

Figure 10.2 Three-dimensional scatter plot provided by the `car` package.

The rather considerable variation of the data points about the regression plane is apparent from Figure 10.2. Also apparent is the downward slope of Reading ability as the number of days Absent increases. The Verbal aptitude effect leads to a less pronounced increase in Reading ability, though the angle of the presentation of this graph tends to obscure this effect. Obtain different perspectives by rotating the graph.

10.3 Indicator Variables

The previous examples of regression analysis involved continuous variables. Categorical variables can also appear as predictor variables in a regression analysis. How is that possible given that categorical variables have non-numeric data values? The answer is to convert the levels, that is, categories, to numeric variables.

binary variable:
Variable with only two unique values.

The numeric versions of a categorical variable are called indicator variables, also sometimes called dummy variables. Create an *indicator variable* for each category. Each indicator variable is a *binary variable*, that is, with only two unique values, such as a 0 and 1. For example, assign a value of 1 if the level is present for a given case and a value of 0 if it is not. Gender has two levels, Male and Female, so two indicator variables could be created for Gender, illustrated in Table 10.1. Score the indicator variable for Male a 1 if a person is a man and 0 if the person is a woman. Similarly, score the indicator variable for a Female a 1 for a woman and a 0 for a man.

Table 10.1 Data table of the categorical variable Gender and its two indicator variables for four people.

Gender	M	F
F	0	1
F	0	1
M	1	0
F	0	1

The benefit of an indicator variable is that despite the non-numeric values of Gender, the 0 and 1 values of the resulting indicator variables are numeric. In general, if there are k categories or levels of the categorical variable, then $k - 1$ indicator variables are needed to describe the values of the categorical variable. The variable Gender has just two levels, so to know the value of either indicator variable for Gender is to know the value of the remaining indicator variable. If the value of one of the Gender indicator variables for a person is a 0 then the value for the remaining indicator is a 1, and vice versa.

Gender can be included in a regression analysis in terms of either one of its two indicator variables. The interpretation of the slope coefficient remains the same as for any regression model, the average change in the response variable for a one unit increase in the corresponding predictor variable, with the values of all other variables in the model held constant. For an indicator variable of Gender that means its slope coefficient represents the average change in the response variable from either moving from Male to Female, or from Female to Male, depending on which indicator variable was entered into the model.

factor variable, Section 1.6.3, p. 22

Employee data table, Figure 1.7, p. 21

The core R regression function is `lm` for "linear model". This function automatically creates these indicator variables from a categorical variable encoded as a `factor` submitted to a regression analysis. The lessR function `Regression` invokes `lm` and then accesses its output, so categorical variables can be entered directly into a function call to `Regression`. In this example the variable Gender from the Employee data set has values M and F.

lessR Input *Regression analysis with a categorical variable*

```
> Regression(Salary ~ Gender)
```

R names the resulting indicator variable `GenderM`, a juxtaposition of the name of the categorical variable and the name of the category or level `M`. By default R orders the levels of a categorical variable, a factor, alphabetically, so `F` is the first level of Gender and `M` is the second. R uses the convention of naming the Gender effect with the last of the two levels. The y-intercept in this analysis is the average value of Salary for the first level of Gender, `F`. The slope coefficient for this indicator variable `GenderM` represents the "male effect", the average change in Salary moving from the first level of Gender, `F`, to the second level, `M`.

factor variable, Section 3.3.2, p. 59

The estimated regression coefficients and analyses appear in Listing 10.6.

	Estimate	Std Err	t-value	p-value	Lower 95%	Upper 95%
(Intercept)	56830.598	4783.005	11.882	0.000	47120.581	66540.615
GenderM	14316.860	6857.494	2.088	0.044	395.406	28238.314

Listing 10.6 Estimated model for Salary regressed on Gender.

The output in Listing 10.6 provides the estimated model.

$$\hat{Y}_{Salary} = \$56830.60 + \$14316.86 X_{GenderM}$$

Both coefficients are significant with *p*-values less than 0.05. In this sample the average increase in Salary for a 1-unit increase in the indicator variable, moving from Female to Male, is $14317. The accompanying scatter plot from the `Regression` function in Figure 10.3 illustrates

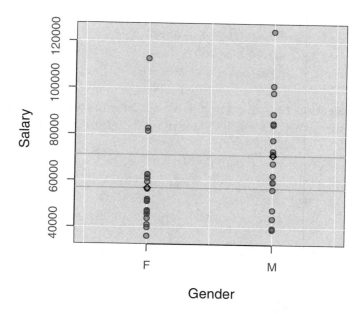

Figure 10.3 Scatter plot of the factor variable Gender with Salary.

this difference between the mean Salary levels with horizontal lines drawn through the mean of each group. This is the default form of the `lessR` scatter plot function when the variable plotted on the horizontal axis is a factor. The `Regression` function automatically provides the call to `ScatterPlot`.

Scatter plot function, Section 8.2.1, p. 182

The estimated slope coefficient $b_1 = \$14317$ is the sample mean difference, $\bar{Y}_M - \bar{Y}_F$. The p-value from a t-test analysis of the mean difference is identical to the sample slope coefficient from a least-squares regression analysis, as are the corresponding confidence intervals. This comparison is from the `Regression` output in Figure 10.6 and the `ttest` output in Listing 10.7.

ttest function, Section 6.3, p. 130

```
Hypothesis Test of 0 Mean Diff:   t = 2.088,   df = 35,   p-value = 0.044

Margin of Error for 95% Confidence Level:   13921.454
95% Confidence Interval for Mean Difference:   395.406 to 28238.314
```

Listing 10.7 Independent groups t-test analysis of the mean difference of Salary for men and women.

This generalization of results also extends to analysis of variance.

 lessR Input *Three equivalent analyses of a mean difference*

```
> ttest(Salary ~ Gender)
> ANOVA(Salary ~ Gender)
> Regression(Salary ~ Gender)
```

Each of these three analyses yields identical results for the hypothesis test of the mean difference of Salary for Men and Women. A summary of the output for all three analyses follows where μ_M and μ_F are the respective population mean Salaries for men and women.

```
Gender effect on Salary:
    t-test for H_0: μ_M − μ_F = 0,  p-value = 0.044 < α = 0.05
    ANOVA for H_0: μ_M = μ_F,  p-value = 0.044 < α = 0.05
    Regression for H_0: β_Gender = 0,  p-value = 0.044 < α = 0.05
```

The result of each analysis is the detection of a difference between average Salary of men and women. That is, the difference is statistically significant. Men have a higher average salary than women at this company.

t-test between groups, Section 6.3.1, p. 130
ANOVA one-way between groups, Section 7.2, p. 150

Of the three analyses, each successive one is more general. The t-test compares the means of the response variable across two groups with the t-value. The one-way ANOVA procedure compares two or more means by a ratio of two variances, which is an F-value. The regression procedure can evaluate the response variable for changes in the value of a continuous variable as well, also with the t-value.

gross effect, Section 10.2, p. 225

This analysis established the difference between average men's and women's Salary at this company. This slope coefficient, however, is a gross effect. How much average Salary changes between the two values of Gender does not separate the direct effect of Gender on Salary from potential indirect effects. That is, the correlation between Salary and Gender could result to some extent from a causal relation of other variables to Salary from which Gender is correlated.

Another question of interest is to assess the net effect of Gender on Salary controlling the values of other potentially confounding variables. One potential such variable is Years experience working at that company. To evaluate the net effect of Gender relative to Years experience, consider the following multiple regression.

```
> Regression(Salary ~ Years + Gender)
```

The output appears in Listing 10.8.

	Estimate	Std Err	t-value	p-value	Lower 95%	Upper 95%
(Intercept)	33103.742	3739.836	8.852	0.000	25494.987	40712.496
Years	3467.771	386.922	8.962	0.000	2680.573	4254.969
GenderM	-5170.610	4373.917	-1.182	0.246	-14069.412	3728.192

Listing 10.8 Estimated multiple regression model of net effects of Years experience and Gender.

From Listing 10.8, write the model as follows.

$$\hat{Y}_{Salary} = \$33103.74 + \$3467.77X_{Years} - \$5170.61X_{GenderM}$$

In particular, the net effect of Gender is not significant.

```
Net effect of Gender on Salary:
```
p-value $= 0.246 > \alpha = 0.05$ for $H_0 : \beta_{Gender} = 0$, `do not reject` H_0

The effect of Years, however, is significant.

```
Net effect of Years on Salary:
```
p-value $= 0.000 > \alpha = 0.05$ for $H_0 : \beta_{Years} = 0$, `reject` H_0

In this sample each additional year of employment at the company leads to an average increase of Salary of \$3468 regardless of Gender. There is a 95% confidence that the true average increase is somewhere from \$2681 to \$4255. This effect is perhaps a direct causal impact on the determination of Salary. The lack of significance for the net effect of Gender indicates that there is no detected difference in Salary for men and women for any group of employees who have worked at the company for the same number of years.

Investigating further, for some reason women in this company have worked fewer years on average than men. The two sample averages for Years employed are $\bar{Y}_M = 12.24$ and $\bar{Y}_F = 6.84$. The corresponding independent groups t-test with the `ttest` function indicates that this difference in average Years worked is significant with a p-value equal to 0.003. The reason for this pattern is not clear from the data. Perhaps management used to be dominated by chauvinists who did not hire women, but now all the old guys are dead, retired, or in jail.

independent groups t-test, Section 6.3, p. 130

The analysis detected no overt discrimination against women in the company at this time. After some number of years, however, the revised data should be analyzed to verify that equal Salary by Gender is in fact becoming the norm as women gain more work experience at the company. Currently the second highest paid employee, Leslie James, is a woman, so perhaps this trend will be realized. As illustrated, the implementation of multiple regression allows for statistical control, which then permits a more sophisticated examination of causal influences.

10.3.1 Prediction from New Data

prediction from new values, Section 9.4.2, p. 214

As discussed in the previous chapter, true forecasting or prediction occurs with new data. The values of the response variable are already known for the data from which the model is estimated. Only by coincidence are the new values of the predictor variables equal to the existing values. The fitted values and corresponding prediction intervals need to be calculated for any specified values of the predictors, not just for existing values in the original data set.

 Scenario *Prediction from new data*
To assess the potential gender discrimination in the company, calculate predicted values of Salary for men and women separately for various Years of experience working in the company. Even though not as many women have extended Years experience as the men, the model provides the values of Salary consistent with additional experience. Are there Gender differences?

X1.new, X2.new options: Obtain predictions for specified values of the predictor variables.

To provide the predictions and 95% prediction intervals for new, specified data values use the X1.new and X2.new options for the Regression function. Use X1.new to specify the values for the first predictor variable, and X2.new for the second predictor variable listed in the function call. These values may be specified up to the arbitrary cutoff of five predictor variables, up to X5.new.

lessR Input *Prediction from new data*

```
> Regression(Salary ~ Years + Gender,
                 X1.new=c(10,15,20), X2.new=c("F","M"))
```

The output from Regression is identical to the previous analysis except for the section that provides the predicted values, which appears in Listing 10.9.

Years	Gender	Salary	fitted	ci:lwr	ci:upr	pi:lwr	pi:upr	width
10.00	M		62610.84	56662.95	68558.74	38441.49	86780.19	48338.70
10.00	F		67781.45	61860.07	73702.84	43618.61	91944.29	48325.68
15.00	M		79949.70	73865.48	86033.92	55746.44	104152.96	48406.52
15.00	F		85120.31	76746.32	93494.30	60242.54	109998.09	49755.55
20.00	M		97288.56	88943.37	105633.74	72420.46	122156.65	49736.19
20.00	F		102459.17	90790.04	114128.30	76287.64	128630.69	52343.05

Listing 10.9 Predicted values and prediction intervals of Salary from Years experience and Gender for specified values of new data.

The output for the predicted values contains no values for the response variable Salary because at this time these values are unknown. The widths of the prediction intervals are around $50000 so prediction is not expected to be accurate. The fitted values, however, are perfectly consistent with the two-predictor-variable model. Based on the current distribution of Salary among men and women at the company, women are predicted to have a larger Salary than men.

The larger predicted Salaries for women indicates from another perspective the information obtained from a multiple regression model, which necessarily assesses the net effects of the predictor variables instead of the gross effects. The predicted Salary for men and then for women based on Gender alone are their respective average Salaries in this sample. The respective men's and women's average Salary is $\bar{Y}_M = \$71147.46$ and $\bar{Y}_F = \$56830.60$, a difference of $14316.86. When the number of Years worked is controlled, however, the Gender effect is no longer significant, although women are predicted to make more than men at all levels of experience. Again, what needs to be verified is that this model remains applicable as women actually gain more experience working at the company.

10.4 Logistic Regression

The previous section showed how categorical predictor variables can be included in a multiple regression model. This section shows how to analyze a model with a categorical response variable that has only two categories. Examples of such binary or yes/no variables include Gender (male, female), Cigarette Use (smoke, do not smoke), Begin Therapy (begin, do not begin), and Home Ownership (own, do not own).

binary variable, Section 10.3, p. 234

To illustrate, consider a data table of various body measurements for 340 motorcyclists, 170 men and 170 women, fitted for motorcycle clothing. The values for the variable Gender are entered in the data file as M or F. As these values are read into R the variable Gender is automatically coded as a factor variable, a non-numerical categorical variable. Measurements are provided for Weight to the nearest pound, Height, Waist, Hips, and Chest to the nearest inch, Hand circumference to the nearest quarter of an inch and Shoe size to the nearest half size. The data table is part of lessR and can be accessed via its name dataBodyMeas or the abbreviation BodyMeas.

factor variable, Section 2.2.2, p. 34

```
> mydata <- Read("BodyMeas", format="lessR")
```

read lessR data, Section 2.3.5, p. 44

The values of a binary variable can be coded as an indicator variable with numeric values 0 and 1. So a model with a binary response variable with this encoding can be submitted for analysis to a traditional least-squares regression program such as Regression. The results of this traditional regression analysis, however, are problematic as shown in Figure 10.4. The response variable Gender is regressed on Hand circumference in inches. (See the note for how to obtain this figure.[1]) The response variable Gender has only two values, 0 and 1, yet the fitted values from the resulting estimated regression line are continuous. What does a fitted value of 0.75 mean? Or how about an out of range value such as $\hat{Y}_{Gender} = -0.38$?

least-squares estimation, Section 9.3, p. 209

Another problem is that the least-squares estimation procedure applied to a binary response variable necessarily violates some assumptions. First, from the mathematics of the variance of a binary variable, the residuals of a binary response variable cannot have the same variance for different values of the predictor variables. Also, the residuals cannot be normally distributed because each residual is calculated with a subtraction from only either 0 or 1.

Residuals for a binary response: $\hat{Y}_i = Y_i - 0 \quad$ or $\quad \hat{Y}_i = Y_i - 1$

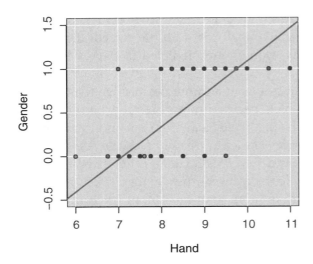

Figure 10.4 Least-squares regression fit and scatter plot of Hand circumference and binary response variable Gender.

Instead of continuously distributed across their range according to a normal distribution, the residuals cluster only around these two values.

10.4.1 The Logistic Regression Model

The key to properly modeling a binary response variable is to switch the focus from the actual values of the response variable to their probabilities. For example, given a Hand circumference, what is the probability that the person is Male? Probabilities vary continuously from and including 0 to 1 so all fitted values in that range would be meaningful. Fitted values, however, would still extend beyond that range.

Rather than directly model the probability of the response variable, invoke the equivalent concept of the *odds* of an event.

odds of an event: Ratio of the probability of the event occurring to the probability of not occurring.

$$\text{odds} = \frac{p}{1-p}$$

Half of the people represented in the BodyMeas data table are men and half are women. The probability of randomly selecting a Male is 0.5, which means that the odds of this selection are $0.5/0.5 = 1$, often expressed as 1 to 1. If 10% of the cases in the data table were from men, then the odds for this selection would be $0.1/0.9 \approx 0.11$ or 0.11 to 1. Similarly, for a probability of 0.9 the associated odds are $0.9/0.1 = 9$ or 9 to 1. The greater the probability of event, the greater its odds. The smallest probabilities yield odds close to 0 and the closer the probability is to 1 the larger the odds.

We wish to model the values of one or more variables over all possible values. To transform the range of odds from 0 to infinity to all values from negative to positive infinity, take the logarithm of the odds. The odds of an event that has a probability of 0.5 is 1, with the corresponding logarithm of 0, the boundary between an event with either less or more than a 0.5 probability. A probability close to zero yields a very large negative value. A probability closer to one yields a very large positive value.

logit: The logarithm of the odds for the occurrence of an event.

This logarithm of the odds is the *logit* transformation, the response variable for the logistic regression. With some algebra the logit transformation can be expressed directly as a linear function of the predictor variables, with ln the natural logarithm of the resulting expression.

$$\text{logit}(p) = \ln\left(\frac{p}{1-p}\right) = b_0 + b_1 X_1 + b_2 X_2 + \ldots b_m X_m$$

The logistic model specifies how the logarithm of the odds change for a one-unit increase in each of the predictor variables, with the values of the other predictor variables held constant. The odds are expressed for obtaining the value of the response variable of 1. This is the model estimated by a logistic regression analysis.

There is no mathematical solution for these estimates by the least-squares principle previously discussed. Fortunately, there is a solution to estimate these coefficients by a method called *maximum likelihood*, which maximizes the conditional probability of the data for any given set of parameters. These conditional probabilities are likelihoods. The likelihood is calculated from the data for one set of initial estimates. Then the estimates are successively adjusted to produce a greater likelihood for each iteration. The output of a logistic regression includes the number of iterations processed before the best solution is reached from the initial estimates.

maximum likelihood solution: Choose estimated values for the model that would have most likely produced the observed data.

10.4.2 Logistic Regression Coefficients

Now apply a logistic regression analysis to the BodyMeas data.

Scenario *Predict Gender from body measurements*
Sometimes a customer's gender is not recorded. How well can Gender be predicted from available body measurements?

Gender is a binary variable so the resulting regression model should be a logistic regression. The lessR function Logit accomplishes this regression. The syntax of Logit is the same as for Regression. By default R orders the levels of the factors alphabetically before converting to a 0 and 1, so the default coding is 0 for Female and 1 for Male. First try a logistic regression model with only a single predictor, here Hand circumference in inches.

lessR Input *Logistic regression with a single predictor*
```
> Logit(Gender ~ Hand)
```

The first part of the output appears in Listing 10.10. The form of the output is identical to that of the usual least-squares regression analyses previously presented. Each estimate of the regression model is presented, with its standard error, hypothesis test that the corresponding population value is 0, and associated 95% confidence interval. What is new is the number of iterations the algorithm required to achieve an optimal maximum likelihood solution.

	Estimate	Std Err	z-value	p-value	Lower 95%	Upper 95%
(Intercept)	-26.9237	2.7515	-9.785	0.000	-32.7130	-21.8940
Hand	3.2023	0.3269	9.794	0.000	2.6047	3.8904

Number of Fisher Scoring iterations: 6

Listing 10.10 Estimated coefficients from logistic regression analysis.

Each estimate is evaluated with the null hypothesis of a zero population value for the corresponding slope coefficient. The sample estimate from the logit model is $b_{Hand} = 3.202$.

$$\text{Effect of Hand size: } p\text{-value} < \alpha = 0.05, \text{ so reject } H_0 : \beta_{Hand} = 0$$

The direct interpretation of each estimated slope coefficient from this model, however, is not straightforward. As shown, although the model for logit(p) is linear, the response variable for this analysis is the logit, the logarithm of the odds. Consistent with the interpretation of a linear model, for a one-unit increase in Hand circumference the expected change in the logistic function is 3.20. But what does this mean?

10.4.3 The Odds Ratio

odds ratio: The ratio of change in the odds that the binary response variable equals 1 as the value of the predictor variable is increased one unit.

exp function: Exponentiation.

− relationship between X and Y: Odds ratio is less than 1.0.

+ relationship between X and Y: Odds ratio is greater than 1.0.

Fortunately, a simple expression permits a straightforward interpretation of how the change in the value of X impacts the odds for the value of 1 for the response variable, here Male. The algebra is to apply the exponential function to each side of the model, accomplished in R with the exp function. The exponential function converts a subtraction to a division, so the comparison of a change in the odds from changing the value of the predictor variable is expressed as a ratio. The result is the *odds ratio*. For example, exponentiate the estimated slope coefficient for Hand with exp(3.2023), which yields 24.59.

An odds ratio of 1.0 indicates no relationship between predictor and response variables. An odds ratio of .5 indicates that a value of 1 for the response variable is half as likely with an increase of the predictor variable by one unit, an inverse relationship. As the predictor value increases the value of the response variable decreases. Values of the odds ratio over 1.0 indicate a positive relationship of the predictor to the probability that the value of the response variable is 1.

The Logit function automatically displays the odds ratios and the corresponding 95% confidence intervals, shown in Listing 10.11.

	Odds Ratio	Lower 95%	Upper 95%
(Intercept)	0.0000	0.0000	0.0000
Hand	24.5883	13.5277	48.9321

Listing 10.11 The estimated odds ratio for each coefficient and associated 95% confidence interval.

The odds ratio in Listing 10.11 is considerably larger than 1.0, so there is a positive relationship of Hand circumference to being Male. The odds are for a value of the response variable equal to 1, that is, that a Male is randomly selected from the sample of 340 people.

These odds are almost 25 times as likely, 24.59, for each additional inch of Hand circumference. In the population this odds ratio, with 95% confidence, is somewhere between 13.53 and 48.93.

The odds ratio is so much larger than 1.0 because of the unit of measurement, inches, as a percentage of hand size. Measuring hand size in inches yields a range of sizes between 6 and 12. Each inch spans a considerable portion of the range from 6 to 12 inches. The result is a dramatic increase of the odds that a random selection of a person from a sample all with the same increased Hand size yields a Male.

To illustrate, convert the Hand measurements from inches to millimeters by multiplying each Hand measurement by 2.54 and re-run the analysis.

```
> mydata <- Transform(Hand.mm=2.540*Hand)
> Logit(Gender ~ Hand.mm)
```

A millimeter is much smaller than an inch, so the size of the resulting odds ratio decreases dramatically, from 24.59 to 3.53. The odds of selecting a Male for each increase of one millimeter in Hand circumference increases, but not as much as for an increase of the much larger inch. There are different units for the two analyses, but the same relationship.

10.4.4 Assessment of Fit

For a traditional least-squares regression analysis, assessment of fit is based on the minimization of the sum of squared residuals. Obtain the standard deviation of the residuals and the R^2 fit statistics from this minimization. For a maximum likelihood solution such as for logistic regression, there is no least-squares minimization from which to obtain these statistics, nor is there a direct analogy to R^2, though there are several possibilities for fit indices (Tjur, 2009).

An intuitive fit index is the percentage of correctly predicted values of the response variable from the corresponding probabilities. If the probability of a 1 for the value of the response variable is greater than or equal to 0.5 assign the case to that group. If the probability is less than 0.5, assign the case to the group with the response variable equal to 0. Then determine how many cases are correctly classified and compare to the baseline probability, which is the larger percentage of cases with either a 1 or with a 0.

For the `BodyMeas` data set both men and women are equally present so the baseline rate of correct predictions, from what could be called the *null model*, is 50%, shown in Listing 10.12 provided by the `Logit` function. The use of Hand circumference to predict Gender increases the percentage of correct predictions from 50% to 88.2%.

null model, Section 9.3.2, p. 211

		Baseline		Predicted		
Gender		Total	%Tot	F	M	%Correct
	F	170	50.0	147	23	86.5
	M	170	50.0	17	153	90.0
	Total	340				88.2

Listing 10.12 Classification table from Height predicting Gender.

The output of `Logit` for a single predictor model also includes a graph, Figure 10.5. The graph is the predicted probability that Gender=1 for each Hand size, that is, the probability of selecting a Male. These probabilities are obtained for the previously provided expression of `logit(p)` from the exponential function. The algorithm inverses the logarithm of the model with the specific estimates of b_0, b_1 and so forth, and then solves for the probability of selecting the value of Gender=1.

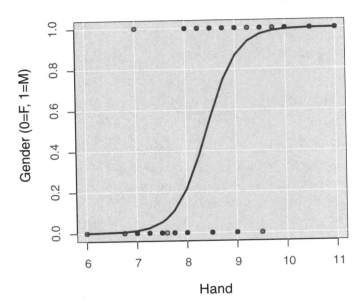

Figure 10.5 Logistic fit expressed as a probability curve and scatter plot of Hand circumference and Gender.

10.4.5 Outliers

outlier analysis,
Section 9.5, p. 216

influence statistics,
Section 9.5.1,
p. 217

The `Logit` function also provides the outlier analysis that accompanies the least-squares regression analyses. Examination of the scatter plot of the data in Figure 10.5 indicates that the most deviant data values are for Males with a Hand circumference of 7 inches, and for Females with a value of 9.5 inches. These are also the four values that have an R-Studentized residual larger in magnitude than 2, shown in Listing 10.13. They also have the largest values of Cook's Distance.

	Hand	Gender	fitted	residual	rstudent	dffits	cooks
183	7.0	M	0.0109	0.9891	3.045	0.1930	0.11740
275	7.0	M	0.0109	0.9891	3.045	0.1930	0.11740
152	9.5	F	0.9706	-0.9706	-2.684	-0.2256	0.07555
170	9.5	F	0.9706	-0.9706	-2.684	-0.2256	0.07555

Listing 10.13 The four cases with the magnitude of the R-Student residual larger than 2 and also the largest values of Cook's Distance.

The information in Listing 10.13 lists the most extreme misclassifications. If a re-examination were possible, it would be advised to double-check the assignment of Gender in these four cases. The data values could be correct but the possibility of a transcription error should be explored if possible.

10.4.6 Logistic Multiple Regression

The potential for improvement of model fit and understanding of the relations among the variables in the model applies to all multiple regression models regardless of their means of estimation, least-squares or maximum likelihood. With additional predictor variables that tend to be uncorrelated with each other but correlated with the response variable, the model will demonstrate improved fit and a richer understanding of the underlying relationships. Here consider a variety of other measurements intended to help differentiate among Male and Female.

> **lessR Input** *Logistic multiple regression*
> ```
> > Logit(Gender ~ Height + Weight + Waist + Hips + Chest + Hand + Shoe)
> ```

The model specifies seven predictors to account for Gender.

The estimated regression coefficients from the logistic regression model, similar to those in Listing 10.10, provide the information needed to compute the odds ratios. For this logistic multiple regression we move directly to this output, which appears in Listing 10.14. The interpretations of these values are similar to that for the one-predictor model already considered, except that each coefficient is interpreted with the values of all remaining predictor variables held constant.

	Odds Ratio	Lower 95%	Upper 95%
(Intercept)	0.0000	0.0000	0.0000
Height	1.1734	0.9546	1.4571
Weight	1.0544	1.0082	1.1066
Waist	1.1671	0.9310	1.4816
Hips	0.5109	0.3752	0.6614
Chest	1.1691	0.9352	1.4885
Hand	9.2634	3.8105	26.3174
Shoe	2.0938	1.2840	3.5690

Listing 10.14 Odds ratios and associated confidence intervals.

As seen from the output in Listing 10.10, the `Logit` function provides the estimated coefficients and hypothesis tests of each regression coefficient. Although not shown here, in this analysis the partial slope coefficients for three variables were not significantly different from 0, that is, the corresponding p-values were all larger than $\alpha = 0.05$. These three variables are Height, Waist, and Chest.

This lack of significance for these variables can also be gleaned from the 95% confidence intervals of the odds ratios reported in Listing 10.14. The confidence intervals of the odds ratios for these three variables with non-significant coefficients all cross the neutral value of 1.0. For example, the lower bound of this interval for Height is 0.9546, which means that for each one-inch increase in Height, the odds of a random selection of a Male decrease by $1 - 0.9546$ or 4.5%, with the values for all other variables held constant. Yet the upper bound of the same confidence interval is 1.4571, which means that the same odds increase by 45.7%. Because the same confidence interval contains values below 1.0 and above 1.0, the corresponding relationship between Height and Gender=1 cannot be shown to exist, with the values of all other variables held constant.

10.4.7 Assessment of Fit

A primary purpose for adding more predictor variables to a model is to enhance the model's ability to predict the response variable. The classification table for this seven-predictor model appears in Listing 10.15. Here the percentage of correct classifications with the one-predictor model compared with the seven-predictor model has increased from 88.2% to 93.2%.

```
                    Baseline              Predicted
         ---------------------------------------------------
                   Total  %Tot      F      M    %Correct
              F     170   50.0     158    12      92.9
  Gender      M     170   50.0      11   159      93.5
         ---------------------------------------------------
             Total   340                            93.2
```

Listing 10.15 Classification table based on seven predictors of Gender.

The addition of six more variables to the original logistic model with just Hand circumference as the predictor variable has enhanced predictive efficiency. Are all seven predictor variables necessary? The logistic multiple regression indicated that three of the variables had non-significant partial slope coefficients. This lack of significance suggests that these three coefficients do not contribute to the predictive efficiency of the model. This concept can be more formally evaluated by comparing the fit of the reduced or nested model with four predictors to the full model with seven predictors.

As with least-squares regression, use the lessR function Nest to conduct this hypothesis test. The null hypothesis is that all of the deleted variables have zero partial slope coefficients. By default the function assumes a least-squares solution. To specify that logit regression is the applicable procedure invoke the method option, set to "logit".

method option: Set to "logit" to indicate a logit analysis for comparing models.

> **lessR Input** *Compare nested models*

```
> Nest(Gender, c(Weight, Hips, Hand, Shoe),
      c(Height, Weight, Waist, Hips, Chest, Hand, Shoe), method="logit")
```

Nest function applied to least-squares solutions, Section 10.2.3, p. 231

The result of the comparison of the two models with Nest is shown in Listing 10.16. The Deviance index is the analogy for a maximum likelihood solution to the sum of the squared residuals for a least-squares solution.

Here the assessment is of the reduction of Deviance from the nested model to the full model, a reduction of 6.5019. The result is not significant, so the addition of the three predictor variables to the nested four-predictor model does not significantly contribute to the reduction in Deviance.

Effect of Height, Waist and Chest: p-value $= 0.090 > \alpha = 0.05$, so do *not* reject $H_0 : \beta_{Height} = \beta_{Waist} = \beta_{Chest} = 0$

```
Model 1: Gender ~ Weight + Hips + Hand + Shoe
Model 2: Gender ~ Height + Weight + Waist + Hips + Chest + Hand + Shoe
   Resid.df  Resid.Dev  df   Deviance   p-value
1      335     117.67
2      332     111.17    3     6.5019    0.0900
```

Listing 10.16 Direct comparison of a nested model to the full model with logistic regression.

The classification table provides further support of the conclusion of the viability of the four-predictor model. Re-running the model only with these four predictors confirms the validity of this analysis. The table is identical to that from the seven-predictor model in Listing 10.15. With Weight, Hips, Hand circumference, and Shoe size already in the model, the addition of Height, Waist, and Chest does not improve model fit.

The odds ratios for these four predictors in Listing 10.17 are not much changed from those from the seven-predictor model presented in Listing 10.14. A one-inch increase in Hand size results in an increase of the Odds of choosing a Male over 8.5 times more likely, with the values of all other predictor variables held constant.

```
             Odds Ratio   Lower 95%   Upper 95%
(Intercept)     0.0000      0.0000      0.0031
     Weight     1.0990      1.0660      1.1406
       Hips     0.5301      0.4079      0.6591
       Hand     8.5671      3.7773     21.9579
       Shoe     2.0647      1.3794      3.2211
```

Listing 10.17 Odds ratios and confidence intervals for the four-predictor model.

10.4.8 Predictions from New Data

Given the acceptance of the four-predictor model, predictions can now be made from new data.

⭐ **Scenario** *Predict Gender from new data with the logistic regression model*
Suppose the Gender of a customer is unknown and so is predicted from his or her corresponding body measurements. Also suppose that it is known that the customer has a medium size glove, but his or her hand size is unknown. Obtain the predicted value of Gender from the known measurements of Weight, Hips, and Shoe size, and then the three Hand circumference values that fit the medium size glove.

The analysis is done with the same set of X1.new, X2.new options and so forth as for the least-squares regression models.

prediction in least-squares models, Section 10.3.1, p. 238

 lessR Input *Logistic regression prediction from new data*
```
> Logit(Gender ~ Weight + Hips + Hand + Shoe,
        X1.new=155, X2.new=39, X3.new=c(8,8.5,9), X4.new=10)
```

The predictions for the three different sets of measurements appear in Listing 10.18. In all three cases the probability is high or very high that Y=1, that is, the person is a Male.

```
   Weight Hips Hand Shoe Ynew predict fitted std.err
1    155   38  8.0   10          1 0.7033 0.09586
2    155   38  8.5   10          1 0.8740 0.05042
3    155   38  9.0   10          1 0.9531 0.02481
```

Listing 10.18 Probabilities of a Male for three sets of new values for the four predictor variables.

In summary, very good differentiation between men and women is obtained simply from knowledge of the circumference of the Hand, with an 88.2% correct classification of Gender on this information alone. Increase this classification accuracy by adding the predictor variables of Weight, Hips, and Shoe size to the model. The result for this sample of 170 men and 170 women is an overall correct classification percentage to Gender of 93.2% on the basis of these five body measurements.

Worked Problems

?dataBodyMeas
for more
information.

1 Return to the `BodyMeas` data set.

> ```
> mydata <- Read("BodyMeas", format="lessR")
> ```

(a) Predict Weight from Height and Waist. Specify the estimated model. Specify the variables with significant partial slope coefficients. Interpret the largest coefficient.
(b) Identify the obvious outlier. What data value most contributes to the status of this case as an outlier?
(c) Using the `Subset` function drop this case from the data table.
(d) Re-estimate the model. Is the model reasonably similar or qualitatively different from the model estimated with the outlier?
(e) Predict Weight from Height, Waist, Hips, Chest, Hand circumference, and Shoe size. Specify the estimated model. Specify the variables with significant partial slope coefficients. Interpret the largest coefficient.
(f) Evaluate collinearity.
(g) Examine all possible subset regressions. List two models with five predictors that have an $R^2_{adj} > 0.80$ and also two such models with only two predictors.
(h) Relate your answers for the two previous questions.

2 The `Cars93` data set contains much information on 93 1993 car models. One variable is Source, which has two values, 0 for a foreign car and 1 for a car manufactured in the USA.

?dataCars93 for
more information.

> ```
> mydata <- Read("Cars93", format="lessR")
> ```

(a) Use the variable HP for horsepower to account for the Source of the automobile. Does horsepower successfully differentiate between non-USA and USA manufactured cars? If the odds ratio is interpretable provide the interpretation.

(b) Use the variable Width to account for the Source of the automobile. Does Width successfully differentiate between foreign and USA manufactured cars? If the odds ratio is interpretable provide the interpretation.

(c) For the one-variable Width predictor variable model what is the predicted Source for a car with a Width of 60.5 inches?

(d) How much improvement in prediction is there with the following predictor variables: Width, PassCap, Wheelbase, Engine, MPGhiway. Are all these predictor variables relevant? Interpret the largest odds ratio.

CHAPTER 11

FACTOR/ITEM ANALYSIS

11.1 Quick Start

First install R and `lessR` as explained in Section 1.2. At the beginning of each R session access `lessR` with `library(lessR)`. Then read your data into an R data frame with `Read()`, the subject of Chapter 2.

Factor analysis provides a relatively small number of abstract variables called factors that account for the relations among a usually much larger set of measured variables. A primary application of factor analysis in social science research is for attitude surveys in which a large number of items are designed to measure a much smaller number of attitudes. The factor analysis computes and relates the factors to the measured variables, the items, so that each factor corresponds to an attitude of interest on the attitude survey.

✓ The factor analysis analyzes the correlations among the measured variables. Prepare the data for the factor analysis by reading the responses to the measured variables, such as attitude items, and then calculate the corresponding correlation matrix.

```
> mydata <- Read()
> mycor <- Correlation()
```

Or, just read a stored correlation matrix directly.

```
> mycor <- corRead()
```

✓ The first consideration is an estimate of the smallest number of factors that reasonably well account for the correlations among the measured variables. The information for determining the number of factors is the scree plot, the plot of the eigenvalues of the correlation matrix plotted in descending order. Obtain this plot with the `lessR` function `scree`.

scree function, Section 11.3.2, p. 256

```
> scree()
```

✓ Run the exploratory factor analysis with the `lessR` function `efa`, which requires the specification of the number of factors to extract from the input correlation matrix. Here two factors are specified. The extraction method is maximum likelihood. The default rotation is the oblique promax method, with the orthogonal varimax rotation also available.

efa function, Section 11.3.2, p. 258

```
> efa(n.factors=2)
```

The factors from the exploratory analysis are often used to define and/or validate multi-item measurement scales. Accordingly, the output of `efa` also includes the code to copy and paste into R for the subsequent confirmatory factor analysis.

cfa function, Section 11.5.2, p. 267

✓   To evaluate the unidimensionality of a set of, for example, multi-item attitude scales, evaluate the corresponding multiple indicator measurement model or MIMM with a confirmatory factor analysis. Specify the variables that define each factor in the call to the `lessR` function `cfa`, here with two factors, each with three items.

```
> cfa(F1=c(X1,X2,X3), F2=c(X4,X5,X6))
```

This confirmatory factor analysis also provides the reliability of each derived scale with Coefficient Alpha and Coefficient Omega.

11.2 Overview of Factor Analysis

A guiding principle of science is *parsimony*, the explanation of relatively complex phenomena in terms of a small number of basic principles. A second guiding principle is that scientific explanations often involve abstract concepts, such as gravity, that themselves are not directly observable. Instead, the existence of these concepts is inferred from measurements and observations of the world in which we live. Factor analysis is a statistical methodology and analysis procedure consistent with these scientific principles.

parsimony: The simplest model to account for the most phenomena.

The purpose of doing a factor analysis is to build a model of the variables of interest expressed in terms of a relatively small number of underlying abstractions, what are called *latent variables*. A classic example of a latent variable in social science research is an attitude such as Machiavellianism or a personality trait such as Extroversion/Introversion. In a factor analysis these latent variables are operationalized as *factors*, abstractions not directly observed, but which can be empirically inferred and validated from the correlations between the corresponding measured variables.

latent variable: Unobserved, abstract variable.
factor: The name of a latent variable in factor analysis.

Many studies in social science research use surveys and questionnaires that consist of many items. Although the items may be presented in a randomized order, each attitude or personality characteristic of interest is typically measured by a set of items called a multi-item scale. Each person's responses to each of the items on such a scale are then summed to form the measurement of the underlying latent variable for that person. In this context the measured variables are the items on the attitude survey, and factor analysis becomes the primary tool for item analysis. *Item analysis* analyzes the relations between the items and scales to guide the construction of the multi-item scales. Each derived scale typically corresponds to a factor from the factor analysis.

item analysis: Analysis of the relations of items and the corresponding scales.

One of the key issues in a factor analysis is how many factors are needed to account for the relations among the measured variables. Usually the researcher begins with a one-to-one correspondence between the factors and the attitudes of interest. For example, consider the social construct of Machiavellianism as operationalized by the Christie and Geis (1970) 20-item Mach IV scale. If the Mach IV scale assesses the construct of Machiavellianism, then presumably there is a factor that would be revealed by a factor analysis that would indicate a measurement model that links each Mach IV item with this one underlying factor. This analysis would be evidence for a unified construct of Machiavellianism.

Mach IV scale, Table 1.2, p. 26

The model that relates each measured variable to the factors is a *measurement model*, a concept first delineated by Charles Spearman (1904) in what has become one of the most influential papers in all of the social sciences. The measurement model that specifies a single Machiavellian factor links each item on the Mach IV scale to this one factor. A one-factor model, called a *unidimensional* model, postulates just a single dimension, or factor, to underlie the 20 Mach IV items.

In the specification of the unidimensional measurement model the response to each scale item is expressed in terms of two attributes. The first attribute is the underlying factor itself, that is, the extent the response to the item is attributable to what is shared with all the other items on the scale. What is not shared with the other items on the scale is unique to a specific item. For the unidimensional model of Machiavellianism the model for each of the 20 Mach IV items can be written with the following regression model.

$$m_i = \lambda_i F + u_i$$

This model specifies that the response to the ith item on the scale for a given respondent is explained in terms of the underlying attribute shared with all the other scale items, the factor F, which presumably is Machiavellianism, plus some unique contribution, u_i, of this item that is, well, unique to that item. The complete unidimensional measurement model in this situation is the set of 20 such equations, one equation for each item.

For example, consider the sixth item on the scale, "Honesty is the best policy in all cases". The associated model for this item follows.

$$m_{06} = \lambda_{06} F + u_{06}$$

This regression coefficient, λ_i, the weight of the underlying factor of the common attribute that underlies the responses to the measured variable, is a *factor pattern* coefficient. The factor analysis of this complete 20-equation model provides an estimate of λ_i for each item, that is, an estimate of how strongly the responses to the item directly depend on the one shared common factor.

The relation between the factors and measured variables in the measurement model is a causal specification. Each factor is theorized to partially account for, or cause, the response to the item. For example, someone with a high Machiavellian attitude would then respond `Agree` or `Strongly Agree` to items that are consistent with Machiavellianism. The extent of the causal impact depends on the quality of the item in terms of its clarity and to the extent that it reflects the Machiavellian attitude.

The analysis also portrays the extent that the responses depend on the unique qualities of the item, the uniqueness. Each unique portion of the response to an item is the *uniqueness* term, the underlying basis of the response to the item not shared with the other items on the scale. By definition the unique component of each item is uncorrelated with the unique components of the remaining items. It consists, in part, of random response error. Each administration of the item potentially changes the *random response* error, much like flipping the same coin 10 times and getting 6 heads, and then flipping the same coin again and getting 4 heads on 10 flips. Random response error is relatively large for ambiguous items. The respondent may infer one meaning on one reading of an ambiguous item and another meaning on another reading. The resulting response to such an item is less a function of the underlying attitude and more a function of random response.

measurement model: Relates the observed measures to the latent variables.

unidimensional model: The observed measures have only one latent variable in common.

regression model, Section 9.2.2, p. 205

factor pattern coefficient: Model coefficient that relates the measured item to a factor.

uniqueness: Variance of an item not shared with any other items.

random response error: Component of a response that is attributable to unexplained randomness.

systematic response error: Stable component of a response that is attributable to the wrong content.

invalidity: The result of systematic error.

The uniqueness component also consists of *systematic error*, the contribution to *invalidity* regarding the measurement of the underlying attitude. The item may measure something stable, but it measures something other than the attitude of interest. Consider the item "I like chocolate ice cream". Presumably this item analyzed as the 21st Mach IV item would result in its corresponding responses demonstrating a low value of λ and a high uniqueness component. The responses to this ice cream item likely have little to do with Machiavellianism, so the responses would not be related in any meaningful sense with the responses to the actual Mach IV items. The factor analysis presumably would quantify the lack of this relationship with an estimated value of the factor pattern coefficient, λ, close to zero.

The factor analysis differentiates between the attributes of each response shared with the remaining items, the factor, and the attribute unique to each item. By definition the items correlate only to the extent that one or more common attributes generate the responses to the items. In particular, the measurement model, which regresses the measured variables, the items, onto the factors, imposes the correlational structure of the measured variables. The factor analysis reverses this process, inferring the underlying factor structure from the correlations among the variables of interest.

11.3 Exploratory Factor Analysis

11.3.1 The Concept of Exploratory Factor Analysis

The two primary types of factor analysis are confirmatory and exploratory, the latter the subject of this section. The models that underlie both types of factor analysis are similar. Both models express each measured variable as a function of the underlying factors and the corresponding uniqueness term. The distinction is that for exploratory factor analysis, introduced by Thurstone (1931), only the number of factors is specified to begin the analysis. Unlike confirmatory analysis, exploratory factor analysis expresses each measured variable as a function of *all* the factors specified in the analysis.

For example, suppose two specified factors account for the correlational structure of six items. Then the measurement model estimated by the corresponding exploratory factor analysis specifies six equations, each with two factors. Each measured variable has a pattern coefficient, a λ coefficient, on each of the two specified factors.

$$X_1 = \lambda_{11}F_1 + \lambda_{12}F_2 + u_1$$
$$X_2 = \lambda_{21}F_1 + \lambda_{22}F_2 + u_2$$
$$X_3 = \lambda_{31}F_1 + \lambda_{32}F_2 + u_3$$
$$X_4 = \lambda_{41}F_1 + \lambda_{42}F_2 + u_4$$
$$X_5 = \lambda_{51}F_1 + \lambda_{52}F_2 + u_5$$
$$X_6 = \lambda_{61}F_1 + \lambda_{62}F_2 + u_6$$

Conducting the exploratory factor analysis provides an estimated value of λ for each factor for each measured variable. Often the goal of such an analysis is to uncover a structure in which the response for each measured variable is causally dependent on a single factor and is not directly dependent on any other factor in the system. For the exploratory analysis, every measured variable is to some extent directly related to every factor. The desired solution, however, would be that for each item there is one relatively large value of λ and the rest of the λ's are reasonably close to zero in value. This style of solution is a *simple structure* solution.

The measurement model for the exploratory factor analysis is *underidentified*, which means that there is no unique solution for each estimated value in the model. The situation here is the same as the examples from high school algebra for systems of equations in which there are more unknown values to solve for than there are equations to provide information on which to base the solution. With underidentification there are many possible equally valid solutions.

Accordingly, an exploratory factor analysis is actually two different analyses. First obtain the initial solution, the *factor extraction*. The criterion for which to extract the factors is to define the first factor such that it is related as strongly as possible to all of the existing variables. The problem with the initial solution is that there is usually a strong general factor such that most of the items tend to highly relate to this general factor and less so with the other factors. Then the second extracted factor is the factor most related to all of the items after the first factor has been extracted. The result is that the initial extraction of the specified number of factors results in a solution that is roughly opposite of the desired goal of simple structure.

The factors from the initial factor extraction solution are uncorrelated. For the usual attitude survey that measures multiple attitudes, however, the attitudes are usually correlated with each other. When the second, rotated solution is obtained, the rotated factors can remain uncorrelated, what are called *orthogonal* factors, or they can be rotated into a correlated solution, resulting in what are called *oblique* factors.

For the study of sets of multi-item attitude scales, the scales present on the attitude survey are typically compared with scales defined by the factor analysis. Define a derived scale for each extracted factor, and then place each item on the scale for which it is most related to the corresponding factor. For the purpose of deriving scales of related items, the choice of orthogonal or oblique factor is not critical as both do reasonably well at this task (Gerbing & Hamilton, 1996).

simple structure: A factor solution in which each item primarily relates to a single factor.

underidentified model: The model has no unique solution from the available data.

factor extraction: First set of factors in an exploratory analysis.

factor rotation: Second set of factors in an exploratory analysis, which are interpreted.

orthogonal rotation: Uncorrelated factors from the rotation.

oblique rotation: Correlated factors from the rotation.

11.3.2 Exploratory Analysis of the Mach IV Scale

The data to which we apply factor analysis are the responses to the Mach IV scale for the measurement of Machiavellianism. The first task is to read the data. The data are included in the lessR package, and so can be read with the format="lessR" option.

Mach IV scale, Section 1.2, p. 26

```
> mydata <- Read("Mach4", format="lessR")
```

Before conducting a factor analysis, the items on a scale should be coded in the same direction. For the Mach IV scale, 11 of the 20 items are written so that agreement with the item indicates low Machiavellianism. These 11 items are reverse scored before computing the item correlations.

reverse score, Section 3.4.1, p. 63

```
> mydata <- Recode(c(m03,m04,m06,m07,m09,m10,m11,m14,m16,m17,m19),
              old=0:5, new=5:0)
```

To do a factor analysis we need the item correlations, the 20×20 correlation matrix, which by default accesses the data in the mydata data frame.

```
> mycor <- Correlation(m01:m20)
```

correlation matrix, Section 8.3, p. 194

In contrast to confirmatory factor analysis, exploratory analysis does not require the specification of a complete measurement model. Exploratory factor analysis only requires that the number of factors that account for item correlations first be specified. Probably the most useful test for the optimal number of factors is the scree plot, based on what are called eigenvalues from the initial factor extraction of the item correlation matrix. The eigenvalues are just a rescaling of the extracted factors, one eigenvalue per factor. The first extracted factor has the largest eigenvalue, the second extracted factor the second largest, and so forth.

scree plot: Plot of successive eigenvalues from the correlation matrix to identify the number of factors.

The word "scree" refers to a geological description of a cliff in which rock and dirt have slid down the face of the cliff, gathering at the bottom. The *scree plot* plots the eigenvalues sequentially in descending order. There are as many eigenvalues as items in the input correlation matrix, but the size of these eigenvalues, when plotted, tends to resemble a scree. Examination of the scree plot attempts to separate the important factors, which correspond to the cliff, from the scree, or rubble, at the bottom of the cliff.

 Scenario *Estimate the number of factors of a correlation matrix*
Analyze a correlation matrix to suggest the number of factors that should be specified for an exploratory factor analysis.

scree function: Obtain a scree plot and plot of eigenvalue differences.

The lessR function corScree, abbreviated scree, provides a scree plot of the eigenvalues of the input correlation matrix. To generate the scree plot for the default correlation matrix mycor, no argument to the function is needed.

 lessR Input *Scree and scree difference plot*
```
> scree()
```

The scree plot for the 20-item Mach IV correlation matrix appears in Figure 11.1. Where does the "cliff" end and the "scree" begin? The answer based on this scree plot is around the 4th eigenvalue, after which the "scree" begins to accumulate. At this point the slope becomes much less steep.

To view this change in slope between the "cliff" and the "scree" more directly, your author also prefers to evaluate the plot of the difference of the successive eigenvalues, to plot the successive changes directly. Accordingly, the scree function also provides this plot, shown in Figure 11.2. Here only the first four eigenvalue differences lie above the flat line, which is automatically provided as part of the plot. After the first four eigenvalue differences, the rate of change is essentially constant, which plots as a flat line. This flat line through the plotted eigenvalue differences represents the scree.

Any purely statistical criterion for the number of factors is at best a guideline for the most useful number. The final decision regarding the number of factors also depends on the interpretability of the resulting exploratory factor analysis. For example, if a five-factor solution is more interpretable than a four-factor solution, then that former solution would be preferred. Perhaps an important concept that corresponds to a factor is only represented by a small number of items, and hence the corresponding factor has a relatively small eigenvalue, but because of its substantive importance the factor should still be included in the results.

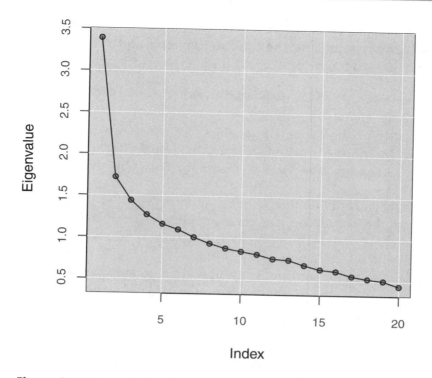

Figure 11.1 Scree plot for the successive eigenvalues of the 20-item Mach IV correlation matrix.

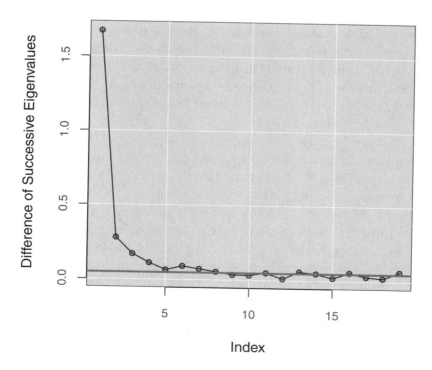

Figure 11.2 Scree plot for the difference of successive eigenvalues of the 20-item Mach IV correlation matrix.

The scree plot, and its associated plot of successive differences, provide a useful starting point for specifying the number of factors that underlie the correlation matrix, and a required starting point for the exploratory factor analysis. Next proceed with the exploratory factor analysis.

⭐ **Scenario** *Exploratory factor analysis*
Given a correlation matrix of the measured variables, such as the items, extract the specified number of factors and then rotate to a correlated factor solution.

The `lessR` exploratory factor analysis routine is `corEFA`, abbreviated `efa`. The specified number of factors is given by the required `n.factors` argument. There are many factor extraction methods. The standard `R` system factor analysis function `factanal`, upon which `efa` relies, does a maximum likelihood extraction.

show.initial
option: If `TRUE`, show the initial extracted factor solution.

Here we proceed with the four-factor maximum likelihood exploratory analysis on the default correlation matrix `mycor`. This initial solution is not displayed by default. To view the initial factors, specify `show.initial=TRUE`.

---

 lessR Input *Exploratory factor analysis for a four-factor model*
```
> efa(n.factors=4)
```

---

promax
rotation: Oblique factor solution.

varimax
rotation: Orthogonal factor solution.

rotate option: Can specify a varimax rotation.

The default rotational method provided by `efa` is *promax*, a rotational method that yields correlated, that is, oblique, factors. The underlying latent variables of interest, such as the attitudes of interest, correspond to the extracted factors. The alternative is to rotate the initially extracted factors to an uncorrelated or orthogonal solution. The orthogonal rotation method `R` provides is *varimax*. To specify, include `rotate="varimax"` in the call to `efa`.

The primary output of the exploratory four-factor solution appears in Listing 11.1. `R` labels the output `Loadings:`, a somewhat ambiguous term in the factor analysis literature. Here the term refers to the pattern coefficients, the λ's of the underlying measurement model. Loadings with a value close to zero, by default values between −0.2 and 0.2, are replaced by blanks to facilitate interpretation of the more important coefficients.

min.loading
option: Specify the minimum loading to display on the output.

sort option: If `FALSE` then the items are not sorted by highest factor loading.

The minimum value to display can be changed by specifying a value other than 0.2 for the `min.loading` option. By default the items are sorted by their highest loading across all the factors, though just the items with loadings of 0.5 or greater are listed first. To suppress sorting, specify the following in the call to `efa`, `sort=FALSE`.

The four factors in this solution define a four-dimensional space, that is, a coordinate system with four axes, and each item can be plotted in that space. In most social science research, however, the interpretation of this loading matrix is usually not based on the factors as abstract dimensions, but rather on the multi-item scales defined from this loading matrix.

In Listing 11.1, we see, for example, that Items `m06`, `m07`, `m10`, `m03` and `m09` all load primarily on the first rotated factor. The interpretation of the underlying factor, and the associated scale of items, is based on the content of these items. This interpretation is explored in the next section.

The relations of the four factors across all the measured variables are shown in Listing 11.2. Here `SS loadings` refers to the sum of the squared factor loadings across all of the items for

```
Loadings:
        Factor1  Factor2  Factor3  Factor4
m06   0.828                        -0.290
m07   0.712
m10   0.539
m05            0.649
m13            0.543   -0.226
m18            0.555   -0.253
m14           -0.402    0.991   -0.401
m11            0.299    0.309   -0.609
m01            0.490
m02                              0.319
m03   0.422   -0.318
m04                     0.426
m08            0.236    0.202
m09   0.323
m12            0.434    0.230
m15   0.207    0.203             0.214
m16                     0.274   -0.455
m17                     0.267
m19
m20            0.237    0.282
```

Listing 11.1 Factor loadings for the rotated four-factor extraction of the correlations of Mach IV items.

each factor. There can be as many factors as there are items, so the total amount of variance to account for is 20. The proportion of variance accounted for by the sum of squared loadings, Proportion Var, for the first factor follows.

Proportion of Variance for Factor #1: 1.933/20 = 0.097

As can be seen, the sum of squared loadings for the first three factors all approximate 2, whereas there is a drop-off for the fourth factor, a value that only approximates 1. As mentioned previously, however, these indices should not be interpreted too literally because perhaps the content of the items that tap into the fourth factor are simply fewer in number than the number of items that tap into the other factors. The issue, again, cannot be reduced solely to statistics, but instead focuses on the interpretability and usefulness of the factors for explaining, in this example, Machiavellianism.

	Factor1	Factor2	Factor3	Factor4
SS loadings	1.933	2.038	1.825	1.099
Proportion Var	0.097	0.102	0.091	0.055
Cumulative Var	0.097	0.199	0.290	0.345

Listing 11.2 The sum of the squared loadings of each factor across the measured variables and the proportion of the total variance accounted for by each factor.

Listing 11.1 and 11.2 are the primary output of the exploratory factor analysis. Now the task is to interpret the meaning of the extracted factors, usually in the form of the corresponding multi-item scales that are defined on the basis of the pattern of factor loadings.

11.4 The Scale Score

Items on a survey may be intended to measure attitudes such as Machiavellianism or Self-Esteem. Measurement of these attitudes is usually accomplished with groups of items that define scales, even though the survey itself may present the items from all the scales in a randomized order. The sum or average of the responses for the items on a scale for each person is referred to as the *total score*, *composite score*, or *scale score*.

Item analysis is the analysis of the relations between the items and the scale scores to guide the construction of the multi-item scales. Both the item responses or the scale scores can be directly observed by, for example, computing a scale score for each person who took an attitude survey. Contrast these scale scores to the factors from the factor analysis that are inferred abstractions, latent variables instead of observed variables.

Accomplish a more sophisticated item analysis with confirmatory factor analysis, as discussed in Section 11.5. The more traditional item analysis described in this section, however, can be considered optional and is somewhat tangential to the more sophisticated confirmatory factor analyses. Conceptually, this analyses of the observed responses and scores complement the focus on abstract factors in an exploratory and also confirmatory factor analysis.

A primary role of exploratory factor analysis in item analysis is the construction of scales based on the factor loadings of the items. There is one scale for each factor. Each item is generally put into the scale on which it has its highest corresponding factor loading, unless the absolute value of its highest loading is less than the value of some minimum value such as 0.2. To facilitate this scale construction process, the last part of the efa output defines the corresponding scales, and then constructs the code, to copy and paste into R, to run the confirmatory factor analysis of the resulting scales.

> **total score**: The sum or average of all the items on multi-item scale.
> *item analysis*, Section 11.2, p. 252

Scenario *Analyze the reliability of a total score and the item-total correlations*
Item analysis procedures evaluate the relation of an item to the overall scale of which the item is a part. The scale score is computed as the sum of the corresponding item scores. Obtain these observed item–scale correlations, the scale–scale correlations and the reliability of each scale score.

The corresponding scales are shown in Listing 11.4. Here, however, we do not pursue the confirmatory analysis, but only analyze the scale scores. Replace the unmodified call to the lessR confirmatory factor analysis function, cfa, with the lessR function scales. The scales function is an abbreviation for a call to cfa with parameter settings to provide for the analysis of the observed scale scores in place of their unobserved, latent counterparts.

> **scales** function: A call to cfa for the analysis of the observed scale scores.

 lessR Input *Analysis of four scales from the exploratory factor analysis*

```
> scales(
    F1=c(m03,m06,m07,m09,m10),
    F2=c(m01,m05,m08,m12,m13,m18),
    F3=c(m04,m14,m17,m20),
    F4=c(m02,m11,m15,m16)
  )
```

In this example, only `m19` was not included in any of the derived multi-item scales, because its highest factor loading from the exploratory factor analysis was below the minimum absolute value of `min.loading=0.2`, the default value of `efa`. Of course, increasing the value of `min.loading` will omit more items from the resulting scales.

11.4.1 Item and Scale Correlations

A person's score on a multi-item scale is the sum of his or her responses to the items that define the scale. The correlation of an item with its own scale score is an *item–total correlation*. The call to `scales` provides the correlations of the items with all of the scale scores shown in Figure 11.3. The item–total correlation of each item with its own scale is highlighted in Figure 11.3.

item–total correlation: Correlation of an item with its own scale score.

```
      m07 m06 m10 m09   m03 m01 m05 m12 m13 m18 m08 m17 m20 m14 m04 m16 m11 m15 m02
F1    .75 .73 .67 .60   .54 .11 .08 .18 .16 .16 .08 .17 .15 .17 .17 .25 .28 .21 .16
F2    .23 .23 .20 .21  -.11 .60 .58 .57 .56 .53 .49 .20 .27 .01 .20 .17 .26 .22 .22
F3    .20 .13 .22 .21   .12 .17 .08 .29 .13 .07 .18 .61 .61 .60 .60 .17 .25 .02 .12
F4    .30 .32 .29 .30   .09 .15 .23 .27 .19 .26 .16 .07 .13 .22 .19 .58 .57 .56 .56
```

Figure 11.3 Annotated item–total correlations from the function `scales` plus the added highlight of the uncorrected correlation of each item with its own scale.

One property of these highlighted item–total correlations, the correlation of an item with its own total score, is an upward bias. The reason for this bias is that the item response is by definition part of the total score and so must necessarily correlate at least to some extent with the total score even if the item correlates zero with all the other items on the multi-item scale. These item–total correlations are usually more useful when the item correlates not with the entire total score, but with the total score calculated without the contribution of the item of interest. This modified correlation is a *part–whole correlation* or the *corrected correlation*. This more sophisticated version of these corrected correlations is presented later, in the form of the correlation of an item with the underlying factor instead of the observed total score.

part–whole correlation: Correlation of an item with the scale without the item's influence.

The correlations of the scales with each other are also part of the `scales` output, here shown in Listing 11.3.

correlation matrix, Section 8.3, p. 194

```
        F1    F2    F3    F4
F1    1.00  0.23  0.27  0.40
F2    0.23  1.00  0.28  0.38
F3    0.27  0.28  1.00  0.25
F4    0.40  0.38  0.25  1.00
```

Listing 11.3 Correlation matrix of the scale scores.

Here the correlation of Scale F_1 with Scale F_2, 0.23, is the observed correlation between the two scale scores. Later we obtain the underlying factor correlation in place of the observed, that is, directly calculated, correlation. The true factor correlation is with measurement error purged, the value corrected for attenuation due to measurement error, and so is larger than the value observed here. With the item uniquenesses remaining in the analysis, the correlations are between the scale scores and not between abstract factors, though `scales` still uses the `F` notation as an abbreviation for Factor instead of something like `S` for scale.

11.4.2 Scale Reliability

reliability:
Consistency of
repeated measures.

A fundamental concept of measurement is that of *reliability*, the consistency of the measured values from measurement to measurement. For example, suppose one morning you wish to measure your weight. You step on the bathroom scale and it registers 148 lbs. Then suppose you step off the scale, wait a few moments for the scale to re-set to 0, and then step back on the same scale. Now it registers 157 lbs. Your weight has not changed, which means that the measuring device, in this case the bathroom scale for measuring weight, is unreliable.

What is the purpose of measuring attitudes with multi-item scales instead of a single item? One reason is that the multi-item scale score, the composite score, is generally more reliable than any of the individual items that define the scale. A primary reason for the use of scale scores in psychological measurement is due to the relatively large amount of error in individual responses. That is, each item by itself may be relatively unreliable. These composite scores provide a level of analysis that is intermediate to the responses to individual components and the factors from a factor analysis.

Measurements at two different points in time provide the data to assess the reliability of the bathroom scale. The analogy for social measurement would be to administer an attitude survey, wait for enough time to pass so that the responses are not memorized but the underlying attitudes have not changed, and then re-administer the survey. Administering a measuring instrument at two different times to assess the consistency of responses forms the basis for *test–retest* reliability.

test–retest reliability:
Correlation of
repeated measures.

Usually the opportunity to administer a survey multiple times does not exist. How, then, to assess consistency over multiple measures at one time period? Assess consistency over multiple items that are all on the same scale to obtain the *internal-consistency reliability*. The most well known index of internal-consistency reliability is Coefficient Alpha, introduced by Cronbach (1951) and sometimes called Cronbach's Alpha. These reliability estimates appear in Listing 11.4.

internal-consistency reliability: Based
on the correlation
of items on the
same scale
administered at the
same time.

```
Reliability Analysis
-------------------
 Scale  Alpha
 -----------
   F1   0.676
   F2   0.550
   F3   0.423
   F4   0.300
```

Listing 11.4 Scale reliabilities for the two scales that correspond to the grouping of the items that define the underlying multiple-indicator measurement model.

All of these four scales have low reliabilities. A rough heuristic is to have a scale reliability of at least 0.7 or 0.8, so even the scale with the highest reliability, 0.677, falls short of this goal. To increase the reliability of the scale score, increase the number of items that assess more or less the same underlying attitude. These low scale reliabilities are not surprising because the Mach IV scale was not written as four separate scales, but as a single scale. Future work, then, would extend the reliability of these subscales by increasing the number of items on each scale. First, however, we wish to refine the scales further with confirmatory factor analysis.

11.5 Confirmatory Factor Analysis

For *confirmatory factor analysis* specify the measurement model in advance of the analysis. One purpose of the analysis is to estimate the parameters of the measurement model, the values of the pattern coefficients, the λ's, and the factor correlations. From these estimates derive the imposed correlation matrix of the measured variables and compare to the actual item correlations. To the extent that the imposed correlations match the actual correlations, the measurement model is empirically confirmed.

confirmatory factor analysis: Analysis of a specified measurement model.

The general process of factor analysis based research for attitude surveys follows a standard pattern. First specify the measurement model and then analyze.

- ○ Gather the responses to the items on the survey
- ○ Calculate the correlations among the items
- ○ Run the factor analysis program on the correlations to estimate the model parameters such as the λ's
- ○ Evaluate the fit of the estimated model by comparing the item correlations implied by the model to the actual item correlation

An explanation of the meaning of these imposed correlations follows.

11.5.1 The Covariance Structure

The confirmatory factor analysis estimates a specified measurement model. We apply our first confirmatory factor analysis to a correlation matrix in which the correct measurement model is known in advance of the analysis. We know the correct model because we define our own measurement model and then derive the item correlations computed not from data but from the corresponding correlation pattern implied by this measurement model. We analyze the resulting correlations imposed by that model, the model's *covariance structure*.[1] This model is devoid of psychological content, but serves as a useful exercise to illustrate the conceptual basis of factor analysis.

covariance structure: Covariances, such as correlations, of the variables implied by the measurement model.

Our model includes six measured variables and two factors, with three variables linked to one factor and the other three variables linked to the other factor. This model contains multiple factors, but each item directly indicates only a single factor, an example of a *multiple indicator measurement model* or MIMM. An MIMM is generally the most useful type of measurement model for scale development because the items on an attitude survey are usually partitioned into multi-item scales. Within this framework each item measures a single attitude, modeled as a factor.

MIMM: A measurement model with each item directly linked to only one factor.

Define this MIMM in terms of six equations that link each of the measured items to one of the two underlying factors. The correlation among the factors must also be specified. Here we specify our own population model, so use the symbol for the population correlation, ρ. Specify a moderate population factor correlation of 0.3, and a sequence of the population pattern coefficients, the λ's, that step from 0.8 to 0.6 to 0.4 for the three indicators of each factor.

$$X_1 = .8F_1 + u_1 \qquad X_4 = .8F_2 + u_4$$

$$X_2 = .6F_1 + u_2 \qquad X_5 = .6F_2 + u_5$$

$$X_3 = .4F_1 + u_3 \qquad X_6 = .4F_2 + u_6$$

$$\rho_{F_1,F_2} = 0.3$$

path diagram: A diagram of causal relationships.

This model can also be presented as a *path diagram*, shown in Figure 11.4. In this diagram the lines with arrowheads at one end represent a causal structure, which specifies that the response to each observed variable is due to the underlying shared factor, plus there is an implied uniqueness term. The curved line with double-headed arrows represents a correlation that has no underlying specification of causality. That is, Factors F_1 and F_2 are correlated, but the model provides no explanation as to why they are correlated.

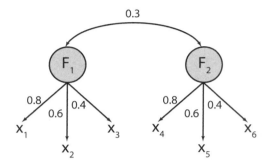

Figure 11.4 Specified population two-factor multiple indicator measurement model, three items per factor.

Now the critical question. How does a measurement model dictate or impose the correlations among the measured variables, here the correlation matrix for variables X_1 through X_6? Matrix algebra provides the general result. Fortunately, for the multiple indicator measurement model, which posits only one factor underlying each item, we can provide these equations without resorting to matrices.

External Consistency

external consistency: Covariance structure of items on a unidimensional scale with respect to other items.

The correlation of two items from different factors defined by a MIMM is provided by the *product rule for external consistency* (Spearman, 1914; Gerbing & Anderson, 1988). The extent of the correlation here depends not only on the strength of the relationship of each item with its own factor, but also on the correlation of the factors. For example, if the factors have a low correlation, then items from these two different factors also have a low correlation.

The corresponding product rule provides the quantitative relationship between two items, one from Factor F_1 and the other from Factor F_2.

product rule for external consistency: $\rho_{X_i X_j} = \lambda_i (\rho_{F_1, F_2}) \lambda_j$

For example, the correlation of Items X_1 and X_5 consistent with the underlying measurement model in Figure 11.4 follows.

$$\rho_{X_1 X_5} = \lambda_1 (\rho_{F_1, F_2}) \lambda_5 = (0.8)(0.3)(0.6) = 0.144$$

internal consistency: Covariance structure of items on a unidimensional scale.

Internal Consistency

A special case of external consistency applies to the correlations of the items of the same factor, that is, for a factor–factor correlation of 1.0. The *product rule for internal consistency* specifies that the correlation of two items that both measure the same factor depends only on their corresponding pattern coefficients or λ's. Here express the rule for Items X_i and X_j.

$$\text{product rule for internal consistency: } \rho_{X_i X_j} = \lambda_i(1.0)\lambda_j = \lambda_i \lambda_j$$

One would expect that higher item correlations would occur for two items more highly related to their common factor. This pattern is shown quantitatively by applying the product rule for internal consistency, here for Items X_1 and X_2.

$$\rho_{X_1 X_2} = \lambda_1 \lambda_2 = (0.8)(0.6) = 0.48$$

Similarly, apply the product rule to the second and third items.

$$\rho_{X_2 X_3} = \lambda_2 \lambda_3 = (0.6)(0.4) = 0.24$$

Apply the product rules to all six items to obtain the correlation matrix presented in Listing 11.5. Each item correlates with itself perfectly, that is, the values of the diagonal elements are all 1's.

```
> mycor
      X1    X2    X3    X4    X5    X6
X1 1.000 0.480 0.320 0.192 0.144 0.096
X2 0.480 1.000 0.240 0.144 0.108 0.072
X3 0.320 0.240 1.000 0.096 0.072 0.048
X4 0.192 0.144 0.096 1.000 0.480 0.320
X5 0.144 0.108 0.072 0.480 1.000 0.240
X6 0.096 0.072 0.048 0.320 0.240 1.000
```

Listing 11.5 Population correlation matrix, the covariance structure, of the six observed variables imposed by their multiple indicator measurement model.

Correlation does not establish causation. A causal pattern, however, does imply correlation. If the items in the measurement model in Figure 11.4 are related to the two underlying factors as specified, then the population correlations of the six items in the model are constrained to those in Listing 11.5.

Communalities

We have considered the correlations of two items from the same and different factors that are consistent with the underlying measurement model. What about the correlation of each item with itself, the diagonal elements in the correlation matrix such as in Listing 11.5? These diagonal elements, which all equal 1, are fundamentally different from, and are all larger than the off-diagonal elements.

The basis of this distinction is that the correlation of two different items directly depends only on the strength of their relationships with the underlying factor or factors. The correlation of an item with itself, however, depends not only on the influence of its underlying factor, but also on the influence of its uniqueness component. The relationship between the pattern coefficient λ and the variance of the item uniqueness attribute for the ith item follows.

$$\rho_{X_i X_i} = 1 = \lambda_i^2 + \sigma_{u_i}^2$$

communality:
Proportion of an item's variance due only to the common factors.

An item's *communality* is the proportion of the correlation of an item with itself that is due only to the shared factors. For a unidimensional model of the type specified here, this communality, here λ_i^2, is due only to the one underlying factor.

The expression of an item's communality is based on a special case of the product rule for internal consistency, applied to the same item twice.

$$\textit{communality of } i^{th} \textit{ item: } \lambda_i\lambda_i = \lambda_i^2$$

To solve for this communality is to extract this common contribution to the full variation of the item, here a value of 1.0. This extraction of the common influence of the factors on item variability, the ability to distinguish between the communality and the uniqueness component of an item, is the solution for the factor pattern coefficient, λ_i. The factor analysis, then, transforms the observed correlation matrix with 1's in the diagonal to the correlation matrix with communalities in the diagonal.

iteration: A computed solution, the results of which are entered back into the model to compute another solution.

The communalities are computed as an iterative process, from one *iteration* to the next. Compute the communalities by starting with the 1's in the diagonal of the input correlation matrix. Then the corresponding pattern coefficients and factor–factor correlations are estimated with one of the many available factor analysis estimation procedures. Next, the resulting estimated pattern coefficients are squared according to the product rule for internal consistency, and then those values inserted into the diagonal. This process is repeated until the solution generally does not change much from iteration to iteration. The result is the final estimated parameters of the model.

11.5.2 Analysis of a Population Model

Now we have the information needed to proceed to the confirmatory factor analysis of the correlation matrix in Listing 11.5. These correlations were generated according to the covariance structure rules imposed by a multiple-indicator measurement model presented in Figure 11.4.

⭐ **Scenario** *Recover the measurement model from the imposed correlations*
Recover the parameters of a measurement model used to construct the correlation matrix. The confirmatory factor analysis of those correlations should return the same parameter values, the pattern coefficients and the factor correlations, originally used to construct the imposed correlations.

calculate correlation matrix, Section 8.3, p.194

The factor analysis begins from the correlations between the variables. One possibility is to use the `Correlation` function to calculate the correlations from the original data table, the data frame, which contains the raw data. The other possibility is to read the already computed correlations from an external file, the only choice available in this example because the correlations were computed directly from the product rules imposed by the model. This is not a standard data analysis to evaluate a posited structure that may or may not fit the data. Instead this is a conceptual exercise, an attempt to recover a known structure from its implied correlations, its covariance structure.

To read a correlation matrix into R, use the `lessR` function `corRead`, abbreviated `rd.cor`. The correlations are on the `lessR` web site.

```
> mycor <- corRead("http://lessRstats.com/data/MIMMperfect.cor")
```

The correlations are stored in a data structure called `mycor`, which is the default name for the input correlation matrix for the `lessR` factor analysis functions.

correlation matrix in R, Section 8.2.1, p. 182

The `lessR` confirmatory factor analysis program `corCFA`, abbreviated `cfa`, analyzes a MIMM. The `cor` in the full name for the procedure indicates that the information entered into the procedure for analysis is not the responses to the items, but their correlations. The required arguments to `cfa` are the lists of items that define each factor. Each factor is named with an F followed by the factor number, beginning with a 1 and continuing to the number of factors, of which 12 is the maximum. By default, `cfa` analyzes the correlations in the `mycor` matrix.

cfa function: Confirmatory factor analysis of a multiple indicator measurement model.

The most general technique to specify a list of items is to use the R combine function `c`, such as in `c(X1,X2,X3)`. If the variables in the list are sequential in the corresponding data frame, then the colon notation, `:`, can be used instead.

c function, Section 1.3.6, p. 15

> **✐ lessR Input** *Confirmatory factor analysis of a two factor MIMM*
> ```
> > cfa(F1=X1:X3, F2=X4:X6)
> ```

The output of `cfa` is primarily text, but also includes one graphic, the heat map of the item-correlation matrix with communalities in the diagonal, as shown in Figure 11.5. The *heat map* displays a patch of color or gray scale for each correlation coefficient. The darker is the color, the stronger the correlation.

heat map: A graph of item correlations.

Item Correlations/Communalities

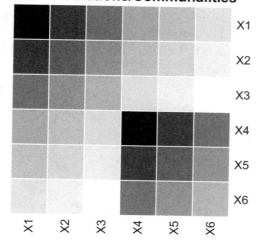

Figure 11.5 Heat map of six-variable correlation matrix with communalities in the diagonal.

The pattern of the two three-item blocks in the heat map, in the top-left corner and bottom-right corner, is the "hierarchical ordering" of the correlations of unidimensional items first noted by Spearman (1904) more than a century ago. The items that more strongly relate to their underlying factor correlate more highly with each other, as indicated by the darker shades of gray. Further, items within each factor correlate more highly than items in different factors, as shown by the lighter shades of gray in the bottom-left corner and top-right corner of Figure 11.5.

The primary output of the confirmatory factor analysis, in Listing 11.6, begins with the estimated pattern coefficients, the λ for each measured variable, as well as its corresponding uniqueness.

```
Indicator Analysis
------------------------------------------------------------------------
Fac   Indi   Pat     Unique   Factors with which an indicator correlates too
tor   cator  tern    ness     highly, and other indicator diagnostics.
------------------------------------------------------------------------
F1    X1     0.800   0.360
F1    X2     0.600   0.640
F1    X3     0.400   0.840

F2    X4     0.800   0.360
F2    X5     0.600   0.640
F2    X6     0.400   0.840
```

Listing 11.6 Estimated factor pattern coefficients, uniquenesses and diagnostics.

misspecification: A specified model that does not match reality.

The confirmatory factor analysis perfectly recovered the underlying true measurement model. The λ's computed by the factor analysis, listed under the heading of `Pattern`, are the exact values used to generate the covariance structure, in this case the item correlation matrix. There is also room for diagnostic information that helps identify aspects of the model that do not fit the data, what are called *misspecifications*. In this example this area is blank because the covariance structure input in the analysis fits the estimated model perfectly, as designed.

item–factor correlation: A correlation of an item with a factor.

The next output, in Figure 11.6, is the complete item–factor correlation matrix with communalities in the diagonal of the item correlations. Here we observe all of the *item–factor correlations*, the correlations of the items, the measured variables, with the factors, the latent variables. Thus we see, for example, that the first item, X_1, correlates 0.8 with its own factor, F_1, and 0.24 with the second factor, F_2. Note that the factor correlation of an item on its own factor for an MIMM is the corresponding pattern coefficient, λ.

	X1	X2	X3	X4	X5	X6	F1	F2
X1	0.64	0.48	0.32	0.19	0.14	0.10	0.80	0.24
X2	0.48	0.36	0.24	0.14	0.11	0.07	0.60	0.18
X3	0.32	0.24	0.16	0.10	0.07	0.05	0.40	0.12
X4	0.19	0.14	0.10	0.64	0.48	0.32	0.24	0.80
X5	0.14	0.11	0.07	0.48	0.36	0.24	0.18	0.60
X6	0.10	0.07	0.05	0.32	0.24	0.16	0.12	0.40
F1	0.80	0.60	0.40	0.24	0.18	0.12	1.00	0.30
F2	0.24	0.18	0.12	0.80	0.60	0.40	0.30	1.00

Figure 11.6 Annotated output correlation matrix with communalities in the diagonal of all measured and latent variables in the analysis.

The factor correlation matrix appears in the bottom right of the complete matrix in Figure 11.6. The correlation of the two factors, F_1 and F_2, is 0.3. This value for the factor correlation specified in the constructed model has also been recovered by the confirmatory factor analysis of the implied population covariance structure, validating the analysis for the estimation and evaluation of measurement models for data analysis.

For an analysis of many variables it may be convenient to list only the item–factor and factor–factor correlations. To display just those correlations on the cfa output, add the item.cor=FALSE option to the function call.

item.cor option: If FALSE, then the item correlations are not displayed.

How well does the model fit? Examine Listing 11.7, where each residual is the difference between the corresponding item correlation and its value imposed by the estimated multiple indicator measurement model.

residual: Difference between the actual correlation and the imposed by the model.

```
Residuals
--------------------
    X1 X2 X3 X4 X5 X6
X1   0  0  0  0  0  0
X2   0  0  0  0  0  0
X3   0  0  0  0  0  0
X4   0  0  0  0  0  0
X5   0  0  0  0  0  0
X6   0  0  0  0  0  0
```

Listing 11.7 Residuals, the difference between observed correlations and those specified by the estimated model.

The analysis perfectly recovered the structure of the underlying model. The fit is perfect. All residuals are zero, as it should be because the correlation matrix was generated to be perfectly consistent with the underlying model.

The preceding analysis was accomplished with the default 25 iterations to obtain the communality estimates. The number of iterations can be specified by setting the iter option. For example, to restrict the analysis to the observed scores, specify 0 iterations, which is the equivalent of specifying the scales function. The result is an analysis of the item and scale (total) correlations. It is as if the scale scores were computed by summing the relevant item scores and then the correlations computed between the items and the scale scores.

iter option: Specify the number of iterations for the estimates.

scales function, Section 11.4, p. 260

11.5.3 Proportionality

An implication of the product rule for external consistency is that for any two items of the same factor, their correlations of all other items, including items from other factors and for the communalities, are proportional. To illustrate, return to Figure 11.6, which lists the item correlations with communalities in the diagonal. Consider the first two items, X_1 and X_2, their correlations with all other items, and the corresponding ratios, shown in Table 11.1.

external consistency, Section 11.5.1, p. 264

How can these proportionality constants help diagnose and suggest measurement models consistent with the data?

 Scenario *Obtain the matrix of proportionalities*

A heuristic aid to specify a multiple indicator measurement model consistent with the data is a matrix of proportionality coefficients, which provides, for each pair of items, the average proportionality of their correlations with all other items.

Table 11.1 Correlations of Items X_1 and X_2 to three decimal digits across all six items in the model and their corresponding ratios, that is, proportions.

Item	X1	X2	Ratio
X1	0.640	0.480	1.333
X2	0.480	0.360	1.333
X3	0.320	0.240	1.333
X4	0.192	0.144	1.333
X5	0.144	0.108	1.333
X6	0.096	0.072	1.333

The `lessR` function `corProp`, abbreviated `prop`, provides the matrix of average proportionalities (Hunter, 1973). Again, the default input correlation matrix is `mycor`. The output of `prop` is in this example not written to a data structure, so the output instead is directed to the console as text output.

🖋 **lessR Input** *Proportionality coefficients*

```
> prop()
```

The output is shown in Figure 11.7.

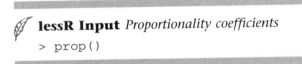

Figure 11.7 Annotated proportionality matrix.

For these perfect correlations according to their fit with the underlying model, the proportionalities of items that measure the same factor are all 1.00.

perfect model, Section 11.5.2, p. 266

Recovering the postulated model from the implied covariance structure is a conceptual exercise. In this situation there is no model specification error because the model is perfectly specified. There is also no sampling error because the implied population correlations are used as the input to the analysis. In the real world of data analysis, even for a well specified model, sampling error ensures that the model parameters are not perfectly recovered. If multiple samples were taken, each sample would generate different estimates because each sample of data is different from every other sample, and no sample perfectly represents the population.

The process of a confirmatory factor analysis with actual data for the analysis of Machiavellianism follows.

11.5.4 Confirmatory Analysis of the Mach IV Scale

One tradition in social science research is to use exploratory factor analysis to define and/or revise a set of multi-item scales. The procedure is straightforward. Define a scale for each extracted factor and then place each item on the scale for which it has the highest factor loading, perhaps only retaining those items that load on the factor at some minimum value such as 0.4. Another part of this tradition, at least as practiced by some researchers, is to stop at this point and declare the scales unidimensional.

The problem here is that exploratory factor analysis defined the factors as dimensions that set up a coordinate system in some multi-dimensional space. A set of coordinate axes is not a set of scales. The construction of the scales from these factors is an ad-hoc procedure without any formal statistical evaluation of dimensionality. Fortunately, exploratory factor analysis can be useful for suggesting multiple indicator measurement models (Gerbing & Hamilton, 1996), but a suggestion is not an evaluation of fit.

The re-emergence of confirmatory factor analysis during the last several decades of social science research has once again provided access to tools for formally testing the dimensionality of the resulting scales.

 Scenario *Evaluate the implied Mach IV measurement model*
A set of four Mach IV subscales was constructed based on an exploratory factor analysis of all 20 Mach IV items. Now formally evaluate the dimensionality of these scales with a confirmatory factor analysis of the resulting multiple indicator measurement model.

The confirmatory factor analysis specification provided by the four-factor exploratory analysis from the `efa` function follows. To run this analysis, copy the instructions for the `cfa` function call at the end of the `efa` output in Listing 11.8, and then paste back into R.

```
> corCFA(
    F1=c(m03,m06,m07,m09,m10),
    F2=c(m01,m05,m08,m12,m13,m18),
    F3=c(m04,m14,m17,m20),
    F4=c(m02,m11,m15,m16)
  )
```

Listing 11.8 Confirmatory factor analysis code from the exploratory factor analysis.

The formal analysis of the corresponding MIMM indicates that the model does not fit well. For example, 10 of the 19 items have loadings on their own factor at 0.4 or less, and 7 of the 19 items in the model correlate more with another factor than they do their own. Clearly the model direct from the exploratory analysis needs refinement. The size of the average absolute value of all the residuals is also large, 0.051.

How to respecify the corresponding measurement model to improve fit? One strategy is delete from the model some of the poor fitting items, such as those with low λ values. Another strategy is to recognize that two items of the same underlying factor have, in the population, the same constant of proportionality across all other variables, both items that also measure the same factor, or items or any other variable from anywhere else.

item proportionality of correlations, Figure 11.7, p. 270

Scenario *Obtain and re-order proportionality coefficients*
As an aid to constructing a multiple indicator measurement model, an MIMM, calculate the proportionality coefficient for each pair of Mach IV items. Then re-order the matrix of proportionality coefficients so that similar items tend to appear next to each other in the matrix. The goal is identify a MIMM that complements the guidance provided by the exploratory factor analysis.

reorder function: Re-order the variables that define a correlation matrix.

To obtain these re-ordered proportionality coefficients, first invoke the `prop` function as before. But now save the new matrix into another R object, here called `myprop`, so that the proportionalities can be re-ordered with the `lessR` function `corReorder`, or just `reord`. The output from `reord` here is not directed to a data structure, so R directs its output to the console for viewing as text output.

 lessR Input *Re-ordered proportionalities*
```
> myprop <- prop()
> reord(myprop)
```

The `reord` function identifies the variable in the matrix that is most strongly related to all the other variables, the variable with the highest sum of squared coefficients. This variable is placed first in the re-ordered matrix. Then the second variable is the variable that has the highest coefficient with the first variable. The third variable has the highest coefficient with the second, and so on. The algorithm is very simple, but is designed to list variables with parallel profiles of correlation coefficients next to each other.

Figure 11.8 lists the proportionality coefficients for the first eight items listed in the output. The gray regions in the figure highlight how this technique isolated two groups of items such that the proportionality coefficients within each group are relatively larger than those coefficients between the groups.

	m09	m10	m07	m06	m11	m16	m04
m09	1.00	0.95	0.93	0.91	0.82	0.80	0.84
m10	0.95	1.00	0.96	0.90	0.82	0.82	0.81
m07	0.93	0.96	1.00	0.97	0.85	0.85	0.77
m06	0.91	0.90	0.97	1.00	0.83	0.82	0.76
m11	0.82	0.82	0.85	0.83	1.00	0.92	0.85
m16	0.80	0.82	0.85	0.82	0.92	1.00	0.85
m04	0.84	0.81	0.77	0.76	0.85	0.85	1.00

Figure 11.8 Annotated proportionality coefficients for the items that define the first two factors in the confirmatory factor analysis of Mach IV.

Integrating the information from the exploratory analysis, the re-ordered proportionality coefficients and the content and meaning of the items, and then formulating several more models lead to the final measurement model advocated by Hunter et al. (1982). The two groups of items delineated in Figure 11.8 are a subset of the final model, of which the corresponding call to the `cfa` function is shown in Listing 11.9.

```
> cfa(F1=c(m06,m07,m09,m10), F2=c(m15,m02),
      F3=c(m04,m11,m16), F4=c(m01,m05,m12,m13))
```

Listing 11.9 Specification of the final four-factor Machiavellianism model.

The average residual of the confirmatory factor analysis of this four-factor model is just 0.036. So the model has reasonable fit, but what does it mean?

 Scenario *List the content of the items for each derived unidimensional scale*
Factor and item analysis are statistical techniques. Ultimately, however, the results need to make conceptual sense, they need to be interpretable. An understanding of content should guide the entire process of scale construction. Display the content for each of the four scales that correspond to the four-factor multiple indicator measurement model.

Variable labels can be read into R with the `labels` option of the `lessR` function `Read`. Here the variable label for each item is its content. The `cfa` function lists the items in each group, and, if the variable labels are present, automatically displays their content. *read variable labels, Section 2.4, p. 45*

The call to `cfa` in Listing 11.9 displays the item content that identifies the four specified distinct content domains of Machiavellianism. The content for the final Mach IV measurement model, as output by the `cfa` function, appears in Listing 11.10 for Deceit, 11.11 for Flattery, 11.12 for Immorality, and 11.13 for Cynicism.

```
F1:    m06   m07   m09   m10
------------------------------
m06: Honesty is the best policy in all cases.
m07: There is no excuse for lying to someone else.
m09: All in all, it is better to be humble and honest than to be important
     and dishonest.
m10: When you ask someone to do something for you, it is best to give the
     real reasons for wanting it rather than giving reasons which carry
     more weight.
```

Listing 11.10 Deceit Machiavellian subdomain.

```
F2:    m15   m02
------------------------------
m15: It is wise to flatter important people.
m02: The best way to handle people is to tell them what they want to hear.
```

Listing 11.11 Flattery Machiavellian subdomain.

The four different subscales are conceptually distinct in terms of the covariance pattern, the structure of the item correlation matrix. The subscales are also distinct in terms of their content.

```
F3:    m04   m11   m16
------------------------------
m04: Most people are basically good and kind.
m11: Most people who get ahead in the world lead clean, moral lives.
m16: It is possible to be good in all respects.
```

Listing 11.12 Immorality Machiavellian subdomain.

```
F4:    m01   m05   m12   m13
--------------------------
m01: Never tell anyone the real reason you did something unless it is
     useful to do so.
m05: It is safest to assume that all people have a vicious streak and it
     will come out when they are given a chance.
m12: Anyone who completely trusts anyone else is asking for trouble.
m13: The biggest difference between most criminals and other people is that
     the criminals are stupid enough to get caught.
```

Listing 11.13 Cynicism Machiavellian subdomain.

Further, the underlying factors correlate moderately, but not excessively. The factor correlation matrix from the `cfa` output is reproduced in Listing 11.14.

```
      F1    F2    F3    F4
F1  1.00  0.50  0.64  0.44
F2  0.50  1.00  0.16  0.51
F3  0.64  0.16  1.00  0.61
F4  0.44  0.51  0.61  1.00
```

Listing 11.14 Factor correlations between the four distinct Machiavellian content domains: Deceit(F_1), Flattery(F_2), Immorality(F_3), and Cynicism(F_4).

scales abbreviation for `cfa`, Section 11.4, p. 260

coefficient alpha, Section 11.4.2, p. 262

These factor correlations are the corresponding observed scale correlations corrected for attenuation due to measurement error. That is, they are the estimated correlations among latent variables, the factors, which are larger than the observed scale–score correlations. The later are obtained by setting `iter=0`, or, equivalently, running the abbreviation `scales` in place of `cfa`.

Another issue aside from the dimensionality of the subscales is the reliability of their respective scale scores. This assessment is provided by several possible reliability coefficients, of which two of the most widely used are Coefficient Alpha and Coefficient Omega. Alpha is historically prior but Omega is more appropriate to the analysis of MIMM's because it incorporates the communality estimates into its underlying calculations, which Alpha ignores.

The reliability of the scales tends to be too low to be of practical use for identifying individuals in terms of the scores on the various subscales. Still, the reliabilities are somewhat higher than for the initial model derived from the exploratory factor analysis, in which only Coefficient Alpha was reported. The factor analysis is accomplished with communalities in the diagonal to partition out the unique variance of each item, which then permits the calculation of Coefficient Omega. The more appropriate Omegas are somewhat larger than the corresponding Alpha coefficients.

```
Scale  Alpha  Omega
-------------------
   F1   0.691  0.701
   F2   0.400  0.400
   F3   0.402  0.421
   F4   0.515  0.517
```

Listing 11.15 Reliability of the four Mach IV scales.

This delineation of unidimensional Machiavellian subscales advances our knowledge of the meaning of this social construct. By itself, however, the uncovering of these subscales does not invalidate Machiavellianism as a generic concept, but does demonstrate that Machiavellianism should not be conceived simply as a unitary construct. To further explore that question could include more advanced analyses than a simple confirmatory factor analysis, methodologies briefly discussed next, but which are beyond the scope of this text in terms of their detail.

11.6 Beyond the Basics

The confirmatory factor analysis function presented here is the `lessR` function `cfa`. The estimation procedure that `cfa` implements is *iterated centroid estimation* or `ICE`, revised from the original Fortran code in John Hunter's program PACKAGE (Hunter & Cohen, 1969). This procedure is the computational basis of the first factor analyses with multiple factors ever done in the 1930s because it is computationally straightforward and so made factor analysis accessible in the pre-computer era of statistics. A *centroid factor* is based on a total score, in this case the sum of the corresponding items that define the factor. This relation to the total score of the item analysis provides a conceptual similarity of factor analysis and item analysis.

iterated centroid estimation: Factor analysis based on centroid factors modified with iteration for communalities.

The `ICE` procedure as implemented here for confirmatory factor analysis is limited to multiple indicator measurement models, defined as measurement models in which the measured variables are partitioned into groups with each group of items postulated as a unidimensional set. The construction of multi-item scales, where each item on the scale measures the same shared or common factor, applies to a measurement model that is applicable to much social science research. Other models, however, are also applicable in other situations, such as the evaluation of multi-trait, multi-method measurement.

centroid factor: Derived from the total score of a set of items.

Confirmatory factor analysis is a specific implementation of the more general concept of structural equation modeling. More general confirmatory factor analysis models, and more general models beyond confirmatory factor analysis, require more general structural equation modeling or SEM software. An ambitious, comprehensive system with many developers is OpenMx (Boker et al., 2012). The installation of this software does not follow the usual `install.packages` function, so check their documentation for installation directions. A more recent R SEM package is `lavaan` (Rossell, 2012a, 2012b).

openmx website, openmx.psyc.virginia.edu

lavaan website, http://lavaan.ugent.be

These packages use more advanced estimation procedures than `cfa`'s ICE, such as full information maximum likelihood. And, statistical tests of fit are generally available for the estimation procedures implemented in these packages. ICE, however, does surprisingly well at estimation precision, almost as well as full information maximum likelihood (Gerbing & Hamilton, 1994). Also, ICE does not spread misspecification errors throughout the system, instead localizing such errors within the misspecified factor. Formal statistical tests are useful, but are literally only appropriate when a respecified model is tested on new data. Re-building a model on the same data means that the statistical tests become heuristic aids to assessing fit, such as the residual analysis provided by `cfa`, and not formal statistical tests. As such, the `cfa` of the ICE procedure is a useful, easy to use procedure applicable to the construction of multiple indicator measurement models for analysis with a confirmatory factor analysis.

Worked Problems

The following `Read` statement reads the attitude data analyzed in Hunter et al. (1982). The ID takes up the first four columns, then Gender coded as 0 for Male and 1 for Female in one column. Then 74 columns of responses, one to each of 74 attitude items. All the responses are already reversed scored where appropriate.

```
> mydata <- Read("http://lessRstats.com/data/Mach4Plus.fwd",
     widths=c(4,1,rep(1,74)),
     col.names=c("ID", "Gender", to("m",20), to("d",20), to("e",10),
               to("i",8), to("p",8), to("c",8)))
```

The 74 columns of responses to the attitude scales consist of, in this order, the Christie and Geis (1970) 20-item Mach IV scale, the Rokeach (1960) 20-item dogmatism scale, the Rosenberg (1965) 10-item self-esteem scale, an 8-item internal locus of control scale, an 8-item powerful others external locus of control scale, and an 8-item chance external locus of control scale from Levenson (1976).

1 Rotter (1966) proposed the concept of Locus of Control. Those with Internal Locus of Control perceive themselves to be in control of their destiny. Those with an External Locus of Control perceive themselves to have their destiny determined by forces outside of their own control. Levenson (1976) proposed to expand the concept of External Locus of Control to two different concepts, control by Powerful Others and Chance. Here we investigate the structure of Locus of Control.

(a) Read the Mach4Plus data file into R (Section 2.3.4).

(b) Create a subset of the data file that retains just the 24 Locus of Control items (Section 3.6).

(c) Compute the correlation matrix of the 24 Locus of Control items (Section 8.3).

(d) Examine the heat map of the correlation matrix. How many groups of items appear to be on the basis of the strength of their correlation? Why?

(e) Run the confirmatory factor analysis on the three-factor structure that corresponds to the three Locus of Control concepts. How well does the model fit? Answer in terms of the residuals and pattern coefficients.

(f) Revise the three-factor model to improve fit. Interpret this solution, including the correlation between the two External Locus of Control factors.

(g) For the 24 × 24 item correlation matrix, obtain the scree plot of the eigenvalues and the plot of the differences of successive eigenvalues. What is the smallest number of factors that appear to reasonably well account for the correlations among the observed variables? Why?

(h) Extract the specified number of factors from the scree plot, and, secondarily, the heat map. Interpret the meaning of the factors.

(i) Run the corresponding confirmatory factor analysis for this number of factors and interpret.

(j) Compare the two competing measurement models. What is your conclusion regarding the measurement model that underlies these Locus of Control items?

2 Consider the Rosenberg (1965) Self-Esteem scale. Does this scale measure one dimension of self-esteem, or are multiple aspects of self-esteem assessed with the scale?

(a) Read the Mach4Plus data file into R (Section 2.3.4).

(b) Create a subset of the data file that retains just the 10 self-esteem items (Section 3.6).

(c) Compute the correlation matrix of the 10 self-esteem items (Section 8.3).

(d) Examine the heat map of the correlation matrix. How many groups of items appear to be on the basis of the strength of their correlation? Why?

(e) Run the confirmatory factor analysis on the one factor structure. How well does the model fit? Answer in terms of the residuals and pattern coefficients.

(f) What revisions, if any, would you make to this model?

(g) Interpret the analysis and provide your conclusion regarding the number of dimensions measured by this self-esteem scale.

APPENDIX

STANDARD R CODE

Except for the confirmatory factor analysis function, cfa, all lessR functions directly depend on one or more standard R functions for the underlying computations. The following R function calls illustrate the use of most of these R functions within lessR. Essentially R provides a tool kit that the lessR functions access for analysis and then the organization and formatting of the resulting output.

The variable references in the following examples are from the Employee data table, read into R with the following statement.

```
mydata <- Read("Employee", format="lessR")
```

After reading the data into the mydata data frame, the following statements illustrate working R instructions.

Chapter 2, Read/Write Data

Task	R function call
browse for a file	ref <- file.choose()
read csv data	mydata <- read.csv(file=ref, na.strings=missing)
read fixed with data	mydata <- read.fwf(file=ref, widths=c(4,1,2))
read SPSS data	mydata <- read.spss(file=ref, to.data.frame=TRUE)
delete rows w/ missing values	mydata <- na.omit(mydata)
detect missing values	is.na(mydata)
write a csv data file	write.csv(mydata, file="Best.csv")
write an R data file	save(list=deparse(substitute(mydata)), file="Best.rda")

Chapter 3, Edit Data

Task	R function call
transform	mydata <- *transform*(mydata, Salary=Salary/1000)
subset	mydata <- *subset*(mydata, Gender=="F")
recode	programming only
merge horizontal	mydata <- *merge*(mydata1, mydata2, by=common.var)
merge vertical	mydata <- *rbind*(mydata1, mydata2)

Chapter 4, Categorical Variables

Task	R function call
bar chart, 1 variable	*barplot*(table(mydata$Dept))
bar chart, 2 variables	*barplot*(table(mydata$Dept, mydata$Gender))
pie chart	*pie*(table(mydata$Dept))
summary stats	*summary*(mydata$Dept)

Chapter 5, Continuous Variables

Task	R function call
histogram	*hist*(mydata$Salary, breaks=seq(0,130000,10000))
scatter plot, one variable	*stripchart*(mydata$Salary)
box plot	*boxplot*(mydata$Salary)
density plot	*plot*(*density*(mydata$Salary))
summary stats	*summary*(mydata$Salary)

Chapter 6, Means, Compare Two Samples

Task	R function call
one-sample mean	*t.test(mydata$Salary)*
mean difference	*t.test(mydata$Salary ~ mydata$Gender)*

Chapter 7, Compare Multiple Samples

Task	R function call

one-way ANOVA
randomized blocks ANOVA
two-way ANOVA
ANOVA table
Tukey HSD
	`fit <- aov(Salary ~ Gender, data=mydata)`
	`fit <- aov(Y ~ X + Blocks, data=mydata)`
	`fit <- aov(Y ~ X1 * X2, data=mydata)`
	`summary(fit)`
	`plot(TukeyHSD(fit))`

Chapter 8, Correlation

Task	R function call
scatter plot correlation correlation matrix	`plot(mydata$Years, mydata$Salary)` `cor(mydata$Years, mydata$Salary)` [no missing data] `mycor <- cor(mydata)` [only numeric variables in mydata]

Chapter 9, Regression I

Task	R function call

one predictor
estimates
confidence intervals
ANOVA table
fitted values
residuals
R-student residuals
Cook's Distance
DFFITS
prediction intervals
	`fit <- lm(Salary ~ Years)`
	`summary(fit)`
	`confint(fit)`
	`anova(fit)`
	`fitted(fit)`
	`residuals(fit)`
	`rstudent(fit)`
	`cooks.distance(fit)`
	`dffits(fit)`
	`predict(fit, interval="prediction"))`

Chapter 10, Regression II

Task	R function call
multiple reg logit	`fit <- lm(Salary ~ Years + Gender)` `fit <- glm(Gender ~ Years, data=mydata, family="binomial")`

Chapter 11, Factor/Item Analysis

Task	R function call
exploratory factor analysis	`fit <- factanal(covmat=mycor, factors=4, rotation="promax")`

NOTES

1 R for Data Analysis

1 Store this `library` function call, and any other R function calls, in a *text* file with the exact name of `.Rprofile` with no file type and a period as the first character. On Macintosh and Linux computers, however, the Unix convention is followed in which files with names that start with a period are hidden in the file directory, rendered invisible to the usual displays of the file directory. Thus a hidden file must be accessed to be re-edited. Google `mac "hidden file"` for more information. Or, to re-edit, just re-compose and re-save `.Rprofile`, once again as a *text* file.

2 The options for the color hues that correspond to the transparency options are `col.fill.pt` and `col.fill.bar`. Similar options also exist for the stroke or outline of plotted areas, `col.stroke.pt` and `col.stroke.fill`. Setting these four options, as well as the transparency options and background color and grid, provides a de facto customized color theme.

3 Full-fledged word processors, such as MS Word or the free and MS Word compatible LibreOffice Write, generally save their files in a non-text format with many hidden codes such as for formatting and paging the document. They also tend to change aspects of the file, such as MS Word's propensity to change straight quotes to curly quotes.

2 Read/Write Data

1 Another data type sometimes encountered is `logical`, which refers to a variable with only two possible values, TRUE and FALSE. When reading data, however, this data type is not typically encountered. The two data values for a logical variable are usually encoded with character codes or the integers 0 and 1 instead of TRUE and FALSE.

2 In some situations, such as a street address, each data value for the variable is a unique character string. These data values would be more meaningfully interpreted by R as variable type `character` instead of type `factor`. To do this when reading the data, explicitly specify the storage type of each variable with the `colClasses` option, which explicitly informs R of the type of variable in each column. See `?read.table` for more information.

3 The read time of a text file can be reduced by specifying the option `colClasses`, which informs R of the type of variable in each column. See `?read.table` for more information.

3 Edit Data

1 An exception when a factor transformation is not desired when reading data is for character strings such as street addresses that represent unique values for each row of data. To not convert character strings to factors, use the `as.is` option or the colClasses option. See `?read.table` for more information.

8 Correlation

1 Because the `car` package has been downloaded in its entirety with `lessR`, the user can directly access all of its functions by entering the statement `library(car)`. Obtain the list of available functions with a brief description with `help(package=car)`.

9 Regression I

1 The exact value for "two" is the t-cutoff value from the t-distribution, which depends on the sample size, or, more technically, the degrees of freedom, which here is the sample size minus two. For $df = 37 - 2$ the exact cutoff value is 2.03, provided by the `lessR` function call `prob.tcut(df=35)`.

10 Regression II

1 A least-squares regression analysis with the `factor` variable Gender as the response variable requires numerical values. To convert use the `as.numeric` function. By default the levels of a factor are alphabetized. For Gender R internally represents an F as a 1 and an M as a 2.

```
> mydata <- Transform(Gender=as.numeric(Gender))
```

Next convert the resulting numeric values of 1 and 2 to a 0 and a 1. To show a positive sloped curve, Females are scored as a 0 and Males are scored as a 1. That is, convert a 1 to 0 and a 2 to a 1.

```
> mydata <- Recode(Gender, old=c(1,2), new=c(0,1))
```

To obtain more control over the plot, the regression line was obtained with the `ScatterPlot` function instead of the `Regression` function.

```
> ScatterPlot(Hand, Gender, fit.line="ls", ylim=c(-.5, 1.5))
```

Here the y-axis extends from −0.5 to 1.5 to provide for the full range of fitted values.

11 Factor/Item Analysis

1 A correlation is a specific type of covariance in which the variables are standardized, that is, with variances of 1.00.

REFERENCES

Belsley, D. A., Kuh, E., & Welsch, R. H. (1980). *Regression diagnostics*. New York: Wiley.

Boker, S. et al. (2012). *Openmx – advanced structural equation modeling*. Retrieved October 2012, from http://openmx.psyc.virginia.edu/

Christie, R., & Geis, F. (1970). *Studies in Machiavellianism*. New York: Academic Press.

Cohen, J. (1969). *Statistical power analysis for the behavioral sciences*. New York: Academic Press.

Cohen, J. (1988). *Statistical power analysis for the behavioral sciences* (2nd ed.). Hillsdale, NJ: Lawrence Erlbaum.

Cronbach, L. J. (1951). Coefficient alpha and the internal structure of tests. *Psychometrika, 16*(3), 297–334.

Dragulescu, A. A. (2012). xlsx: Read, write, format excel 2007 and excel 97/2000/xp/2003 files [Computer software manual]. Retrieved from http://CRAN.R-project.org/package=xlsx (R package version 0.5.0)

Faraway, J. J. (2004). *Linear models with R*. New York: Chapman and Hall.

Fox, J., & Weisberg, S. (2011). *An R companion to applied regression* (2nd ed.). Thousand Oaks CA: Sage. Retrieved from http://socserv.socsci.mcmaster.ca/jfox/Books/Companion

Gerbing, D. W., & Anderson, J. C. (1988). An updated paradigm for scale development incorporating unidimensionality and its assessment. *Journal of Marketing Research, 25*(2), 186–192.

Gerbing, D. W., & Hamilton, J. G. (1994). The surprising viability of a simple alternate estimation procedure for the construction of large-scale structural equation measurement models. *Structural Equation Modeling: A Multidisciplinary Journal, 1*, 103–115.

Gerbing, D. W., & Hamilton, J. G. (1996). Viability of exploratory factor analysis as a precursor to confirmatory factor analysis. *Structural Equation Modeling: A Multidisciplinary Journal, 3*, 62–72.

Hunter, J. E. (1973). Methods of reordering the correlation matrix to facilitate visual inspection and preliminary cluster analysis. *Journal of Educational Measurement, 10*, 51–61.

Hunter, J. E., & Cohen, S. H. (1969). Package: A system of computer routines for the analysis of correlational data. *Educational and Psychological Measurement, 29*, 697–700.

Hunter, J. E., Gerbing, D. W., & Boster, F. J. (1982). Machiavellian beliefs and personality: Construct invalidity of the Machiavellian dimension. *Journal of Personality and Social Psychology, 43*(6), 1293–1305.

Kelley, K., & Lai, K. (2012). MBESS [Computer software manual]. Retrieved from http://www.nd.edu/~kkelley, (R package version 3.3.3)

Kirk, R. E. (2013). *Experimental design* (4th ed.). Thousand Oaks CA: Sage.

Levenson, H. (1976). Multidimensional locus of control in sociopolitical activists of conservative and liberal ideologies. *Journal of Personality and Social Psychology, 33*, 199–208.

Lumley, T., & Miller, A. (2009). leaps: Regression subset selection [Computer software 300 manual]. Retrieved from http://CRAN.R-project.org/package=leaps (R package version 2.9)

Machiavelli, N. (1902/1513). *The prince.* (W. K. M. (Translator), Ed.). New York: Alfred A. Knopf, Inc.

Rokeach, M. (1960). *The open and closed mind.* New York: Basic Books.

Rosenberg, M. (1965). *Society and the adolescent self-image.* Princeton, NJ: Princeton University Press.

Rosseel, Y. (2012a). laavan: An R package for structural equation modeling. *Journal of Statistical Software, 48*(2), 1–36.

Rosseel, Y. (2012b). *lavaan – latent variable analysis.* Retrieved October, 2012, from http://lavaan.ugent.be/

Rotter, J. (1966). Generalized expectancies for internal versus external control of reinforcement. *Psychological Monographs, 80*(1), Whole No. 609.

Spearman, C. (1904). "General intelligence," objectively determined and measured. *The American Journal of Psychology, 15*, 201–292.

Spearman, C. (1914). Theory of two factors. *Psychological Review, 21*, 105–115.

Thurstone, L. L. (1931). Multiple factor analysis. *Psychological Review, 38*, 406–427.

Tjur, T. (2009). Coefficients of determination in logistic regression models—a new proposal: The coefficient of discrimination. *The American Statistician, 63*(4), 366–372.

Tukey, J. W. (1977). *Exploratory data analysis.* New York: Addison-Wesley.

US Census Bureau. (2012). *World population.* Retrieved November, 2012, from http://www.census.gov/population/international/data/

Wickham, H. (2007). Reshaping data with the reshape package. *Journal of Statistical Software, 21*(12), 1–20. Retrieved from http://www.jstatsoft.org/v21/i12/

Wickham, H. (2009). *ggplot2: Elegant graphics for data analysis* (2nd ed.), New York: Springer Science.

INDEX

==, 69
$ notation, 14

all possible subsets, 230
alpha criterion, 82
alpha level, 90
ANOVA, 150
arguments, 13
assignment operator, 9, 62, 152, 184

balanced, 161
between-subjects, 131
bins, 100
blocks, 142
box plot, whisker, 113
Brown–Forsythe test, 133
browse, 33
bubble plot, 191

case, 21, 37
case-deletion statistics, 218
causal relation, 139
cell, 166
central limit theorem, 127
centroid factor, 275
chi-square test, 81
code integration, 19
collinear, 228
command history, 4
communality, 266
concordant, 201
confidence interval, 128
confirmatory factor analysis, 263
console, 4
control
    experimental, 138
    statistical, 225
Cook's Distance, 218

correlation
    corrected, 261
    item–total, 261
    Kendall, 201
    part–whole, 261
    Spearman, 200
correlation coefficient, 184
correlation matrix, 194
covariance structure, 263
CRAN, 3
cross-tabulation, 88
cross-tabulation table, three-way, 94
cross-validated, 233
csv data file, 24
current working directory, 49

data, 1
    cross-sectional, 118
    interval, 23, 61
    long format, 160
    longitudinal, 118
    nominal, 23, 60
    ordinal, 24, 60
    ratio, 23
    stacked, 151
    unstacked , 151
    wide format, 159
data analysis, 1
data file, 20
data format
    csv, 31
    fwd, 42
data frame, 32
data point, 205
data storage type, 34
data table, wide format, 21, 31
data validation, 22
data value, 20

decimal separator, 41
default, 13
delimiter, 40
density, bandwidth, 116
density plot, 114
dependent-samples, 142
DFFITS, 218
discordant, 201

effect size, 126, 135
empirical, 1
error
    modeling, 213
    prediction, 213
    sampling, 213
experiment, 138, 151

factor, 34
factor extraction, 255
factor pattern, 253
factorial design, 166
factors, 252
fitted value, 163, 207
fixed width format, 27
formula, 95
frequency
    cumulative, 104
    joint, 88
    marginal, 88
frequency distribution, 101
function, 4, 204
    addmargins *R*, 79
    args *R*, 69
    BarChart *lessR*, 79
    barplot *R*, 79
    bin.start *lessR*, 103
    c *R*, 37, 43, 63, 67, 267
    chisq.test *R*, 79
    corReorder *lessR*, 272
    CountAll, 78, 100
    CountAll *lessR*, 12
    data analysis, 13
    data modification, 13
    factanal *R*, 258
    fix *R*, 55
    head *R*, 36
    Histogram *lessR*, 10
    install.packages *R*, 5
    label *lessR*, 85
    levels *R*, 189
    library *R*, 6

LineChart *lessR*, 118
ls *R*, 185
matrix *R*, 91
mosaic *vcd*, 94
na.omit *R*, 232
options *R*, 41
par *R*, 83
print *R*, 36
prob.tcut *lessR*, 280
q *R*, 12
Read *lessR*, 33
Read2 *lessR*, 41
Recode *lessR*, 63
rep *R*, 42
rnorm *R*, 184
row.name *R*, 70
scales *lessR*, 260
set *lessR*, 16, 39, 109
setwd *R*, 50
showColors *lessR*, 17
Sort *lessR*, 66
Subset *lessR*, 68
table *R*, 79, 93
tail *R*, 36
to *lessR*, 43
Transform *lessR*, 56
update.packages *R*, 5
utility, 13
values *lessR*, 10
with *R*, 14, 93

global environment, 184
grand total, 88
gross effect, 225
group
    control, 151
    experimental, 151
grouping variable, 132

heat map, 198, 267
heteroscedasticity, 220
histogram
    cumulative, 104
    undersmoothed, 103
hold-out sample, 72

independent events, 89
independent-samples, 131
inferential statistics, 124
interaction, 167
interquartile range, 112

IQR, 106
item analysis, 252, 260
item–factor correlation, 268
iterated centroid estimation, 275
iteration, 266

kurtosis, 106

latent variable, 252
least-squares estimation, 209
levels, 39
Likert scale, 27
linear relationship, 184
listwise deletion, 197
loess curve, 184
logit, 241

Machiavellianism, 26
main effect, 167
manipulation, 138
matrix, 195
maximum likelihood estimation, 241
mean, 105
    cell, 168
    grand, 153
    marginal, 169
measurement model, 253
median, 106
merge, 72
    horizontal, 72
    vertical, 73
MIMM, 263
missing data, 25
missing data code, 36, 37
misspecification, 268
model, 206
model overfit, 231
model selection, 230
mosaic chart, 94
multiple regression, 224

nested model, 231
net effect, 225
non-parametric, 135
normality test, 116
null hypothesis, 81, 89, 154
null model, 210, 243

oblique, 255
observation, 21, 37
odds, 240
odds ratio, 242

omnibus F-test, 156
one-tailed test, 126, 188
option
    addtop *lessR*, 83
    alternative *R*, 126
    angle *R*, 83
    as.numeric *R*, 280
    bin.start `lessR`, 103
    bin.width `lessR`, 103
    breaks *R*, 102
    brief *lessR*, 14
    c *R*, 83, 87
    center.line *lessR*, 119
    cex *R*, 189
    colors *lessR*, 83
    columns *lessR*, 69
    data *lessR*, 82
    dec *R*, 41
    density *R*, 83
    direction *lessR*, 67
    exp *R*, 242
    format *lessR*, 49
    gap *lessR*, 83
    ghost *lessR*, 16
    horiz *R*, 83
    item.cor *lessR*, 269
    iter *lessR*, 269
    labels *R*, 59
    levels *R*, 59
    main *R*, 18, 80, 83
    min.loading *lessR*, 258
    missing *lessR*, 50
    n *R*, 36
    n.cat *lessR*, 109
    ordered *R*, 61
    OutDec *R*, 41
    over.grid *lessR*, 83
    paired *lessR*, 143
    prop *lessR*, 83, 102
    quiet *lessR*, 14
    random.col *lessR*, 83
    row.names *lessR*, 68
    row.names *R*, 50
    rows *lessR*, 69, 71
    scatter.3D *lessR*, 233
    sep *R*, 41
    shape.points *lessR*, 120
    shape.pts *lessR*, 189
    show.initial *lessR*, 258
    skip *R*, 42

option (*Cont'd*)
    sort *lessR*, 258
    standardize *lessR*, 207
    time.by *lessR*, 120
    time.reverse *lessR*, 121
    time.start *lessR*, 120
    type *lessR*, 119
    wilcox.test *R*, 136
    X2.new *lessR*, 238
    xlab *R*, 18
    xlim *R*, 186
    ylab *R*, 18
    ylim *R*, 186
order statistic, 106
orthogonal, 255
outlier, 106, 111, 216
    actual, 111, 112
    bivariate, 216
    potential, 111, 112

p-value, 81, 89, 128
package, 5
    car, 185
    contributed, 5
    reshape2, 151
pairwise deletion, 197
parametric statistic, 105
parsimony, 231, 252
partial slope coefficients, 224
path diagram, 264
pie chart, 85
post-hoc, 156
power, 142
prediction interval, 213
probability, conditional, 92
product rule
    external consistency, 264
    internal consistency, 264
prompt
    command, 4
    continuation, 4

qualitative variable, 23
quartile, 106

R-Student, 218
random assignment, 138
randomized block design, 159
recode, 62
regression
    explain, 204
    predict, 204

regression line, 205
regression plane, 233
relation, 182
relationship
    negative, 182
    positive, 182
reliability, 262
    test–retest, 262
reliability: internal consistency, 262
reproducible code, 19
research design, 124
residual, 157, 209
response
    invalid, 254
    random, 253
response variable, 132, 151
rotation
    promax, 258
    varimax, 258
row name, 35
run chart, 118

sampling error, 89
scatter plot, 182
    one-variable, 110
scatter plot matrix, 198
score
    composite, 260
    scale, 260
    total, 260
scree plot, 256
Shapiro–Wilk statistic, 116
significant difference, 128
simple structure, 255
skewness, 106
slope coefficient, 205
slope, meaning, 206
split-plot factorial design, 176
standard deviation, 106
standard error
    mean, 127
    mean difference, 133
    regression coefficient, 208
standardization, 57
standardized mean difference, 135
statistical decision, 128
sunflower plot, 193
syntax highlighting, 19
systematic error, 254

t-cutoff, 127
test sample, 212
text editor, 19
text file, 19, 24, 27, 42
tolerance, 230
training sample, 212
treatment variable, 151
two-tailed test, 126

underidentified, 255
unidimensional, 253
uniqueness, 253
unit of the analysis, 20
user's workspace, 184

value labels, 60
variable, 21
   binary, 234
   categorical, 23

confounding, 138
continuous, 22
indicator, 234
predictor, 95, 204
quantitative, 23
response, 95, 138, 204
treatment, 138
variable label, 46
variable list, 195
variable name, 21
variance ratio test, 133
VIF, 230

Wilcoxon rank sum test, 136

Y-intercept, 205

z-scores, 57

Taylor & Francis

eBooks

FOR LIBRARIES

ORDER YOUR
FREE 30 DAY
INSTITUTIONAL
TRIAL TODAY!

Over 22,000 eBook titles in the Humanities,
Social Sciences, STM and Law from some of the
world's leading imprints.

Choose from a range of subject packages or create your own!

Benefits for
you

▶ Free MARC records
▶ COUNTER-compliant usage statistics
▶ Flexible purchase and pricing options

Benefits
for your
user

▶ Off-site, anytime access via Athens or referring URL
▶ Print or copy pages or chapters
▶ Full content search
▶ Bookmark, highlight and annotate text
▶ Access to thousands of pages of quality research
at the click of a button

For more information, pricing enquiries or to order
a free trial, contact your local online sales team.

UK and Rest of World: **online.sales@tandf.co.uk**

US, Canada and Latin America:
e-reference@taylorandfrancis.com

www.ebooksubscriptions.com

ALPSP Award for
BEST eBOOK
PUBLISHER
2009 Finalist

Taylor & Francis eBooks
Taylor & Francis Group

A flexible and dynamic resource for teaching, learning and research.